Advance Praise for *Testing Applications on the Web*

Testing Applications on the Web by Hung Q. Nguyen is an absolute must for anyone who has a serious interest in software testing, especially testing web applications.

This book covers nearly every aspect of the error-finding process, moving from basic definitions and terminology, through detailed and easy-to-understand explanations of most testing strategies in use today. It finishes with a chapter on Web testing tools and appendices with test documentation templates.

This book is written with the practitioner in mind, but can equally well be used by students in software engineering curriculums. It presents both theory and practice in a thorough and clear manner. It illustrates both concepts and practical techniques with numerous realistic examples. This is a very good book on testing Web applications.

—*Steve Schuster*
Director, Quality Engineering
Carrier Applications Group
Phone.Com, Inc.

Testing Applications on the Web is a long-overdue and much needed guide to effectively testing web applications. The explosion of e-commerce businesses in the last couple of years has brought new challenges to software testers. There is a great need for knowledge in this area, but little available. Nguyen's class, Testing Web Applications, was the only class I could find of its kind and I was immediately able to put what I learned to use on the job. Nguyen's first book, *Testing Computer Software*, is required reading for my entire test team, and *Testing Applications on the Web* will now be added to that list.

Nguyen provides a combination of in-depth technical information and sound test planning strategies, presented in a way that will benefit testers in real world situations. *Testing Applications on the Web* is a fabulous reference and I highly recommend it to all software testers.

—*Debbie Goble*
Software Quality Control Manager
SBC Services, Inc.

Testing Applications on the Web contains a wealth of practical information. I believe that anyone involved with web testing will find this book invaluable. Hung's writing is crisp and clear, containing plenty of real-world examples to illustrate the key points. The treatment of gray-box testing is particularly insightful, both for general use, and as applied to testing web applications.

—*Christopher Agruss*
Quality Engineering Manager
Discreet (a division of Autodesk)

Years ago I was looking for a book like this. Internet software must work in all kinds of configurations. How can you test them all? Which do you choose? How should you isolate the problems you find? What do you need to know about the Internet technologies being used? *Testing Applications on the Web* answers all these questions. Many test engineers will find this book to be a godsend. I do!

—*Bret Pettichord*
Editor
Software Testing Hotlist

If you want to learn about testing Web applications, this book is a 'must-have.' A Web application comprises many parts—servers, browsers, and communications—all (hopefully) compatible and interacting correctly to make the right things happen. This book shows you how all these components work, what can go wrong, and what you need to do to test Web applications effectively. There are also plenty of examples and helpful checklists. I know of no other place where you can get a gold mine of information like this, and it's very clearly presented to boot!

—*Bob Stahl*
President
The Testing Center

I won't test another Web app without first referring to *Testing Applications on the Web*! The test design ideas are specific and would provide excellent support for any tester or test planner trying to find important problems fast.

This is really one of the first testing books to cover the heuristic aspects of testing instead of getting caught up in impractical rigor. It's like climbing into the mind of a grizzled veteran of Web testing. It's nice to see a testing book that addresses a specific problem domain.

—*James Bach*
Principal
Satisfice, Inc.

Testing Applications on the Web

Test Planning for Internet-Based Systems

Hung Q. Nguyen

Wiley Computer Publishing

John Wiley & Sons, Inc.

NEW YORK · CHICHESTER · WEINHEIM · BRISBANE · SINGAPORE · TORONTO

Publisher: Robert Ipsen

Executive Editor: Carol Long

Associate Editor: Margaret Hendrey

Managing Editor: Angela Smith

Text Design & Composition: North Market Street Graphics

Designations used by companies to distinguish their products are often claimed as trademarks. In all instances where John Wiley & Sons, Inc., is aware of a claim, the product names appear in initial capital or ALL CAPITAL LETTERS. Readers, however, should contact the appropriate companies for more complete information regarding trademarks and registration.

This book is printed on acid-free paper. ∞

Published by John Wiley & Sons, Inc.

Published simultaneously in Canada.

This publication is designed to provide accurate and authoritative information in regard to the subject matter covered. It is sold with the understanding that the publisher is not engaged in professional services. If professional advice or other expert assistance is required, the services of a competent professional person should be sought.

Library of Congress Cataloging-in-Publication Data:

ISBN 0-471-39470-X

Printed in the United States of America.
10 9 8 7 6 5 4 3 2 1

CONTENTS

Edited by:

Michael Hackett

Chris Thompson

T esting on the Web is a puzzle for many testers whose focus has been black-box, stand-alone application testing. This book's mission is to present the new challenges, along with a strategy for meeting them, in a way that is accessible to the traditional black-box tester.

In this book, Hung Nguyen's approach runs technically deeper and closer to the system than the black-box testing that we present in *Testing Computer Software.* Several people have bandied about the phrase "gray-box testing" over the years. Hung's book represents one thoughtful, experience-based approach to define and use a gray-box approach. I think that this is the first serious book-length exploration of gray-box testing.

In Hung's view of the world, Web testing poses special challenges and opportunities:

- First, the Web application lives in a much more complex environment than a mainframe, stand-alone desktop, or typical client-server environment. If the application fails, the problem might lie in the application's (app's) code, in the app's compatibility with other system components, or in problems of interactions between components that are totally outside of the app developer's control. For example, to understand the application's failures, it is important to understand the architecture and implementation of the network. Hung would say that if we aren't taking into account the environment of the application, we face a serious risk of wasting time on a lot of work that doesn't generalize.

- Second, much of what appears to be part of a Web application really belongs to complex third-party products. For example, the customer has a browser, a Java interpreter, and several graphics display and audio playback programs. The application presents its user interface through these tools, but it is not these tools, and it does not include these tools. Similarly, the database server and the Web server are not part of most applications. The app just uses these server-side components, just like it uses the operating system and the associated device drivers. There's a limit to the degree to which the application developer will want to test the client-side and server-side tools—she or he didn't write them, and the customer might update them or replace them at any time. Hung would say that if we don't have a clear idea of the separation between our app and the user-supplied third-party components, we face a serious risk of wasting time on a lot of work on the wrong components, seeking to manage the wrong risks.

- Third, because Web applications comprise so many bits and pieces that communicate, we have new opportunities to apply or create test tools that let us read and modify intermediate events. We can observe and create messages between the client and the server at several points in the chain. The essence of testability is visibility (what's going on in the software under test) and control (we can change the state or data of the software under test). Hung would say that this environment provides tremendous opportunities for a technically knowledgeable, creative tester to develop or use tools to enhance the testability of the application.

The gray-box tester is a more effective tester because he or she can

- Troubleshoot the system environment more effectively
- Manage the relationship between the application software and the third-party components more efficiently
- Use tools in new ways to discover and control more aspects of the application under test

This book applies these ideas to develop thematic analyses of the problems of Web testing. How do we test for database issues, security issues, performance issues, and so on? In each case, we must think about the application itself, its environment, its associated components, and tools that might make the testing more effective.

Another special feature of this book is that it was written by the president of an independent test lab, LogiGear, that tests other companies' Web applications and publishes a Web application of its own. Hung knows the design trade-offs that were made in his product and in the planning and execution of the testing of this product. He also knows the technical support record of the product in the field. The examples in this book are directly based on real experience with a real product that had real successes and real challenges. Normally, examples like the ones in this book would run afoul of a publisher's trade-secret policies. It is a treat seeing this material in print.

Cem Kaner, J.D., Ph.D.
Professor of Computer Sciences
Florida Institute of Technology

Testing Applications on the Web introduces the essential technologies, testing concepts, and techniques that are associated with browser-based applications. It offers advice pertaining to the testing of business-to-business applications, business-to-end-user applications, Web portals, and other Internet-based applications. The primary audience is black-box testers, software quality engineers, quality assurance staff, test managers, project managers, IT managers, business and system analysts, and anyone who has the responsibility of planning and managing Web-application test projects.

Testing Applications on the Web begins with an introduction to the client-server and Web system architectures. It offers an in-depth exploration of Web application technologies such as network protocols, component-based architectures, and multiple server types from the testing perspective. It then covers testing practices in the context of various test types from user interface tests to performance, load, and stress tests. Chapters 1 and 2 present an overview of Web testing. Chapters 3 through 5 cover methodology and technology basics, including a review of software testing basics, a discussion on networking, and an introduction to component-based testing. Chapters 6 through 8 discuss testing planning fundamentals, a sample application to be used as an application under test (AUT) illustrated throughout the book, and a sample test plan. Chapters 9 through 16 discuss test types that can be applied to Web testing. Finally, Chapters 17 and 18 offer a survey of Web testing tools and suggest where to go for additional information.

Testing Applications on the Web answers testing questions such as, "How do networking hardware and software affect applications under test?" "What are Web application components, and how do they affect my testing strategies?" "What is the role of a back-end database, and how do I test for database-related errors?" "What are performance, stress, and load tests—and how do I plan for and execute them?" "What do I need to know about security testing, and what are my testing responsibilities?"

With a combination of general testing methodologies and the information contained in this book, you will have the foundation required to achieve these testing goals—maximizing productivity and minimizing quality risks in a Web application environment.

Testing Applications on the Web assumes that you already have a basic understanding of software testing methodologies such as test planning, test-case design, and bug report writing. Web applications are complex systems that involve numerous components: servers, browsers, third-party software and hardware, protocols, connectivity, and much more. This book enables you to apply your existing testing skills to the testing of Web applications.

This book is not an introduction to software testing. If you are looking for fundamental software testing practices, you will be better served by reading *Testing Computer*

Software 2nd ed., by Kaner et al. (1993). If you are looking for scripting techniques or ways to use test automation effectively, I recommend you read *Software Test Automation* by Fewster and Graham (2000). For additional information on Web testing and other testing techniques and resources, visit www.QAcity.com.

I have enjoyed writing this book and teaching the Web application testing techniques that I use every day to test Web-based systems. I hope that you will find here the information you need to plan for and execute a successful testing strategy that enables you to deliver high-quality applications in an increasingly distributed-computing, market-driven, and time-constrained environment of this Internet era.

Acknowledgments

While my name appears on the cover, over the years, many people have helped with the development of this book. I want to particularly thank Cem Kaner and Bob Johnson for their dedication in providing thorough reviews and critical feedback, and Jesse Watkins-Gibbs and Chris Agruss for their thoughtful suggestions. I also want to thank the following people for their contributions (listed in alphabetical order): Joel Batts, James Bach, Kevin Carlson, William Coleman, Debbie Goble, Thomas Heinz, Heather Ho, Ioana Ilie, Susan Kim, Johnson Leong, Jeffrey Mainville, Denny Nguyen, Kevin Nguyen, Wendy Nguyen, Cathy Palacios, Bret Pettichord, Myvan Quoc, Steve Schuster, Karri Simpson, Louis (Rusty) Smith, Lynette Spruitenburg, Bob Stahl, and Joe Vallejo. Finally, I would like to thank my colleagues, students, and staff at LogiGear Corporation for their discussions and evaluations of the Web testing training material, which made its way into this book.

Certainly, any remaining errors in the book are mine.

About the Author

Hung Q. Nguyen is the president and CEO of LogiGear Corporation, a Silicon Valley company that he founded in 1994, whose mission is to help software development organizations deliver the highest-quality products possible while juggling limited resources and schedule constraints. Today, LogiGear is a multimillion-dollar firm that offers many value-added services, including application testing, automated testing, and Web load and performance testing for e-business and consumer applications. The Testing Services division specializes in Web application, handheld communication device, and consumer electronic product testing. LogiGear also offers a comprehensive "Practical Software Testing Training Series" and TRACKGEAR™, a powerful, flexible, and easy-to-use Web-based defect tracking solution. Hung Nguyen develops training materials and teaches software testing to the public at universities and conferences, as well as at numerous well-known domestic and international software companies. In the past 2 decades, Hung has held management positions in engineering, quality assurance, testing, product development, and information technology. Hung is coauthor of the best-selling book, *Testing Computer Software* (Wiley, 1999). He holds a Bachelor of Science in Quality Assurance from Cogswell Polytechnical College, and is an ASQ-Certified Quality Engineer and active senior member of American Society for Quality. You can reach Hung at hungn@logigear.com, or obtain more information about LogiGear Corporation and his work at www.logigear.com.

PART ONE

Introduction

CHAPTER 1

Welcome to Web Testing*

Why Read This Chapter?

The goal of this book is to help you effectively plan for and conduct the testing of Web-based applications. This book will be more helpful to you if you understand the philosophy behind its design.

Software testing practices have been improving steadily over the past few decades. Yet, as testers, we still face many of the same challenges that we have faced for years. We are challenged by rapidly evolving technologies and the need to improve testing techniques. We are also challenged by the lack of research on how to test for and analyze software errors from their behavior, as opposed to at the source code level. Finally, we are challenged by the lack of technical information and training programs geared toward serving the growing population of the not-yet-well-defined software testing profession. Yet, in today's world on *Internet time,* resources and testing time are in short supply. The quicker we can get the information that we need, the more productive and more successful we will be at doing our job. The goal of this book is to help you do your job effectively.

---

* During the writing of this book, I attended the Ninth Los Altos Workshop on Software Testing (LAWST) in March 2000. The topic of discussion was gray-box testing. I came away with a firmed thought and a comfortable feeling of a discovery that the testing approach I have been practicing is a version of gray-box testing. I thank the LAWST attendees—III, Chris Agruss, Richard Bender, Jaya Carl, Ibrahim (Bob) El-Far, Jack Falk, Payson Hall, Elisabeth Hendrickson, Doug Hoffman, Bob Johnson, Mark Johnson, Cem Kaner, Brian Lawrence, Brian Marick, Hung Nguyen, Noel Nyman, Bret Pettichord, Drew Pritsker, William (B.J.) Rollison, Melora Svoboda, and James Whitaker—for sharing their views and analyses.

Topics Covered in This Chapter

- Introduction
- The Evolution of Software Testing
- The Gray-Box Testing Approach
- Real-World Software Testing
- Themes of This Book

Introduction

This chapter offers a historical perspective on the changing objectives of software testing. It touches on the gray-box testing approach and suggests the importance of having a balance of product design, both from the designer's and the user's perspective, and system-specific technical knowledge. It also explores the value of problem analysis to determine what to test, when to test, and where to test. Finally, this chapter will discuss what assumptions this book has about the reader.

The Evolution of Software Testing

As the complexities of software development have evolved over the years, the demands placed on software engineering, information technology (IT), and software quality professionals, have grown and taken on greater relevance. We are expected to check whether the software performs in accordance with its intended design and to uncover potential problems that might not have been anticipated in the design. Test groups are expected to offer continuous assessment on the current state of the projects under development. At any given moment, they must be prepared to report explicit details of testing coverage and status, and all unresolved errors. Beyond that, testers are expected to act as user advocates. This often involves anticipating usability problems early in the development process so those problems can be addressed in a timely manner.

In the early years, on mainframe systems, many users were connected to a central system. Bug fixing involved patching or updating the centrally stored program. This single fix would serve the needs of hundreds or thousands of individuals who used the system.

As computing became more decentralized, minicomputers and microcomputers were run as stand-alone systems or on smaller networks. There were many independent computers or local area networks and a patch to the code on one of these computers updated relatively fewer people. Mass-market software companies sometimes spent over a million dollars sending disks to registered customers just to fix a serious defect. Additionally, technical support costs skyrocketed.

As the market has broadened, more people use computers for more things, they rely more heavily on computers, and the consequences of software defects rise every year. It is impossible to find all possible problems by testing, but as the cost of failure has gone up, it has become essential to do risk-based testing. In a risk-based approach, you ask questions like these:

- Which areas of the product are so significant to the customer or so prone to serious failure that they must be tested with extreme care?
- For the average area, and for the program as a whole, how much testing is enough?
- What are the risks involved in leaving a certain bug unresolved?
- Are certain components so unimportant as to not merit testing?
- At what point can a product be considered adequately tested and ready for market?
- How much longer can the product be delayed for testing and fixing bugs before the market viability diminishes the return on investment?

Tracking bugs and assessing their significance are priorities. Management teams expect development and IT teams, testing and quality assurance staff, to provide quantitative data regarding test coverage, the status of unresolved defects, and the potential impact of deferring certain defects. To meet these needs, testers must understand the products and technologies they test. They need models to communicate assessments of how much testing has been done in a given product, how deep testing will go, and at what point the product will be considered adequately tested. Given better understanding of testing information, we make better predictions about quality risks.

In the era of the Internet, the connectivity that was lost when computing moved from the mainframe model to the personal computer (PC) model, in effect, has been reestablished. Personal computers are effectively networked over the Internet. Bug fixes and updated builds are made available—sometimes on a daily basis—for immediate download over the Internet. Product features that are not ready by ship date are made available later in *service packs.* The ability to distribute software over the Internet has brought down much of the cost that is associated with distributing some applications and their subsequent bug fixes.

Although the Internet offers connectivity for PCs, it does not offer the control over the client environment that was available in the mainframe model. The development and testing challenges with the Graphical User Interface (GUI) and event-based processing of the PC are enormous because the clients attempt remarkably complex tasks on operating systems (OSs) as different from each other as Unix, Macintosh OS, Linux, and the Microsoft OSs. They run countless combinations of processors, peripherals, and application software. Additionally, the testing of an enterprise client-server system may require the consideration of thousands of combinations of OSs, modems, routers, and server-software packages. Web applications increase this complexity further by introducing browsers and Web servers into the mix.

Software testing plays a more prominent role in the software development process than it ever has before (or at least it should). Companies are allocating more money and resources for testing because they understand that their reputations rest on the quality of their products. The competitiveness of the computing industry (not to mention the savvy of most computer users) has eliminated most tolerance for buggy software. Yet, many companies believe that the only way to compete in *Internet time* is to develop software as rapidly as possible. Short-term competitive issues often outweigh quality issues. One consequence of today's accelerated development schedules is the industry's tendency to push software out into the marketplace as early as possible. Development teams get less and less time to design, code, test, and undertake process improvements. Market constraints and short development cycles often do not allow time for reflection on past experience and consideration of more efficient ways to produce software.

The Gray-Box Testing Approach

Black-box testing focuses on software's external attributes and behavior. Such testing looks at an application's expected behavior from the user's point of view. White-box testing (also known as glass-box testing), on the other end of the spectrum, tests software with knowledge of internal data structures, physical logic flow, and architecture at the source code level. White-box testing looks at testing from the developer's point of view. Both black-box and white-box testing are critically important complements of a complete testing effort. Individually, they do not allow for balanced testing. Black-box testing can be less effective at uncovering certain error types, such as data-flow errors or boundary condition errors at the source level. White-box testing does not readily highlight macrolevel quality risks in operating environment, compatibility, time-related errors, and usability.

Gray-box testing incorporates elements of both black-box and white-box testing. It considers the outcome on the user end, system-specific technical knowledge, and operating environment. It evaluates application design in the context of the *interoperability* of system components. The gray-box testing approach is integral to the effective testing of Web applications because Web applications comprise numerous components, both software and hardware. These components must be tested in the context of system design to evaluate their functionality and compatibility.

> Gray-box testing consists of methods and tools derived from the knowledge of the application internals and the environment with which it interacts, that can be applied in black-box testing to enhance testing productivity, bug finding, and bug analyzing efficiency. —Hung Q. Nguyen

Here are several other unofficial definitions for gray-box testing from the Los Altos Workshop on Software Testing (LAWST) IX. For more information on LAWST, visit www.kaner.com.

> Gray-box testing—Using inferred or incomplete structural or design information to expand or focus black-box testing —Dick Bender

> Gray-box testing—Tests designed based on the knowledge of algorithms, internal states, architectures, or other high-level descriptions of program behavior —Doug Hoffman

> Gray-box testing—Tests involving inputs and outputs, but test design is educated by information about the code or the program operation of a kind that would normally be out of scope of the view of the tester —Cem Kaner

Gray-box testing is well suited for Web application testing because it factors in high-level design, environment, and interoperability conditions. It will reveal problems that are not as easily considered by a black-box or white-box analysis, especially problems of end-to-end information flow and distributed hardware/software system configuration and compatibility. Context-specific errors that are germane to Web systems are commonly uncovered in this process.

Another point to consider is that many of the types of errors that we run into in Web applications might be well discovered by black-box testers, if only we had a better model of the types of failures for which to look and design tests. Unfortunately, we are still developing a better understanding of the risks that are associated with the new application and communication architectures. Therefore, the wisdom of traditional books on testing [e.g., *Testing Computer Software* (Kaner et al., 1993)] will not fully prepare the black-box tester to search for these types of errors. If we are equipped with a better understanding of the system as a whole, we'll have an advantage in exploring the system for errors and in recognizing new problems or new variations of older problems.

As testers, we get ideas for test cases from a wide range of knowledge areas. This is partially because testing is much more effective when we know what types of bugs we are looking for. We develop ideas of what might fail, and of how to find and recognize such a failure, from knowledge of many types of things [e.g., knowledge of the application and system architecture, the requirements and use of this type of application (domain expertise), and software development and integration]. As testers of complex systems, we should strive to attain a broad balance in our knowledge, learning enough about many aspects of the software and systems being tested to create a battery of tests that can challenge the software as deeply as it will be challenged in the rough and tumble of day-to-day use.

Finally, I am not suggesting that *every* tester in a group be a gray-box tester. I have seen a high level of success in several test teams that have a mix of different types of testers, with different skill sets (e.g., subject matter expert, database expert, security expert, API testing expert, test automation expert, etc.). The key is, within that mix, at least some of the testers must understand the system as a collection of components that can fail in their interaction with each other, and these individuals must understand how to control and how to see those interactions in the testing and production environments.

Real-World Software Testing

Web businesses have the potential to be high-profit ventures. Venture capitalists can support a number of losing companies as long as they have a few winners to make up for their losses. A CEO has 3 to 4 years to get a start-up ready for IPO (6 months to prove that the prototype works, 1 or 2 years to generate some revenue—hence, justifying the business model—and the remainder of the time to show that the business can be profitable someday). It is always a challenge to find enough time and qualified personnel to develop and deliver quality products in such a fast-paced environment.

Although standard software development methodologies such as Capability Maturity Model (CMM) and ISO-9000 have been available, they are not yet well accepted by aggressive start-up companies. These standards and methods are great practices, but the fact remains that many companies will rely on the efforts of a skilled development and testing staff, rather than a process that they fear might slow them down. In that situation, no amount of improved standards and process efficiencies can make up for the efforts of a skilled development and testing staff. That is, given the time and resource constraints, they still need to figure out how to produce quality software.

The main challenge that we face in Web application testing is learning the associated technologies to have a better command over the environment. We need to know how Web technologies affect the interoperability of software components, as well as Web systems as a whole. Testers also need to know how to approach the testing of Web-based applications. This requires being familiar with test types, testing issues, common software errors, and the quality-related risks that are specific to Web applications. We need to learn, and we need to learn fast. Only with a solid understanding of software testing basics and a thorough knowledge of Web technologies can we competently test Web-based systems.

Themes of This Book

The objective of this book is to introduce testers into the discipline of gray-box testing, by offering readers information about the interplay of Web applications, component architectural designs, and their network systems. I expect that this will help testers develop new testing ideas, enabling them to uncover and troubleshoot new types of errors and conduct more effective root-cause analyses of software failures discovered during testing or product use. The discussions in this book focus on determining what to test, where to test, and when to test. As appropriate, real-world testing experiences and examples of errors are included.

To effectively plan and execute the testing of your Web application, you need to possess the following qualities: good software testing skill; knowledge of your application, which you will need to provide; knowledge of Web technologies; understanding of the types of tests and their applicability to Web application; knowledge of several types of Web application-specific errors (so you know what to look for); and knowledge of some of the available tools and their applicability, which this book offers you. (See Figure 1.1.)

Based on this knowledge and skill set, you can analyze the testing requirements to come up with an effective plan for your test execution. If this is what you are looking for, this book is for you. It is assumed that readers have a solid grasp of standard software testing practices and procedures.

TESTER RESPONSIBILITIES

- Identifying high-risk areas that should be focused on in test planning
- Identifying, analyzing, and reproducing errors effectively within Web environments (which are prone to multiple environmental and technological variables)

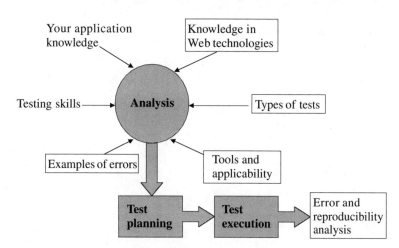

Figure 1.1 Testing skill and knowledge.

- Capitalizing on existing errors to uncover more errors of the same class, or related classes

To achieve these goals, you must have high-level knowledge of Web environments and an understanding of how environmental variables affect the testing of your project. The information and examples included in this book will help you to do just that.

There is one last thing to consider before reading on. Web applications are largely platform-transparent. However, most of the testing and error examples included in this book are based on Microsoft technologies. This allows me to draw heavily on a commercial product for real examples. While I was researching this book, my company built TRACKGEAR™, a Web-based defect-tracking solution that relies on Microsoft technologies. As the president of that company, I can lay out engineering issues that were considered in the design and testing of the product that testing authors cannot normally reveal (because of nondisclosure contracts) about software that they have developed or tested. My expectation, however, is that the testing fundamentals should apply to technologies beyond Microsoft.

CHAPTER 2

Web Testing versus Traditional Testing

Why Read This Chapter?

Web technologies require new testing and bug analysis methods. It is assumed that you have experience in testing applications in traditional environments; what you may lack, however, is the means to apply your experience to Web environments. To effectively make such a transition, you need to understand the technology differences between traditional testing and Web testing.

Topics Covered in This Chapter

- Introduction
- The Application Model
- Hardware and Software Differences
- The Differences between Web and Traditional Client-Server Systems
- Web Systems
- Your Bugs Are Mine
- Back-End Data Accessing
- Thin Client versus Thick Client
- Interoperability Issues
- Testing Considerations
- Bibliography

Introduction

This chapter presents the application model and shows how it applies to mainframes, PCs, and ultimately, Web/client-server systems. It explores the technology differences between mainframes and Web/client-server systems, as well as the technology differences between PCs and Web/client-server systems. Testing methods that are suited to Web environments are also discussed.

Although many traditional software testing practices can be applied to the testing of Web-based applications, there are numerous technical issues that are specific to Web applications that need to be considered.

The Application Model

Figure 2.1 illustrates how humans interact with computers. Through a user interface (UI), users interact with an application by offering input and receiving output in many different forms: query strings, database records, text forms, and so on. Applications take input, along with requested logic rules, and manipulate data; they also perform file reading and writing [input/output (I/O)]. Finally, results are passed back to the user through the UI. Results may also be sent to other output devices, such as printers.

In traditional mainframe systems, as illustrated in Figure 2.2, all of an application's processes, except for UI functions, occur on the mainframe computer. User interface functions take place on dumb terminals that simply echo text from the mainframe. No processing occurs on the terminals themselves. The network connects the dumb terminals to the mainframe. Dumb-terminal UIs are text-based (nongraphical). Users send data and commands to the system via keyboard inputs.

Desktop PC systems, as illustrated in Figure 2.3, consolidate all processes—from UI, through rules, to file systems—on a single physical box. No network is required for a desktop PC. Desktop PC applications can support either a text-based UI (command-

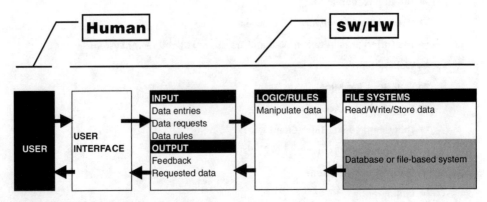

Figure 2.1   The application model.

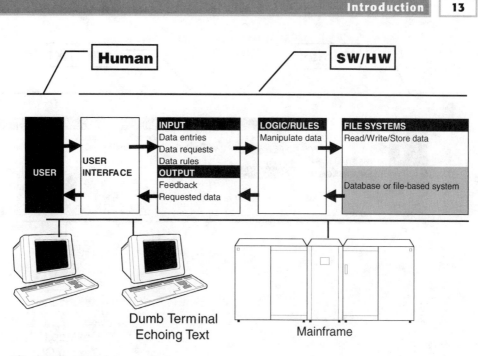

Figure 2.2 Mainframe systems.

line) or a Graphical User Interface (GUI). In addition to keyboard input events, GUI-based applications also support mouse input events such as click, double-click, mouse-over, drag-and-drop, and so on.

Client-server systems, upon which Web systems are built, require a network and at least two machines to operate: a *client* computer and a *server* computer, which serves requested data to the client computer. With the vast majority of Web applications, a Web browser serves as the UI on the client computer.

The server receives input requests from the client and manipulates the data by applying the application's *business logic rules.* Business logic rules are the processes that an application is designed to carry out based on user input—for example, sales tax might be charged to any e-commerce customer who enters a California mailing address. Another example includes customers over age 35 who respond to a certain online survey being mailed a brochure automatically. This type of activity may require reading or writing to a database. Data is sent back to the client as output from the server. The results are then formatted and displayed in the client browser.

The client-server model, and consequently the Web application model, is not as neatly segmented as that of the mainframe and the desktop PC. In the client-server model, not only can either the client or the server handle some of the processing work, but server-side processes can be divided between multiple physical boxes (application server, Web server, database server, etc.). Figure 2.4, one of many possible client-server models, depicts I/O and logic rules handled by an *application server* (the server in the center) while a *database server* (the server on the right) handles data storage. The dotted lines in the illustration indicate processes that may take place on

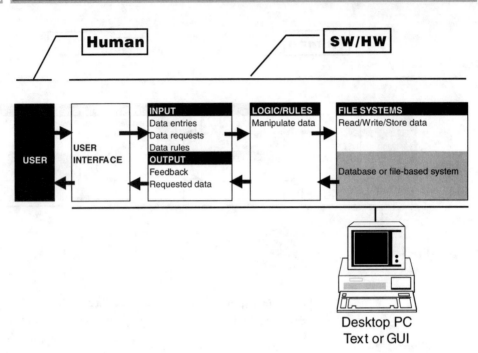

Figure 2.3   Desktop PC systems.

either the client side or the server side. See Chapter 5, "Web Application Components," for information regarding server types.

A Web system may comprise any number of physical server boxes, each handling one or more server types. Later in this chapter, Table 2.1 illustrates some of the possible three-box server configurations. Note that the example is relatively a basic system. A Web system may contain multiple Web servers, application servers, and multiple database servers (such as a *server farm*, a grouping of similar server types that share workload). Web systems may also include other server types, such as e-mail servers, chat servers, e-commerce servers, and user profile servers. See the Chapter 5, "Web Application Components," for more information.

Keep in mind that it is software, not hardware, that defines clients and servers. Simply put, clients are software programs that request services from other software programs on behalf of end users. Servers are software programs that offer services. Additionally, *client-server* is also an overloaded term. It is only useful from the perspective of describing a system. A server may, and often does, become a client in the chain of requests.

Hardware and Software Differences

Mainframe systems (Figure 2.5) are traditionally *controlled* environments—meaning that hardware and software are primarily supported, end to end, by the same manufacturer. A mainframe with a single operating system, and applications sold and sup-

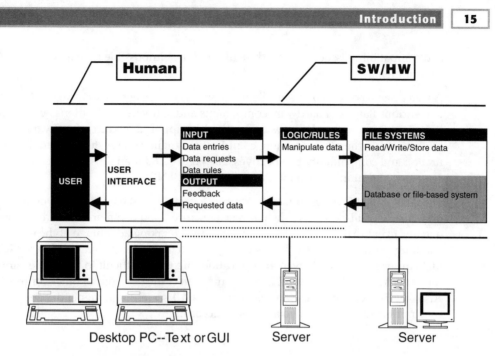

Figure 2.4   Client-server systems.

ported by the same manufacturer, can serve multiple terminals from a central location. Compatibility issues can be readily managed in such an environment.

A single desktop PC system comprises *mixed* hardware and software—multiple hardware components built and supported by different manufacturers, multiple operating systems, and nearly limitless combinations of software applications. Configuration

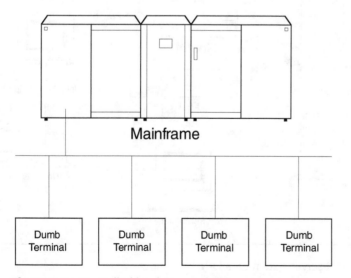

Figure 2.5   Controlled hardware and software environment.

and compatibility issues become difficult or almost impossible to manage in this environment.

A Web system consists of many clients as well as server hosts (computers). The system various flavors of hardware components and software applications begin to multiply. The server side of Web systems may also support a mixture of software and hardware and, therefore, are more complex than mainframe systems, from the configuration and compatibility perspectives. See Figure 2.6 for an illustration of a client-server system running on a local area network (LAN).

The GUI of the PC makes multiple controls available on screen at any given time (e.g., menus, pull-down lists, help screens, pictures, and command buttons.). Consequently, event-driven browsers are also produced, taking advantage of the event-handling feature offered by the operating system (OS). However, event-based GUI (data input coupled with events) applications are more difficult to test. For example, each event applied to a control in a GUI may affect the behavior of other controls. Also, special dependencies can exist between GUI screens; interdependencies and constraints must be identified and tested accordingly.

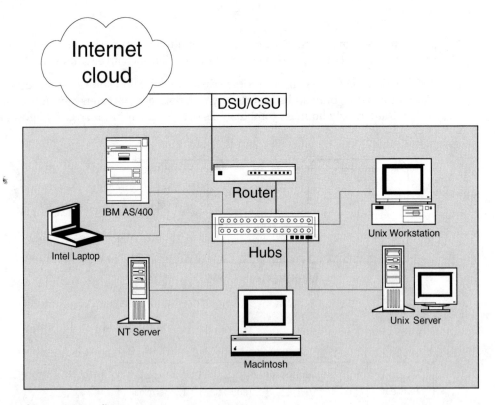

Figure 2.6 A client-server system on a LAN.

The Differences between Web and Traditional Client-Server Systems

The last two sections point out the application architecture, and hardware and software differences among the mainframe, PC, and Web/client-server systems. This section will continue that theme. We will begin to explore additional differences between Web and traditional systems so that appropriate considerations can be formulated specifically for testing Web applications.

Client-Side Applications

As illustrated in Figure 2.7, most client-server systems are data access applications. A client typically enables users, through the UI, to send input data, receive output data, and interact with the back end (for example, sending a query command). Clients of traditional client-server systems are platform-specific. That is, for each supported client platform (e.g., Windows 16- and 32-bit, Solaris, Linux, Macintosh, etc.), a client application will be developed and tested for that target platform.

Most Web-based systems are also data access applications. The browser-based clients are designed to handle similar activities to those supported by a traditional client. The main difference is that the Web-based client is running in the context of a Web

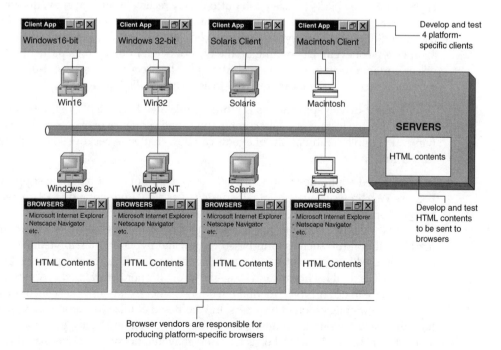

Figure 2.7 Client-server versus Web-based clients.

browser. Web browsers consist of platform-specific client software running on a client computer. It renders static HyperText Markup Language (HTML) as well as active contents to display Web page information. Several popular browsers also support active content such as client-side scripting, Java applet, ActiveX control, cascading style sheet (CSS), dynamic HTML, security features, and other goodies. To do this, browser vendors must create rendering engines and interpreters to translate and format HTML contents. In making these software components, incompatibility issues are introduced among various browsers and their releases. See Chapters 9, "User Interface Tests," and 14, "Configuration and Compatibility Tests," for more information.

From the application producer's perspective, there is no need to develop platform-specific clients. Delivering platform-specific Web browsers is, rather, a responsibility of Web browser vendors (e.g., Netscape, Microsoft, AOL, etc.). In theory, if your HTML contents are designed to conform with HTML 3.0 standard, your client application should run properly in any browser that supports HTML 3.0 standard from any vendor.

In practice, we will find ourselves working laboriously to address vendor-specific incompatibility issues introduced by each browser and its various releases. At the writing of this book, the golden rule is "Web browsers are not created equal."

Event Handling

In the GUI and event-driven model, inputs are driven by *events*. Events are actions taken by users, such as mouse movements and clicks, or the input of data through a keyboard. Some objects (e.g., a push button) may receive mouse-over events whenever a mouse passes over them. A mouse single-click is an event. A mouse double-click is a different kind of event. A mouse-click with a modifier key such as Ctrl is yet another type of event. Depending on the type of event initiated on a particular UI object, certain procedures in an application may be executed. In an event-driven environment, these procedures are referred to as *event-handling code*.

Testing event-driven applications is more complicated because it's very labor intensive to cover the testing of many combinations and sequence of events. Simply identifying all possible combinations of events can be a challenge because some actions trigger multiple events.

Browser-based applications introduce a different flavor of event-handling support. Because Web browsers were originally designed as a data presentation tool, there was no need for interactions other than single-clicking for navigation and data submission, and mouse-over ALT attribute for an alternate description of graphic. Therefore, standard HTML controls such as form-based control and hyperlinks are limited to single-click events. Although script-based events can be implemented to recognize other events such as double-clicking and drag-and-drop, it's not natural in the Web-based user interface to do so. Not to mention that those other events also cause incompatibility problems among different browsers. In Web-based applications, users may click links that generate simulated dialog boxes (the server sending back a page that includes tables, text fields, and other UI objects). Users may interact with browser-based UI objects in the process of generating input for the application. In turn, events are generated. Some of the event-handling code is in scripts that are embedded in the HTML page and executed on the client side. Some are in UI components (such as Java applets and ActiveX controls) embedded in the HTML page and executed on the client side. Others are executed on the server side. Understanding where (client or server side) each event is handled enables you to develop useful test cases as well as reproduce errors effectively.

Browser-based applications offer very limited keyboard event support. You can navigate within the page using Tab and Shift-Tab keys. You can activate a hyperlink to jump to another link or push a command button by pressing the Enter key while the hyperlink text, graphic, or a button is highlighted. Supports for keyboard shortcuts and access keys, such as Alt-[key] or Ctrl-[key], are not available.

Another event-handling implication in browser-based applications is in the one-way request and submission model. The server generally does not receive commands or data until the user explicitly clicks a button such as "Submit" to submit form data, or the user may request data from the server by clicking a link. This is referred to as the *explicit submission model.* If the user simply closes down a browser but does not explicitly click on a button to save data or to log off, data will not be saved and the user is still considered logged on (on the server side).

Application Instance and Windows Handling

Standard event-based applications may support multiple instances, meaning that the same application can be loaded into memory many times as separate processes. Figure 2.8 shows two instances of Microsoft Word application.

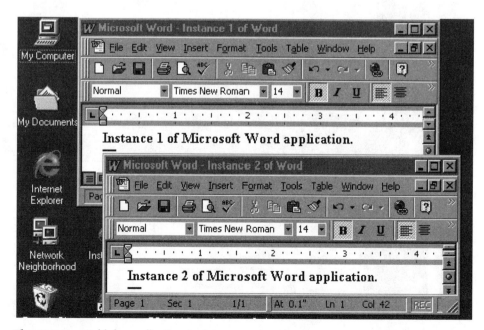

Figure 2.8 Multiple application instances.

Similarly, multiple instances of a browser can run simultaneously. With multiple browser instances, users may be able to log into the same Web-based application and access the same data table—on behalf of the same user or different users. Figure 2.9 illustrates two browser instances, each accessing the same application and data using the same or different user ID and password.

From the application's perspective, keeping track of multiple instances, the data, and the users who belong to each instance can be problematic. For example, a regular user has logged in using one instance of the browser. An Admin user has also logged into the same system using another instance for the browser. It's common that the application server may mistakenly receive data from and send data to one user thinking that the data belongs to the other users. Test cases that uncover errors surrounding multiple-instance handling should be thoroughly designed and executed.

Within the same instance of a standard event-based application, multiple windows may be opened simultaneously. Data altered in one of an application's windows may affect data in another of the application's windows. Such applications are referred to as *multiple document interface* (MDI) applications (Figure 2.10). Applications that allow only one active window at a time are known as *single document interface* (SDI) applica-

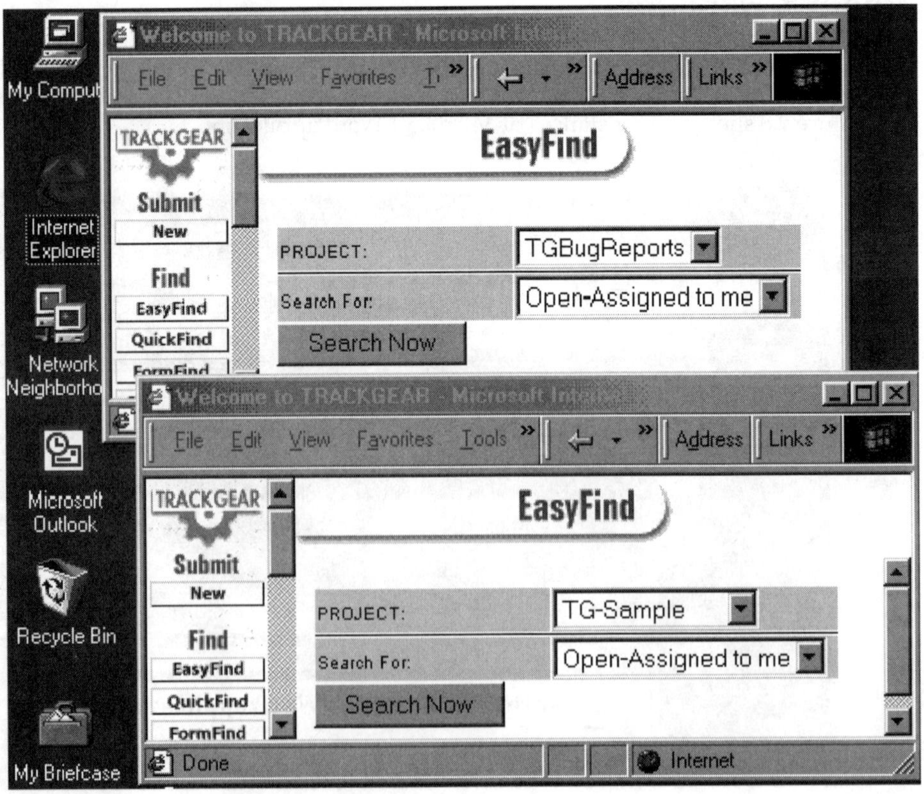

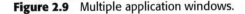

Figure 2.9 Multiple application windows.

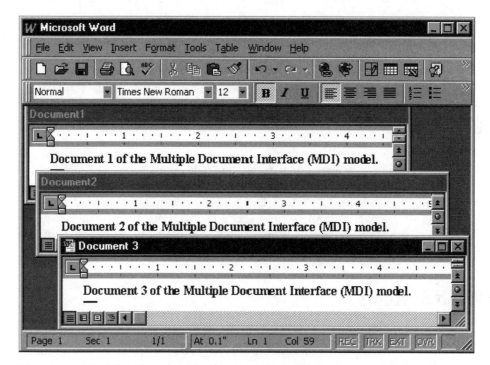

Figure 2.10   Multiple document interface (MDI) application.

tions (Figure 2.11). Single document interface applications allow users to work with only one document at a time.

Microsoft Word (Figure 2.10) is an example of an MDI application. Notepad (Figure 2.11) is an example of a SDI application.

Multiple document interface applications are more interesting to test because they might fail to keep track of events and data that belong to multiple windows. Test cases designed to uncover errors caused by the support of multiple windows should be considered.

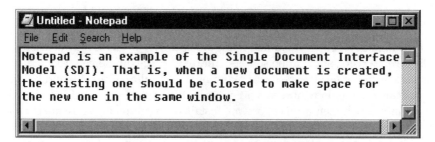

Figure 2.11   Single document interface (SDI) application.

Multiple document interface or multiple windows interface is only available for clients in a traditional client-server system. The Web browser interface is *flat* and *nonlinear;* therefore, it does not support MDI. It's flat because it can only display one page at the time. It's nonlinear (there is no hierarchical structure) because one can easily jump to several links and quickly lose track of the original position.

UI Controls

In essence, an HTML page that is displayed by a Web browser consists of text, hyperlinks, graphics, frames, tables, forms, and balloon help text (ALT tag). Basic browser-based applications do not support dialog boxes, message boxes, toolbars, status bars, and other common UI controls. Extra effort can be put in to take advantage of Java applets, ActiveX controls, scripts, CSS, and other helper applications to go beyond the basic functionality. However, there will be compatibility issues among different browsers.

Web Systems

The complexities of the PC model are multiplied exponentially in Web systems (Figure 2.12). In addition to the testing challenges that are presented by multiple client PCs, the server side of Web systems involves hardware of varying types and a software mix of OSs, service processes, server packages, and databases.

Hardware Mix

With Web systems and their mixture of flavors of hardware to support, the environment can become very difficult to control. Web systems have the capacity to use machines of different platforms, such as Unix, Windows NT, and Macintosh boxes. A Web system might include a Unix server that is used in conjunction with other servers that are either Windows-based or Macintosh-based. Web systems may also include mixtures of models from the same platform (on both the client and server sides). Such hardware mixtures present testing challenges because different computers in the same system may employ different OSs, CPU speeds, buses, I/O interfaces, and more. Each variation can potentially cause problems.

Software Mix

At the highest level, as illustrated in Figure 2.12, Web systems may consist of various OSs, Web servers, application servers, middleware, e-commerce servers, database servers, major enterprise resource planning (ERP) suites, firewalls, and browsers. Application development teams often have little control over the kind of environment into which their applications are installed. In producing software for mainframe systems, development was tailored to one specific system. Today, for Web systems, software is often designed to run on a wide range of hardware and OS combinations, and risks of software incompatibility are always present. An example is

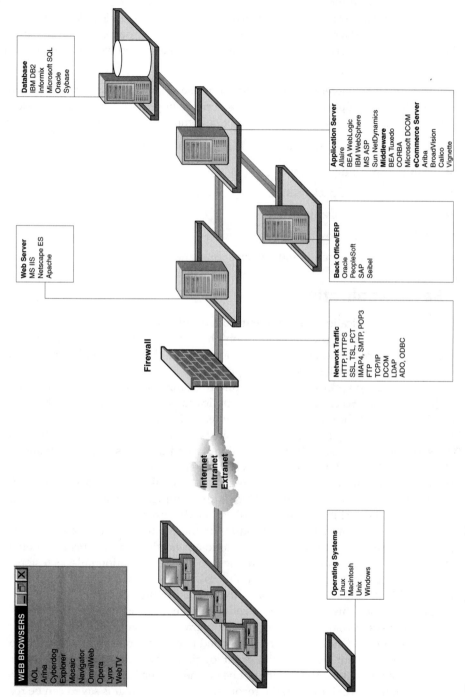

Figure 2.12 Web system architecture.

that different applications may not share the same versions of a database server. On the Microsoft platform, a missing or incompatible DLL (dynamic link library) is another example. (Dynamic link libraries are software components that can exist on both the client and server sides whose functions can be called by multiple programs on demand.)

Another problem inherent in the simultaneous use of software from multiple vendors is that when each application undergoes a periodic upgrade (client or server side), there is a chance that the upgrades will not be compatible with preexisting software.

A Web system software mix may include any combination of the following:

- Multiple operating systems
- Multiple software packages
- Multiple software components
- Multiple server types, brands, and models
- Multiple browser brands and versions

Server-Based Applications

Server-based applications are different from client applications. For one, server-based applications are programs that don't have a UI with which the end users of the system interact. End users only interact with the client-side application. In turn, the client interacts with server-based applications to access functionality and data via communication protocols, application programming interface, and other interfacing standards. Second, server-based applications run unattended. That is, when a server-based application is started, it's intended to stay up, waiting to provide services to client applications whether there is any client out there requesting services. In contrast, to use a client application, an end user must explicitly launch the client application and interact with it via a UI. Therefore, to black-box testers, server-based applications are black boxes. You may ask: "So it also is with desktop applications. What's the big deal?" Here is an example. When a failure is caused by an error in a client-side or desktop application, the users or testers can provide essential information that helps reproduce or analyze the failure because they are right in front of the application. Server-based applications or systems are often isolated away from the end users. When a server-based application fails, as testers or users from the client side, we often don't know when it failed, what happened before it failed, who was or how many users were on the system at the time it failed, and so on. This makes bug reproducibility even more challenging for us. In testing Web systems, we need a better way to track what goes on with applications on the server side. One of the techniques used to enhance our failure reproducibility capability is event logging. With event logging, server-based applications can record activities to a file that might not be normally seen by an end user. When an application uses event logging, the recorded information that is saved can be read in a reliable way. Have discussions with your developers and information technology staff to determine how event logging can be incorporated into the testing process.

Distributed Server Configurations

Server software can be distributed among any number of physical server boxes, which further complicates testing. Table 2.1 illustrates several possible server configurations that a Web application may support. You should identify the configurations that the application under test claims to support. Matrices of all possible combinations should be developed, and testing should be executed on each configuration to ensure that application features are intact.

The Network

The network is the glue that holds Web systems together. It connects clients to servers and servers to servers. This variable introduces new testing issues including reliabil-

Table 2.1 Distributed Server Configurations

	BOX 1	BOX 2	BOX 3
One-box model	NT-based Web server		
	NT-based application server		
	NT-based database server		
Two-box model	NT-based Web server	NT-based database server	
	NT-based application server		
Three-box model	NT-based Web server	NT-based Web server	Unix-based database server
	NT-based application server	NT-based application server	
One-box model	Unix-based Web server		
	Unix-based application server		
	Unix-based database server		
Two-box model	Unix-based Web server	Unix-based database server	
	Unix-based application server		
Three-box model	NT-based Web server	NT-based Web server	NT-based database server
	NT-based application server	NT-based application server	

ity, inaccessibility, performance, security, configuration, and compatibility. As illustrated in Figure 2.12, the network traffic may consist of several protocols supported by the TCP/IP network. It's also possible to have several networks using different net OSs connecting to each other by gateways. Testing issues related to the network can be a challenge or beyond the reach of black-box testing. However, understanding the testing-related issues surrounding the network enables us to better define testing problems and ask for appropriate help. See Chapter 4, "Network Basics," for more information.

Your Bugs Are Mine

It is common for Web applications to be built of preexisting objects or components that have been strung together. They may also be built of preexisting applications that have been strung together. In either scenario, the newly created systems are subject to whatever bugs may have existed in the original objects.

One of the important benefits of both *object-oriented programming* (OOP) and *component-based programming* is reusability. (The difference between OOP and component-based software is in the deliverable: OOP features are delivered in source, and classes are created or derived from the base class. Component-based software components, however, are delivered in binary forms, such as DLLs). As to reusability, a developer can take advantage of preexisting features created by other developers (with proper permission) by incorporating those features into his or her own application—rather than writing the code from scratch. In effect, code is recycled, eliminating the need to rewrite existing code. This model helps accelerate development time, reduces the amount of code that needs to be written, and maintains consistency between applications.

The potential problem with this shared model is that bugs are passed along with components. Web applications, due to their component-based architecture, are particularly vulnerable to the sharing of bugs.

At the low level, the problem has two major impacts on testing. First, existing objects or components must be tested thoroughly before their functionality can be used by other applications or objects. Second, regression testing (see "Regression Testing" in Chapter 3, "Software Testing Basics," for more information) must be executed comprehensively. Even a small change in a parent object can alter the functionality of an application or object that uses it.

This problem is not new. Object-oriented programming and component-based software have long been used in PCs. With the Web system architecture, however, the problem is multiplied due to the fact that components are shared across servers on a network. The problem is further exacerbated by the demand that software be developed in increasingly shorter time.

At the higher level, bugs in server packages such as Web servers and database servers, and bugs in Web browsers themselves, will also have an effect on the software under test. See Chapter 5, "Web Application Components," for more information.

Back-End Data Accessing

Data in a Web system is often distributed. That is, it resides on one or more (server) computers other than the client computer. There are several methods of storing data on a back-end server. For example, data can be stored in flat files, in a nonrelational database, in a relational database, or in an object-oriented database. In a typical Web application system, it's common that a relational database is employed so that data accessing and manipulation can be more efficient comparing to flat-file database.

In a flat-file system, when a query is initiated, the results of that query are dumped into files on a storage device. An application then opens, reads, and manipulates data from these files and generates reports on behalf of the user. To get to the data, the applications need to know exactly where files are located and what their names are. Access security is usually imposed at the application level.

In contrast, a database, such as a relational database, stores data in tables of records. Through the database engine, applications access data by getting a set of records without knowing where the physical data files are located or what they are named. Data in relational databases are accessed via database names (not to be mistaken with file names) and table names. Relational database files can be stored on multiple servers. Web systems using a relational database can impose security at the application server level, the database server level, as well at the database user level.

Thin-Client versus Thick-Client Processing

Thin client versus thick client is concerned with where applications and components reside and execute. Components may reside on a client machine and on one or more server machines. The two possibilities are:

Thin client. With thin-client systems, the client PC does very little processing. Business logic rules are executed on the server side. Some simple HTML Web-based applications and hand-held devices utilize this model. This approach centralizes processing on the server and eliminates most client-side incompatibility concerns. (See Table 2.2.)

Thick client. The client machine runs the UI portion of the application as well as the execution of business logic. In this case, the browser not only has to format the HTML page, but it also has to execute other components such as Java applet and ActiveX. The server machine houses the database that processes data requests from the client. Processing is shared between client and server. (See Table 2.3.)

Table 2.2 Thin Client

DESKTOP PC	SERVER
THIN CLIENT	
UI	Application rules
	Database

Table 2.3 Thick Client

DESKTOP PC	SERVER
THICK CLIENT	
UI	Database
Application rules	

The PC doing much of a system's work (i.e., executing business logic rules, DHTML, Java applets, ActiveX controls, or style sheets on the client side) is referred to as *thick-client processing.* Thick-client processing relieves processing strain on the server and takes full advantage of the client processor. With thick-client processing, there are likely to be more incompatibility problems on the client side.

Thin-client versus thick-client application testing issues revolve around the compromises among feature, compatibility and performance issues.

For more information regarding thin-client versus thick-client application, please see Chapter 5, "Web Application Components."

Interoperability Issues

Interoperability is the ability of a system or components within a system to interact and work seamlessly with other systems or other components. This is normally achieved by adhering to certain application program interfaces (APIs), communication protocol standards, or to interface-converting technology such as Common Object Request Broker Architecture (CORBA) or Distributed Common Object Model (DCOM). There are many hardware and software interoperability dependencies associated with Web systems. It is essential that our test-planning process include study of the system architectural design.

Interoperability issues—it is possible that information will be lost or misinterpreted in communication between components. Figure 2.13 shows a simplified Web system that includes three box servers and a client machine. In this example, the client requests all database records with zip code 94444 from the server side. The application server in turn queries the database server. Now, if the database server fails to execute the query, what will happen? Will the database server tell the application server that the query has failed? If the application server gets no response from the database server, will it resend the query? Possibly, the application server will receive an error message that it does not understand. Consequently, what message will be passed back to the client? Will the application server simply notify the client that the request must be resent or neglect to inform the client of anything at all? All of these scenarios need to be investigated in the study of the system architectural design.

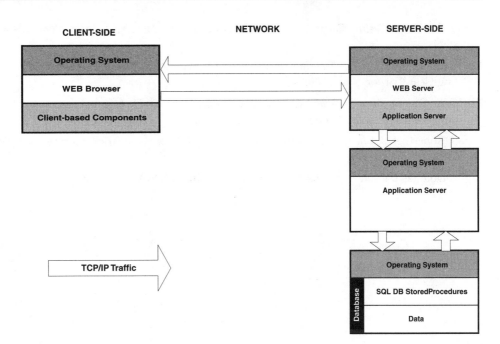

Figure 2.13 Interoperability.

Testing Considerations

The key areas of testing for Web applications beyond traditional testing include:

- Web UI implementation
- System integration
- Server and client installation
- Web-based help
- Configuration and compatibility
- Database
- Security
- Performance, load, and stress

For definitions for these tests, see Chapter 3 ("Software Testing Basics"). In addition, see Chapters 9 through 16 for in-depth discussions on these tests.

Bibliography

Bourne, Kelly C. *Testing Client/Server Systems.* New York: McGraw-Hill, 1997.

Coffman, Gayle. *SQL Server 7: The Complete Reference.* Berkeley, CA: Osborne/McGraw-Hill, 1999.

Kaner, Cem, et al. *Testing Computer Software,* second edition. New York: John Wiley & Sons, 1999.

LogiGear Corporation. *QA Training Handbook: Testing Web Applications.* Foster City, CA: LogiGear Corporation, 2000.

LogiGear Corporation. *QA Training Handbook: Testing Windows Desktop and Server-Based Applications.* Foster City, CA: LogiGear Corporation, 2000.

Orfali, Robert, et al. *Client/Server Survival Guide, Third Edition.* New York: John Wiley & Sons, 1999.

Reilly, Douglas J. *Inside Server-Based Applications.* Redmond, WA: Microsoft Press, 2000.

PART TWO

Methodology
and Technology

CHAPTER 3

Software Testing Basics

Why Read This Chapter?

In general, the software testing techniques that are applied to other applications are the same as those that are applied to Web-based applications. Both types of testing require basic test types such as functionality tests, forced-error tests, boundary condition and equivalence class analysis, and so forth. The difference between the two types of testing is that the technology variables in the Web environment multiply. Having the basic understanding in testing methodologies, combined with a domain expertise in Web technology, will enable you to effectively test Web applications.

Introduction

This chapter includes a review of some of the more elemental software testing principals upon which this book is based. Basic testing terminology, practices, and test-case

---

Topics Covered in This Chapter

- Introduction
- Basic Planning and Documentation
- Common Terminology and Concepts
- Test-Case Development
- Bibliography

development techniques are covered. However, a full analysis of the theories and practices that are required for effective software testing is not a goal of this book. For more detailed information on the basics of software testing, please refer to *Testing Computer Software* (Kaner et al., 1999).

Basic Planning and Documentation

Methodical record keeping builds credibility for the testing team and focuses testing efforts. Records should be kept for all testing. Complete test-case lists, tables, and matrices should be collected and saved. Note that Chapter 6, "Test Planning Fundamentals," details many practical reporting and planning processes.

There are always limits to the amount of time and money that can be invested into testing. There are often scheduling and budgetary constraints on development projects that severely restrict testing—for example, adequate hardware configurations may be unaffordable. For this reason, it is important that cost justification, including potential technical support and outsourcing, be factored into all test planning.

To be as efficient as possible, look for redundant test cases and eliminate them. Reuse test suites and locate preexisting test suites when appropriate. Become as knowledgeable as possible about the application under test and the technologies supporting that application. With knowledge of the application's technologies, you can avoid wasted time and identify the most effective testing methods available. You can also keep the development team informed about areas of possible risk.

Early planning is key to the efficiency and cost savings that can be brought to the testing effort. Time invested early in core functionality testing, for example, can make for big cost savings down the road. Identifying functionality errors early reduces the risk of developers having to make risky fixes to core functionality late in the development process when the stakes are higher.

Test coverage (an assessment of the breadth and depth of testing that a given product will undergo) is a balance of risk and other project concerns such as resources and scheduling (complete coverage is virtually impossible). The extent of coverage is a negotiable concept over which the product team will be required to give input.

Common Terminology and Concepts

Following are some essential software testing terms and concepts.

Test Conditions

Test conditions are critically important factors in Web application testing. The test conditions are the circumstances in which an application under test operates. There are two categories of test conditions, *application-specific* and *environment-specific,* which are described in the following text.

1. *Application-specific conditions.*   An example of an application-specific condition includes running the same word processor spell-checking test while in normal view and then again when in page view. If one of the tests generates an error and the other does not, then you can deduce that there is a condition that is specific to the application that is causing the error.

2. *Environment-specific conditions.*   When an error is generated by conditions outside of an application under test, the conditions are considered to be environment-specific.

In general, I find it useful to think in terms of two classes of operating environments, each having its own unique testing implications:

1. *Static environments* (i.e., configuration and compatibility errors).   An operating environment in which incompatibility issues may exist regardless of variable conditions such as processing speed and available memory.

2. *Dynamic environments* (i.e., RAM, disc space, memory, etc.).   An operating environment in which otherwise compatible components may exhibit errors due to memory-related errors and latency conditions.

Static Operating Environments

The compatibility differences between Netscape Navigator and Internet Explorer illustrate a static environment.

Configuration and *compatibility* issues may occur at any point within a Web system: client, server, or network. Configuration issues involve various server software and hardware setups, browser settings, network connections, and TCP/IP stack setups. Figures 3.1 and 3.2 illustrate two of the many possible physical server configurations, one-box and two-box, respectively.

Dynamic Operating Environments

When the value of a specific environment attribute does not stay constant each time a test procedure is executed, it causes the operating environment to become dynamic. The attribute can be anything from resource-specific (available RAM, disk space, etc.) to timing-specific (network latency, the order of transactions being submitted, etc.).

Resource Contention Example

Figure 3.3 and Table 3.1 illustrate an example of a dynamic environment condition that involves three workstations and a shared temp space. Workstation C has 400Mb of temporary memory space on it. Workstation A asks Workstation C if it has 200Mb of memory available. Workstation C responds with an affirmative response. What happens though if, before Workstation A receives an answer to its request, Workstation B writes 300Mb of data to the temp space on Workstation C? When Workstation A finally receives the response to its request it will begin writing 200Mb of data to Workstation C—even though there will only be 100Mb of memory available. An error condition will result.

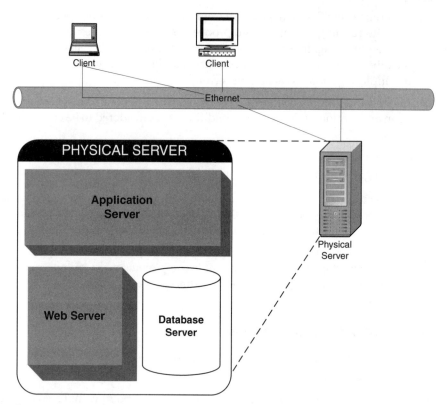

Figure 3.1 One-box configuration.

Test Types

Test types are categories of tests that are designed to expose a certain class of error or verify the accuracy of related behaviors. The analysis of test types is a good way to divide the testing of an application methodically into logical and manageable groups of tasks. They are also helpful in communicating required testing time and resources to other members of the product team.

Following are a number of common test types. See Chapter 6, "Test Planning Fundamentals," and Chapter 8, "Sample Test Plan," for information regarding the selection of test types.

Acceptance Testing

The two common types of acceptance tests are development acceptance tests and deployment acceptance tests.

Development Acceptance Test

Release acceptance tests and functional acceptance simple tests are two common classes of test used during the development process. There are subtle differences in the application of these two classes of tests.

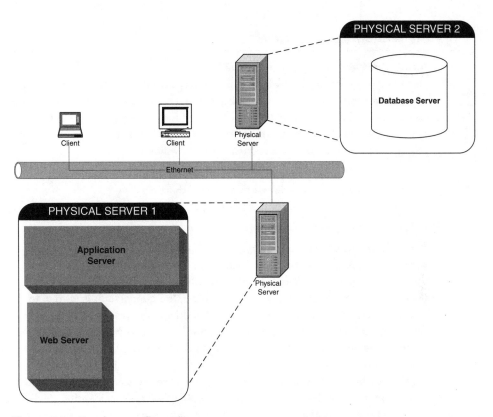

Figure 3.2 Two-box configuration.

Release Acceptance Test

The *release acceptance test* (RAT), also referred to as a *build acceptance* or *smoke test,* is run on each development release to check that each build is stable enough for further testing. Typically, this test suite consists of entrance and exit test cases plus test cases that check mainstream functions of the program with mainstream data. Copies of the RAT can be distributed to developers so that they can run the tests before submitting builds to the testing group. If a build does not pass a RAT test, it is reasonable to do the following:

- Suspend testing on the new build and resume testing on the prior build until another build is received.
- Report the failing criteria to the development team.
- Request a new build.

Functional Acceptance Simple Test

The functional acceptance simple test (FAST) is run on each development release to check that key features of the program are appropriately accessible and functioning properly on at least one test configuration (preferably the minimum or common configuration). This test suite consists of simple test cases that check the lowest level of

Testing the Sample Application

STATIC OPERATING ENVIRONMENT EXAMPLE

This sample application illustrates incompatibility between a version of Netscape Navigator and a version of Microsoft Internet Explorer. (See Chapter 7, "Sample Application," for more information.) The application has charting functionality that enables users to generate metrics reports, such as bar charts and line charts. When a user requests a metrics report, the application server pseudocode runs as follows:

1. Connect to the database server and run the query.

2. Write the query result to a file named c:\temp\chart.val.

3. Execute the chart Java applet. Read and draw a graph using data from c:\temp\chart.val.

4. Send the Java applet to the browser.

During testing of the sample application, it was discovered that the charting feature works on one of the preceding configurations, but not the other. The problem occurred only in the two-box configuration. After examining the code, it was learned that the problem was in steps 2 and 3. In step 2, the query result is written to c:\temp\chart.val of the database server local drive. In step 3, the chart Java applet is running on the application server, which is not in the same box as the database server. When the database server attempts to open the file c:\temp\chart.val on the application server local drive, the file is not found. It should not be inferred from this example that we should read the code every time we come across an error—leave the debugging work for the developers. It is essential, however, to identify which server configurations are problematic and include such information in bug reports. You should consider running a cursory suite of test cases on all distributed configurations that are supported by the application server under test. You should also consider replicating every bug on at least two configurations that are extremely different from each other when configuration-dependency is in suspect.

functionality for each command—to ensure that task-oriented functional tests (TOFTs) can be performed on the program. The objective is to decompose the functionality of a program down to the command level and then apply test cases to check that each command works as intended. No attention is paid to the combination of these basic commands, the context of the feature that is formed by these combined commands, or the end result of the overall feature. For example, FAST for a File/Save As menu command checks that the Save As dialog box displays. However, it does not validate that the overall file-saving feature works nor does it validate the integrity of saved files.

Typically, errors encountered during the execution of FAST are reported through the standard issue-tracking process. Suspending testing during FAST is not recommended.

Consider the compatibility issues involved in the following example.

- The home directory path for the Web server on the host **myserver** is mapped to **C:\INETPUB\WWWROOT**.

- When a page is requested from **http://myserver/**, data is pulled from **C:\INETPUB\WWWROOT**.

- A file name, **mychart.jar**, is stored at **C:\INETPUB\WWWROOT\MYAPP\BIN**.

- The application session path (*relative path*) points to **C:\INETPUB\WWWROOT\MYAPP\BIN**, and a file is requested from **.\LIB**.

Using Internet Explorer version 3.x, the Web server looks for the file in **C:\INETPUB\WWWROOT\MYAPP\BIN\LIB**, because the browser understands relative paths. This is the desired behavior and the file will be found in this scenario.

Using Netscape Navigator version 3.x, which uses absolute paths, the Web server looks for the file in **C:\INETPUB\WWWROOT\LIB**. This is a problem because the file (**mychart.jar**) will not be found. The feature does not work with this old version of Netscape Navigator (which some people still use).

Bringing up the Java Console, you can see the following, which confirms the finding: **#Unable to load archive http://myserver/lib/mychart.jar:java.io.IOException:<null>**.

This is not to say that Internet Explorer is better than Netscape Navigator. It simply means that there are incompatibility issues between browsers. Code should not assume that relative paths work with all browsers.

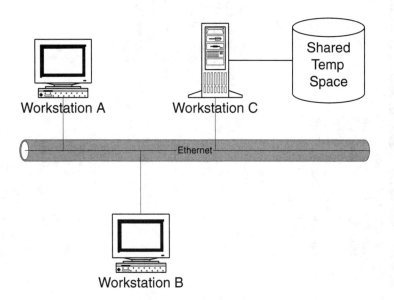

Figure 3.3 Resource contention diagram.

Table 3.1 Resource Contention Process

STEP	WORKSTATION A	WORKSTATION B	BEFORE WORKSTATION C: SHARED TEMP SPACE AVAILABLE MEMORY	AFTER WORKSTATION C: SHARED TEMP SPACE AVAILABLE MEMORY
1	Workstation A needs to write 200Mb of data to the shared temp space on Workstation C. Workstation A asks Workstation C if the needed space is available. Workstation C tells Workstation A that it has the available memory space. Note that Workstation A did not reserve the space.		400Mb	400Mb
2		Workstation B needs to write 300Mb of data to the shared temp space on Workstation C. Workstation B asks Workstation C to GIVE it the needed space. Workstation C tells Workstation B that it has the available memory space and it reserves the space for Workstation B. Workstation B writes the data to Workstation C.	400Mb	100Mb
3	Workstation A finally gets its response from Work-station C and begins to write 200Mb of data. Workstation C however now has only 100Mb of temp space left. Without proper error handling, Work-station A crashes.			0Mb

Bug Analyzing and Reproduction Tips

To reproduce an *environment-dependent* error, both the exact sequence of activities and the environment conditions (e.g., operating system, browser version, add-on components, database server, Web server, third-party components, client-server resources, network bandwidth and traffic, etc.) in which the application operations must be replicated.

Environment-independent errors on the other hand are easier to reproduce—they do not require replicating the operating environment. With environment-independent errors, all that need to be replicated are the steps that generate the error.

BROWSER BUG ANALYZING TIPS

- Check if the client operating system (OS) version and patches meet system requirements.
- Check if the correct version of the browser is installed on the client machine.
- Check if the browser is properly installed on the machine.
- Check the browser settings.
- Check with different browsers (e.g., Netscape Navigator versus Internet Explorer).
- Check with different supported versions of the same browsers (e.g., 3.1, 3.2, 4.2, 4.3, etc.).

Note that it depends on the organization for which you work. Each might have different rules in terms of which test cases should belong to RAT versus FAST, and when to suspend testing or to reject a build.

Deployment Acceptance Test

The configurations on which the Web system will be deployed will often be much different from develop-and-test configurations. Testing efforts must consider this in the preparation and writing of test cases for installation time acceptance tests. This type of test usually includes the full installation of the applications to the targeted environments or configurations. Then, FASTs and TOFTs are executed to validate the system functionality.

Feature-Level Testing

This is where we begin to do some serious testing, including boundary testing and other difficult but valid test circumstances.

Task-Oriented Functional Test

The task-oriented functional test (TOFT) consists of positive test cases that are designed to verify program features by checking the task that each feature performs against specifications, user guides, requirements, and design documents. Usually, features are organized into list or test matrix format. Each feature is tested for:

- The validity of the task it performs with supported data conditions under supported operating conditions
- The integrity of the task's end result
- The feature's integrity when used in conjunction with related features

Forced-Error Test

The forced-error test (FET) consists of negative test cases that are designed to force a program into error conditions. A list of all error messages that the program issues should be generated. The list is used as a baseline for developing test cases. An attempt is made to generate each error message in the list. Obviously, tests to validate error-handling schemes cannot be performed until all the handling and error messages have been coded. However, FETs should be thought through as early as possible. Sometimes, the error messages are not available. The error cases can still be considered by walking through the program and deciding how the program might fail in a given user interface (UI) such as a dialog or in the course of executing a given task or printing a given report. Test cases should be created for each condition to determine what error message is generated (if any).

USEFUL FET EXECUTION GUIDELINES

Check that the error-handling design and the error communication methods are consistent.

Check that all common error conditions are detected and handled correctly.

Check that the program recovers gracefully from each error condition.

Check that the unstable states of the program (e.g., an open file that needs to be closed, a variable that needs to be reinitialized, etc.) caused by the error are also corrected.

Check each error message to ensure that:

- Message matches the type of error detected.
- Description of the error is clear and concise.
- Message does not contain spelling or grammatical errors.
- User is offered reasonable options for getting around or recovering from the error condition.

Boundary Test

Boundary tests are designed to check a program's response to extreme input values. Extreme output values are generated by the input values. It is important to check that a program handles input values and output results correctly at the lower and upper boundaries. Keep in mind that you can create extreme boundary results from non-extreme input values. It is essential to analyze how to generate extremes of both types. In addition, sometimes you know that there is an intermediate variable involved in processing. If so, it is useful to determine how to drive that one through the extremes and special conditions such as zero or overflow condition.

System-Level Test

System-level tests consist of batteries of tests that are designed to fully exercise a program as a whole and check that all elements of the integrated system function properly. System-level test suites also validate the usefulness of a program and compare end results against requirements.

Real-World User-Level Test

These tests simulate the actions customers may take with a program. Real-world user-level testing often detects errors that are otherwise missed by formal test types.

Exploratory Test

Exploratory tests do not involve a test plan, checklists, or assigned tasks. The strategy here is to use past testing experience to make educated guesses about places and functionality that may be problematic. Testing is then focused on those areas. Exploratory testing can be scheduled. It can also be reserved for unforeseen downtime that presents itself during the testing process.

Load/Volume Test

Load/volume tests study how a program handles large amounts of data, excessive calculations, and excessive processing. These tests do not necessarily have to push or exceed upper functional limits. Load/volume tests can, and usually must, be automated.

FOCUS OF LOAD/VOLUME TESTING

- Pushing through large amounts of data with extreme processing demands
- Requesting many processes simultaneously
- Repeating tasks over a long period of time

Load/volume tests, which involve extreme conditions, are normally run after the execution of feature-level tests, which prove that a program functions correctly under normal conditions.

Stress Test

Stress tests force programs to operate under limited resource conditions. The goal is to push the upper functional limits of a program to ensure that it can function correctly and handle error conditions gracefully. Examples of resources that may be artificially manipulated to create stressful conditions include memory, disk space, and network bandwidth. If other memory-oriented tests are also planned, they should be performed here as part of the stress test suite. Stress tests can be automated.

Performance Test

The primary goal of performance testing is to develop effective enhancement strategies for maintaining acceptable system performance. Performance testing is a capacity analysis and planning process in which measurement data are used to predict when load levels will exhaust system resources.

The testing team should work with the development team to identify tasks to be measured and to determine acceptable performance criteria. The marketing group may even insist on meeting a competitor's standards of performance. Test suites can be developed to measure how long it takes to perform relevant tasks. Performance tests can be automated.

Regression Test

Regression testing is used to confirm that fixed bugs have, in fact, been fixed and that new bugs have not been introduced in the process, and that features that were proven correctly functional are intact. Depending on the size of a project, cycles of regression testing may be performed once per milestone or once per build. Some bug regression testing may also be performed during each acceptance test cycle, focusing on only the most important bugs. Regression tests can be automated.

CONDITIONS DURING WHICH REGRESSION TESTS MAY BE RUN

Issue fixing cycle.   Once the development team has fixed issues, a regression test can be run to validate the fixes. Tests are based on the step-by-step test cases that were originally reported.

- If an issue is confirmed as fixed, then the issue report status should be changed to *Closed*.
- If an issue is confirmed as fixed, but with side effects, then the issue report status should be changed to *Closed*. However, a new issue should be filed to report the side effect.
- If an issue is only partially fixed, then the issue report resolution should be changed back to *Unfixed,* along with comments outlining the outstanding problems.

Open-status regression cycle.   Periodic regression tests may be run on all open issues in the issue-tracking database. During this cycle, issue status is confirmed either *the report is reproducible as is with no modification, the report is reproducible with additional comments or modifications,* or *the report is no longer reproducible.*

Closed-fixed regression cycle.   In the final phase of testing, a full-regression test cycle should be run to confirm the status of all fixed-closed issues.

Feature regression cycle.   Each time a new build is cut or is in the final phase of testing, depending on the organizational procedure, a full-regression test cycle should be run to confirm that the proven correctly functional features are still working as expected.

Compatibility and Configuration Test

Compatibility and configuration testing is performed to check that an application functions properly across various hardware and software environments. Often, the strategy is to run FASTs or a subset of TOFTs on a range of software and hardware configurations. Sometimes, another strategy is to create a specific test that takes into account the error risks associated with configuration differences. For example, you might design an extensive series of tests to check for browser compatibility issues. You might not run these as part of your normal RATs, FASTs, or TOFTs.

Software compatibility configurations include variances in OS versions, input/output (I/O) devices, extensions, network software, concurrent applications, online services, and firewalls. Hardware configurations include variances in manufacturers, CPU types, RAM, graphic display cards, video capture cards, sound cards, monitors, network cards, and connection types (e.g., T1, DSL, modem, etc.).

Documentation Test

Testing of reference guides and user guides check that all features are reasonably documented. Every page of documentation should be keystroke-tested for the following errors:

- Accuracy of every statement of fact
- Accuracy of every screen shot, figure, and illustration
- Accuracy of placement of figures and illustrations
- Accuracy of every tutorial, tip, and instruction
- Accuracy of marketing collateral (claims, system requirements, and screen shots)
- Accuracy of downloadable documentation (PDFs, HTML, or text files)

Online Help Test

Online help tests check the accuracy of help contents, correctness of features in the help system, and functionality of the help system.

Utilities/Toolkits and Collateral Test

If there are utilities and software collateral items to be tested, appropriate analysis should be done to ensure that suitable and adequate testing strategies are in place.

Install/Uninstall Test

Web systems often require both client-side and server-side installs. Testing of the installer checks that installed features function properly—including icons, support documentation, the README file, and registry keys. The test verifies that the correct directories are created and that the correct system files are copied to the appropriate directories. The test also confirms that various error conditions are detected and handled gracefully.

Testing of the uninstaller checks that the installed directories and files are appropriately removed, that configuration and system-related files are also appropriately removed or modified, and that the operating environment is recovered in its original state.

User Interface Tests

Ease-of-use UI testing evaluates how intuitive a system is. Issues pertaining to navigation, usability, commands, and accessibility are considered. User interface *functionality* testing examines how well a UI operates to specifications.

AREAS COVERED IN UI TESTING

- Usability
- Look and feel
- Navigation controls/navigation bar
- Instructional and technical information style
- Images
- Tables
- Navigation branching
- Accessibility

External Beta Testing

External beta testing offers developers their first glimpse at how users may actually interact with a program. Copies of the program or a test URL, sometimes accompanied with a letter of instruction, are sent out to a group of volunteers who try out the program and respond to questions in the letter. Beta testing is black-box, real-world testing. Beta testing can be difficult to manage, and the feedback that it generates normally comes too late in the development process to contribute to improved usability and functionality. External beta-tester feedback may be reflected in a README file or deferred to future releases.

Ongoing Y2K Testing

A program's ability to handle the year change from 1999 to 2000 has been tested to ensure that internal systems were not scrambled or shut down on 01 January 2000. However, Y2K-related considerations will remain an issue well beyond the year 2000 due to future leap-year and business-calendar changeovers.

Security Tests

Security measures protect Web systems from both internal and external threats. E-commerce concerns and the growing popularity of Web-based applications have made security testing increasingly relevant. Security tests determine whether a company's security policies have been properly implemented; they evaluate the functionality of existing systems, not whether the security policies that have been implemented are appropriate.

PRIMARY COMPONENTS REQUIRING SECURITY TESTING

- Application software
- Databases
- Servers
- Client workstations
- Networks

Unit Tests

Unit tests are positive tests that evaluate the integrity of software code units before they are integrated with other software units. Developers normally perform unit testing. Unit testing represents the first round of software testing—when developers test their own software and fix errors in private.

Phases of Development

The software development process is normally divided into phases. Each phase of development entails different test types, coverage depth, and demands on the testing effort. Refer to Table 6.1, "Test Types and Their Place in the Software Development Process," for a visual representation of test phases and corresponding test types.

Development phases should be defined by clearly communicated and measurable criteria that are agreed upon. Often, people on the same development team may have different understandings of how particular phases are defined. For example, it might be defined that an application cannot officially begin its beta phase of development until all crash or data loss bugs have been fixed. Alternatively, *beta* is also commonly defined as being a product that is functionally complete (though bugs may still be present, all features have been coded).

Disagreement over how a phase is defined can lead to problems in perception of completeness and product stability. It is often the role of the test team to define the milestone or completion criteria that must be met for a project to pass from one phase to another. Defining and agreeing upon milestone and completion criteria allows the testing, development, and marketing groups to work better as a team. The specifics of the milestones are not as important as the fact that they are clearly communicated. It is also a concern that the developers usually consider that they have made the milestone when the build is done. In practice, testing still must confirm if this is true, and the confirmation process may take from a few days to a few weeks.

COMMON PHASES OF SOFTWARE DEVELOPMENT

Alpha.   A significant and agreed-upon portion (if not all) of the product has been completed (the product includes code, documentation, additional art, or other content, etc.). The product is ready for in-house use.

Pre-beta (or beta candidate).   A build that is submitted for beta acceptance. If the build meets the beta criteria (as verified by the testing group), then the software is accepted into the beta phase of development.

Beta.   Most, or all, of the product is complete and stable. Some companies send out review copies (beta copies) of software to customers once software reaches this phase.

UI freeze.   Every aspect of the application's UI is complete. Some companies accept limited changes to error messaging and repairs to errors in help screens during this phase.

Prefinal [or golden master candidate (GMC)].   A final candidate build has been submitted for review to the testing team. If the software is complete and all GMC tests are passed, then the product is considered ready for final testing.

Final test.   This is the last round of testing before the product is migrated to the live Web site, sent to manufacturing, or posted on the Web site.

Release (or golden master).   The build that will eventually be shipped to the customer, posted on the Web, or migrated to the live Web site.

Other Software Testing Terms

Test case.   A test that (ideally) executes a single well-defined test objective (i.e., a specific behavior of a feature under a specific condition). Early in testing, a test case might be extremely simple; later, however, the program is more stable, so we need more complex test cases to provide us with useful information.

Test script.   Step-by-step instructions that describe how a test case is to be executed. A test script may contain one or more test cases.

Test suite.   A collection of test scripts or test cases that is used for validating bug fixes (or finding new bugs) within a logical or physical area of a product. For example, an acceptance test suite contains all the test cases that are used to verify that software has met certain predefined acceptance criteria. A regression suite, on the other hand, contains all the test cases that are used to verify that all previously fixed bugs are still fixed.

Test specification.   A set of test cases, input, and conditions that are used in the testing of a particular feature or set of features. A test specification often includes descriptions of expected results.

Test requirement.   A document that describes items and features that are tested under a required condition.

Test plan.   A management document outlining risks, priorities, and schedules for testing. (See Part Three for more information.)

Test-Case Development

There are many methods available for analyzing software in an effort to develop appropriate test cases. The following sections focus on several methods of establishing coverage and developing effective test cases. A combination of most, if not all, of the following test design methods should be used to develop test cases for the application under test.

Equivalence Class Partitioning and Boundary Condition Analysis

Equivalence class partitioning is a timesaving practice that identifies tests that are equivalent to one another; when two inputs are equivalent, you expect them to cause the identical sequence of operations to take place or they cause the same path to be executed through the code. When two or more test cases are seen as equivalent, the resource savings associated with not running the redundant tests normally outweighs the risk.

An example of an equivalence class includes the testing of a data-entry field in an HTML form. If the field accepts a five-digit ZIP code (e.g., 22222) then it can reasonably be assumed that the field will accept all other five-digit ZIP codes (e.g., 33333, 44444, etc.). Because all five-digit ZIP codes are of the same equivalence class, there is little benefit in testing more than one of them.

In equivalence partitioning, both valid and invalid values are treated in this manner. For example, if entering six letters into the ZIP code field just described results in an error message, then it can reasonably be assumed that all six-letter combinations will result in the same error message. Similarly, if entering a four-digit number into the ZIP code field results in an error message, then it should be assumed that all four-digit combinations will result in the same error message.

EXAMPLES OF EQUIVALENCE CLASSES

- Ranges of numbers (such as all numbers between 10 and 99, which are of the same two-digit equivalence class)
- Membership in groups (dates, times, country names, etc.)
- Invalid inputs (placing symbols into text-only fields, etc.)
- Equivalent output events (variation of inputs that produce the same output)
- Equivalent operating environments
- Repetition of activities
- Number of records in a database (or other equivalent objects)
- Equivalent sums or other arithmetic results
- Equivalent numbers of items entered (such as the number of characters entered into a field)
- Equivalent space (on a page or on a screen)
- Equivalent amounts of memory, disk space, or other resources available to a program

Boundary values mark the transition points between equivalence classes. They can be limit values that define the line between supported inputs and nonsupported inputs, or they can define the line between supported system requirements and nonsupported system requirements. Applications are more susceptible to errors at the boundaries of equivalence classes, so boundary condition tests can be quite effective at uncovering errors.

Generally, each equivalence class is partitioned by its boundary values. Nevertheless, not all equivalence classes have boundaries. For example, given the following four browser equivalent classes (Netscape Navigator 4.6 and 4.6.1, and Microsoft Internet Explorer 4.0 and 5.0), there is no boundary defined among each class.

Each equivalence class represents potential risk. Under the equivalent class approach to developing test cases, at most, nine test cases should be executed against each partition. Figure 3.4 illustrates how test cases can be built around equivalence class partitions. In Figure 3.4, *LB* stands for *lower boundary* and *UB* stands for *upper boundary*. The test cases include three tests clustered around each of the boundaries: one test

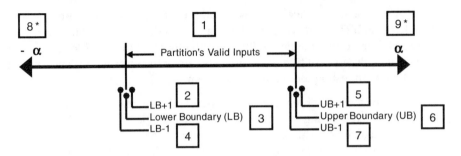

Figure 3.4 Boundary condition test cases. *, Smallest/largest possible values allowed via UI.

Source: © 1998–2000 LogiGear Corporation. All rights reserved.

that falls within the partition's boundaries, and two tests that fall well beyond the boundaries.

Figure 3.5 illustrates another boundary condition test-case design example taken from the sample application. (See Chapter 7, "Sample Application," for more information.)

To develop test cases via equivalence class partitioning and boundary class analysis, one must do the following:

- Identify the equivalence classes.
- Identify the boundaries.
- Identify the expected output(s) for valid input(s).
- Identify the expected error handling (ER) for invalid inputs.
- Generate a table of test cases (maximum of nine for each partition).

Test Case	Input	Output
Value Class Partition		
1	Any Valid Input	Functional Result
2	2	Functional Result
3	1	Functional Result
4	0	Error Handling
5	10000	Error Handling
6	9999	Functional Result
7	9998	Functional Result
8	-99999...	Error Handling
9	99999...	Error Handling
Number of Character Class Partition		
1	Any Valid Input	Functional Result
2	2	Functional Result
3	1	Functional Result
4	NULL	Error Handling
5	5	Error Handling
6	4	Functional Result
7	3	Functional Result
8	N/A	N/A
9	99999	Error Handling

Valid Values: 1 to 9999 or 1 to 4-digit value

Figure 3.5 Sample application test cases.

Note that this example is an oversimplified one. It indicates only two equivalent classes. In reality, there are many other equivalent classes such as invalid character class (nonalphanumeric characters), special cases such as numbers with decimal points, leading zeros of leading spaces, and so on. Chapter 10, "Functionality Tests," contains additional information regarding boundary analysis.

State Transition

State transition involves analysis of the transitions between an application's states, the events that trigger the transitions, and the results of the transitions.

GENERAL STEPS FOR STATE TRANSITION TEST-DESIGN ANALYSIS

1. Identify all of an application's supported states.

2. For each test case, define the following:

   - The starting state

   - The input events that cause the transitions

   - The output results or events of each transition

   - The end state

3. Draw a diagram that illustrates the relationships between the states, events, and actions of the application.

4. Generate a table of test cases that addresses each state transition.

Condition Combination

A long-standing challenge in software testing is having enough time to execute all possible test cases. There are numerous approaches that can be taken to strategically

Testing the Sample Application

Figures 3.6 and 3.7 show two different states that are available within the sample application. (See Chapter 7, "Sample Application," for details regarding the sample application.) Figure 3.6 shows the application in Edit View mode. Available navigation options from this state include Full View, First, Previous, Next, and Last. Figure 3.7 shows the application in Full View. Available navigation options from this state include Edit View and the Report Number hyperlink. Figure 3.8 diagrams the transitions, events, and actions that interconnect these two states.

Figure 3.9 is a table of test cases that targets each of the transition states. Each test case has a beginning state (Start View mode), an event or input (Navigation Command), and an event (End View Mode).

Continues

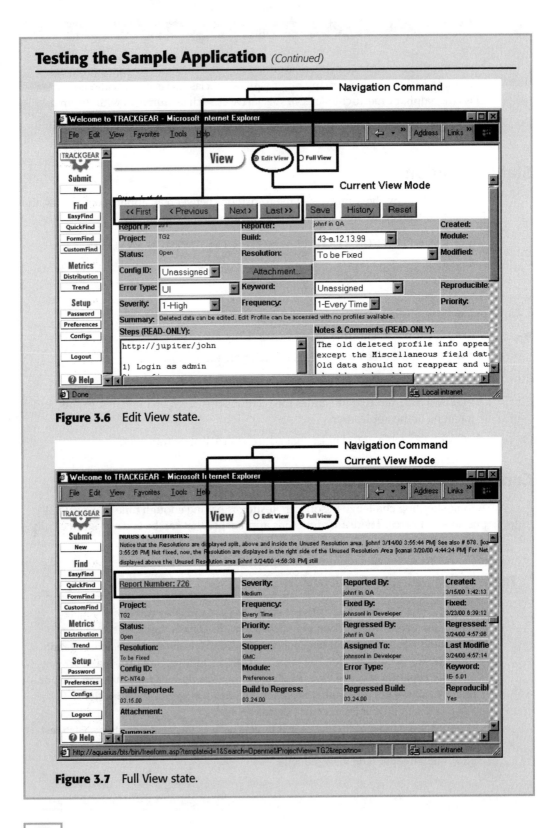

Figure 3.6 Edit View state.

Figure 3.7 Full View state.

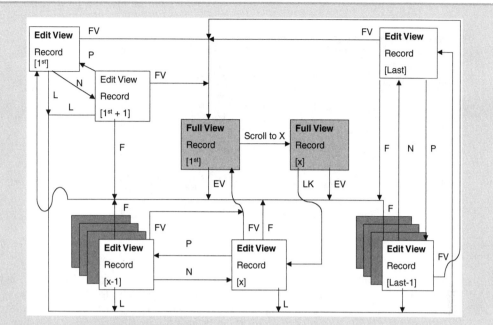
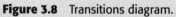

Figure 3.8 Transitions diagram.

Code	VIEW MODE (State)		NAVIGATION COMMAND (Event)	
a	Edit View-Record [1st]	Edit View displaying the 1st record	F	First
b	Edit View-Record [1st + 1]	Edit View displaying the 2nd record	P	Previous
c	Edit View-Record [x]	Edit View displaying the record [x]	N	Next
d	Edit View-Record [x - 1]	Edit View displaying the record [x-1]	L	Last
e	Edit View-Record [Last]	Edit View displaying the last record	FV	Full View
f	Edit View-Record [Last - 1]	Edit View displaying the next to last record		
g	Full View Record [1st]	Full View displaying the 1st record	EV	Edit View
h	Full View Record [x]	Full View displaying record [x]	LK	Record ID Link

TEST CASE NO.	1	2	3	4	5	6	7	8	9	10	11	12	13	14	15
Start View Mode	a	a	a	b	b	b	b	c	c	c	c	d	d	d	d
Navigation Command (input)	N	L	FV	F	P	L	FV	F	P	L	FV	F	N	L	FV
End View Mode	b	e	g	a	a	e	g	a	d	e	g	a	c	e	g

TEST CASE NO.	16	17	18	19	20	21	22	23	24	25
Start View Mode	e	e	e	f	f	f	f	g	h	h
Navigation Command (input)	F	P	FV	F	N	L	FV	EV	EV	LK
End View Mode	a	f	g	a	e	e	g	a	a	c

Figure 3.9 Test matrix.

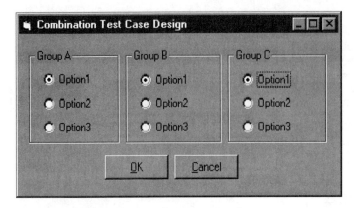

Figure 3.10 Simplified application example.

reduce the number of test cases to a manageable amount. The riskiest approach is to randomly reduce test cases without a clear methodology. A better approach is to divide the total test cases over a series of software builds.

The *condition combination* approach involves the analysis of combinations of variables, such as browser settings. Each combination represents a condition to be tested with the same test script and procedures. The condition combination approach involves the following:

- Identifying the variables
- Identifying the possible unique values for each variable
- Creating a table that illustrates all the unique combinations of conditions that are formed by the variables and their values

Figures 3.10 and 3.11 illustrate an application that includes three variables with three possible unique values each. The number of complete combinations formed by the variables is $3 \times 3 \times 3 = 27$. The 27 unique combinations (test cases) formed by the three variables *A*, *B*, and *C* are listed in Table 3.2. To execute the test cases calculated by these unique combinations, set the values for each *A*, *B*, and *C* variable using the variables listed in the corresponding rows of the tables. Execute the procedures and verify expected results.

The Combinatorial Method

The combinatorial method is a thoughtful means of reducing test cases via a pairwise shortcut. It involves analyzing combinations of variables, such as browser settings, one

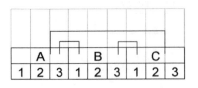

Figure 3.11 Unique combinations.

Table 3.2 Total Unique Combinations

Case	A	B	C
1	1	1	1
2	1	1	2
3	1	1	3
4	1	2	1
5	1	2	2
6	1	2	3
7	1	3	1
8	1	3	2
9	1	3	3

Case	A	B	C
10	2	1	1
11	2	1	2
12	2	1	3
13	2	2	1
14	2	2	2
15	2	2	3
16	2	3	1
17	2	3	2
18	2	3	3

Case	A	B	C
19	3	1	1
20	3	1	2
21	3	1	3
22	3	2	1
23	3	2	2
24	3	2	3
25	3	3	1
26	3	3	2
27	3	3	3

pair at a time. Each unique combination pair represents a condition to be tested. By examining and testing pair combinations, the number of total conditions to be tested can be dramatically reduced. This technique is useful when complete condition combination testing is not feasible. The the combinatorial method involves the following:

- Identifying the variables
- Identifying the possible unique values for each variable
- Identifying the unique combinations formed by the variables, one pair at a time
- Creating a table that illustrates all of the unique combinations of conditions that are formed by the variables and their values
- Generating the unique combinations formed by the first pair, A-B. As illustrated in Table 3.3, arrange the values in the C column to cover the combinations of the B-C and A-C pairs without increasing the number of cases. Set the value of the variables A, B, and C using the information listed in each row of the table, one at a time. Execute the test procedure and verify the expected output.

Table 3.3 The Combinatorial Method

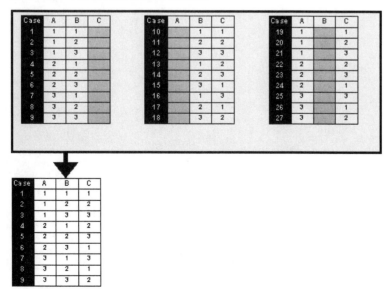

For more information on this technique, go to AR GREENHOUSE at www
.argreenhouse.com. For a paper on this topic, *The AETG System: An Approach to Testing
Based on Combinatorial Design* (Cohen et al., 1997), go to www.argreenhouse.com/
papers/gcp/AETGieee97.shtml.

Bibliography

Kaner, Cem, et al. *Testing Computer Software,* second edition. New York: John Wiley & Sons,
1999.

LogiGear Corporation. *QA Training Handbook: Testing Web Applications.* Foster City, CA:
LogiGear Corporation, 2000.

LogiGear Corporation. *QA Training Handbook: Testing Windows Desktop and Server-Based Applications.* Foster City, CA: LogiGear Corporation, 2000.

LogiGear Corporation. *QA Training Handbook: Testing Computer Software.* Foster City, CA:
LogiGear Corporation, 2000.

Cohen, D. M., et al. "The AETG System: An Approach to Testing Based on Combinatorial
Design." *IEEE Transactions On Software Engineering,* Vol. 23, no. 7 (July 1997).

Networking Basics

Why Read This Chapter?

Networks hold Web systems together; they provide connectivity between clients and servers. The reliability, bandwidth, and latency of network components such as T1 lines and routers directly influence the performance of Web systems.

Having knowledge of the networking environment enables you to identify configuration and compatibility requirements for your test planning, and to enhance your bug-analysis abilities.

Introduction

This chapter delivers a brief introduction to networking technologies; the information supports the effective planning, testing, analysis of errors, and communication that is required for the testing of Web applications. Network topologies, connection types,

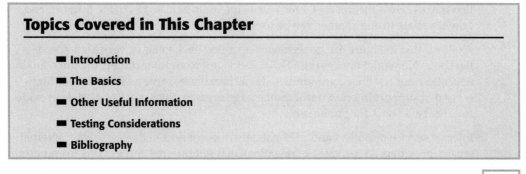

Topics Covered in This Chapter

- ■ Introduction
- ■ The Basics
- ■ Other Useful Information
- ■ Testing Considerations
- ■ Bibliography

and hardware components are also discussed. The chapter also offers test examples and testing considerations that pertain to networking.

POSSIBLE ENVIRONMENTAL PROBLEMS THAT MAY BE THE CAUSE OF AN APPLICATION NOT OPERATING CORRECTLY

- The client or server may be inaccessible because they are not connected to the network.
- There may be a failure in converting a Domain Name Service (DNS) name to an Internet Protocol (IP) address.
- A slow connection may result in a time-out.
- There may be an authentication process failure due to an invalid ID or password.
- The server or client may be incorrectly configured.
- Firewall may block all or part of the transmitted packets.
- Childproofing software may be blocking access to certain servers or files.

The Basics

The following sections deliver introductions to network types, connectivity services, and hardware devices, as well as other useful information such as TCP/IP, IP addresses, DNS, and subnetting/supernetting.

The Networks

Networks are the delivery system offering connectivity that glues clients, servers, and other communication devices together.

The Internet

The Internet's infrastructure is built of regional networks, Internet service providers (ISPs), high-speed backbones, network information centers, and supporting organizations [e.g., the Internet Registry and, recently, the Internet Corporation for Assigned Names and Numbers (ICANN)]. Web systems don't exist without the Internet and the networked structures of which the Internet is composed. Understanding how information moves across the Internet, how client-side users gain access to the Internet, and how IPs relate to one another, can be useful in determining testing requirements.

As illustrated in Figure 4.1, government-operated backbones or very high-speed Backbone Network Services (vBNSs) connect supercomputer centers together, linking education and research communities. These backbones serve as the principle highways that support Internet traffic. Some large organizations, such as NASA, provide Internet backbones for public use.

Internet service providers and regional networks connect to the backbones. Internet service providers are private organizations that sell Internet connections to end users;

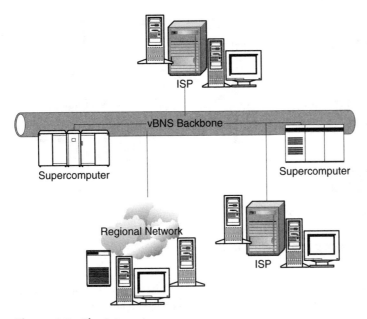

Figure 4.1 The Internet.

both individuals and companies can gain Internet access through ISPs. Online services such as America Online sell access to private sectors of the Internet—in addition to the general Internet. Regional networks are groups of small networks that band together to offer Internet access in a certain geographical area. These networks include companies and online services that can provide better service as groups than they can independently.

Local Area Networks (LANs)

Web-based applications operating over the Internet normally run on *local area networks* (LANs). The LANs are relatively small groups of computers that have been networked to one another. Local area networks are often set up at online services; government, business, and home offices; and other organizations that require numerous computers to regularly communicate with one another. Two common types of LANs are *Ethernet networks* and *token-ring networks*. Transmission Control Protocol/Internet Protocol (TCP/IP), the suite of network protocols enabling communication among clients and servers on a Web system, runs on both of these popular network topologies. On an Ethernet LAN, any computer can send packets of data to any other computer on the same LAN simultaneously. With token-ring networks, data is passed in *tokens* (packets of data) from one host to the next, around the network, in a ring or star pattern. Figure 4.2 illustrates simple token-ring and Ethernet networks, respectively.

Typically, a LAN is set up as a private network. Only authorized LAN users can access data and resources on that network. When a Web-based system is hosted on a private LAN (its services are only available within the LAN) and application access is

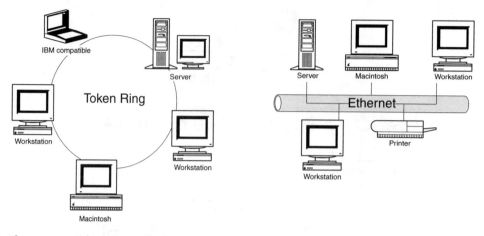

Figure 4.2 Token-ring and Ethernet networks.

only available to hosts (computers) within the LAN or to trusted hosts connected to the LAN [e.g., through remote-access service (RAS)], the Web-based system is considered as an *intranet* system.

Wide Area Networks (WANs)

Multiple LANs can be linked together through a *wide area network* (WAN). Typically, a WAN connects two or more private LANs that are run by the same organization in two or more regions. Figure 4.3 is an illustration of an X.25 (X.25 is one of several available *packet-routing service standards*) WAN connecting computers on a token-ring LAN in one

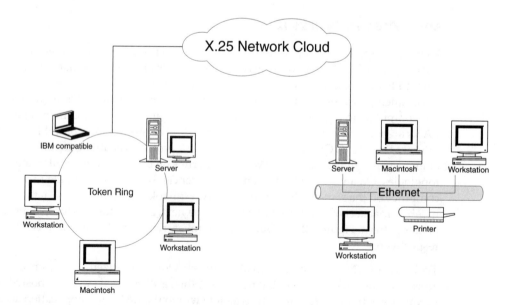

Figure 4.3 Wide area networks (WANs).

geographic region (San Jose, California, for example) to computers on another Ethernet LAN in a different geographic region (Washington, D.C., for example).

Connecting Networks

There are numerous connectivity services and hardware options available for connecting networks to the Internet, as well as to each other; countless testing-related issues may be affected by these components.

Connectivity Services

The two common connection types are dial-up connection and direct connection, which we will discuss in turn in this section.

Dial-Up Connection

One of the very familiar connection service types is the dial-up connection through a telephone line.

Plain Old Telephone Service (POTS).   Plain Old Telephone Service is the standard analog telephone line used by most homes and businesses. A POTS network is often also called the *public switched telephone network* (PSTN). Through an analog modem, a POTS connection offers a transmission rate of up to 56 kilobits per second (Kbps).

Integrated Services Digital Network (ISDN).   The ISDN lines are high-speed dial-up connections over telephone lines. The ISDN lines with which we are familiar can support a data transmission rate of 64 Kbps (if only one of the two available wires is used) or 128 Kbps (if both wires are used). Although not widely available, there is a broadband version (as opposed to the normal baseband version) of ISDN, called *B-ISDN*. The B-ISDN supports a data transmission rate of 1.5 megabits per second (Mbps) but requires fiber-optic cable.

Direct Connection

In contrast to dial-up, another series of connection service type is direct connection such as leased-line, including T1, T3, cable modem, and DSL.

T1 connection.   T1s (connection services) are dedicated, leased telephone lines that provide point-to-point connections. They transmit data using a set of 24 channels across two-wire pairs. One-half of each pair is for sending, the other half is for receiving; combined, the pairs supply a data rate of 1.54 Mbps.

T3 connection.   T3 lines are similar to T1 lines except that, instead of using 24 channels, T3 lines use 672 channels (an equivalent of 28 T1 lines), enabling them to support a much higher data transmission rate: 45 Mbps. Internet service providers and Fortune 500 corporations that connect directly to the Internet's high-speed backbones often use T3 lines. Many start-up Internet companies require bandwidth comparable with a T3 to support their e-business infrastructures, yet they cannot afford the associated costs; the alternative for these smaller companies is to share expensive high-speed connections with larger corporations.

DS connection services.   DS connection services are fractional or multiple T1 and T3 lines. T1 and T3 lines can be subdivided or combined for fractional or multiple levels of service. For example, DS-0 provides a single channel (out of 24 channels) of bandwidth that can transmit 56 Kbps (kilobits per second). DS-1 service is a full T1 line; DS-1C is two T1 lines; DS-2 is four T1 lines; DS-3 is a full T3 line.

Digital subscriber line (DSL).   The DSL offers high-bandwidth connections to small businesses and homes via regular telephone lines. There are several types of DSL, including Asymmetric Digital Subscriber Line (ADSL), which is more popular in North America, and Symmetric Digital Subscriber Line (SDSL). The ADSL supports a downstream transmission rate (receiving) of 1.5 to 9 Mbps and an upstream transmission rate (sending) of 16 to 640 Kbps. The DSL lines carry both data and traditional voice transmissions; the data portion of the bandwidth, however, is always connected.

Cable connection services.   Through a cable modem, a computer can be connected to a local cable TV service line, enabling a data transmission rate, or throughput, of about 1.5 Mbps upstream (sending) and an even much higher rate for downstream (receiving). However, cable modem technology utilizes a shared medium in which all of the users served by a node (between a couple hundred to couple thousand homes, depending on the provider) share bandwidth. Therefore, the throughput can be affected by the number of cable modem users in a given neighborhood and the types of activities in which those users are engaged on the network. In most cases, cable service providers supply the cable modems and Ethernet interface cards as part of the access service.

Internet Connection Hardware

To connect a terminal or a network to the Internet, a hardware device such as a modem must be used to enable the communication between each side of the connection. With POTS dial-up connections, analog modems are used. With ISDN, ISDN (digital) modems are used. With DSL and cable connections, DSL modems and cable modems are used.

With leased lines such as T1, T3, and other DS connection services, a channel service unit/data service unit (CSU/DSU) device is used. They are actually two different units but often a packaged as one. You may think of CSU/DSU as an expensive and powerful version of a modem that is required at both ends of the leased-line connection.

Other Network Connectivity Devices

Local area networks employ several types of connectivity devices to link them together. Some of the common hardware devices include:

Repeaters.   Used to amplify data signals at certain intervals to ensure that signals are not distorted or lost over great distances.

Hubs.   Used to connect groups or segments of computers and devices to one another so that they can communicate on a network, such as a LAN. A hub has multiple ports. When a data packet arrives at one port, it is replicated to the other ports so that computers or devices connected to other ports will see the data packet. Generally, there are three types of hubs.

■ *Bridges.*   Used to connect physical LANs that use the same protocol as one another into a logical network. Bridges examine incoming messages and pass the messages on to the appropriate computers—on either a local LAN or a remote LAN.

- *Routers.* Used to ensure that data are delivered to the correct destinations. Routers are like bridges, except that they support more features. Routers determine how to forward packets—based on IP address and network traffic. When they receive packets with a destination address of a host that is outside of the network or subnetwork, they route the packets to other routers outside of the network or subnetwork so that the packets will eventually reach their destination. Routers are often not necessary when transmitting data within the same network, such as over a LAN.
- *Gateways.* Used like routers, except that they support even more features than routers. For example, a gateway can connect two different types of networks, enabling users from one network (Novell IPX/SPX, for example) to exchange data with users on a different network type (for example, TCP/IP).

Figure 4.4 illustrates a sample configuration in which a bridge, router, or gateway is used to connect the two networks or subnetworks.

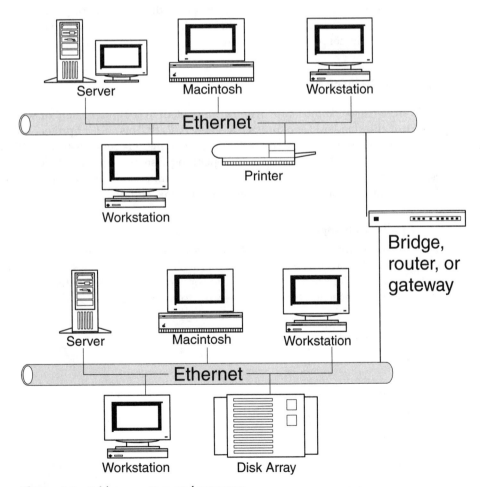

Figure 4.4 Bridges, routers, and gateways.

TCP/IP Protocols

The Internet is a *packet-switched* network—meaning that all transmitted data objects are broken up into small packets (each of less than 1500 characters). The packets are sent to the receiving computer where they are reassembled into the original object.

The TCP is responsible for breaking up information into packets and reassembling packets once they reach their destination. Each packet is given a header that contains information regarding the order in which packets should be reassembled and a *checksum*—which records the precise amount of information in each packet. Checksums are used to determine, on the receiving end, if packets were received in their entirety.

The IP is responsible for routing packets to their correct destination. The IP puts packets into separate IP *envelopes* that have unique headers. The envelope headers provide such information as the receiver's and the sender's addresses. The IP envelopes are sent separately through routers to their destination. The IP envelopes of the same transmission may travel different routes to reach the same destination—often arriving out of order. Before reassembling the packets on the receiving end, TCP calculates the checksum of each packet and compares it with the checksum of the original TCP headers. If the checksums do not match, TCP discards the unmatched packets and requests the original packets to be resent.

The TCP/IP Architecture

For computers to communicate over the Internet, each computer, client or server, must utilize a standard set of protocols called TCP/IP. This suite of protocols is referred to as a TCP/IP *stack* or *socket*. There are numerous versions of TCP/IP stack available, for every target platform and operating system (UNIX, PC, Macintosh, handheld devices, etc.). The TCP/IP stack, as illustrated in Figure 4.5, is composed of five layers: application, transport, Internet, data link, and physical.

The Application Layer

The top layer of the TCP/IP protocol is the *application layer*. End-user applications interact with this layer. The protocols in this layer perform activities such as enabling end-user applications to send, receive, and convert data into their native formats, and establishing a connection (session) between two computers.

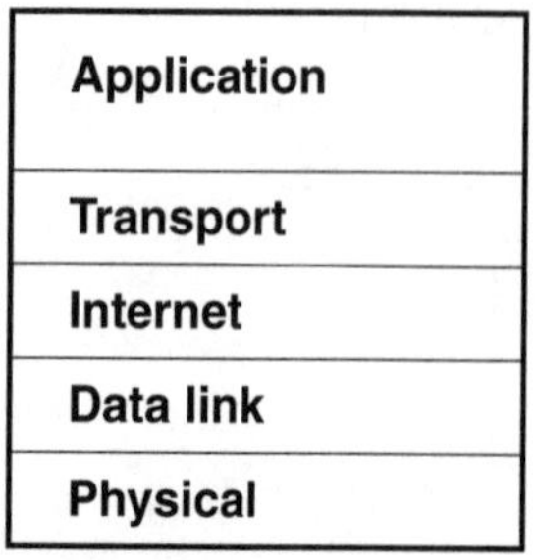

Application
Transport
Internet
Data link
Physical

Figure 4.5 TCP/IP stack architecture.

Examples of several common protocols associated with the application layer with which you may be familiar include:

HyperText Transfer Protocol (HTTP).   Commonly used in browsers to transfer Web pages and other related data between client and server across the Internet.

File Transfer Protocol (FTP).   Commonly used in browsers or other applications to copy files between computers by downloading files from one remote computer and uploading them to another computer.

Network News Transfer Protocol (NNTP).   Used in news reading applications to transfer USENET news articles between servers and clients, as well as between servers.

Simple Mail Transfer Protocol (SMTP).   Used by e-mail applications to send e-mail messages between computers.

Dynamic Host Configuration Protocol (DHCP).   Used in server-based applications to allocate shared IP addresses to individual computers. When a client computer requires an IP address, a DHCP server assigns the client an IP address from a pool of shared addresses.

For example, a network may have 80 workstations, but only 54 IP addresses available. The DHCP allows the 80 workstations to share the 54 IP addresses in a way that is analogous to an office with 80 employees who share a phone system with only 54 trunk lines. In this scenario, it is expected that in normal operation no more than 54 employees will be on the phone at the same time. That is, the 55th employee and beyond will not be able to get onto the system.

The Transport Layer

The *transport layer* breaks data into packets before sending them. Upon receipt, the transport layer ensures that all packets arrive intact. It also arranges packets into the correct order.

Examples of two common protocols associated with the transport layer that you may be familiar with are Transmission Control Protocol (TCP) and User Datagram Protocol (UDP). Both TCP and UDP are used to transport IP packets to applications and to flow data between computers. With TCP, it ensures that no transported data is dropped during transmissions. Error checking and sequence numbering are two of TCP's important functions. Transmission Control Protocol uses IP to deliver packets to applications and it provides a reliable stream of data between computers on networks. Once a packet arrives at its destination, TCP delivers confirmation to the sending and receiving computers regarding the transmitted data. It also requests that packets be resent if they are lost.

■ TCP is referred to as a *connection-oriented* protocol. Connection-oriented protocols require that a channel be established (a communications line established between the sending and receiving hosts, such as in a telephone connection) before messages are transmitted.

■ UDP is considered a *connectionless protocol.* This means that data can be sent without creating a connection to the receiving host. The sending computer simply places messages onto the network with the destination address and hopes that the messages arrive intact.

UDP does not check for dropped data. The benefit of being connectionless is that data can be transferred more quickly; the drawback is that data can more easily be lost during transmission.

The Internet Layer

The *Internet layer* receives data packets from the transport layer and sends them to the correct network address using the IP. The Internet layer also determines the best route for data to travel.

Examples of several common protocols associated with the Internet layer that you may be familiar with include the following:

Internet Protocol (IP). Responsible for basic network connectivity. Every computer on a TCP/IP network has a numeric IP address. This unique network ID enables data to be sent to and received from other networks, similar to the way that a traditional street address allows a person to send and receive snail mail.

Address Resolution Protocol (ARP). Responsible for identifying the address of a remote computer's network interface card (such as an Ethernet interface) when only the computer's TCP/IP address is known.

Reverse Address Resolution Protocol (RARP). The opposite of ARP. When all that is known is a remote computer's network interface card hardware address, RARP determines the computer's IP address.

The Data Link Layer

The *data link layer* moves data across the physical link of a network. It splits outgoing data into frames and establishes communication with the receiving end to validate the successful delivery of data. It also validates that incoming data are received successfully.

The Physical Layer

The *physical layer* is the bottom layer of the TCP/IP stack. It supports the electrical or mechanical interface of the connection medium. It is the hardware layer—composed of a network interface card and wiring such as coaxial cable, 10/100-Based-T wiring, satellite, or leased-line.

Testing Scenarios

With Web-based systems, we may not normally have to be concerned with issues related to connection services, connectivity devices, or how the TCP/IP stack may affect the applications. When an HTTP-based (i.e., Web browser-based) application runs within the context of a third-party browser (e.g., Netscape Navigator or Microsoft Explorer), one can argue that how a TCP/IP connection is established, which hardware components are used on the network, or the connection throughput does not seem to matter. However, understanding the basics of the technologies helps us better decide on the parts that need testing focus, as well as on other parts that can be left alone.

Generally, the two classes of testing-related issues that need coverage are (1) configuration and compatibility and (2) performance. By carefully analyzing the delivered features and the supported system configurations, we can reasonably determine the testing requirements for configuration and compatibility as well as for performance.

Connection Type Testing

Usually, the issues with various types of connection revolve around throughput and performance rather than configuration and compatibility.

How TCP/IP Protocols Work Together

Figure 4.6 illustrates a simplified version of the data-flow processes that occur when a user sends an e-mail message. The process on the sender's end begins at the top layer, the application layer, and concludes at the physical layer, where the e-mail message leaves the sender's network.

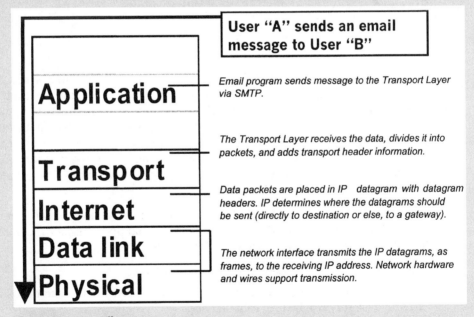

Figure 4.6 E-mail sent.

The process continues on the receiver's end, working in reverse order. The physical layer receives the sender's message and passes it upward until it reaches the receiver's application layer. (See Figure 4.7.)

Continues

How TCP/IP Protocols Work Together *(Continued)*

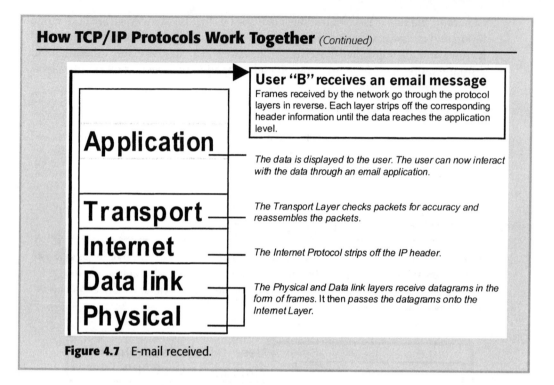

User "B" receives an email message
Frames received by the network go through the protocol layers in reverse. Each layer strips off the corresponding header information until the data reaches the application level.

Application

The data is displayed to the user. The user can now interact with the data through an email application.

Transport

The Transport Layer checks packets for accuracy and reassembles the packets.

Internet

The Internet Protocol strips off the IP header.

Data link

Physical

The Physical and Data link layers receive datagrams in the form of frames. It then *passes the datagrams onto the Internet Layer.*

Figure 4.7 E-mail received.

For example, login fails to authenticate with dial-up connections, but it works properly with direct connection. This symptom may be caused by a number of problems. However, one common issue is that the slow connection causes a time-out in the login or authentication process. With slow connections such as dial-up, it may take too long (longer than the script time-out value) for the client-server to send/receive packets of data; the script will eventually time-out, causing the login or authentication process to fail. The problem could not be reproduced when the same procedure is retried on an Intranet or a LAN connection.

As described earlier, the two types of connection we often work with that offer us various throughput rates are direct connections and dial-up connections. Common direct connection configurations to consider include:

- Standard LAN and/or WAN connections (Intranet)
- Standard LAN and/or WAN connections with a gateway to the Internet using T1, T3, and DS services; DSL; or cable services
- Stand-alone connections to the Internet using DSL or cable services

Common dial-up connection configurations to consider include:

- Stand-alone connections to the Internet through an ISP directly, using POTS lines or ISDN lines (see Figure 4.8 for an example).

In the standard dial-up model (Figure 4.8), a client is a PC that is connected to a modem. Through a local telephone line or ISDN, a connection is made to an ISP. Depending on

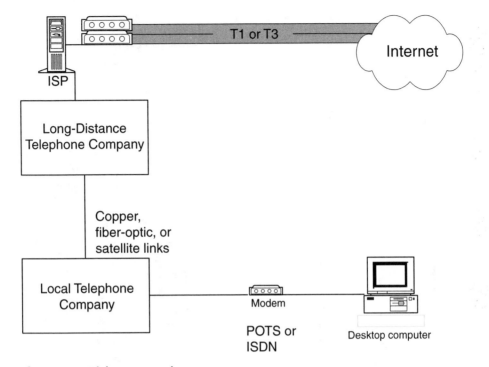

Figure 4.8 Dial-up connection.

whether the ISP is local or not, the local phone company may have to connect (via satellite, copper, or fiber-optic cable) to the ISP through a long-distance carrier. The ISP also has a modem to receive the phone call and to establish a connection to the PC.

- Stand-alone connections to the intranet (LAN) through RAS, using POTS lines or ISDN lines
- Stand-alone connections to the intranet (LAN) through virtual private network (VPN) services, using POTS lines or ISDN lines
- Stand-alone connections to the intranet (LAN) through RAS, using POTS lines or ISDN lines, and then to the Internet using a leased line. (See Figure 4.9 for an example.)

Differing from the model where the client dials up through an ISP is the model of the client dialing up through an RAS. If a LAN is connected directly to the local phone company, there is no need for a long-distance telephone connection. In Figure 4.9, the modem on the server side receives the connection from the local phone company and translates it for the RAS; after proper authentication, LAN resources are made available to the user. If the LAN has a leased line, the user can link to an ISP and, ultimately, to the Internet through the local phone company.

Potential Modem Compatibility Issues

Users of the Web system under test may be dialing in with a modem that translates digital computer signals into analog signals; the analog signals are carried over POTS

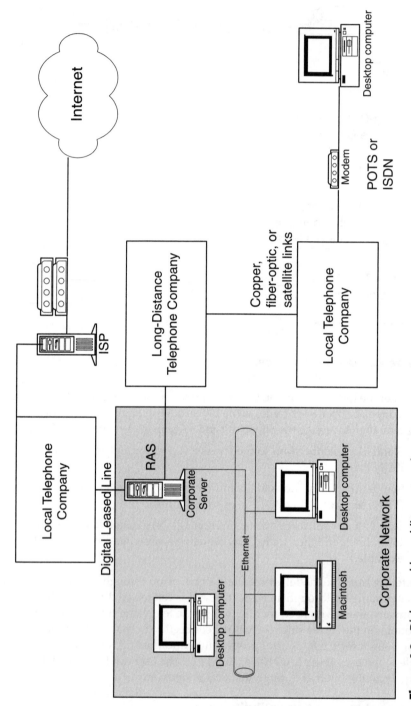

Figure 4.9 Dial-up and leased-line connections.

lines. The brand names and baud rates (generally ranging from 14.4 to 56 Kbps) of these modems may affect the perceived performance of the Web system under test.

Generally, modem is a "don't care" to a Web application. However, if your application is an embedded browser that also provides drivers for users to connect to certain modems, then the connection type and modem brands may be an issue for testing. If modem compatibility issues are a concern for the system under test, then both client- and server-side modems should be tested.

Potential Dialer Compatibility Issues

Dialer compatibility testing is often required when a Web system interacts with a dialer. Some ISPs, such as EarthLink and AOL, supply users with proprietary dialers. Dialup Networking has more than one version of its dialer. Some ISPs supply their new users with CD-ROMs that replace existing browsers and dialers so that users can connect to their services. Such CDs often install new components, which can cause incompatibility or conflict problems that may lead to errors such as a system crash.

Some dialers also offer users a couple of protocol options from which to choose. Two common dial-up protocols are *Serial Line Internet Protocol* (SLIP) and *Point-to-Point Protocol* (PPP). The SLIP is the older of the two. Point-to-Point Protocol is the most popular, as well as the most stable; it enables point-to-point connections and, when necessary, can retransmit garbled data packets. If the Web application under test is an embedded application and also delivers a dialer that supports more than one dial-up protocol, compatibility testing should be considered. Otherwise, this is usually a "don't care" issue to standard browser-based application testing.

Connectivity Device Testing

Do we need to test our HTTP-based application with various brands and models of hubs, repeaters, bridges, routers, and gateways under various configurations? I hope that the answer is No, because a standard Web browser-based application does not interact directly with such devices. However, if a Web application under test is a custom-embedded application that supports several protocols at different layers of the TCP/IP stacks, incompatibility issues may be introduced in interactions with the connectivity devices. For example, an embedded HTTP-based application uses Reverse Address Resolution Protocol (RARP) at the Internet layer of the TCP/IP stacks to determine the computer's IP address, compatibility tests should be conducted with connectivity devices that support RARP, such as routers and gateways.

Many hardware devices do interact with different layers of the TCP/IP stack. Figures 4.10 and 4.11 illustrate the differences in intelligence and network layer interaction that these devices exhibit. Understanding the implementation and support of Web-based applications in the context of TCP/IP layering allows you to determine if configuration and compatibility testing of hardware devices (such as gateways and routers) will be necessary.

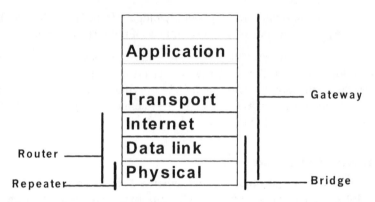

Figure 4.10 Network layer/device interaction.

Other Useful Information

This section offers an overview of how IP addresses, DNS, and network subnet work with the intent to help testers be better at analyzing errors, as well as troubleshooting network/Web related issues.

IP Addresses and DNS

Every network device that uses TCP/IP must have a unique domain name and IP address. Internet Protocol addresses are 32-bit numbers—4 fields of 8 bits each, each field separated by a dot (Figure 4.13). To better understand IP addresses, it is helpful to review the binary model of computer data storage (Figure 4.12).

Binary is *base two*; it differs from the standard numerical system, which is *base ten*. Base two (binary) dictates that each digit, or *bit*, may have one of two values: 1 (meaning *on*) and 0 (meaning *off*). The value of a bit depends on its position. Figure 4.12 includes four examples of standard numerals expressed in the binary model: 1, 3, 133, and 255.

	Hubs	Repeaters	Bridges	Routers	Gateways
Network Layer Protocols					
Application	No	No	No	No	Yes
Transport	No	No	No	No	Yes
Internet	No	No	No	Yes	Yes
Data Link	No	No	Yes	Yes	Yes
Physical	Yes	Yes	Yes	Yes	Yes
Addresses Recognized					
IP	No	No	No	Yes	Yes
Hardware Interface	No	No	Yes	Yes	Yes

Figure 4.11 Network layer protocols and recognized addresses.

Binary Numbers:		128	64	32	16	8	4	2	1
	Position Value	128	64	32	16	8	4	2	1
	On-bit	1	1	1	1	1	1	1	1
	8-bit number								

		0	+0	+0	+0	+0	+0	+0	+1
Example 1:	Decimal Value	1							
	Binary Value	0	0	0	0	0	0	0	1
	8-bit number								

		0	+0	+0	+0	+0	+0	+2	+1
Example 2:	Decimal Value	3							
	Binary Value	0	0	0	0	0	0	1	1
	8-bit number								

		128	+0	+0	+0	+0	+4	+0	+1
Example 3:	Decimal Value	133							
	Binary Value	1	0	0	0	0	1	0	1
	8-bit number								

		128	+64	+32	+16	+8	+4	+2	+1
Example 4:	Decimal Value	255							
	Binary Value	1	1	1	1	1	1	1	1
	8-bit number								

Figure 4.12 Binary model of computer data storage.

Starting from right to left, each of the 8 bit positions represents a different number. Depending on the numeral being expressed, each bit is set either to *on* or *off*. To calculate the expressed numeral, the *on* bit positions must be added up. In the fourth example, note that all positions are set to *on*, and the resulting value—the maximum value for an 8-bit number—is 255.

IP Address

Internet Protocol addresses are segmented into two numbers: a *network number* and a *host number*. The network number identifies a specific organization's network that is connected to the Internet. Within that network there are specific host computers on individual desktops. These host computers are identified by host numbers. The amount of hosts that a network can support depends on the *network class* of the network. Figure 4.13 is an example of a Class C IP address.

Network Classes

The Internet is running low on available IP addresses. This is not due to a limitation of the Internet itself or even of software; it is rather a limitation of the naming convention, or *dotted-decimal notation,* the industry has established to express IP addresses. Simply put, there are mathematical limitations to the amount of numbers that can be expressed in the 32-bit model.

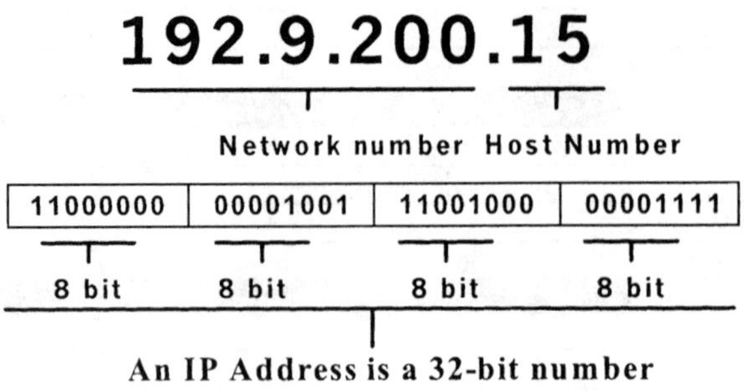

192.9.200.15

Network number Host Number

11000000	00001001	11001000	00001111

8 bit   8 bit   8 bit   8 bit

An IP Address is a 32-bit number

Figure 4.13 Class C IP address.

THREE CLASSES OF TCP/IP NETWORKS

- *Class A networks.* There are only 126 class A network addresses available. Class A networks can support an enormous amount of host devices—16,777,216. Not many organizations require access to such a large number of hosts. America Online, Pacific Bell, and AT&T are some of the organizations that have class A networks. Class A networks use only the first 8 bits of their IP addresses as the network number. The remaining 24 bits are dedicated to host numbers.

- *Class B networks.* Class B networks can support about 65,000 hosts. The Internet can support a maximum of 16,384 class B networks. Class B networks are quite large, but nowhere near as large as class A. Universities and many large organizations require class B networks. Class B networks use the first 16 bits of their IP addresses as the network number. The remaining 16 bits are dedicated to host numbers.

- *Class C networks.* Class C networks are the most common and the smallest network class available. There are over 2 million class C networks on the Internet. Each class C network can support up to 254 hosts. Class C networks use the first 24 bits of their IP addresses as the network number. The remaining 8 bits are dedicated to host numbers.

Domain Name System (DNS)

Although identifying specific computers with unique 32-bit numbers (IP addresses) makes sense for computers, the practice makes it very challenging for humans to remember network and host names. That is why Sun Microsystems developed Domain Name Service (DNS) in the early 1980s. Domain Name Service associates alphabetic aliases with numeric IP addresses. The *DNS servers* match simple alphabetic *domain names*, such as logigear.com and netscape.com, with the 32-bit IP addresses that the names represent. With this method, Internet users only have to remember the domain names of the Internet sites they wish to visit. If a domain server does not have a certain IP address/domain name match listed in its database, that server will route a request to another DNS that will hopefully be able to figure out the IP address associated with the particular domain name.

E-mail addresses are made up of two main components that are separated by an @ symbol. The far right of every e-mail address includes the most general information, and the far left includes the most specific. The far left of every e-mail address is the user's name. The second part, to the right of the @ symbol, is the domain name. In the example webtester@qacity.com, *webtester* is the user name, and *qacity.com* is the domain name.

The domain name itself can be broken down into at least two components, each separated by a period. The far right component of the domain name is the *extension*. The extension defines the domain as being commercial (.com), network-based (.net), educational (.edu), governmental (.gov), or military (.mil). Countries outside the United States have their own extensions: Canada (.ca), Great Britain (.uk), and Japan (.jp) are a few of these.

To the left of the domain extension is the name of the host organization, or ISP (.logigear, .compuserve, etc.). Often, domain names are further subdivided, as in webtester@montreal.qacity.com. In this example, *montreal* is the *host name;* this is the specific host computer that acts as the "post office" for webtester's e-mail. Figure 4.14 shows examples of domain names.

When an e-mail is sent to webtester@montreal.qacity.com, a DNS server translates the letters of the domain name (qacity.com) into the associated numerical IP address. Once in numeric form, the data is sent to the host computer that resides at the domain. The host computer (montreal) ultimately sends the e-mail message to the specific user (webtester).

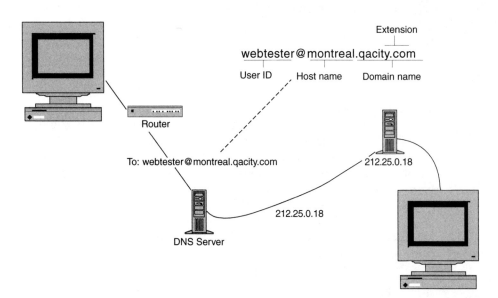

Figure 4.14 Domain names.

Missing a DNS Entry

When you are outside of the intranet and click on the QA Training or TRACKGEAR button in the page illustrated, the browser appears to hang or you don't get any response from the server. However, when you report the problem, your developer who accesses the same links could not reproduce it. One of the possible problems is the DNS entry for the server referenced in the link is only available in the DNS table on the intranet, and is not known to the outside world. (See Figure 4.15.)

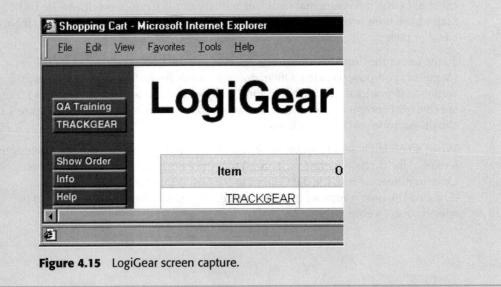

Figure 4.15 LogiGear screen capture.

Subnet

Subnets divide a single network into smaller networks, or network segments. Routers are used to send information from one subnet to another. Subnets are useful in managing IP address allotment. For example, an organization has a class C network and, therefore, only 254 IP addresses are available to distribute to its employees. There are two physical locations. This organization could request a second class C network to service the second location. What if the organization is not currently using all of its IP addresses? Getting a second network address would be wasteful. A subnet, in this case, allows this organization to partition its existing class C network into two subnetworks. Figure 4.17 shows a network divided into two subnets with two IP addresses (192.9.200.100 and 192.9.200.200)

The benefits of subnetting an existing network rather than getting an additional network include:

- Retaining the same network number for multiple locations.
- The outside world will not be aware that the network has been subdivided.

TIPS

1. **Use the View Source menu command to inspect the HTML source.**

2. **Look for the information that's relevant to the links.**

```
...
<td>
<map name=01b238de91a99ed9>
<area shape=rect coords="0,0,88,20" href=https://authorize.qacity
  .com/training-login.asp?>
<area shape=rect coords="0,20,88,40" href=https://authorize.qacity
  .com/trackgear-login.asp?>
...
...
</td>
...
```

Figure 4.16   Tip: ping authorize.qacity.com.

In this example, you will find that clicking on the QA Training and the TRACKGEAR button will result in requests to the server authorized in the *qacity.com* domain.

3. **Try to ping authorize.qacity.com to see if it can be pinged (Figure 4.16).**

4. **If the server cannot be pinged, tell your developer or IS staff so the problem can be resolved.**

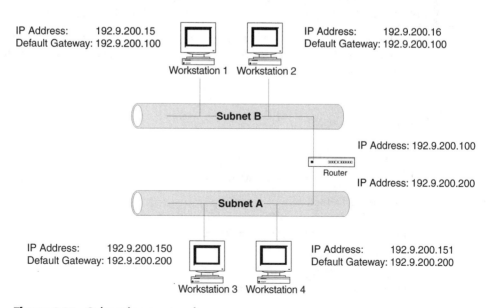

IP Address: 192.9.200.15
Default Gateway: 192.9.200.100

Workstation 1   Workstation 2

IP Address: 192.9.200.16
Default Gateway: 192.9.200.100

Subnet B

IP Address: 192.9.200.100

Router

IP Address: 192.9.200.200

Subnet A

IP Address: 192.9.200.150
Default Gateway: 192.9.200.200

IP Address: 192.9.200.151
Default Gateway: 192.9.200.200

Workstation 3   Workstation 4

Figure 4.17   Subnetting a network.

- A department's network activities can be isolated from the rest of the network—contributing to the stability and security of the network as a whole.

- Network testing can be isolated within a subnet, thereby protecting the network from testing-based crashes.

- Smaller networks are easier to maintain.

- Network performance may improve due to the fact that most traffic remains local to its own subnet (for example, the network activities of business administration and engineering could be divided between two subnets).

Subnet Masks

Subnet addresses are derived from the main network's *network number* plus some information from the host section in the network's IP address. *Subnet masks* tell the network which portion of the host section of the subnet address is being used as the network address.

Subnet masks, like IP addresses, are 32-bit values. The bits for the network section of the subnet address are set to 1, and the bits for the host section of the address are set to 0. Each network class has its own default subnet mask (Figure 4.18). Every computer on a network must share the same subnet mask—otherwise, the computers will not know that they are part of the same network.

As stated earlier, class C IP addresses have 24 bits to the left devoted to network address. Class B IP addresses have 16 bits, and class A IP addresses have 8 bits. Internet Protocol addresses that are included in incoming messages are filtered through the appropriate subnet mask so that the network number and host number can be identified. As an example, applying the class C subnet mask (255.255.255.0) to the class C address (126.24.3.11) results in a network number of 126.4.3 and a host number of 11.

The value of 255 is arrived at when all bits of an IP address field are set to 1, or *on*. If all values in an IP address are set to 255, as in the default subnet masks, then there are no subnets at all.

Default Subnet Masks

    Class A Default
    255.0.0.0 or
11111111.00000000.00000000.00000000

    Class B Default
    255.255.0.0 or
11111111.11111111.00000000.00000000

    Class C Default
    255.255.255.0 or
11111111.11111111.11111111.00000000

Figure 4.18   Subnet masks.

Custom Subnets

Subnet masks may be customized to divide networks into several subnets. To do this, some of the bits in the host portion of the subnet mask will be set to 1's. For example: Consider an IP address of 202.133.175.18, or 11001010.10000101.10101111.00010010. Using the default mask of 255.255.255.0, or 11111111.11111111.11111111.00000000, the network address will be 202.133.175.0, and the host address IP address is 18. If a custom mask such as 255.255.255.240, or 11111111.11111111.11111111.11110000, is used, the network address will then be 202.133.175.16 (because 28 bits are used for the subnet address instead of 24 as in the default mask), and the host address will still be 18.

A Testing Example

Following is an example of an embedded HTTP-based application handheld device that involves testing the host name and IP address resolution logics.

Host Name and IP Resolution Tests

CONSIDERATIONS FOR THE SYSTEM UNDER TEST

- Adapter address
- IP address
- Subnet mask
- Host name resolved by DNS, WINS, or other technologies
- Dynamic Host Configuration Protocol (DHCP)
- Default gateway IP address

By the way, you often need to configure your network stack with the correct information for each of the items previously listed to enable your computer or any devices connected to the network to operate properly.

TESTING EXAMPLE SPECIFICATIONS

- There are two applications—one running on the remote host and the other running on the target host.
- The product supports Windows 95, 98, NT 4.0, or Chameleon TCP/IP stack.
- The remote host connects to the private network via a dial-in server.
- The product supports RAS and several popular PPP- or TCP/IP-based dial-in servers.
- From the remote host, a user enters the phone number, user name, and password that are required to connect to the desired dial-in server.
- The remote host then establishes a connection with the target host. Therefore, information about the target host name, IP, and subnet mask must be registered on the remote host.
- The product supports static-based, as well as dynamic-based, IP addresses.
- The product also supports WINS- and DNS-based name/IP resolution.

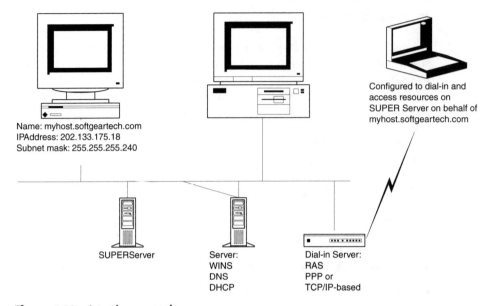

Name: myhost.softgeartech.com
IPAddress: 202.133.175.18
Subnet mask: 255.255.255.240

Configured to dial-in and
access resources on
SUPER Server on behalf of
myhost.softgeartech.com

SUPERServer

Server:
WINS
DNS
DHCP

Dial-in Server:
RAS
PPP or
TCP/IP-based

Figure 4.19   A testing example.

When the target host IP changes, the product has code that relies on the host name alone, or the host name and the subnet mask information, to dynamically determine the new IP address.

In developing test cases to validate the functionality under various possible scenarios that the system under test can be exposed to, I examine the following attributes:

The host name.   May be available on the device or may not.

IP address.   May be available on the device or may not.

Subnet mask.   May be standard mask or may be custom mask.

Name server—IP/name resolving.   Either configured to use WINS or DNS.

Type of IP address.   May be static or may be dynamic.

A table is then developed to represent various unique combinations formulated by these five attributes and the possible values for each attribute. There are 32 combinations generated. (See Table 4.1.) Each combination is then configured and tested accordingly. Figure 4.19 shows a testing example.

In considering testing for compatibility issues, six operating environments were identified: three of them are Windows 95, 98, and NT 4.0 with Microsoft default TCP/IP stack; the other three are the same set of operating systems with the latest version of Chameleon TCP/IP stack.

Table 4.1   The 32 Unique Combinations

No=0 | Yes=1
No=0 | Yes=1
No=0 | Yes=1
WINS=0 | DNS=1
Static=0 | Dynamic=1

	1	2	3	4	5	6	7	8	9	10	11	12	13	14	15	16	17	18	19	20	21	22	23	24	25	26	27	28	29	30	31	32
Host Name	0	0	1	1	0	0	1	1	0	0	1	1	0	0	1	1	0	0	1	1	0	0	1	1	0	0	1	1	0	0	1	1
IP	0	1	0	1	0	1	0	1	0	1	0	1	0	1	0	1	0	1	0	1	0	1	0	1	0	1	0	1	0	1	0	1
Subnet Mask	0	0	0	0	1	1	1	1	0	0	0	0	1	1	1	1	0	0	0	0	1	1	1	1	0	0	0	0	1	1	1	1
Name Server	0	0	0	0	0	0	0	0	1	1	1	1	1	1	1	1	0	0	0	0	0	0	0	0	1	1	1	1	1	1	1	1
Static/Dynamic IP	0	0	0	0	0	0	0	0	0	0	0	0	0	0	0	0	1	1	1	1	1	1	1	1	1	1	1	1	1	1	1	1

Validating Your Computer Connection

Ensure that your test machines are properly configured and connected to the network before you begin testing. To check host connection and configuration in a Windows environment, read the following instructions. Windows NT offers a utility named `ipconfig`. Windows 9x has `winipcfg`, which has more of a user interface.

1a. *For Windows NT.*   Run IPCONFIG/ALL.

1b. *For Windows 9x.*   Run WINIPCFG.

2. Ping the exact value that is received from IPCONFIG and WINIPCFG. To make sure the DNS is working properly, ping by the domain name also. If positive responses are received, then there is a good TCP/IP connection.

3. To ensure that there is a proper TCP/IP connection, ping the loop-back IP address: PING 127.0.0.1 or PING YourMachineIPAddress.

Testing Considerations

- If the application under test runs in its own embedded browser, analyze the application to determine if it utilizes any protocols beyond ones at the application level. If it does, how would it affect your configuration and compatibility testing requirements with respect to connectivity devices?

- Determine the hardware and software configuration dependencies of the application under test. Develop a test plan that covers a wide mix of hardware and software configurations.

- Examine the Web application as a whole and consider the connection dial-up and direct connection methods. How would each type of connection affect the performance and functionality of the product?

- Will users be accessing the system via dial-up connections through an ISP? If so, connectivity may be based upon proprietary ISP strings, such as the parsing of a login script. Will there be remote users accessing through an RAS?

- Will the application be installing any special modules, such as a dialer and associated components, that may introduce conflicts? Consider dialer platforms, versions, and brand names.

Bibliography

Comer, Douglas. *Internetworking with TCP/IP Vol. I: Principles, Protocols, and Architecture,* fourth edition. Upper Saddle River, NJ: Prentice-Hall PTR, 2000.

Gralla, Preston. *How the Internet Works.* Emeryville, CA: Ziff-Davis Press, 1997.

LogiGear Corporation. *QA Training Handbook: Testing Web Applications.* Foster City, CA: LogiGear Corporation, 2000.

LogiGear Corporation. *QA Training Handbook: Testing Windows Desktop and Server-Based Applications.* Foster City, CA: LogiGear Corporation, 2000.

LogiGear Corporation. *QA Training Handbook: Testing Computer Software.* Foster City, CA: LogiGear Corporation, 2000.

Orfali, Robert, et al. *Client/Server Survival Guide, Third Edition.* New York: John Wiley & Sons, 1999.

CHAPTER 5

Web Application Components

Having an understanding of a Web application's internal components and how those components interface with one another, even if only at a high level, leads to better testing. Such knowledge allows for the analysis of a program from its developer's perspective—which is invaluable in determining test strategy and identifying the cause of errors. Furthermore, analyzing the relationship among the components gives an understanding of the interaction of the work product of several independent developers, not only from the individual developer's perspective. You analyze the work product from a perspective that is not evident from the analysis of any individual component. You are asking how all these components interact with each other to make up the system. The gray-box tester provides this strength. You look at the sys-

Topics Covered in This Chapter

tem at a level that is different from the developer's look. Just like the black-box tester, you add a different perspective, and, therefore, you add value.

Generally, we learn about an application's architecture from its developers during walk-throughs. An alternate approach is to do our own analysis by tracing communication traffic between components. For example, tests can be developed that hit a database server directly, or on behalf of actual user activities, via browser-submitted transactions. Regardless, we need to have a firm grasp of typical Web-based application architecture at the component level if we are to know what types of errors to look for and what questions to ask.

Introduction

This chapter explores the software and hardware components of a typical Web-based system—from client-based components on the *front end* (such as Web browsers, plug-ins, and embedded objects) to server-side components on the *back end* (such as application server components, database applications, third-party modules, and cross-component communication). It offers insight into what typically happens when users click buttons on browser-based interfaces. It also explores pertinent testing issues such as:

- Which types of plug-ins are used by the application under test? What are the testing implications associated with these plug-ins? What issues should be considered during functionality and compatibility testing once these plug-ins have been integrated into the system?

- How should the distribution of server-side components affect test design and strategy?

- Which Web and database servers are supported by the application? How is Web-to-database connectivity implemented, and what are the associated testing implications?

- How can testing be partitioned to focus on problematic components?

Overview

A Web-based system consists of hardware components, software components, and users. This chapter focuses on the software components of Web-based systems.

Distributed Application Architecture

In a distributed architecture, components are grouped into clusters of related services. Distributed architectures are used for both traditional client-server systems and Internet-based client-server systems.

Traditional Client-Server Systems

A database access application typically consists of four elements:

1. *User interface (UI) code.* The end-user or input/output (I/O) devices interact with this for I/O operations.
2. *Business logic code.* Applies rules, computes data, and manipulates data.
3. *Data access service code.* Handles data retrieval and updates to the database, in addition to sending results back to the client.
4. *Data storage.* Holds the information.

Thin- versus Thick-Client Systems

When the majority of processing is executed on the server side, a system is considered to be a *thin-client* system. When the majority of processing is executed on the client side, a system is considered to be a *thick-client* system.

In a thin-client system (Figure 5.1), the user interface runs on the client host while all other components run on the server host(s). By contrast, in a thick-client system (Figure 5.2), most processing is done on the client side; the client application handles data processing and applies logic rules to data. The server is responsible only for providing data access features and data storage.

Web-Based Client-Server Systems

Web-based client-server systems typically group components into three related tiers: (1) *User service components* (client), (2) *business service components* (server), and (3) *data service components* (server). Processing, performance, scalability, and system maintenance are all taken into account in the design of such systems.

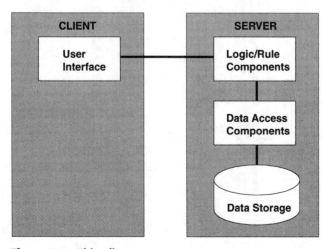

Figure 5.1 Thin-client system.

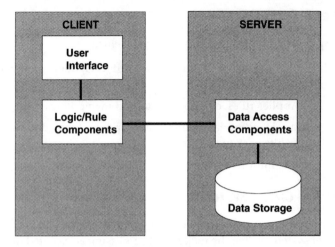

Figure 5.2 Thick-client system.

An example of a three-tiered Web application is shown in Figure 5.3. The components shown in this example are discussed in later sections of this chapter.

Figures 5.4 and 5.5 illustrate thin-client and thick-client Web applications, respectively. In the thin-client example, the server is responsible for all services. After retrieving and processing data, only a plain HTML page is sent back to the client. In the thick-client example, however, components such as ActiveX controls and Java applets, which are required for the client to process data, are hosted and executed on the client machine. Each of these models calls for a different testing strategy.

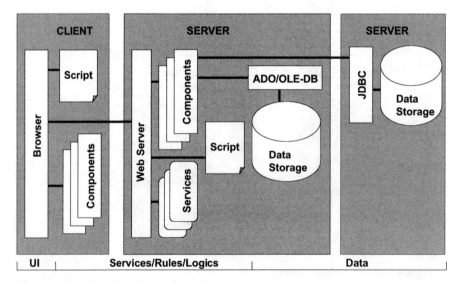

Figure 5.3 Three-tiered Web-based system.

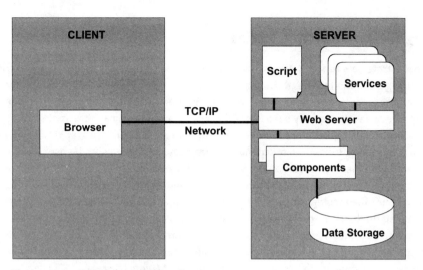

Figure 5.4 A Web-based thin client.

In thick-client system testing, tests should focus on performance and compatibility. If Java applets are used, the applets will be sent to the browser with each request (unless the same applet is used within the same instance of the browser). If the applet is a few hundred kilobytes in size, it will take a fair amount of bandwidth to download it with reasonable response time.

Although Java applets are, in theory, designed to be platform independent, they should be tested with various supported browsers because they may have been created with different versions of the *software development kit* (SDK). Each SDK supports a different set of features. In addition, applets need to be interpreted by a *Java Virtual*

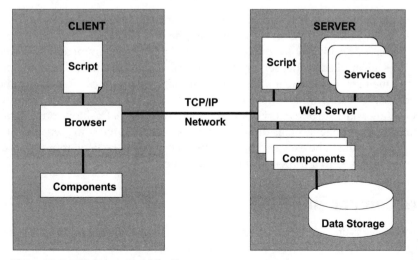

Figure 5.5 Web-based thick client.

Testing the Sample Application

To illustrate how functionality implementation can affect testing efforts, consider the metric generation feature of the sample application (See Chapter 7, "Sample Application," for more information). The sample application enables users to generate bug-report queries that specify search criteria such as bug severity and the names of engineers. Query results are tabulated and ultimately plugged into graphic charts, which are displayed to users. This functionality is implemented by having the user send a query to the Web server (via a Web browser). The Web server in turn submits the query to a database. The database executes the query and returns results. The Web server then sends the resulting data along with a Java applet or ActiveX control that is to be installed on the client machine. The client side, after downloading the component, converts the data into a graphically intuitive format for the user. If the downloaded component executes on the client machine, then the system is a thick-client system. If the processing is done on the server [i.e., the Structured Query Language (SQL) server gets results from the database, a GIF graphic is created on the server-side, and the GIF is sent back to the browser], then the system is a thin-client system. These alternate functionality implementations will have different consequences on the testing effort.

Machine (JVM). Different browsers, on different platforms and their respective versions, have different built-in JVMs, which may contain bug incompatibilities with each other. With ActiveX controls, the performance hit should occur only once. There may, however, be incompatibility issues with browsers other than Microsoft Internet Explorer and platforms other than Microsoft Windows.

In thin-client systems, incompatibility issues are less of a concern. Performance issues, however, need to be considered on the server side where requests are processed and data transfer takes place (sending bitmaps to the browser).

The thin-client model is designed to solve incompatibility problems as well as processing power limitations on the client side (the thin-client model concentrates work on the server). Additionally, it ensures that updates happen immediately because the updates are applied at that server only. *Personal digital assistants* (PDAs), for example, due to their small size, are not capable of handling much processing. The thin-client model serves PDAs well because it pushes the work to servers, which perform the processing and return results back to the client (the PDA). Desktop computers (in which the operating systems deliver a lot of power and processing) enable much more processing to be executed locally; therefore, the thick-client approach is commonly employed to improve overall performance.

Software Components

A *component* is any identifiable part of a larger system that provides a specific function or group of related functions. Web-based systems, such as e-business systems, are composed of a number of hardware and software components. *Software components* are integrated application and third-party modules, service-based modules, the operating system (and its service-based components), and application services (packaged servers such as Web servers, SQL servers, and their associated service-based components). *Component testing* is the testing of individual software components, or logical groups of components, in an effort to uncover functionality and interoperability problems. Some key software components include operating systems, server-side application service components, client-side application service components, and third-party components.

Operating Systems

Operating systems extend their services and functionality to applications. The functionality is often packaged in binary form, such as standard dynamic link libraries (DLLs). When an application needs to access a service, the application does it by calling a predefined *application program interface* (API) set. In addition, with object-based technology, these components extend their functionality by also exposing events (e.g., when a certain applied event is double-clicked, perform the following action), properties (e.g., when the background color is white and the foreground color is black), and methods (e.g., remove or add a certain entry to the scroll list) for other applications to access.

Application Service Components

Server-side packaged servers. A *server* is a software program that provides services to other software programs from either a local host or a remote host. The hardware box that a server software program runs in is also often referred to as a *server.* Physical hardware boxes, however, can support multiple client programs, so it is more accurate to refer to the software as the *server,* as opposed to the hardware that supports it. Packaged servers offer their services and extend their functionality to other applications in a manner that is similar to the extended model of operating systems. Two common packaged servers that are used in Web-based systems are *Web servers* and *database servers.* Web servers typically store HTML pages that can be sent, or served, to Web clients via browsers. It is common for packaged Web servers to offer functionality that enables applications to facilitate database activities. Such features can be packaged in a binary module such as a DLL. Access to these features is achieved via predefined APIs. See Table 5.1 for examples of server-side service components.

Client-side services. On the client side, a typical browser supports a variety of services, including Java VM, which runs Java applets, script interpreters that execute scripts. See Table 5.1 for examples of client-side services.

Third-Party Components

Software applications are subdivided into multiple components, otherwise referred to as *units* or *modules.* In object-oriented programming and distributed software engineering, components take on another meaning: *reusability.* Each component offers a

Table 5.1   Possible Scenario of Software Component Segmentation

APPLICATION SERVICE COMPONENTS	THIRD-PARTY COMPONENTS
Server side	Java components
Web server	ActiveX controls
Scripting	Standard EXEs
Java VM	Standard DLLs
Database server	CGIs
Data access service	etc.
Transaction service	
Client Side	
Web browser	
Scripting	
Java VM	
etc.	
INTEGRATED APPLICATION COMPONENTS	
HTML, DHTML, JavaScript, VBScript, Jscript, perl Script, etc.	
Standard EXEs	
CGIs	
API-based components	
Java components	
ActiveX controls	
Standard DLLs	
etc.	

template, or self-contained piece to a puzzle that can be assembled with other components, to create other applications. Components can be delivered in two formats: (1) *source-based*, such as in object-oriented programming class, and (2) *binary-based*, such as in a DLL or Java Archive file format (JAR). Binary-based components are more relevant to the testing concerns of this book.

Integrated Application Components

An *integrated application* consists of a number of components, possibly including a database application running on the server side, or a Java-based chart generation application running on the server side in an HTML page that is running on the client side, as shown in Figure 5.6. In the Java applet example shown in Figure 5.6, the software component executes within the context of the Web browser, or a *container*. A container can also be a Web-server-based application, a database application, or any other application

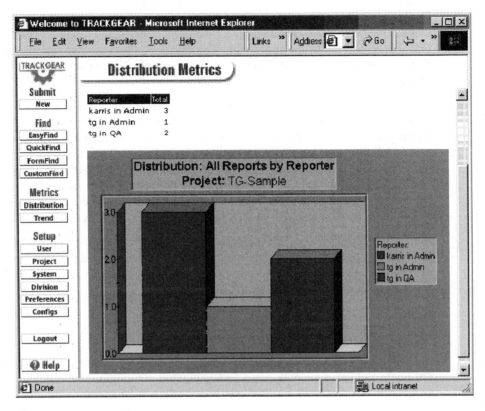

Figure 5.6 Java applet.

that can communicate with the component via a standard interface or protocol. Typically, software components are distributed across different servers on a network. They, in turn, communicate with each other via known interfaces or protocols to access needed services. See Table 5.1 for a sample list of integrated software components.

Dynamic Link Library (DLL)

Understanding DLLs and the potential errors that may be associated with them is essential in designing useful test cases. In the early years of software development, the only way that a developer could expose created functionality to another developer was to package the functionality in an object file (.OBJ) or library files (.LIB). This method required the other developer to link with the .OBJ or .LIB file. The functionality was therefore locked in with the executable. Some of the implications of this approach were that if several executables used the same set of functionality, each executable had to individually link to the object. This was repetitive, and the linked code added to the size of the executable file, which resulted in more memory requirements at runtime. More important, if new versions of the object or library files became available, the new code had to be relinked, which led to the need for much retesting.

Dynamic link library was introduced to improve the method of sharing functionality. A DLL is a file that contains functions and resources that are stored separately from and linked to on demand by the applications that use them. The operating system maps the DLL into the application's address space when the application, or another DLL, makes an explicit call to a DLL function. The application then executes the functions in the DLL.

Files with .DLL extensions contain functions that are either exported or available to other programs. Multiple applications or components may share the same set of functionality and, therefore, may also share the same DLLs at runtime. If a program or component is linked to a DLL that must be updated, in theory all that needs to be done is replace the old DLL with the new DLL. Unfortunately, it is not this simple. There are situations where errors may be introduced with this solution. For example, if a DLL that is referenced in the import library links to a component that is not available, then the application will fail to load. (See the error message example in Figure 5.10.)

Here is another example. The DLL caller application illustrated in Figure 5.7 is a Visual Basic application. It uses a few functions that are exported by the system DLL named KERNEL32.DLL. After loading the application, clicking the Show Free Memory button displays the current available physical memory.

To implement this feature, the code that handles the click event on the Show Free Memory button needs to be written. Because there is an exported function named *GlobalMemoryStatus*, which is available in the Windows system DLL named KERNEL32.DLL, a developer can simply call this function to retrieve the information. The process of using a function in a DLL is illustrated in Figures 5.8 and 5.9. Call the DLL function when there is a click event on the Show Free Memory button.

Potential DLL-Related Errors

Missing required DLL.   For example, when the application DLLCALLER.EXE is executed on the developer's machine, everything works fine. When it is first exe-

Figure 5.7   DLL caller program.

```
              Data Structure
              |
Type MEMORYSTATUS
         dwLength As Long
         dwMemoryLoad As Long
         dwTotalPhys As Long
         dwAvailPhys As Long
         dwTotalPageFile As Long
         dwAvailPageFile As Long
         dwTotalVirtual As Long
         dwAvailVirtual As Long
End Type
```

Figure 5.8 DLL function declaration.

cuted on a system other than the developer's, however, the error message shown in Figure 5.10 displays.

As it turns out, the application was created with Visual Basic 4.0 and depends on the DLL named VB40032.DLL. If that DLL is not installed, the application will not load properly. The application did not complain about KERNEL32.DLL, because it is a system DLL, which is expected to be there. Otherwise, even the operating system would not work.

API-incompatible DLL.   There may be two versions of the same DLL, but the data type, structure, or number of parameters has been changed from one version to another. And so, an error results.

Other incompatibility issues.   One of the benefits of using DLL is that when the author of a DLL needs to change the implementation of a function (to improve performance, for example) but not change the API, the change should be transparent to the DLL callers. No problems should result. This is, however, not always the case. You need to test to confirm the compatibility with your application.

See the section entitled "Testing Considerations" later in this chapter for more DLL-related issues. The preceding section is not intended to suggest that you should start testing at the API level, unless you are specifically asked to do so. It is intended to

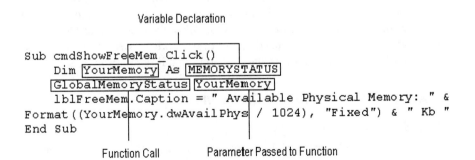

Figure 5.9 DLL function call.

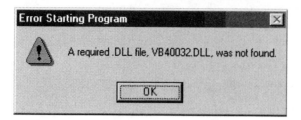

Figure 5.10 Error caused by missing DLL.

give you enough background information to design powerful test cases that focus on interoperability issues.

Web Application Component Architecture

Generally, Web applications consist of server-side and client-side components, including operating systems, browsers, packaged servers, and other associated software. A sampling of these components, along with their associated testing issues, follows.

Server-Side Components

Any computer that provides services to other computers is a *server*. A single physical computer can house multiple servers (software programs). Servers can also be distributed across multiple physical computers. Testing considerations vary depending on the number and distribution of servers and other software components associated with a system.

Web systems often have several servers included at their back end—allowing users to gain access from a client computer (via a browser) and get the services they need (Web page content or database records). On the hardware side, the characteristics that distinguish server host quality are similar to those qualities considered favorable in all computers: high performance, high data throughput, scalability, and reliability.

Server operating systems need to be more robust than desktop workstation operating systems. Windows 95 and Windows 98, for example, do not offer the reliability or performance required by most servers. Operating systems such as Unix, Windows NT, and Windows 2000 Advanced Server offer strong security features and administrator tools, in addition to the scalability and reliability required by servers.

Core Application Service Components

Web Servers

Web servers, or HTTP servers, store Web pages or HTML files and their associated contents. Web servers make their contents available to client computers. Web servers are the most essential type of server for Web-based systems. Many software companies develop Web servers: Novel, Netscape, Microsoft, Sun Microsystems, and others. Web servers also serve advanced technology components such as Java Servlets, ActiveX controls, and back-end database connectors. Web servers may work with protocols such as FTP and Gopher to pass data back to users.

Database Servers

Database servers act as data repositories for Web applications. Most Web systems use *relational database servers* (RDBSs). Database servers introduce a variety of testing complexities, which are discussed in Chapter 11, "Database Tests."

Prominent database server manufacturers include Microsoft, Oracle, and Sybase. Structured Query Language (SQL) is the coding language used in relational database management servers (RDBMS). Refer to Chapter 11, "Database Tests," for more information regarding SQL and databases.

Application Servers

Application server is a term used to refer to a set of components that extend their services to other components (e.g., ASP) or integrated application components as discussed earlier. Web applications support users by giving them access to data that is stored on database servers. Web applications coordinate the functionality of Web servers and database servers so that users can access database content via a Web browser interface.

The sample application, a Web-based bug-tracking system, is an example of an application server that utilizes component-based technologies. See Chapter 7, "Sample Application," for more information.

Web-to-Database Connectivity

The value of data access applications is that they allow interaction between users and data. Communication between users, Web servers, and database servers is facilitated by certain extensions and scripting models.

On the back end, data resides in a database. On the front end, the user is represented by requests sent from the Web server. Therefore, providing connectivity between Web server requests and a database is the key function of Web-based applications. There are several methods that can be employed to establish such connectivity. The most common are Common Gateway Interface– (CGI) based programs with embedded SQL commands, Web server extension-based programs, and Web server extension-based scripts.

Common Gateway Interface (CGI)

The CGI is a communications protocol that Web servers use to communicate with other applications. *Common Gateway Interface scripts* allow Web servers to access databases (among other things); *CGI applications*, on the other hand, receive data from servers and return data through the CGI. The CGI applications are usually written in *Practical Extraction and Reporting Language* (perl), although they can be written in other programming languages, such as C, C++, and Visual Basic.

Once a CGI program has been written, it is placed in a Web server directory called a *CGI bin*. Web server administrators determine which directories serve as CGI bins.

Common Gateway Interface programs must be placed in their correct directories if they are to run properly. This security feature makes it easier to keep track of CGI programs and to prevent outsiders from posting damaging CGI programs.

After a CGI program has been placed in a CGI bin, a link to the bin is embedded in a URL on a Web page. When a user clicks the link, the CGI program is launched. The CGI program contacts a database and requests the information that the user has requested. The database sends the information to the CGI program. The CGI program receives the information and translates it into a format that is understandable to the user. This usually involves converting the data into HyperText Markup Language (HTML), so that the user can view the information via a Web browser.

The main drawback of CGI scripts is that they run as separate executables on Web servers. Each time a user makes a request of a database server by invoking a CGI script, small amounts of system resources are tied up. The net effect of running a single CGI script is negligible, but consider the effect of 1000 concurrent users launching CGI scripts simultaneously; the effect of 100,000 simultaneous CGI scripts running on a Web server would likely have disastrous consequences to system memory and processing resources.

Web Server Extension-Based Programs

An alternate, and sometimes more efficient, means of supplying Web-to-database connectivity is to integrate with *Web server–exported library functions.* The NSAPI/ISAPI-based applications, for example, are *in-process* applications that take advantage of Web servers' native API. Library functions work off of features and internal structures that are exposed by Web servers to provide different types of functionality, including Web-to-database connectivity.

The NSAPI/ISAPI-based applications can be DLLs that run in the same memory space as Web server software. Netscape Server uses NSAPI. Microsoft Internet Information Server uses ISAPI. Both NSAPI and ISAPI effectively offer a similar solution; they are APIs that offer functions in DLL format. These APIs expose the functionality of the Web server software of which they are a part so that required processes can be performed by the server software itself, rather than by a separate executable (such as a CGI script).

Web server extension-based applications, although more efficient from a resource perspective, are not always the best choice for invoking Web server functionality. For example, a Web application may be distributed to multiple server platforms. It often makes sense to write different code for each platform. A CGI script might be written to interface with a Unix server, whereas NSAPI code might be used to invoke functions on a Netscape server running in the same system. A third server (e.g., Microsoft Internet Information Server) might require either a CGI script or ISAPI code. The development of every Web system, as far as Web-to-database connectivity goes, requires a careful balance between tolerable performance levels, compatibility, and perceived effort of execution.

A drawback of Web server extension-based applications is that, because they are written in compiled languages such as C, C++, or Visual Basic, they are binary. Whenever changes are made to code—for example, during bug fixing—the code has to be recompiled. This makes remote changes to the code more cumbersome. Furthermore, scripting language is easier to use and, therefore, many new developers can quickly be trained.

Web Server Extension-Based Scripts

Active Server Page (ASP) is a Microsoft technology that allows for the dynamic creation of Web pages using scripting language. The ASP is a programming environment that provides the ability to combine HTML, scripting, and components into powerful Internet applications. Also, ASP can be used to create Web sites that combine HTML, scripting, and other reusable components. Active Server Page script commands can also be added to HTML pages to create HTML interfaces. In addition, with ASP, business logic can be encapsulated into reusable components that can be called from scripts or other components.

Active Server Page scripts typically run on servers. Unlike the binary code model, ASP scripts do not have to be compiled. Therefore, ASP scripts can be easily copied from distributed software unless encryption measures are undertaken; encryption measures add more components and processing requirements to Web servers, however—not to mention the need for additional testing. The ASP scripts interact with the DLL layer through an interpreter (asp.dll). The DLL layer in turn interacts with the ISAPI layer to provide functionality, such as gateway connectivity. An HTML page that contains a link to an ASP file often has the file name suffix of .ASP.

Java Server Page (JSP) is a Sun Microsystems technology similar to ASP for the dynamic creation and control of the Web page content or appearance through the use of servlets, small programs that run on the Web server to generate the Web page before it is sent to the requested user. Java Server Page technology is also referred to as the servlet API. Unlike ASP, which is interpreted, JSP calls a Java program (servlet) that is run on the Java Web Server. An HTML page that contains a link to a Java servlet often has the file name suffix of .JSP.

ASP/JSP versus CGI

- The CGI programs require Web server operating systems to launch additional processes with each user request.
- As an in-process component, ASP/JSP can run in the same memory space as Web server applications—eliminating additional resource drain and improving performance.

ASP/JSP versus Web Server Extension-Based Programs

- Because NSAPI/ISAPI applications are in-process applications that use a Web server's native API, they run at a speed comparable with that of ASP.
- NSAPI/ISAPI applications must be compiled.

- ASP/JSP uses scripting languages.
- ASP/JSP is faster to develop and deploy than NSAPI/ISAPI.

Other Application Service Components

Search Servers

Often referred to as *search engines, search servers* catalog and index data that is published by Web servers. Not all Web systems have search servers. Search servers allow users to search for information on Web systems by specifying *queries*. A query, simply put, is a request (to find certain data) that has been submitted to a search server by a user. Users submit queries so that they can define the goal and scope of their searches—often specifying multiple search criteria to better refine search results.

As new information is introduced into a Web system, search servers update their indices. Robust search servers have the ability to handle large amounts of data and return results quickly, without errors.

Proxy Servers and Firewalls

Proxy servers are sometimes employed by companies to regulate and track Internet usage. They act as intermediaries between networks and the Internet by controlling packet transmissions. Proxy servers can prevent files from entering or leaving networks, log all traffic between networks and the Internet, and speed up the performance of Internet services. They log IP addresses, URLs, durations of access, and numbers of bytes downloaded.

Most corporate Web traffic travels through proxy servers. For instance, when a client computer requests a Web page from the Internet, the client computer contacts the network's proxy server with the request. The proxy server then contacts the network's Web server. The Web server sends the Web page to the proxy server, which in turn forwards the page to the client computer.

Proxy servers can speed up performance of Internet services by *caching* data. Caching involves keeping copies of requested data on local servers. Through caching, proxy servers can store commonly viewed Web pages so that subsequent users can access the pages directly from the local server, rather than accessing them at slower speeds over the Internet.

Firewalls are shields that protect private networks from the Internet. They prevent unauthorized users from accessing confidential information, using network resources, and damaging system hardware—while allowing authorized insiders access to the resources they require. Firewalls are combinations of hardware and software—making use of routers, servers, and software to shield networks from exposure to the Internet. Two common types of firewalls are *packet-filtering* firewalls (such as routers) and *proxy-based* firewalls (such as gateways).

See Chapter 15, "Security Tests," for more information regarding proxy servers and firewalls.

Communication-Related Servers

Numerous communication server types are available to facilitate information exchange between users, networks, and the Internet. If a Web system under test includes a remote-access server, e-mail, a bulletin board, or chat feature, then communication server components are present and should be tested.

E-Commerce-Related Servers

E-commerce servers (though not truly a separate type of server, but rather a specialized use of Web server technologies) provide functionality for retail operations. Via Web applications, they allow both merchants and customers to access pertinent information through client-side Web browsers.

TASKS PERFORMED BY E-COMMERCE SERVERS

- Order taking and order processing
- Inventory tracking
- Credit card validation
- Account reconciliation
- Payment/transaction posting
- Customer orders/account information

COMMON E-COMMERCE SERVER BRANDS

- Ariba
- BroadVision
- Calico
- Vignette

Multimedia-Related Servers

Multimedia servers provide support for high-speed multimedia streaming, enabling users to access live or prerecorded multimedia content. Multimedia servers make it possible for Web servers to provide users with computer-based training (CBT) materials.

Client-Side Components

The client side of a Web system often comprises a wide variety of hardware and software elements. Multiple brand names and product versions may be present in a single system. The heterogeneous nature of hardware, networking elements, operating systems, and software on the client side can make for challenging testing.

Web Browsers

Web browsers are applications that retrieve, assemble, and display Web pages. In the client-server model of the Web, browsers are clients. Browsers request Web pages from Web servers. Web servers then locate requested Web pages and forward them to the browsers, where the pages are assembled and displayed to the user. There are multiple browsers and browser versions available for PCs, Macintosh computers, and Unix computers.

Browsers issue HTML requests (although they can also issue requests for ASP, DHTML, and more). The HTML code instructs browsers how to display Web pages to users. In addition to HTML, browsers can display material created with Java, ActiveX, and scripting languages such as JavaScript and VB Script.

When Web pages present graphics and sound files, the HTML code of the Web pages themselves does not contain the actual multimedia files. Multimedia files reside independently of HTML code, on multimedia servers. The HTML pages indicate to Web browsers where requested sounds, graphics, and multimedia are located.

In the past, browsers required that separate applications, known as *helper applications,* be launched to handle any file type other than HTML, GIF, and JPEG. *Plug-ins,* such as RealPlayer and QuickTime, are more popular today. They allow streaming media and other processes to occur directly within browser windows. RealPlayer, by RealNetworks, is a popular streaming sound and video plug-in. Windows Media Player is a sound and video plug-in that is built into Windows operating systems. QuickTime, made by Apple, can play synchronized content on both Macintosh computers and PCs.

Newer browsers are bundled with complete suites of Internet applications, including plug-ins, e-mail, utilities, and *What You See Is What You Get* (WYSIWYG) Web page authoring tools. Netscape Communicator, of which Netscape Navigator is a component, is such a suite. Internet Explorer 4.x and 5.x allow users to view their entire desktops using HTML; Web links are used to interact with the operating system and live Web content can be delivered directly to the user desktop.

Add-on/Plug-in Components

Additional software may reside on the client side to support various forms of interactivity and animation within Web pages. *Java applets* and *ActiveX controls* are examples of such add-on applications. Java, a full-featured object-oriented programming language, can be used to create small applications, known as *applets,* within Web pages. ActiveX is a Microsoft technology that behaves similarly to both Java applets and plug-ins. ActiveX controls offer functionality to Web pages. Unlike applets, however, they are downloaded and stored on the user's hard disk and run independently of Web browsers. Microsoft Internet Explorer is the only browser that supports ActiveX controls. Java applets and ActiveX controls can also reside on and be executed from servers.

Communication-Related Components

The client sides of Web systems often contain applications that facilitate various methods of communication. Such applications take advantage of server-based communication components such as remote-access dial-up, chat (IRC), discussion groups, bulletin boards, and videoconferencing.

Testing Discussion

The following component architecture example is useful in illustrating effective testing strategies. Figure 5.11 details the chart generation example that was mentioned earlier in the section, "Distributed Application Architecture," in this chapter. The pseudodesign for the transaction process runs as follows:

- User submits a request for a trend chart that compares daily totals of open bugs with closed bugs over the past 5 days.
- Web server requests the file named trend.asp.
- trend.dll is called to do some processing work.
- trend.dll connects to the database server and calls a stored procedure named sp_trend to pull the requested data.
- trend.dll, upon receiving the requested data, calls plot.dll and passes the data for calculation and formatting in preparation for drawing the trend chart.
- The formatted data is then written to a file named data.tmp in comma-delimited format.
- A third-party Java charting component is requested with the file name data.tmp so that a line chart can be drawn.
- The JavaApplet is sent to the client and data.tmp is then deleted.
- The Java applet is loaded into the user's browser and a trend chart with the appropriate data is drawn.

Based on the program logic and its component architecture, we will analyze this design to determine potential problems. Then, we will design test cases around the potential problems in an effort to expose possible faults and errors. Note that the

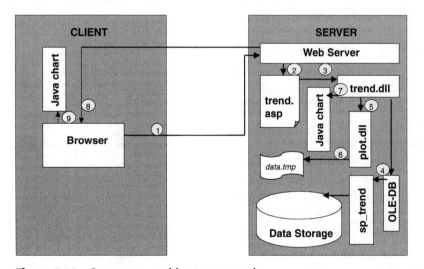

Figure 5.11 Component architecture example.

potential issues and test cases discussed in this section are by no means definitive. They are designed to encourage you to think more about the possibility of errors in component-based systems. They will help you to think beyond black-box testing from the end user's point of view. Some of the testing issues mentioned in this example are discussed in great detail in later chapters.

Test-Case Design Analysis

Submitting the request.

- *What happens if the input data is invalid?*

  You want to determine if there is any error handling code. Hopefully, there is. You will then need to devise test cases that test the error handling logic, which consist of three parts: (1) error detection, (2) error handling, and (3) error communication. You also want to know if errors are handled on the client side, the server side, or both. Each approach has unique implications. You may want to know if error handling is done through scripts or through an embedded component (e.g., if a Java applet or an ActiveX control is used for the input UI).

- *What happens if there is too much data for the last 5 days?*

  Look for potential boundary condition errors in the output.

- *What happens if there is no data for the last 5 days?*

  Look for potential boundary condition errors in the output.

- *What happens if there is a firewall in front of the Web server?*

  Look for potential side effects caused by the firewall such as dropping or filtering out certain data packets, which would invalidate the request.

trend.asp is requested.

- *Is the Web server environment properly set up to allow ASP to be executed?*

  The environment can be set up manually by the system administrator or programmatically via an installation program or setup utility. Regardless, if a script is not allowed to execute, trend.asp will fail.

- *Will the ASP be encrypted? If so, has it been tested in encrypted mode?*

  The application under test may be using third-party technology to encrypt the ASP files. Incompatibility, performance, time-related, and other environment-related issues may affect functionality.

trend.dll is called.

- *Is trend.dll a standard DLL or a COM-based DLL? If it is a COM-based object, how is it installed and registered?*

- *What are the exported functions in the DLLs upon which trend.dll depends? Are they all available on the local and remote host(s)?*

  There are numerous errors related to DLLs that should be considered. See "Dynamic Link Library" in this chapter for more information.

Calling sp_trend.

- *The application needs to make a connection to the SQL server before it can execute the stored procedure sp_trend on the database. What issues might cause the connection to fail?*

There are numerous reasons why this process might fail. For example, there may be an error in authentication due to a bad ID, password, or data source name.

- *When an attempt to connect to the database fails, how is the error condition communicated back to the user?*

    The user may receive anything from a cryptic error message to no message at all. What are acceptable standards for the application under test?

Testing the Sample Application

Please see Chapter 7 for details on the sample application. Following is an example of a real bug that was discovered in the testing of the sample application. trend.dll crashed an ISAPI-based DLL that, in turn, generated error messages on the application server console. However, the end user at the client side received no communication regarding the error. The user was not notified of the error condition.

- *Is the stored procedure properly precompiled and stored in the database?*

    This is typically done through the installation procedure. If for some reason the stored procedure is dropped or fails to compile, then it will not be available.

- *How do you know that the data set returned by the stored procedure is accurate?*

    The chart might be drawn correctly but the data returned by the stored procedure may be incorrect. You need to be able to validate the data. See Chapter 11, "Database Tests," for more information.

Calling plot.dll. The functions in this DLL are responsible for calculating and formatting the raw data returned by sp_trend in preparation for the Java chart application.

- *Is data being plotted correctly to the appropriate time intervals (daily, weekly, and monthly)?*

    Based on the user's request, the data will be grouped into daily, weekly, and monthly periods. This component needs to be thoroughly tested.

- *Does the intelligence that populates the reports with the appropriate time periods reside in plot.dll or in sp_trend?*

    Based on what was described earlier, some of the logic can be implemented in the stored procedure and should be tested accordingly.

Write data to file data.tmp.

- *What happens if the directory to which the text file will be written is write-protected?*

    Regardless if the write-protected directory is a user error or a program error, if data.tmp is not there, the charting feature will not work.

- *What happens if plot.dll erroneously generates a corrupt format of the comma-delimited file?*

    The data formatting logic must be thoroughly tested.

- *What happens if multiple users request the trend chart simultaneously or in quick succession?*

Multiuser access is what makes the Web application and client-server architectures so powerful. Yet, this is one of the main sources of errors. Test cases that target multiuser access need to be designed.

Testing the Sample Application

A hard-to-reproduce bug that resulted in a blank trend chart was discovered during the development of the sample application. It was eventually discovered that the data.tmp file was hard-coded. Whenever more than one user requested the chart simultaneously, or in quick succession, the earlier request resulted in incomplete data, or data intended for the subsequent request. The application's developer later designed the file name to be uniquely generated with each request.

Calling the Java charting program.

- *What happens if a chart program is not found?*

    The Java applet must be physically placed somewhere, and the path name in the code that requests the applet must point to the correct location. If the applet is not found, the charting feature will not work.

- *What happens if there is a missing cls (class) in a JAR?*

    A jar file often contains the Java classes that are required for a particular Java application. There is a dependency concept involved with Java classes that are similar to what is described in "Dynamic Link Library" in this chapter. If one or more of the required classes are missing, the application will not function.

Sending results back to the client.   The Java applet is sent to the browser and the data in data.tmp is also sent, so that the applet can draw the chart in the browser. data.tmp is then deleted from the server.

- *What is the minimum bandwidth requirement that the application under test supports? How big is the applet? Is performance acceptable with the minimum bandwidth configuration?*

    Check the overall performance in terms of response time under the minimum requirement configuration. This test should also be executed with multiple users (for example, a million concurrent users if that is what the application under test claims to support). See Chapter 16, "Performance, Load, and Stress Tests," for more information.

- *Is the temp file properly removed from the server?*

    Each charting request leaves a new file on the server. These files unnecessarily take up space.

Formatting and executing the client-side component.   The browser formats the page, loads the Java applet, and displays the trend chart.

- *Is the applet compatible with all supported browsers and their relative versions?*

Testing the Sample Application

The sample application utilizes a third-party Java charting component that enables the generation of charts. Because the component offers numerous user interaction features, it is a rather large object to be sent to a browser. Because the sample application required only basic charts, the developer decided to remove some of the classes in the jar that were not required by the application. The size of the jar was thereby slimmed down to about half its original size and performance was greatly improved.

After about a week of testing, in which the testing team had no idea that the number of Java classes had been reduced, the test team discovered a unique condition that required some handling by the applet. The applet, in turn, was looking for the handling code in one of the classes that had been removed. The test team wrote up a bug report and subsequently talked to the developer about the issue. The developer explained what he had done and told the test team that they should make sure that this type of error be detected in the future. Several test cases that focused on this type of error were subsequently designed. The test team ultimately found five more errors related to this optimization issue.

Each browser has its own version of the sand box, or JVM, and does not necessarily have to be compatible with all other browsers. This incompatibility may have an effect on the applet.

■ *What happens when security settings, either on the browser side or on the network firewall side, prohibit the applet from downloading? Will there be any communication with the user?*

Look for error conditions and see how they are handled.

Test Partitioning

Given the distributed nature of the Web system architecture, it is essential that test partitioning be implemented. For example, at the configuration and compatibility level, if the application under test requires Microsoft IIS 3.0, 4.0, and 5.0, and Microsoft SQL versions 6.5 and 7.0, then the test matrix for the configuration should look something like this:

TEST CONFIGURATION ID	MS-IIS	MS-SQL
1	3.x	6.5
2	3.x	7.0
3	4.x	6.5
4	4.x	7.0
5	5.0	6.5
6	5.0	6.0

Regarding performance, you might wish to compare SQL 6.5 with SQL 7.0. Such a test matrix would look something like this:

TEST CONFIGURATION ID	MS-IIS	MS-SQL
1	Don't Care	6.5
2	Don't Care	7.0

On a more micro level, if a component in the system under test is updated at the last minute and testing must be completed in a hurry, how much testing should be repeated? Should everything be retested, or should only specific features be retested?

Using the sample application's charting feature as an example (Figure 5.6), say that PLOT.DLL is recompiled with a later version of the compiler, but other than that, not a single line of code has been changed. How can test requirements be determined? Here are a few suggestions:

- Reexamine the specific functionality that PLOT.DLL offers and look for error scenarios.
- For each potential error scenario, consider the consequences.
- Use a utility such as Dependency Walker to determine any new dependencies that PLOT.DLL has and the potential implications of those dependencies.
- Examine other components to make sure that TREND.DLL is the only component using PLOT.DLL.
- Focus testing on the creation of DATA.TMP and the data integrity.
- Confine testing to the context of the trend chart features only.
- Retest all other functionality.
- Retest browser compatibility (the Java applet remains the same, so there is no need to be concerned with its compatibility).
- Focus testing on the stored procedure sp_trend (because nothing has changed there).

DIFFERENT CONCEPTUAL LEVELS OF PARTITIONING

- *High-level partitioning.* If the goal of testing is to measure server-side response time, then there is no need to run data through the Internet, firewall, proxy servers, and so on. With a load-testing tool (see Chapter 16, "Performance, Load, and Stress Tests," for more information), a load generator can be set up to hit the Web server directly and collect the performance data. Figure 5.12 shows an example of high-level partitioning.
- *Physical-server partitioning.* If the goal of testing is to measure per-box performance, then each physical server can be hit independently with a load generator to collect performance data.
- *Service-based partitioning.* If the goal of testing is to test the functionality of the data application and the overall performance of the database server that is providing services to the application, then testing should focus on the database server.

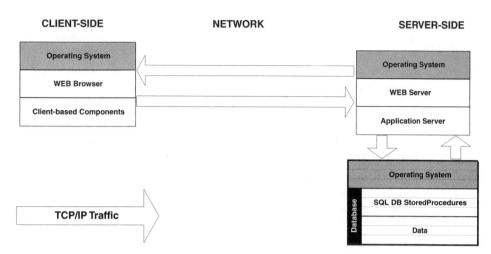

Figure 5.12 High-level partitioning.

- *Application/component-based partitioning.* The focus of such testing is on the component level (refer to the preceding Java chart generation tests for examples). The testing here is focused at the component level as previously described in the charting example.

Testing Considerations

- Determine the server hardware requirements of the system under test. Then, generate a matrix of the supported configurations and make sure that these configurations are tested.

- Determine the server software component requirements (Web servers, database servers, search servers, proxy servers, communications servers, application servers, e-commerce servers, multimedia servers, etc.) and design interoperability tests to look for errors.

- Determine how the server software components are distributed and design interoperability tests to look for errors.

- Determine how the server software components interact with one another and design interoperability tests to look for errors.

- Determine how the Web-to-database connectivity is implemented (CGI, NSAPI/ISAPI, ASP, or other technologies) and design interoperability tests to look for errors.

- Determine the hardware/software compatibility issues and test for those classes of errors.

- Determine how the processing is distributed between client and server (thin client versus thick client).

- Test partitioning involves the testing of pieces of a system both individually and in combination. Test partitioning is particularly relevant in the testing of Web systems due to the communication issues involved. Because Web systems involve multiple components, testing them in their entirety is neither an easy or effective means of uncovering bugs at an early stage.

- Design test cases around the identified components that make up the client side of a Web application, including browser components, static HTML elements, dynamic HTML elements, scripting technologies, component technologies, plug-ins, and so on.

- One way of evaluating integration testing and test partitioning is to determine where the components of an application reside and execute. Components may be located on a client machine or on one or more server machines.

DLL Testing Issues

- Use a utility such as Microsoft Dependency Walker to generate a list of DLLs upon which the application under test (and its components) depends. For each DLL, determine its version number and where it is located. Determine if the version number is the latest shipping version.

Here is an example of a component-recursive dependency tool, Microsoft Dependency Walker. If the utility is run and DLL.CALLER.EXE is loaded in (the example DLL mentioned in "Dynamic Link Library" in this chapter), its dependencies will be analyzed (as shown in Figure 5.13). To download Dependency Walker and other related utilities, go to the Microsoft site and search for Dependency Walker. Or visit the URL www.microsoft.com/msdownload/platformsdk/sdktools.htm.

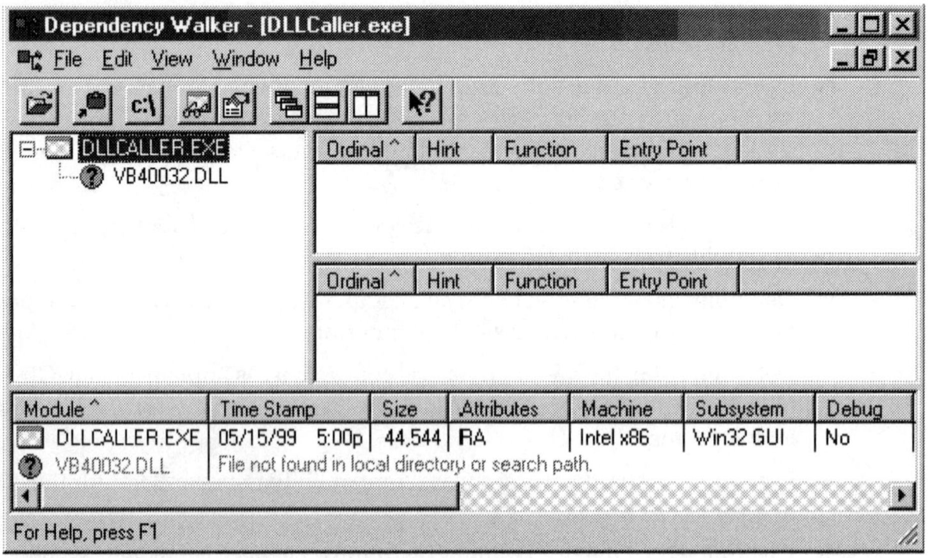

Figure 5.13 Component-recursive dependency tool.

A comparable utility called QuickView is available for Windows 9.x and NT systems. To access this utility, right-click on a component that you would like to view and choose QuickView from the context menu list.

There are at least four categories of DLLs and components:

1. *Operating system-based DLLs.* In Windows environments, this includes USER32.DLL, GDI32.DLL, and KERNEL32.DLL.

2. *Application service-based DLLs.* In Windows environments, this includes ASP.DLL, CTRL3D32.DLL, VB40032.DLL, and so forth.

3. *Third-party DLLs.* For example, CHART.DLL offers charting functionality to other applications.

4. *Company-specific DLLs.* For example, Netscape Navigator includes the NSJAVA32.DLL.

In testing for DLL-related errors, look for the following issues:

- Ensure that nonsystem DLLs are properly installed and that their paths are properly set so that they can be found when the components call them.

- Look for potential incompatibility errors, such as API incompatibility, or functional incompatibility among various versions of the same DLL.

- If there are other applications installed on the system that share the same DLL with components, how will the installation and uninstallation processes be handled?

- What if the DLL is accidentally erased or overwritten by a newer or older version of the same DLL?

- What happens if more than one version of the same DLL coexists on the same machine?

- Explicitly loaded DLLs must be unloaded when applications and processes no longer need them. Typically, this should occur upon the termination of the calling application.

- Test with a *clean* environment (a system with only the operating system installed on it), as well as a *dirty* environment (a system loaded with common applications).

- What if a third-party DLL needs certain files that are not available (printer initialization, for example)?

- With Windows-based applications, consider looking for errors related to the creation and removal of DLL keys during installation and uninstallation.

Bibliography

Binder, Robert V. *Testing Object-Oriented Systems: Models, Patterns, and Tools.* Reading, WA: Addison Wesley Longman, 2000.

LogiGear Corporation. *QA Training Handbook: Testing Web Applications.* Foster City, CA: LogiGear Corporation, 2000.

LogiGear Corporation. *QA Training Handbook: Testing Windows Desktop and Server-Based Applications.* Foster City, CA: LogiGear Corporation, 2000.

Orfali, Robert, et al. *Client/Server Survival Guide, Third Edition.* New York: John Wiley & Sons, 1999.

Reilly, Douglas J. *Inside Server-Based Applications.* Redmond, WA: Microsoft Press, 2000.

CHAPTER 6

Test Planning Fundamentals

Why Read This Chapter?

A crucial skill required for the testing of Web applications is the ability to write effective test plans that consider the unique requirements of those Web applications. These skills are also required to write up the sample test plan for the sample application. (See Chapter 7, "Sample Application," and Chapter 8, "Sample Test Plan," for details.)

Introduction

This chapter discusses test documentation, including test plan templates and section definitions. It also explains the efficiencies of the *LogiGear One-Page Test Plan*, details the components of issue and weekly status reports, and lists some helpful testing considerations.

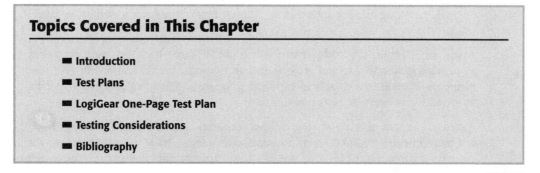

Topics Covered in This Chapter

- Introduction
- Test Plans
- LogiGear One-Page Test Plan
- Testing Considerations
- Bibliography

Test planning for Web applications is similar to test planning for traditional software applications; careful planning is always critically important to effective structuring and management. Test planning is an evolutionary process that is influenced by numerous factors: development schedules, resource availability, company finances, market pressures, quality risks, and managerial whim.

Test planning begins with the gathering and analysis of information. First, the product under test is examined thoroughly. Schedules and goals are considered. Resources are evaluated. Once all associated information has been pulled together, test planning begins.

Despite the complex and laborious nature of the test planning process, test teams are not generally given much direction by management. If a company-approved test-plan template does not exist, test teams are often simply instructed to "come up with a test plan." The particulars of planning, at least for the first draft of the test plan, are normally left up to the test team.

Test Plans

A test plan is a document, or set of documents, that details testing efforts for a project. Well-written test plans are comprehensive and often voluminous in size. They detail such particulars as testing schedules, available test resources, test types, and personnel who will be involved in the testing project. They also clearly describe all intended testing requirements and processes. Test plans often include quite granular detail—sometimes including test cases, expected results, and pass/fail criteria.

One of the challenges of test planning is the need for efficiency. It takes time to write these documents. Although some or all of this time might be essential, it is also time that is no longer available for finding and reporting bugs. There is always a tradeoff between depth/detail and cost, and in many of the best and most thoughtful test groups, this trade-off is difficult and uncomfortable.

Another challenge of test planning is that it comes so early in the development process that, more than likely, there is no product built yet on which to base planning. Planning, instead, is based on product specifications and requirements documents (if such documents exist, and to whatever extent that they are accurate, comprehensive, and up-to-date). As a consequence, planning must be revised as the product develops, often moving in directions that are different than those suggested by original specifications.

Assuming that they are read (which is often not the case), test plans support testing by providing structure to test projects and improving communication between team members. They are invaluable in supporting the testing team's primary responsibility—finding as many bugs as possible.

A central element of test planning is the consideration of test types. Although every test project brings with it its own unique circumstances, most test plans include the same basic categories of tests: acceptance tests, functionality tests, unit tests, system tests, configuration tests, and regression tests. Other test types (installation tests, help tests, database tests, usability, security, load, performance, etc.) may be included in test plans depending on the type of Web application under test. Sometimes, testing groups also need to determine how much automation and which automated testing tools will be used. How will test coverage be measured, and what tools will be used? Other tasks that testing groups are often asked to do include designing and implementing defect tracking, configuration management, and build-process ownership.

Table 6.1 details when standard test types are normally performed during the software development process. See Chapter 3, "Software Testing Basics," for definitions of these test types. Note that Release Acceptance Tests (RATs), Functional Acceptance Simple Tests (FASTs), and Task-Oriented Functional Tests (TOFTs) are generally run in each phase of testing. Web systems may require additional test types, such as security, database, and load/stress.

The next phase of test planning is laying out the tasks. After all available resources and test types have been considered, one can begin to piece together a *bottom-up* schedule that details which tests will be performed and how much time each test will require (later, delegation of tasks to specific personnel should be incorporated into the test plan). A bottom-up schedule is developed by associating tasks with the time

Table 6.1 Test Types and Their Place in the Software Development Process

TIME →		
Begin Alpha Testing	Begin Beta Testing	Begin Final Testing
Alpha Phase	Beta Phase	Final Phase

TYPES OF TESTS RECOMMENDED		
TOFT FAST RAT Configuration Compatibility * Boundary Test Stress Installation Test Exploratory Test	TOFT FAST RAT Real World User Test Exploratory Test Forced-Error Test Full Configuration Compatibility Test Volume Test Stress Test Install/Uninstall Test Performance Test User Interface Regression Documentation	TOFT FAST RAT Install/Uninstall Test Real World User- Level Test Exploratory Test

* Test one representative from each equivalence class.

needed to complete them—with no regard to product ship date. A *top-down* schedule, on the other hand, begins with the ship date and then details all tasks that must be completed if the ship date is to be met. Negotiations regarding test coverage and risk often involve elements of both top-down and bottom-up scheduling.

Test plans must undergo peer management and project management review. Like engineering specs, test plans need to be approved and signed before implemented. During a test-plan review, the testing group may need to negotiate with management over required resources—including schedule, equipment, and personnel. Issues of test coverage and risk-based quality or life-critical and 24/7 up-time quality may also come into play (See Chapter 1, "Welcome to Web Testing," for more information on test coverage and risk-based quality). Ultimately, a test plan will be agreed upon, and testing can begin.

Test-Plan Documentation

Test-plan documentation should detail all required testing tasks, offer estimates of required resources, and consider process efficiencies. Unless one is creating a test plan with the intention of distributing it to a third party—either to prove that proper testing was performed or to sell it along with software—it is best to keep test plans focused on only those issues that support the effort of finding bugs. Enormous, heavily detailed test plans—unless required by a customer or third-party regulating body—are only valuable in so far as they help you find bugs.

The unfortunate reality is that the majority of test plans sit unread on shelves during most of the testing process. This is because they are unwieldy and dense with information that does not support the day-to-day effort of finding bugs. Even if they are read, they are seldom updated as regularly as they should be—reflecting current changes to schedule, delegation of tasks, test coverage, and so on.

The LogiGear One-Page Test Plan (included later in this chapter) is designed specifically to avoid the troubles that more traditional test plans suffer; one-page test plans are more easily read and updated.

When read, test-plan documentation improves communication regarding testing requirements by explaining the testing strategy to all members of the product development team. Documentation is of course also valuable in conveying the breadth of a testing job to testing staff and in providing a basis for delegating tasks and supervising work.

Documentation generates feedback from testing team members and members of other departments. Debates are often sparked over the contents of test documentation. For example, project managers may insist on different levels of testing than those that are proposed by the testing group. It is always a good idea to make test plans available for review as early in the development process as possible so that managers, programmers, and members of the marketing team can assess risk and priorities before testing begins. Debates are also more fruitful when team members can focus discussions on a clearly laid-out test plan that includes specific goals.

Issues of test coverage often arise midway through the testing process. Requiring managers to approve and sign test plans (before testing begins) brings managers into the test coverage decision process; it places responsibility on management to approve any compromises of test coverage that may arise from test-plan negotiations.

Accountability is also increased by good test documentation. Clearly defined responsibilities make it easier for both managers and staff to stay focused. Detailed lists of tests that must be performed, along with clearly defined expectations, go a long way toward ensuring that all foreseeable areas of risk are addressed.

Proper test documentation requires a systematic analysis of the Web system under test. Your understanding of the interdependencies of a system's components must be detailed and thorough if test planning is to be effective. As a test project is analyzed, a comprehensive list of program features should be compiled. It is common for a feature list to detail the complete set of product features, all possible menu selections, and all branching options. It is a good idea to begin writing up a feature list as early in the test planning phase as possible.

Test plans take into consideration many of the risks and contingencies that are involved in the scheduling of software development projects. For example, product documentation (e.g., online help, printed manuals) testing cannot be completed until the documentation itself nears completion. Documentation, however, cannot be in its final phase until after the user interface (UI) has been frozen. The UI, in turn, cannot be frozen until at some point in beta testing when functional errors affecting the UI have been fixed. Another example of testing interdependency includes not being able to execute performance testing until all debugging code has been removed.

A list of features that are *not* to be tested will also be of value. A list of features that are not to be tested sometimes smokes out resistance within the product team that might not otherwise have been voiced until midway through the testing process. It also clearly marks what you believe to be out of scope.

For more in-depth information regarding test planning, refer to *Testing Computer Software* by Kaner et al. (1999).

Test-Plan Templates

One effective means of saving time and ensuring thoroughness in test-plan documentation is to work from a *test-plan template.* A test-plan template is essentially a fill-in-the-blank test plan into which information that is specific to the system under test is entered. Because they are generic and comprehensive, test-plan templates force one to consider questions that might not otherwise be considered at the beginning of a test project. They prompt one to consider numerous test types—many of which may not be appropriate for the test project—in addition to pertinent logistical issues, such as which test tools will be required and where testing will take place. Test templates can also impose a structure on planning, encouraging detailed specifications on exactly which components will be tested, who will test them, and how testing will proceed. See Appendix A of this book for the complete LogiGear Test Plan Template.

There are many test templates available. After looking over the LogiGear Test Plan Template, one should consider other test-plan templates. A good place to begin looking for a test-plan template is the LogiGear Test Resource Web site (www.qacity.com).

A standard test-plan template that is used by the software testing industry is the *ANSI/IEEE Standard 829-1983 for Software Test Documentation.* It defines document types that may be included in test documentation, including test cases, feature lists, and platform matrices. It also defines the components that the IEEE believes should be included in a standard test plan; so among other uses, it serves as a test-plan template. For information regarding the *ANSI/IEEE Standard 829-1983,* visit www .computer.org, or phone (202) 371-0101.

Test-Plan Section Definitions

The following lists gives a number of standard test-plan sections that are appropriate for most test projects.

OVERVIEW SECTION

Test-plan identifier. Unique alphanumeric name for the test plan. See the LogiGear Test Plan Template (Appendix A) for details.

Introduction. Discussion of the overall purpose of the project. References all related product specifications and requirements documents.

Objective. Goals of the project, taking quality, scheduling constraints, and cost factors into consideration.

Approach. The overall testing strategy: Who will conduct testing, what tools will be utilized, scheduling issues that must be considered, and feature groups that will be tested.

TESTING SYNOPSIS SECTION

Test items. Lists every feature and function of the product. References specifications and product manuals for further detail on features. Includes descriptions of all software application, software collateral, and publishing items.

Features to be tested. Cross-references features and functions that are to be tested with specific test design specifications and required testing environments.

Features not to be tested. Features of the product that will not undergo testing. May include third-party items and collateral.

System requirements. Specifications on hardware and software requirements of the application under test: Computer type, memory, hard-disk size, display type, operating system, peripheral, and drive type.

Entrance/exit. *Application-specific:* Description of the application's working environment; how to launch and quit the application. *Process-specific:* Description of criteria required for entering and exiting testing phases, such as alpha and beta testing.

Standard/reference. List of any standards or references used in the creation of the test plan.

Types of tests. Tests to be executed. May include acceptance tests, feature-level tests, system-level tests, regression tests, configuration and compatibility tests, documentation tests, online help tests, utilities and collateral tests, and install/uninstall tests.

Test deliverables. List of test materials developed by the test group during the test cycles that are to be delivered before the completion of the project. Includes the test plan itself, the bug tracking system, and an End of Cycle or Final Release report.

TEST PROJECT MANAGEMENT SECTION

The product team. List of product team members and their roles.

Testing responsibilities. Responsibilities of all personnel associated with the testing project.

Testing tasks. Testing tasks to be executed: The order in which tasks will be performed, who will perform the tasks, and dependencies.

Development plan and schedule. Development milestone definitions and criteria—detailing what the development group will deliver to testing, and when it will be delivered.

Test schedule and resource. Dates by which testing resources will be required. Estimates on amount of tester hours and personnel required to complete project.

Training needs. Personnel and training requirements. Special skills that will be required and amount of personnel who may need to be trained.

Environmental needs. Hardware, software, facility, and tool requirements of testing staff.

Integration plan. How the integration plan fits into overall testing strategy.

Test suspension and resumption. Possible problems or test failures that justify the suspension of testing. Basis for allowing testing to resume.

Test completion criteria. Criteria that will be used to determine the completion of testing.

The issue-tracking process. Description of the process, the issue-tracking database, bug severity definitions, issue report formats (see "Issue Reports" in this chapter for an example).

Status tracking and reporting. How status reports will be communicated to the development team, and what the content of status reports will be (see "Weekly Status Reports" in this chapter for an example).

Risks and contingencies. All risks and contingencies, including deliverables, tools, and assistance from other groups—even those risks and contingencies that are detailed in other parts of the test plan.

Approval process. Test-plan approval and final release approval.

LogiGear One-Page Test Plan

It is often a challenge for testing groups to communicate their needs to other members of the software development team. The myriad test types, the testing sequence, and scheduling considerations can be overwhelming when not organized into a comprehensible plan that others can read at a glance. The LogiGear One-Page Test Plan is a distillation of test types, test coverage, and resource requirements that meets this need.

The LogiGear One-Page Test Plan is task oriented. It lists only testing tasks—because some members of the product team may not be interested in "testing approach," "features not to be tested," and so on. They just want to know what is going to be tested and when. Because one-page test plans are so easy to reference, if they are adequate for your process, they are less likely to be disregarded by impatient team members.

The LogiGear One-Page Test Plan does not require additional work. It is simply a distillation of the standard test-plan effort into an easily digestible format. The LogiGear One-Page Test Plan is effective because it details the testing tasks that a testing team should complete, how many times the tasks should be performed, the amount of time each test task may require, and even a general idea of when the tasks should be performed during the software development process.

The LogiGear One-Page Test Plan is easy to reference and read. Twenty-page test plans are regularly ignored throughout projects, and 100-page test plans are rarely read. One-page test plans, on the other hand, are straightforward and can easily be used as negotiating tools when it comes time to discuss testing time and coverage—the usual scenario being, "What testing time can be cut?" The test team can point to test tasks listed on a one-page test plan and ask, "Are we prepared to accept the risk of not performing some of these tests to their described coverage?"

Developing a One-Page Test Plan

The process of completing a one-page test plan is described in the following steps.

Step 1: Test Task Definition

Review the standard test types that are listed in Chapter 3, "Software Testing Basics," and in Table 6.1.

Select the test types that are required for the project. Decisions should be based on the unique functionality of the system under test. Discussions with developers, analysis of system components, and an understanding of test types are required to accurately determine which test types are needed.

Step 2: Task Completion Time

Calculate the time required to perform the tests. The most difficult aspect of putting together a test plan is estimating the time required to complete a test suite. With new testers, or with tests that are new to experienced testers, the time estimation process involves a lot of guesswork. The most common strategy is divide and conquer. That is, break the tasks down into smaller subtasks. The smaller subtasks are easier to estimate. You may then sum up from those. As you gain experience, you miss fewer tasks and you gain a sense of percentage of tasks that you typically miss so you can add an n percent for contingency or missing-tasks correction.

Informed estimates may also be arrived at if testing tasks are similar to those of a past project. If time records of similar past testing are not available, estimates may be unrealistic. One solution is to update the test plan after an initial series of tests has been completed.

A 20 percent contingency or missing-tasks correction is included in this example. As testing progresses, if this contingency does not cover the inevitable changes in your project's schedule, the task completion time will need to be renegotiated.

Step 3: Placing the Test Tasks into Context

Once the task list has been developed and test times have been estimated, place the tasks into the context of the project. The development team will need to supply a build schedule.

Determine how many times tests will be run during development. For example, documentation testing may only be performed once, or it may be reviewed once in a preliminary phase and then again later after all edits are complete. A complete cycle of functionality tests may be executed once per development phase, or possibly twice. Acceptance tests are run on every build. Often, a full bug regression occurs only once per phase, though partial regression tests may happen with each build.

Step 4: Table Completion

Finally, multiply the numbers across the spreadsheet. Total the hours by development phase for an estimate of required test time for the project. Add time for management, including test-plan writing/updating, test-case creation, bug database management, staff training, and other tasks that are needed for the test team and for completion of the project.

Step 5: Resource Estimation

Take the total number of hours required for the alpha phase, divide that by the total number of weeks in the alpha phase, and then divide that by 30 hours per week. That gives you the number of testers needed for that week. For example, if you need total testing hours for alpha of 120, a 4-week alpha phase, and testers have a third-hour testing week, your project requires only one tester $[(120 \div 4) \div 30 = 1]$. Apply this same process to arrive at estimates for the beta phase and project management also.

Note that I use only 30-hour testing week for a full-time tester because by experience, know that the other 10 (overhead) hours are essentially used for meeting, training, defect tracking, researching, special projects, and so on.

LogiGear One-Page Test Plan

The LogiGear One-Page Test Plan can be invaluable in negotiating testing resource and testing time requirements with members of the product team. Figure 6.1 provides

Milestone	Type of Test	# of Cycles	Hrs. per Cycle	Est. Hours
Alpha				
			Total:	
Beta				
			Total:	#
Final				
			Total:	#
	Testing Project Management			
	Test Planning & Test Case Design			
	Training			
	Test Automation			
			Total:	#

PROJECT TOTAL DAYS	xx
PERSON WEEKS	xx
20% Contingency (wks)	xx
Total person weeks	**XX**
Testers for Alpha	**XX**
Testers for Beta	**XX**
Testers for Final	**XX**
Project Management	**XX**

Figure 6.1 LogiGear One Page Test Plan.

an example of the LogiGear One-Page Test Plan. Descriptions of each of the tests are included in Chapter 3, "Software Testing Basics."

Testing Considerations

As part of the test planning process, you should consider how the bug reporting/resolution cycle will be managed and the procedure for status reporting. In addition, you should give some thoughts on how to manage milestone criteria, as well as whether to implement an automated testing program. This section touches on those issues.

Issue Reports

An *issue report*, or *test incident report*, is submitted whenever a problem is uncovered during testing. Figure 6.2 shows an example of an online issue report that is generated by the sample application. The following list details the entries that may be included in a complete issue report.

ISSUE REPORT FIELDS

Project.   A project may be anything from a complex client-server system with multiple components and builds, to a simple 10-page user's guide.

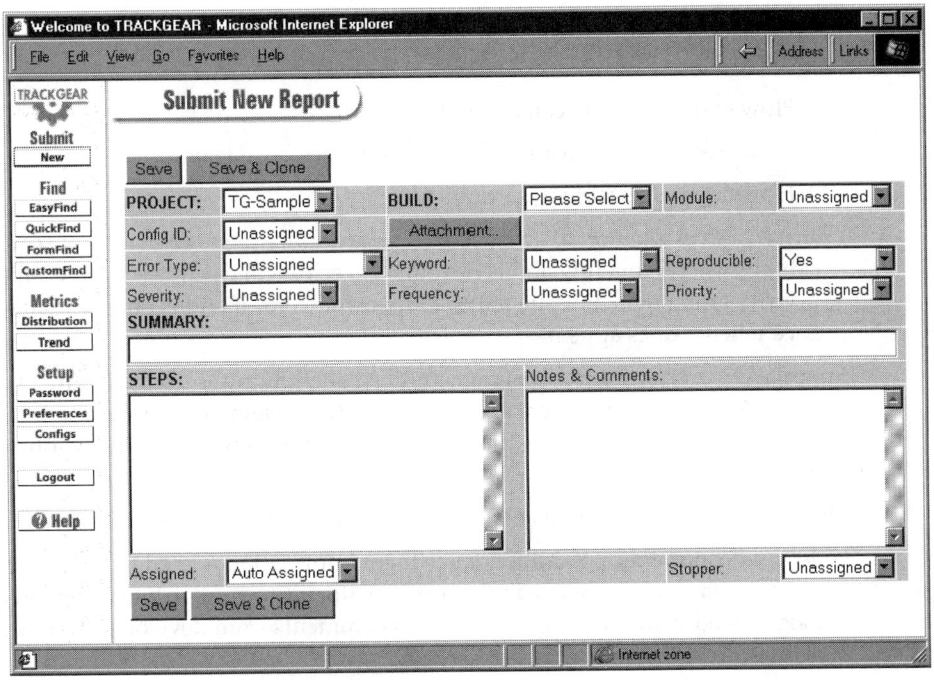

Figure 6.2   Online issue report form.

Build.   Builds are versions or redesigns of a project that is in development. A given project may undergo numerous revisions, or builds, before it is released to the public.

Module.   Modules are parts, components, units, or areas that comprise a given project. Modules are often thought of as units of software code.

Configuration.   Configuration testing involves checking an application's compatibility with many possible configurations of hardware. Altering any aspect of hardware during testing creates a new testing configuration.

Uploading attachments.   Attachments are uploaded along with issue reports to assist QA and developer groups in identifying and recreating reported issues. Attachments may include keystroke captures or macros that generate an issue, a file from a program, a memory dump, a corrupted file that an issue report is predicated on, or a memo describing the significance of an issue.

Error types.   The category of error into which an issue report falls (e.g., software incompatibility, UI, etc).

Keyword.   Keywords are an attribute type that can be associated with issue reports to clarify and categorize an issue's exact nature. Keywords are useful for sorting reports by specific criteria to isolate trends or patterns within a report set.

Reproducible.   Specifies whether a reported issue can be recreated: *Yes, No,* with *Intermittent* success, or *Unconfirmed.*

Severity.   Specifies the degree of seriousness that an issue represents to users. For example, a typo found deep within an online help system might be labeled with a severity of *low,* and a crash issue might qualify for a severity of *high.*

Frequency.   Frequency, or how often an issue exhibits itself, is influenced by three factors:

1. How easily the issue can be reached.

2. How frequently the feature that the issue resides in is used.

3. How often the problem is exhibited.

Priority.   An evaluation of an issue's severity and frequency ratings. An issue that exhibits itself frequently and is of a high severity will naturally receive a higher priority rating than an issue that seldom exhibits itself and is only of mild annoyance when it does appear.

Summary.   A brief summary statement that concisely sums up the nature of an issue. A summary statement should convey three elements: (1) symptoms, (2) actions required to generate the issue, and (3) operating conditions involved in generating the issue.

Steps.   Describes the actions that one must perform to recreate the issue.

Notes and comments.   Additional pertinent information related to the bug that has not been entered elsewhere in the report. Difficult-to-resolve bugs may develop long, threaded discussions consisting of comments from developers, project managers, QA testers, and writers.

Assigned.   Assigned individuals who are accountable for addressing an issue.

Milestone stopper. An optional bug report attribute that is designed to prevent projects from achieving future development milestones. By associating critical bugs with production milestones, milestone stoppers act as independent criteria by which to measure progress.

Weekly Status Reports

At the conclusion of each week during testing, the testing team should compile a status report. The sections that a status report normally includes follow.

Weekly status reports can take on critical importance because they are often the only place where software changes are tracked. They detail such facts as prerequisite materials not arriving on time, icons not loading onto desktops properly, and required documentation changes. Once archived, they, in effect, document the software development process.

Consideration needs to be given to what information will be included in weekly status reports and who will receive the reports. Just as test plans need to be negotiated at the beginning of a project, so do weekly status reports need to be negotiated. The manner in which risks will be communicated to the development team needs to be carefully considered because information detailed in these reports can be used against people to negative effect. Possibly only milestone status reports should be disseminated to the entire product team, leaving weekly status reports to be viewed only by a select group of managers, testers, and developers. See Appendix B for the "Weekly Status Report Template."

Following are descriptions of sections that are typically included in weekly status reports.

TESTING PROJECT MANAGEMENT

Project schedule. Details testing and development milestones and deliverables.

Progress and changes since last week. Tests that have been run and new bugs that have been discovered in the past week.

Urgent items. Issues that require immediate attention.

Issue bin. Issues that must be addressed in the coming weeks.

To-do tasks by next report. Tasks that must be completed in the upcoming week.

PROBLEM REPORT STATUS

Bug report tabulation. Totals of open and closed bugs, how totals have changed in past week.

Summary list of open bugs. Summary lines from issue reports associated with open bugs.

TREND ANALYSIS REPORT

Stability trend chart. Graph that illustrates the stability of a product over time.

Quality trend chart. Graph that illustrates the quality of a product over time.

Note that there are numerous other document types that may be included in test-plan documentation. For definitions of other test documentation types (including test-design, test-procedure, and test-case specifications; test transmittal reports; and test logs), refer to *Testing Computer Software* by Kaner et al. (1999).

Automated Testing

The sample one-page test plan (See Chapter 8, "Sample Test Plan," for details) can be analyzed to uncover areas that may be well suited to automated testing. Considerations regarding staffing, management expectations, costs, code stability, UI/functionality changes, and test hardware resources should be factored into all automated testing discussions.

Table 6.2 categorizes the testing tasks called for in the sample one-page test plan by their potential adaptability to automated testing; further evaluation would be required to definitively determine whether or not these testing tasks are well suited to automation.

When evaluating test automation, you should do the following:

- Look for the tests that take the most time.
- Look for tests that could otherwise not be run (e.g., server tests).
- Look for application components that are stable early in development.
- Consider acceptance tests.
- Consider compatibility/configuration quick-look tests.

Milestone Criteria and Milestone Tests

Milestone criteria and milestone tests should be agreed upon and measurable (for example, alpha testing might not begin until all code is testable and installable, and all UI screens are complete—even if they contain errors). Such criteria can be used to

Table 6.2 Test Types Suited for Automation Testing

IDEALLY SUITED	NOT SUITABLE
RAT	Documentation
FAST	Boundary
Performance, load, and stress	Installation
Metrics/charting	Most functionality
Regression	Exploratory
Database population	Import utility
Sample file generation	Browser compatibility
	Forced-error

verify whether code should be accepted or rejected when it is submitted for milestone testing. Milestone criteria and accompanying tests should be developed for all milestones, including *completion of testing, entrance,* and *exit.* Ideally, these tests will be developed by the test team and approved by the development team; this approach may reduce friction later in the development project.

Bibliography

Kaner, Cem, et al. *Testing Computer Software,* second edition. New York: John Wiley & Sons, 1999.

LogiGear Corporation. *QA Training Handbook: Lead Software Test Project with Confidence.* Foster City, CA: LogiGear Corporation, 2000.

LogiGear Corporation. *QA Training Handbook: Testing Web Applications.* Foster City, CA: LogiGear Corporation, 2000.

LogiGear Corporation. *QA Training Handbook: Testing Windows Desktop and Server-Based Applications.* Foster City, CA: LogiGear Corporation, 2000.

LogiGear Corporation. *QA Training Handbook: Testing Computer Software.* Foster City, CA: LogiGear Corporation, 2000.

CHAPTER 7

Sample Application

Why Read This Chapter?

Some of the testing concepts covered in this book may seem abstract until they are applied in practice to an actual Web application. By seeing how the features of the sample application are accounted for in the sample test plan (See Chapter 8, "Sample Test Plan," for details) readers can gain insights into effective Web application test planning.

Introduction

This chapter details the features and technologies that are associated with the sample application, including system overview and application functionality.

The sample application is helpful in illustrating test planning issues that relate to browser-based Web systems; it places many of the issues that are raised in upcoming

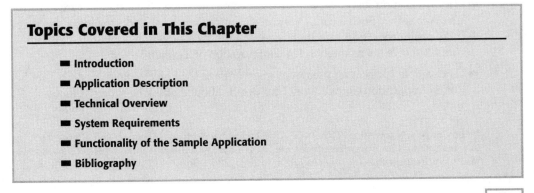

Topics Covered in This Chapter

- Introduction
- Application Description
- Technical Overview
- System Requirements
- Functionality of the Sample Application
- Bibliography

chapters into context. The sample application is TRACKGEAR* 1.0, a Web-based defect-tracking system that is produced by LogiGear Corporation. In Chapter 8, "Sample Test Plan," the sample application serves as a baseline from which a high-level test plan is developed.

Application Description

The sample application (TRACKGEAR) is a problem-tracking system designed for software development teams. It is used to manage the processing and reporting of change requests and defects during software development. The sample application allows authorized Web users, regardless of their hardware platform, to log into a central database over the Internet to remotely create and work with defect reports, exchange ideas, and delegate responsibilities. All software development team members (project management, marketing, support, QA, and developers) can use the sample application as their primary communications tool.

The sample application offers a relatively complex system from which to explore test planning. The sample application requires a database server, a Web server, and an application server. It also supports both administrator and user functionality.

The sample application's features include:

- Defect tracking via the Internet, intranet, or extranet
- Customizable workflow that enforces accountability between team members
- Meaningful color metrics (charts, graphs, and tables)
- E-mail notification that alerts team members when defects have changed or require their attention

Technical Overview

Following are some key technical issues that relate directly to the testing of the sample application.

- The application server should be installed on the same physical hardware box as the Web server. Such a configuration eliminates potential performance issues that may result from the application accessing the Web server on a separate box. Figure 7.1 shows the recommended configuration of a system.
- The sample application uses Active Server Page (ASP) technology (See Chapter 5, "Web Application Components," for details about ASP). Web servers process ASP

---

* At the time of this writing, TRACKGEAR™ 2.0 has been released. This version offers many new features and improvements to release 1.0. For the latest information on this product, please visit www.logigear.com.

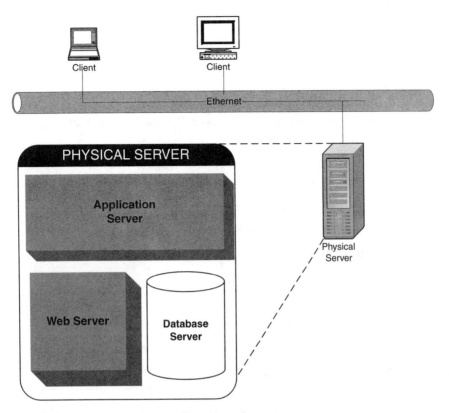

Figure 7.1 Recommended configuration of a system.

scripts, based on user requests, before sending customized pages back to the user. The ASP scripts are similar to server-side includes and Common Gateway Interface (CGI) scripts in that they run on the Web server rather than on the client side. The ASP scripts do not involve a client-side install. This thin-client model involves the browser sending requests to the Web server where ASP computes and parses requests for the application, database server, and Web server.

- The CGI scripts are not used in the sample application.

- The database activities (queries and stored procedures) are supported via Microsoft SQL 6.5 or higher.

- A single Java applet runs on the client browser to display defect metrics (charts and graphics). Only fourth-generation browsers (4.0 or higher) are supported by the sample application.

- Both the Web server and the application server must utilize Microsoft technology (IIS, NT, etc.).

System Requirements

The hardware and software requirements of the sample application are as follows:

SERVER REQUIREMENTS

- *Computer.* PC with a Pentium processor (Pentium II recommended)
- *Memory.* 64Mb (128 recommended)
- *Disk space.* 100Mb for the server application and 200Mb for the database
- *Operating system.* Microsoft Windows NT Server 4.0 with most recent service pack
- *Web server software.* Microsoft Internet Information Server (IIS) 4.0
- *SQL server software.* Microsoft SQL Server 6.5 or higher with service pack

CLIENT REQUIREMENTS

- Active LAN or Internet connection
- Netscape Navigator 4.x
- Microsoft Internet Explorer 4.x or higher

Functionality of the Sample Application

Following are several sections that help detail the functionality of the sample application.

Installing the Sample Application

The sample application utilizes a standard InstallShield-based installation program that administrators (or IS personnel) must run to set up the databases that are required by the application. This installation wizard automates the software installation and database configuration process, allowing administrators to identify preexisting system components (Web server, IIS server, physical hardware boxes, etc.), determine where new components should be installed, and how much disk space should be allocated for databases.

Getting Started

The sample application allows users to define workflow processes that are customized for their organization's defect-tracking needs. Workflow dictates, among other things, who has the privilege to assign resolutions (i.e., defect states) and who is responsible for addressing defect-related concerns. The sample application allows administrators to hardwire such resolution management process and to enforce accountability. User, group, division, and project assignments dictate the screen layouts and functionality that administrators and different user types can access.

The administrator of the application has access to administrator-level functions, such as user setup, project setup, and database setup, in addition to all standard user functionality, including report querying, defect report submission, and metrics generation.

Division Databases

The sample application acts as an information hub, controlling data flow and partitioning defect-tracking data. A company may use as many division-specific databases as it wishes. Some information is shared globally—for example, the application itself. Other information, including reports and functional groups, is relevant only to specific projects or divisions, and therefore is not shared globally across division databases.

Importing Report Data

The sample application comes with an import utility (a separate executable) that allows administrators to import existing databases. Specifically, the program allows the import of comma-separated values (CSV) files. These CSV files can be exported from other database programs, such as Microsoft Access, Excel, and Oracle. In order for the sample application to properly process imported data, it is important that certain guidelines be adhered to when creating the CSV files.

System Setup

Many of the sample application's attributes can be customized. Customizable system attributes include the following:

- Keywords
- Error types
- Resolutions
- Severity
- Phases
- Milestone stoppers
- Frequency
- Priority
- Workflow (the method by which reports are routed)

Project Setup

The key components of every project are project name, project members, project modules, project builds, and optional e-mail notification.

E-Mail Notification

The sample application utilizes e-mail to notify and inform individuals of their responsibilities regarding defects that are tracked. E-mail notification settings are flexible and can be customized for each project. For example, one project team might require notification for all defects that may prevent their product from going beta. This team's e-mail notification settings could then be set up to only alert them when a received defect has a milestone-stopper value of *beta.* Likewise, a team whose product is nearing release date could choose to have hourly summaries of every defect report in the system sent to them.

The sample application uses the Simple Mail Transfer Protocol (SMTP) to deliver notifications (most popular e-mail clients are compatible: Eudora, Microsoft Exchange, Microsoft Outlook Express, and others).

Submitting Defect Reports

Users of the sample application must go to the report screen to submit new defect reports (Figure 7.2). The report screen includes fields for recording relevant defect-tracking information. To get to the report screen, users click the New button on the navigation bar.

Generating Metrics

The sample application includes a third-party Java applet that allows users to generate metrics (charts, graphs, and tables of information) to gain global perspective over defect reports. Project managers, developers, and software-quality engineers in particular may gain insight into defect-fixing trends, personnel workload, and process efficiency by viewing trend and distribution metrics.

The sample application generates two types of metrics: (1) distribution metrics and (2) trend metrics. Figure 7.3 shows the distribution metrics setup screen. Figure 7.4

Figure 7.2 Sample application report screen.

PROJECT: TG2 ▼

Template: Closed by Report Validity ▼

Generate Metrics

Figure 7.3 Distribution metrics setup screen.

shows a typical distribution metric. Figure 7.5 shows the trend metrics setup screen. Figure 7.6 shows a typical trend metric.

Documentation

Documentation for the sample application comes in the following three forms:

1. *Administrator's guide.* A printed manual that provides administrators with the information they need to set up and manage the sample application.

Distribution: Closed by Report Validity

Project: TG2
User: karris
Date: 04/06/00

Report Validity	Total
Invalid	90
Valid	704

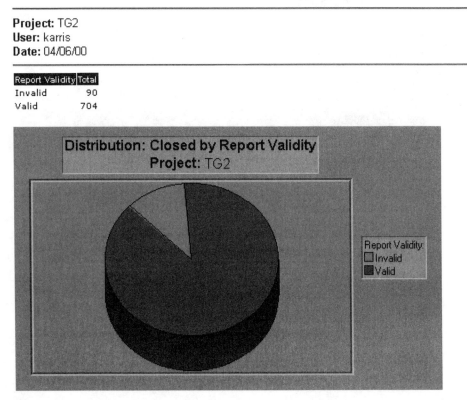

Figure 7.4 Distribution metric example.

PROJECT:	TG2 ▼
Template:	Total vs. Open vs. Closed - Over time ▼
Period:	○ Daily ⦿ Weekly ○ Monthly
Start Date:	⦿ Use the first submitted report date ○ Month: 4 ▼ Day: 6 ▼ Year: 00 ▼
End Date:	⦿ Today ○ Month: 4 ▼ Day: 6 ▼ Year: 00 ▼

Generate Metrics

Figure 7.5 Trend metrics setup screen.

Trend: Total vs. Open vs. Closed - Over Time

Project: TG2
Weekly: From 09/29/99 To 11/8/99
User: karris
Date: 04/06/00

Date	Closed	Open	Total
10/03/99	14	7	21
10/10/99	48	11	59
10/17/99	54	18	72
10/24/99	54	18	72
10/31/99	54	18	72
11/07/99	54	18	72

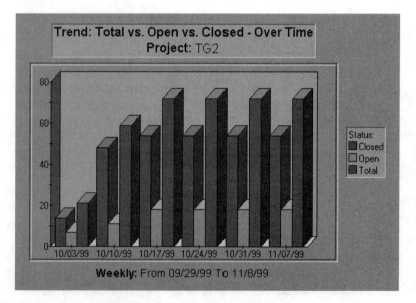

Figure 7.6 Trend metric example.

2. *User's guide.*   A printable Adobe Acrobat Reader .pdf manual that provides software testers and product team members with the information they need to submit reports, find reports, and advance workflow.

3. *Online help.*   A context-sensitive help system that resides within the sample application. The help system is accessible via the Help button on the navigation bar.

Bibliography

LogiGear Corporation. *QA Training Handbook: Testing Web Applications.* Foster City, CA: LogiGear Corporation, 2000.

LogiGear Corporation. *TRACKGEAR Administrator Guide.* Foster City, CA: LogiGear Corporation, 1999.

CHAPTER 8

Sample Test Plan

Why Read This Chapter?

Many of the test planning considerations discussed in this book may seem abstract until they are applied in practice to an actual Web application. By examining the test planning process for the sample application (see Chapter 7, "Sample Application," for details), readers gain insights into effective test planning practices that can be applied to Web applications.

The test types that are listed in this chapter are explored in more detail in the upcoming chapters of Part Four. The sample application is also referenced throughout upcoming chapters.

Introduction

This chapter discusses the test types that are appropriate for the sample application. It includes both a test schedule and a one-page test plan that are designed for the

---

Topics Covered in This Chapter

- Introduction
- Gathering Information
- Sample One-Page Test Plan
- Bibliography

---

sample application. Note that the sample test plan is *high level* by design. A complete test plan for the sample application is not feasible within the constraints of this book.

Many of the principles employed in this chapter are discussed in Chapter 6, "Test Planning Fundamentals." It is recommended that both Chapters 6 and 7 be read before proceeding with this chapter.

The information conveyed in Chapter 7 serves as a technical baseline for the test planning purposes of this chapter. As far as planning for other projects is concerned, getting involved early in the development process and discovering reliable sources of information is the best way to gather required technical data. Product prototypes, page mock-ups, preliminary documentation, specifications, and any marketing requests should be evaluated; such information, combined with experience and input from application developers, is the best means of determining required testing. Input from the project team should focus the test-plan effort on potential problem areas within the system under test.

Preliminary project schedules and an estimated number of builds should be considered in the development of any testing schedule.

With basic QA knowledge, the information about Web testing conveyed in this book, input from the development team, and an understanding of product functionality, a test planner can confidently develop a list of test types for the system under test (see Table 6.1 for details on test scheduling). Once a list of test types has been developed, staffing needs can be evaluated by considering the number of hours and types of skills that will be required of the testing team. Required tester hours and skills will undoubtedly fluctuate as development progresses. Estimates of testing hours required for testing the sample project are detailed later in this chapter.

Gathering Information

The information gathering process consists of four steps: (1) Establishing testing-task definitions, (2) estimating time required to complete the testing tasks, (3) entering the information into the project plan, and (4) calculating the overall resource requirements.

Step 1: Testing-Task Definition for the Sample Application

Step 1 in the one-page test planning process involves assembling a list of tasks for the project at hand. First, define the test types. The basic tests for Web applications are acceptance [both release acceptance test (RAT) and functional acceptance simple test (FAST)], functionality [task-oriented functional test (TOFT)], installation, user interface (UI), regression, forced-error, configuration and compatibility, server, security, documentation, and exploratory.

By reviewing the product description detailed in Chapter 7, "Sample Application," you can see a need for specific test types that are not included in the preceding list of basic test types. For example, tests should be developed that test the functionality of the databases, data import utility, e-mail notification, and third-party Java applet (metrics charting). The screen shots indicate functionality that should be tested. Some security features that should be tested are also mentioned (login/logout, views, and user permissions). By reviewing the product's system requirements, you can also glean information about test platforms, possible configuration tests, and other technologies that will require testing {Java applets, Microsoft NT [required], Active Server Page [ASP] [rather than Common Gateway Interface (CGI)]}.

The general descriptions offered by Chapter 7 alone do not offer enough information to help you develop an informed testing schedule and list of testing tasks. Much more detail than can be conveyed in this book is required to make such projections. For example, information regarding the number of error messages (and their completion dates) would be required, as would details of the installation process. Complete product descriptions, specifications, and marketing requirements are often used as a starting point from which you can begin to seek out the specific technical information that is required to generate test cases.

Step 2: Task Completion Time

The test times listed in Table 8.1 reflect the actual testing of the sample application. These test times were derived with input from the test team.

As part of evaluating tasks for completion time, you should evaluate resources such as hardware/software and personnel availability. Some test types require unique resources, tools, particular skill sets, assistance from outside groups, and special planning. Such test types include:

- *Configuration and compatibility testing.* Configuration and compatibility testing require a significant amount of computer hardware and software. Because the cost of outfitting a complete test lab exceeds the financial means of many companies, outsourcing solutions are often considered. See Chapter 14, "Configuration and Compatibility Tests," for more information.

- *Automated testing.* Automated testing packages (such as Segue™ SilkTest™) are valuable tools that can, when implemented correctly, save testing time, tester enthusiasm, and other resources. See Chapter 17, "Web Testing Tools," for information about available automated testing tools.

- *Milestone tests.* Milestone tests are performed prior to each development milestone. They need to be developed, usually from TOFT tests, and scheduled according to the milestone plan.

- *Special functionality tests (TOFT).* In addition to the specified functionality of the application, SMTP tests (e-mail notification) are also included in the TOFT suite. These tests may require assistance from other groups or special skill sets.

- *Web- and client-server-specific tests.* Performance, load, and stress tests, in addition to security and database tests, normally require specialized tools and skills.

Table 8.1 Task Completion Time

TEST TYPE	FUNCTIONAL AREA	TIME ESTIMATE	NOTES
RAT		30 minutes for each build	
FAST		2 hours for each build	
TOFT	**Admin functionality** User setup Project setup System setup Division setup **User functionality** Submit new report Easy find Quick find Form find Custom find Configuration profiles Preferences Metrics **Miscellaneous** Upload attachments Password Editing reports Views Tabular layouts	80 hours for a complete run.	These tests represent the majority of testing that must be performed. The entire suite of TOFT tests should be run once during alpha testing, twice during beta testing, and once during final testing. Testing should be segmented as coding is completed and as bugs are fixed.
Installation	Full installation Uninstaller Database initialization Division creation	40 hours	Test functionality, not compatibility. These tests should be performed once at the end of alpha testing, once during beta testing when the known installer bugs have been closed, and once again during final testing. Often, installers are not ready to be tested until well into alpha testing, or even at the beginning of the beta phase.
Data import utility		16 hours	CSV test data is required.

Table 8.1 *(Continued)*

TEST TYPE	FUNCTIONAL AREA	TIME ESTIMATE	NOTES
Third-party functionality testing	Metrics/chart generation feature	20 hours	Sample input data is required for the metrics function to generate charts.
Exploratory		16 hours per build	These are unstructured tests.
User interface	Every screen		Tested while testing functionality.
Regression		4 hours	Test suites are built as errors are uncovered.
Forced-error	Confirm all documented error messages	20 hours	Run suite twice. Can only be performed after all messages have been coded. There are 50 error messages in the sample application.
Configuration and compatibility	**Browser settings** 　Cookies 　Security settings 　Java 　Preferences **Browser types for Macintosh, Windows, and Unix** 　Netscape Navigator 　Internet Explorer **Browser functions** 　Back 　Reload 　Print 　Cache settings 　Server installation 　Compatibility 　Hardware 　　compatibility 　E-mail notification	80 hours	Quick look tests must be developed. A matrix of browsers, operating systems, and hardware equivalent classes must be developed.
Server	Performance, load, and stress tests	100 hours	
Documentation	Printed manual Online help system Downloadable user guide (PDF file)	80 hours	Functionality and content

Continues

Table 8.1 *(Continued)*

TEST TYPE	FUNCTIONAL AREA	TIME ESTIMATE	NOTES
Y2K and boundary testing			Test cases included in functionality tests (TOFT)
Database	Database integrity	20 hours	
Security	Login Logout Permissions Views Allowable IP addresses (firewall) Trusted servers (intranet) Password Preferences	40 hours	

All required tests should be identified as early in the development process as possible so that resource needs for tools, staffing, and outsourcing can be evaluated.

Step 3: Placing Test Tasks into the Project Plan

For the purposes of the sample test plan, a development schedule of 20 calendar weeks has been assumed. Testable code is expected early in July. According to the development team, there will be one build per week.

PRELIMINARY BUILD SCHEDULE

Alpha   12 weeks

Beta   6 weeks

Final   2 weeks

From Table 6.1, you can see which test phases are appropriate for each test type. (See Table 8.2.) Note that test types from Table 8.2 are examined in detail in the upcoming chapters of Part Four.

WHERE TO FIND MORE INFORMATION

- For information about RAT, FAST, TOFT, regression, and forced-error tests, please see Chapter 10, "Functional Tests."
- For information about configuration and compatibility tests, please see Chapter 14, "Configuration and Compatibility Tests."
- For information about install tests, please see Chapter 13, "Installation Tests."
- For information about database tests, please see Chapter 11, "Database Tests."

Table 8.2 Development Phases and Test Planning

7/12/2000	TIME LINE	11/26/2000
7/12/2000 **TWELVE WEEKS =** **60 BUSINESS DAYS** **ALPHA PHASE**	**10/04/2000** **SIX WEEKS =** **30 BUSINESS DAYS** **BETA PHASE**	**11/15/2000** **TWO WEEKS =** **10 BUSINESS DAYS** **FINAL PHASE** **SHIP**
	Types of Tests to Be Executed	
RAT	RAT	RAT
FAST	FAST	FAST
TOFT (User and Admin)	TOFT (User and Admin)	TOFT
Configuration & Compatibility	Server Testing: Stress/Load/Performance	Regression
Install	Complete Configuration & Compatibility	Exploratory
Exploratory	Regression	
	Install	
	Forced-Error	
	Documentation	
	Database	
	Exploratory	
	Third-party component integration	
	Security	

- For information about exploratory tests and an example of a third-party component, please see Chapter 3, "Software Testing Basics."

- For information about security testing, please see Chapter 15, "Web Security Concerns."

- For information about documentation tests, please see Chapter 12, "Help Tests."

- For information about server testing, please see Chapter 16, "Performance, Load, and Stress Tests."

Step 4: Calculate Hours and Resource Estimates

Multiply and total test times (refer to "Developing a One-Page Test Plan" in Chapter 6, "Test Planning Fundamentals," for details). Then calculate resource estimates. The one-page test plan is now complete!

Sample One-Page Test Plan

Table 8.3 is a one-page test plan that addresses the special needs of the sample application. Note that time has been budgeted for issue reporting, research, meetings, and more.

Table 8.3 Sample Test Plan

MILESTONE	TYPE OF TEST	# OF CYCLES	HRS. PER CYCLE	EST. HOURS
Alpha	RAT: Release Acceptance Test	12	0.5	6
	FAST: Functional Acceptance Simple Test	12	2	24
	TOFT: Task Oriented Functional Test	2	80	160
	Configuration Compatibility	1	80	80
	Install	1	40	40
	Exploratory Testing	12	16	192
			Total:	**502**
Beta	RAT: Release Acceptance Test	6	0.5	3
	FAST: Functional Acceptance Simple Test	6	2	12
	TOFT: Task Oriented Functional Test	1	80	80
	Server Tests (Performance, Stress and Load)	2	100	200
	Compatibility/Configuration (Browser, Install)	1	80	80
	Regression Testing	6	4	24
	Install	1	40	40
	Forced Error Test	2	20	40
	Documentation/Help (function and content)	1	80	80
	Database Integrity Test	1	20	20
	Exploratory Testing	6	16	96
	Data Import	1	16	16
	Third-party Component Integration	3	20	60
	Security	1	40	40
			Total:	**791**

Table 8.3 *(Continued)*

MILESTONE	TYPE OF TEST	# OF CYCLES	HRS. PER CYCLE	EST. HOURS
Final	RAT: Release Acceptance Test	2	0.5	1
	FAST: Functional Acceptance Simple Test	2	2	4
	TOFT: Task Oriented Functional Test	1	80	80
	Regression Testing	1	20	20
	Exploratory Testing	1	16	16
			Total:	**121**
Testing Project Management	Test Planning & Test Case Design		40	40
	Training		20	20
			Total:	**60**
	PROJECT TOTAL HOURS			1474
	PROJECT TOTAL DAYS			184
	Person Weeks (30hr/wk)			49
	20% Contingency Weeks			10
	Total person weeks			59
	Testers for Alpha			1.25
	Testers for Beta			4.4
	Testers for Final			2
	Project Management			1

Bibliography

Kaner, Cem, et al. *Testing Computer Software,* second edition. New York: John Wiley & Sons, 1999.

LogiGear Corporation. *QA Training Handbook: Lead Software Test Project with Confidence.* Foster City, CA: LogiGear Corporation, 2000.

LogiGear Corporation. *QA Training Handbook: Testing Computer Software.* Foster City, CA: LogiGear Corporation, 2000.

PART THREE

Testing Practices

9

User Interface Tests

Why Read This Chapter?

To effectively test the user interface (UI) design and implementation of a Web application, we need to understand both the UI designer's perspective (the goals of the design) and the developer's perspective (the technology implementation of the UI). With such information, we can develop effective test cases that target the areas within an application's design and implementation that are most likely to contain errors.

Introduction

This chapter explores the two primary classes of UI testing issues: (1) the *design* of UI components and (2) the *implementation* of UI components. Web technologies that are used to deliver UI components or controls (graphic objects that enable users to inter-

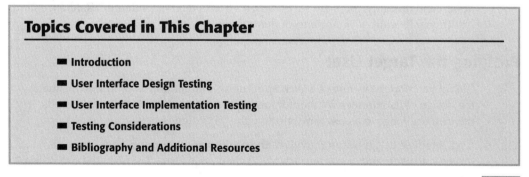

Topics Covered in This Chapter

- ■ Introduction
- ■ User Interface Design Testing
- ■ User Interface Implementation Testing
- ■ Testing Considerations
- ■ Bibliography and Additional Resources

act with applications) are also discussed, as are considerations for the effective testing of both UI design and implementation.

User interface testing normally refers to a type of integration testing in which we test the interaction between units. User interface testing is often done in conjunction with other tests instead of independently. As testers, we sometimes explicitly conduct UI and usability testing, but more often, we consider UI issues while running other types of testing, such as functionality testing, exploratory testing, and task-oriented functional testing (TOFT).

User Interface Design Testing

User interface design testing evaluates how well a design takes care of its users, offers clear direction, delivers feedback, and maintains consistency of language and approach. Subjective impressions of *ease of use* and *look and feel* are carefully considered in UI design testing. Issues pertaining to navigation, natural flow, usability, commands, and accessibility are also assessed in UI design testing.

During UI design testing, you should pay particular attention to the suitability of all aspects of the design. Look for areas of the design that lead users into errors or that do not clearly indicate what is expected of users.

Consistency of aesthetics, feedback, and interactivity directly affect an application's usability—and should therefore be carefully examined. Users must be able to rely on the cues they receive from an application to make effective navigation decisions and understand how best to work with an application. When cues are unclear, communication between users and applications can break down.

It is essential to understand the purpose of the software under test (SUT) before beginning UI testing. The two main issues to consider are:

1. Who is the application's target user?
2. What design approach has been employed?

With answers to these questions, you will be able to identify program functionality and design that do not behave as a reasonable target user would expect they should. Keep in mind that UIs serve users, not designers or programmers. As testers, we represent users and must be conscious of their needs. To learn more about Web UI design and usability, there are several useful books recommended in "References and Additional Resources" at the end of this chapter.

Profiling the Target User

Gaining an understanding of a Web application's target user is central to evaluating the design of its interface. Without knowing the user's characteristics and needs, it can be a challenge to assess how effective the UI design is.

User interface design testing involves the profiling of two target-user types: (1) server-side users and, more important, (2) client-side users. Users on the client side generally interact with Web applications through a Web browser. More than likely they do not have as much technical and architectural knowledge as users on the server side of the same system. Additionally, the application features that are available to client-side users often differ from the features that are available to server-side users (who are often system administrators). Therefore, client-side UI testing and server-side UI testing should be evaluated by different standards.

When creating a user profile, consider the following four categories of criteria (for both client-side and server-side users).

Computer Experience

How long has the intended user been using a computer? Do they use a computer professionally or only casually at home? What activities are they typically involved with? What assumptions does the SUT make about user skill level, and how well do the expected user's knowledge and skills match those assumptions?

For client-side users, technical experience may be quite limited, but the typical user may have extensive experience with a specific type of application, such as a spreadsheet, word processor, desktop presentation program, drawing program, or instructional development software. In contrast, system administrators and information services (IS) personnel who install and set up applications on the server side probably possess significant technical experience, including in-depth knowledge of system configuration and script-level programming. They may also have extensive troubleshooting experience, but limited experience with typical end-user application software.

Web Experience

How long has the user been using the Web system? Web systems occasionally require client-side users to configure browser settings. Therefore, some experience with Web browsers will be helpful. Is the user familiar with Internet jargon and concepts, such as *Java, ActiveX, HyperText Markup Language* (HTML), *proxy servers*, and so on? Will the user require knowledge of related helper applications such as Acrobat reader, File Transfer Protocol (FTP), and streaming audio/video clients? How much Web knowledge is expected of server-side users? Do they need to modify Practical Extraction and Reporting Language (perl) or Common Gateway Interface (CGI) scripts?

Domain Knowledge

Is the user familiar with the subject matter with which the application is associated? For example, if the program involves building formulas into spreadsheets, it is certainly targeted at client-side users with math skills and some level of computing expertise. It would be inappropriate to test such a program without the input of a tester who has experience working with spreadsheet formulas. Another example includes the testing of a music notation–editing application. Determining if the program is designed for experienced music composers who understand the particulars of musical notation, or for novice musicians who may have little to no experience with music notation, is critical to evaluating the effectiveness of the design. Novice users want elementary tutorials, and expert users want efficient utilities. Is the user of an e-commerce system a retailer who has considerable experience with credit card–processing practices? Is the primary intended user of an online real estate system a realtor who understands real estate listing services, or is it a first-time home buyer?

Application-Specific Experience

Will users be familiar with the purpose and abilities of the program because of past experience? Is this the first release of the product, or is there an existing base of users in the marketplace who are familiar with the product? Are there other popular products in the marketplace that have a similar design approach and functionality? (See "Design Approach" later in this chapter for information.)

Keep in mind that Web applications are still a relatively new class of application. It is possible that you are testing a Web application that is the first of its kind to reach the marketplace. Consequently, target users may have substantial domain knowledge but no application-specific experience.

With answers to these questions, you should be able to identify the target user for whom an application is designed. There may be several different target users. With a clear understanding of the application's target users, you can effectively evaluate an application's interface design and uncover potential UI errors.

Table 9.1 offers a means of grading the four attributes of target-user experience. User interface design should be judged, in part, by how closely the experience and skills of the target user match the characteristics of the SUT.

Once we have a target-user profile for the application under test, we will be able to determine if the design approach is appropriate and intuitive for its intended users. We will also be able to identify characteristics of the application that make it overly difficult or simple. Overly simplistic design can result in as much loss of productivity

Table 9.1 Evaluating Target-User Experience

Experience Grades None = 0 Low = 1 Medium = 2 High = 3	
ATTRIBUTE	**MINIMUM EXPERIENCE**
Computer experience	
Web experience	
Domain knowledge	
Application experience	

Testing the Sample Project

Consider the target user of the sample application. The sample application is designed to support the efforts of software development teams. When we designed the sample application, we assumed that the application's target user would have, at a minimum, intermediate computing skills, at least beginning-level Web experience, and intermediate experience in the application's subject matter (bug tracking). We also assumed that the target user would have at least beginning experience with applications of this type. Beyond these minimum experience levels, we knew that it was also possible that the target user might possess high experience levels in any or all of the categories. Table 9.2 shows how the sample application's target user can be rated.

Table 9.2 Evaluating Sample Application Target User

Experience Grades
None = 0
Low = 1
Medium = 2
High = 3

ATTRIBUTE	MINIMUM EXPERIENCE
Computer experience	2–3
Web experience	2–3
Domain knowledge	1–3
Application experience	0

as an overly complex design can. Consider the bug-report screen in the sample application. It includes numerous data-entry fields. Conceivably, the design could have broken up the functionality of the bug-report screen over multiple screens. Although such a design might serve novice users, it would unduly waste the time of more experienced users—the application's target.

Considering the Design

The second step in preparing for UI design testing is to study the design employed by the application. Different application types and target users require different designs.

For example, in a program that includes three branching options, a novice computer user might be better served by delivering the three options over the course of five interface screens, via a *wizard*. An information services (IS) professional, on the other hand, might prefer receiving all options on a single screen, so that he or she could access them more quickly.

TOPICS TO CONSIDER WHEN EVALUATING DESIGN

- Design approach (discussed in the following section)
- User interaction (data input)
- Data presentation (data output)

Design Approach

Design metaphors are cognitive bridges that can help users understand the logic of UI flow by relating them to experiences that users may have had in the real world, or in other places. An example of an effective design metaphor includes Web directory sites that utilize a design reminiscent of a library card catalog. Another metaphor example includes scheduling applications that visually mirror the layout of a desktop calendar and address book. Microsoft Word uses a document-based metaphor for its word-processing program—a metaphor that is common to many types of applications.

EXAMPLES OF TWO DIFFERENT DESIGN METAPHORS

- Figure 9.1 depicts an application that utilizes a document-based metaphor. This metaphor includes a workspace where data can be entered and manipulated in a way that is similar to writing on a piece of paper.
- Figure 9.2 exemplifies a device-based metaphor. This virtual calculator includes UI controls that are designed to receive user input and perform functions.

TWO DIFFERENT APPROACHES TO CONVEY IDENTICAL INFORMATION AND COMMANDS

- Figure 9.3 conveys navigation options to users via radio buttons at the top of the interface screen.

Figure 9.1 Document-based metaphor.

Figure 9.2 Device-based metaphor.

■ Figure 9.4 conveys the same options via an ActiveX pull-down menu.

Neither design approach is more correct than the other. They are simply different.

Regardless of the design approach employed, it is usually not our role as testers to judge which design is best. However, that does not mean that we should overlook design errors, especially if we work for an organization that really cares about subjective issues such as usability. Our job is to point out as many design deficiencies early in the testing as possible. Certainly, it is our job to point out *inconsistency* in the implementation of the design. That is, if the approach is using a pull-down menu as opposed to using radio buttons, a pull-down menu should then be used consistently in all views.

Think about these common issues:

■ Keep in mind that the UI tags, controls, and objects supported by HTML are primitive compared with those available through the Graphical User Interface (GUI) available on Microsoft Windows or Macintosh operating systems. If the designer intends to use the Windows UI metaphor, look for design deficiencies.

■ If you have trouble figuring out the UI, chances are it's a UI error because your end users would go through the same experience.

■ The UI was inadvertently designed for the designers or developers rather than for the end users.

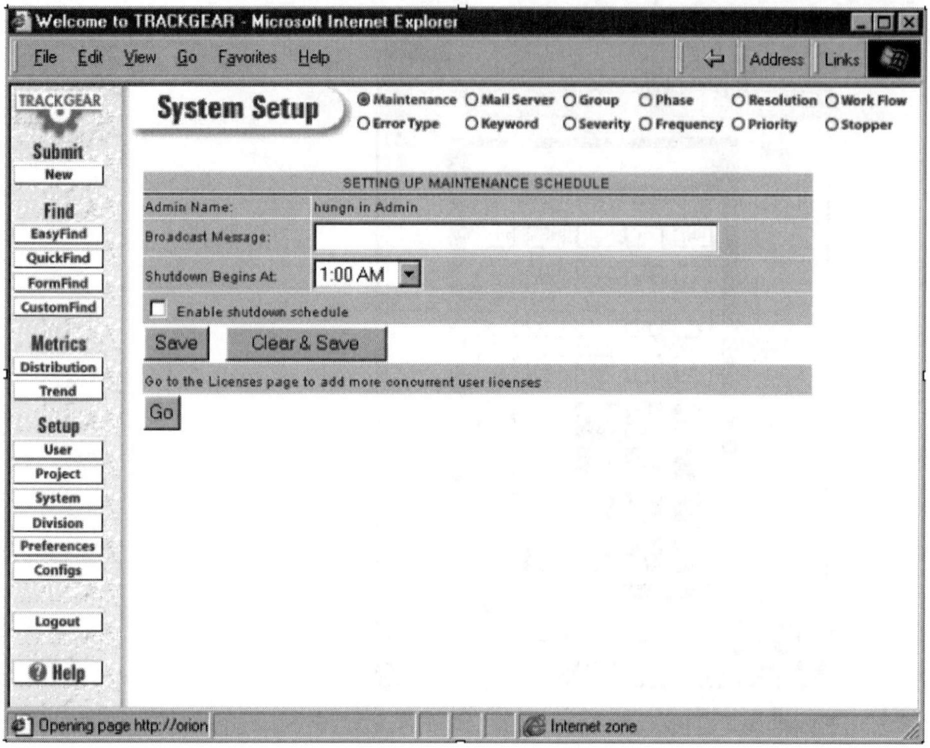

Figure 9.3 Navigation options via radio buttons.

- The important features are misunderstood or hard to find.
- Users are forced to think in terms of the design metaphor from the designer's perspective, although the metaphor itself is difficult to relate to in real-life experience.
- Different terms were used to describe the same functionality.

Ask yourself these questions:

- Is the design of the application under test appropriate for the target audience?
- Is the UI intuitive (you don't have to think too much to figure out how to use the product) for the target audience?
- Is the design consistently applied throughout the application?
- Does the interface keep the user in control, rather than reacting to unexpected UI events?
- Does the interface offer pleasing visual design (look and feel) and cues for operating the application?
- Is the interface simple to use and understand?
- Is help available from every screen?

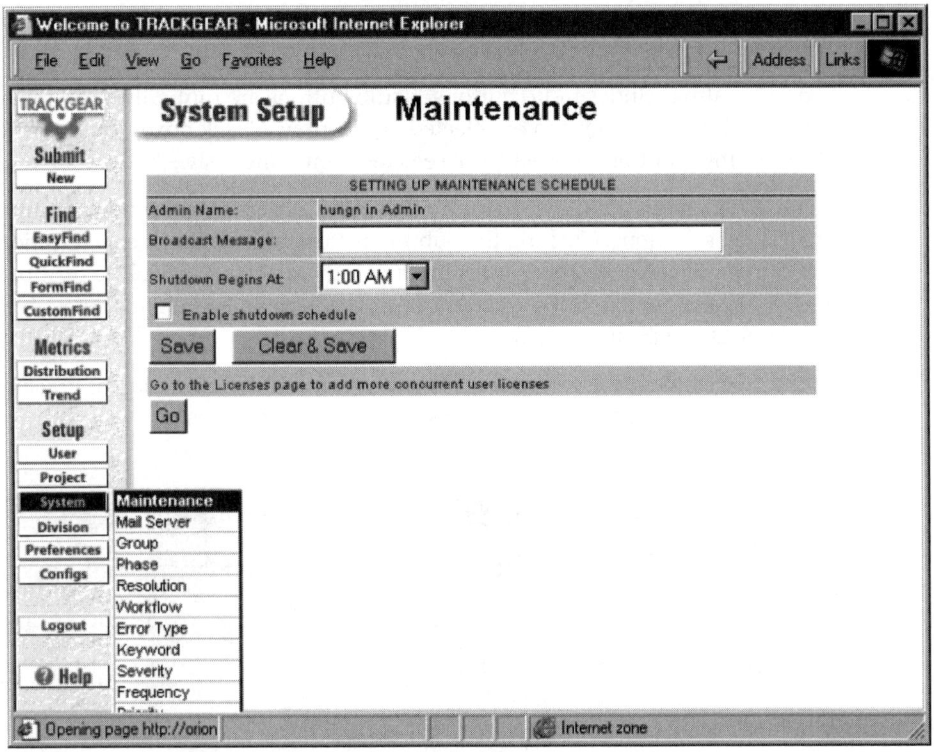

Figure 9.4 Navigation options via pull-down menu.

■ Will usability tests be performed on the application under test? If yes, will you be responsible for coordinating or conducting the test? This is a time-consuming process, and it has to be very well planned.

User Interaction (Data Input)

Users can perform various types of data manipulation through keyboard and mouse events. Data manipulation methods are made available through on-screen UI controls and other technologies, such as cut-and-paste and drag-and-drop.

User Interface Controls

User interface controls are graphic objects that enable users to interact with applications. They allow users to initiate activities, request data display, and specify data values. Controls, commonly coded into HTML pages as form elements, include radio buttons, check boxes, command buttons, scroll bars, pull-down menus, text fields, and more.

Figure 9.5 includes a standard HTML text box that allows limited text input from users, and a scrolling text box that allows users to enter multiple lines of text. Clicking the Submit button beneath these boxes submits the entered data to a Web server. The Reset buttons return the text boxes to their default state.

Figure 9.5 also includes radio buttons. Radio buttons are mutually exclusive—only one radio button in a set can be selected at one time. Check boxes, on the other hand, allow multiple options in a set to be selected simultaneously.

Figure 9.6 includes a pull-down menu that allows users to select one of multiple predefined selections. Clicking the Submit button submits the user's selection to the Web server. The Reset button resets the menu to its default state. The pushbuttons (Go Home and Search) initiate actions (e.g., CGI scripts, search queries, submit data to a database, hyperlinks, etc.).

Figure 9.6 also includes examples of images (commonly referred to as *graphics* or *icons*) that can serve as hyperlinks or simulated pushbuttons.

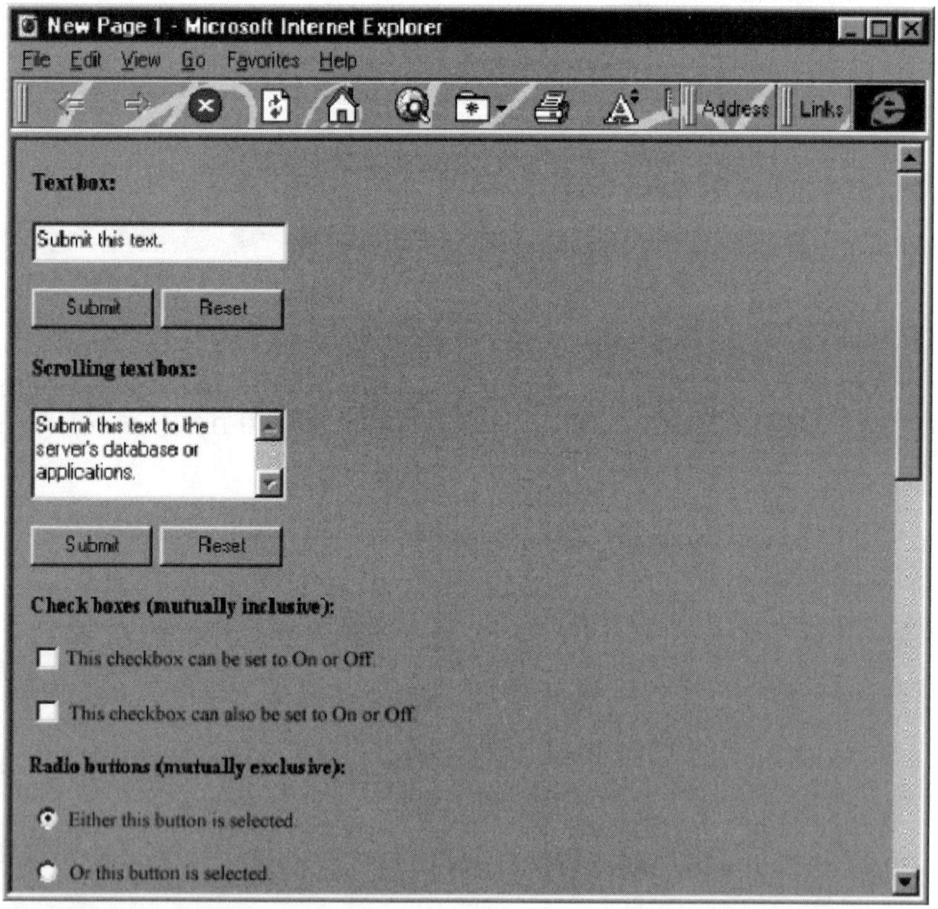

Figure 9.5 Form-based HTML UI controls, including a standard HTML text box and a scrolling text box.

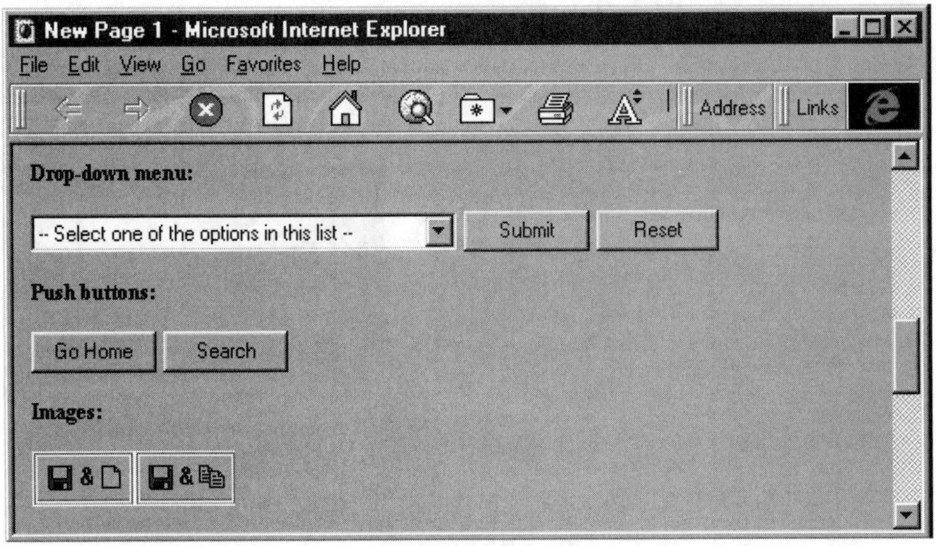

Figure 9.6 Form-based HTML UI controls: including a pull-down menu.

Figures 9.7 and 9.8 illustrate the implementation of several standard HTML UI controls on a Web page. Figure 9.7 shows the objects (graphic link, mouse-over link titles or ALT, and a text link) as they are presented to users. Figure 9.8 shows the HTML code that generates these objects.

Standard HTML controls, such as tables and hyperlinks, can be combined with images to simulate conventional GUI elements such as those found in Windows and Macintosh applications (navigation bars, command buttons, dialog boxes, etc.). The left side of Figure 9.9 (taken from the sample application) shows an HTML frame that has been combined with images and links to simulate a conventional navigation bar.

Dynamic User Interface Controls

The HTML multimedia tags enable the use of dynamic UI objects, such as Java applets, ActiveX controls, and scripts (including JavaScript and VBScript).

Scripts

Scripts are programming instructions that are executed by browsers when HTML pages load or when they are called based on certain events. Some scripts are a form of object-oriented programming, meaning that program instructions identify and send instructions to individual elements of Web pages (buttons, graphics, HTML forms, etc.), rather than to pages as a whole. Scripts do not need to be compiled and can be inserted directly into HTML pages. Scripts are embedded into HTML code with <SCRIPT> tags.

Scripts can be executed on either the client side or the server side. Client-side scripts are often used to dynamically set values for UI controls, modify Web page content, validate data, and handle errors.

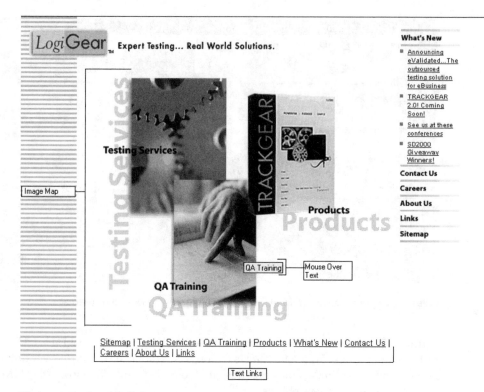

Figure 9.7 Graphic links, mouse-over text, and text links.

Figure 9.8 HTML code for graphic links, mouse-over text, and text links.

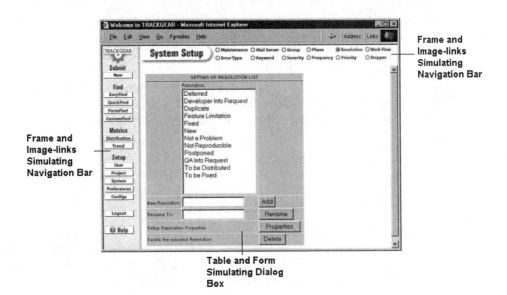

Frame and
Image-links
Simulating
Navigation Bar

Frame and
Image-links
Simulating
Navigation Bar

Table and Form
Simulating Dialog
Box

Figure 9.9 Tables, forms, and frames simulating Windows-based UI controls.

There are a number of scripting languages supported by popular browser. Some browsers support particular scripting languages and exclude others. JavaScript, produced by Netscape, is one of the more popular scripting languages. Other popular scripting languages include Microsoft's version of JavaScript (Jscript) and Visual Basic Script (VBScript).

Java

Java is a computing language developed by Sun Microsystems that allows applications to run over the Internet (though Java objects are not limited to running over the Internet).

Java is a compiled language, which means that it must be run through a compiler to be translated into a language that computer processors can use. Unlike other compiled languages, Java produces a single compiled version of itself, called *Java bytecode*. Bytecode is a series of tokens and data that are normally interpreted at runtime. By compiling to this intermediate language rather than to binaries that are specific to a given type of computer, a single Java program can be run on several different computer platforms for which there is a Java Virtual Machine (Java VM). Once a Java program has been compiled into bytecode, it is placed on a Web server. Web servers deliver bytecode to Web browsers, which interpret and run the code.

Java programs designed to run inside browsers are called *applets*. When a user navigates to a Web site that contains a Java applet, the applet automatically downloads to the user's computer. Browsers require Java bytecode interpreters to run applets. Java-enabled browsers, such as Netscape Navigator and Internet Explorer, have Java bytecode interpreters built into them.

Precautions are taken to ensure that Java programs do not download viruses onto the user's computers. Java applets must go through a verification process when they are first downloaded to users' machines—to ensure that their bytecode can be run safely. After verification, bytecode is run within a restricted area of RAM on users' computers.

ActiveX

ActiveX is a Windows custom control that runs within ActiveX-enabled browsers (such as Internet Explorer), rather than off servers. Similar to Java applets, ActiveX controls support the execution of event-based objects within a browser.

One major benefit of ActiveX controls is that they are components. Components can be easily combined with other components to create new, features-rich applications. Another benefit is that once a user downloads an ActiveX control, he or she will not have to download it again in the future; ActiveX controls remain on users' systems, which can speed up load time for frequently visited Web pages.

Some disadvantages of ActiveX are that it is dependent on the Windows platform, and some components are so big that they use too much system memory. ActiveX controls, because they reside on client computers and generally require an installation and registration process, are considered by some to be intrusive.

Figure 9.10 shows a calendar system ActiveX control. Figure 9.11 shows the HTML code that generated the page in Figure 9.10. An HTML <OBJECT> tag gives the browser the ActiveX control class ID so that it can search the registry to determine the location of the control and load it into memory.

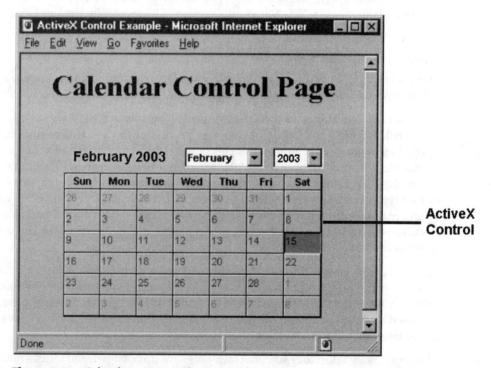

ActiveX Control

Figure 9.10 Calendar system ActiveX control.

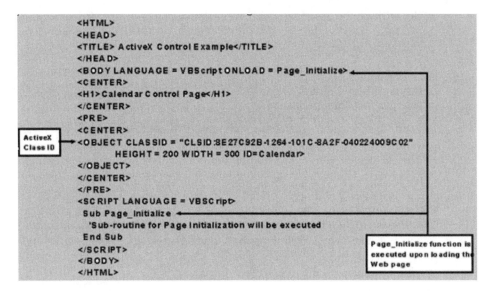

```
<HTML>
<HEAD>
<TITLE> ActiveX Control Example</TITLE>
</HEAD>
<BODY LANGUAGE = VBScript ONLOAD = Page_Initialize>
<CENTER>
<H1>Calendar Control Page</H1>
</CENTER>
<PRE>
<CENTER>
<OBJECT CLASSID = "CLSID:8E27C92B-1264-101C-8A2F-040224009C02"
        HEIGHT = 200 WIDTH = 300 ID=Calendar>
</OBJECT>
</CENTER>
</PRE>
<SCRIPT LANGUAGE = VBScript>
   Sub Page_Initialize
      'Sub-routine for Page Initialization will be executed
   End Sub
</SCRIPT>
</BODY>
</HTML>
```

(ActiveX Class ID)

(Page_Initialize function is executed upon loading the Web page)

Figure 9.11 HTML code that generated the ActiveX control shown in Figure 9.10.

Sometimes, multiple ActiveX controls are required on the same HTML page. In such instances, controls may be stored on the same Web server, or on different Web servers.

Server-Side Includes

Server-side includes (SSIs) are directives to Web servers that are embedded in HTML comment tags. Web servers can be configured to examine HTML documents for such comments and to perform appropriate processes when they are detected. The SSIs are typically used to pull additional content from other sources into Web pages—for example, the addition of current date and time information. Following is an example of an SSI (enclosed between HTML comment tags) requesting that the Web server call a CGI script named *mytest.cgi*.

```
<!--#exec cgi="/cgi-bin/mydir/mytest.cgi"-->
```

Style Sheet

Style sheets are documents that define style standards for a given set of Web pages. They are valuable in maintaining style consistency across multiple Web pages. Style sheets allow Web designers to define design issues such as fonts and colors from a central location, thus freeing designers from concerns over inconsistent graphic presentation that might result from browser display differences or developer oversight.

Style sheets set style properties for a variety of HTML elements: text style, font size and face, link colors, and more. They also define attribute units such as length, percentage, and color.

The problem with traditional style sheets is that they do not take the dynamic nature of Web design into account. Web pages themselves offer multiple means of defining styles without the use of style sheets—for example, style properties can be defined in an HTML page's header, or inline in the body of an HTML document. Such dynamic style definition can lead to conflicting directives.

Cascading style sheets (CSS) is the most common and most mature style sheet language. Cascading style sheets offer a system for determining priority when multiple stylistic influences are directed onto a single Web page element.

Cascading style sheets dictate the style rules that are to be applied when conflicting directives are present. Cascading style sheets allow Web designers to manage multiple levels of style rules over an unlimited number of Web pages. For example, a certain line of text on a Web page might be defined as blue in the page's header, as red in the page's body text (inline), and as black in an external style sheet. In this scenario, CSS could establish a hierarchy of priority for the three conflicting style directives. The CSS could be set up to dictate that inline style commands take priority over all other style commands. Following that in priority might be "page-wide" style commands (located in page headers). Finally, external style sheet commands might hold the least influence of the three style command types.

There are different means of referencing style sheets. The browser takes all style information (possibly conflicting) and attempts to interpret it. Figure 9.12 shows a mixture of styles applied to a page. Some of the approaches may be incompatible with some browsers. For more information about CSS, see WebReview's *Overview of the CSS Specification* at http://webreview.com/pub/guides/style/glossary.html. The W3C's *CSS Validator* is available for download at http://jigsaw.w3.org/css-validator/.

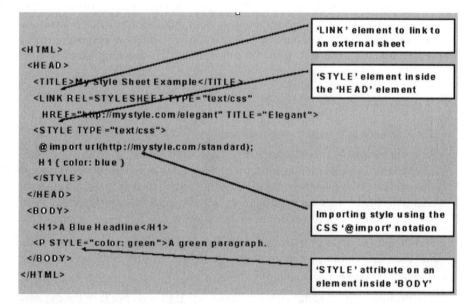

Figure 9.12 Mixed styles.

Some errors that you should look for include:

- The default state of UI controls is incorrect.

- Poor choice of default state.

- The updated state of UI control is incorrect.

- The default input value is incorrect.

- Poor choice of default value.

- The updated input value is incorrect.

- The initial input focus is not assigned to the most commonly used control.

- The most commonly used action button is not the default one.

- The form or dialog box is too big under minimum support display resolution (e.g., 800 × 600).

- The HTML code is often generated dynamically. It's essential to understand how the HTML code is generated. Don't assume that you have already tested "that" page, so you won't have to do it again until something changes.

- Set View Text Size to Largest and the Smallest to see how each setting may affect the UI.

- Check for the existence of ALT attributes.

- Check for correct descriptions in ALT attributes.

- Avoid reporting multiple broken links or missing images used by the same error (e.g., the same image used in 20 HTML pages is missing).

- Invalid inputs are not detected and handled at client side.

- Invalid inputs are not detected and handled at server side.

- Scripts are normally used to manipulate standard (e.g., set input focus, set default state, etc.) UI (form) controls. This is a tedious program chore and the process normally produces errors. Look for them.

- Scripts, CSS, Java applets, and ActiveX controls commonly cause incompatibility errors among different releases of browser produced by different vendors. Make sure to run compatibility tests for all supported browsers. See Chapter 14, "Configuration and Compatibility Tests," for more information.

- If your application uses scripts, Java applets, and ActiveX controls, and the users might have disabled one or more of these features, can your application function at some capacity (or it will simply stop functioning)?

- To test for script (such as JavaScript) incompatibility problems between different browser brands and versions, we first need to identify which pages use script, and for what purposes. Once these pages are cataloged, run these pages through one of the HTML authoring tools that has built-in support for checking script incompatibility based on static analysis method. The one that I am familiar that provides this support with is Macromedia's Dreamweaver.

- Will the Web pages display correctly on handheld devices which often do not support graphics, and have relatively small screen "real estate"?

Navigation Methods

Navigation methods dictate how users navigate through a program—from one UI control to another within the same page (screen, window, or dialog box), and from one page to the next. User navigation is achieved through input devices, such as keyboard and mouse. Navigation methods are often evaluated by how easily they allow users to get to commonly used features and data.

Ask yourself these questions:

- Is the application's navigation intuitive?
- Is accessibility to commonly used features and data consistent throughout the program?

Testing the Sample Application

User navigation within the sample application is achieved via standard UI controls (keyboard and mouse events). Data updates are *submission based,* meaning that they are achieved by clicking action buttons, such as Submit. Figure 9.13 diagrams how users navigate through the sample application's trend metrics and distribution metrics features.

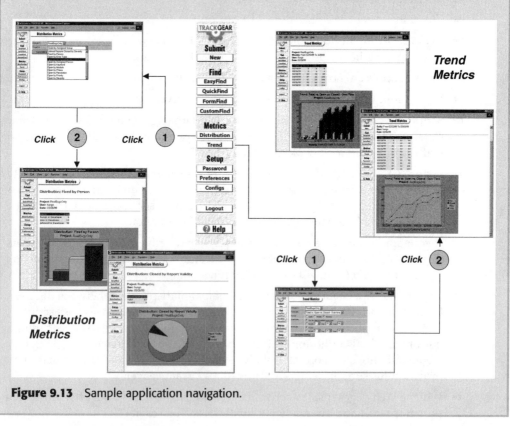

Figure 9.13 Sample application navigation.

- Can users always tell where they are in the program and what navigation options are available to them?

- How well is information presented to the user?

- If the program utilizes a central workspace, does the workspace remain consistent from screen to screen?

- Do navigation conventions remain consistent throughout the application (navigation bars, menus, hyperlinks, etc.)?

- Examine the application for consistent use of mouse-over pop-ups, clicks, and object dragging. Do the results of these actions offer differing results from one screen to the next?

- Do the keyboard alternatives for navigation remain consistent throughout the application?

- Are all features accessible via both mouse and keyboard action?

- Click the Tab button repeatedly and examine the highlight path that is created. Is it logical and consistent?

- Click the Shift-Tab button repeatedly and examine the highlight path that is created. Is it logical and consistent?

- Look at the keyboard shortcuts that are supported. Are they functioning? Is there duplication among them?

- If the user clicks a credit card payment button on an e-commerce site numerous times while he or she is waiting for server response, will the transaction erroneously be submitted numerous times?

Mouse/Keyboard Action Matrices

Appendices D and E contain test matrices that detail mouse and keyboard actions. These matrices can be customized to track navigation test coverage for the Web system under test.

Action Commands

Occasionally, the names of on-screen commands are not used consistently throughout an application. This is partially attributable to the fact that the meaning of command names often varies from one program to the next. If the nomenclature of certain commands varies within a single program, user confusion is likely to result. For example, if a Submit command is used to save data in one area of a program, then the Submit command name should be used for all saving activities throughout the application.

Consideration should be given to the action commands that are selected as the default commands. Default action commands should be the least risky of the available options (the commands least likely to delete user-created data).

Table 9.3 lists a number of common confirming-action and canceling-action commands, along with their meanings and the decisions that they imply.

Table 9.3   Confirming and Canceling Commands

	DECISION	IMPLIED DECISION
Common confirming-action commands		
Done	Dismiss the current dialog box, window, or page.	
Close	Dismiss the current dialog box, window, or page.	
OK	I accept the settings.	Dismiss the current dialog box, window, or page.
Yes	I accept the stated condition.	Proceed and dismiss the current dialog box, window, or page.
Proceed	I accept the stated condition.	Proceed and dismiss the current dialog box, window, or page.
Submit	Submit the data in the form, page, or dialog box.	
Common canceling-action commands		
Cancel	I do not accept the settings or stated condition.	Return to the previous state and dismiss the current dialog box, window, or page.
No	I do not accept the settings or stated condition.	Proceed and dismiss the current dialog box, window, or page.
Reset	Return the settings to their previous state.	Clear all unsubmitted changes in current dialog box, window, or page.

Feedback and Error Messages

Consistency in audible and visible feedback is essential for maintaining clear communication between users and applications. Messages (both visible and audible), beeps, and other sound effects must remain consistent and user friendly to be effective. *Error messaging* in particular should be evaluated for clarity and consistency. In Chapter 10, "Functional Tests," see the section entitled "Task-Oriented Functional Test (TOFT)" for more information regarding error messages.

Examine the utilization of interface components within feedback for unusual or haphazard implementations. One can identify commonly accepted guidelines within each computing platform for standard placement of UI elements, such as placing OK and Cancel buttons in the bottom right corner of dialog boxes. Alternate designs may make user interaction unnecessarily difficult.

Two types of message-based feedback are available. Figure 9.14 illustrates a typical *client-based error message* (generated by error-checking JavaScript on the client side) that utilizes a browser-based message box. Figure 9.15 shows typical *server-based feedback.*

Client-based error messages are generally more efficient and cause less strain on servers than do server-based error messages. Server-based error messages require that data first be sent from the client to the server and then returned from the server back to the client where the error message is displayed to the user.

Client-based error messages, on the other hand, using script (such as JavaScript) embedded in an HTML page, can prevent such excessive network traffic by identifying errors and displaying error messages locally, without requiring contact with the server. Because scripting languages such as JavaScript behave differently with each browser version, testing of all supported platforms is essential.

As a general rule, simple errors such as invalid inputs should be detected and handled at the client side. The server, of course, has to detect and handle error conditions that do not become apparent until they interfere with some process being executed on the server side.

Another consideration is that, sometimes, the client might not understand the error condition being responded to by the server, and it might therefore ignore the condition, or display the wrong message, or display a message that no human can understand.

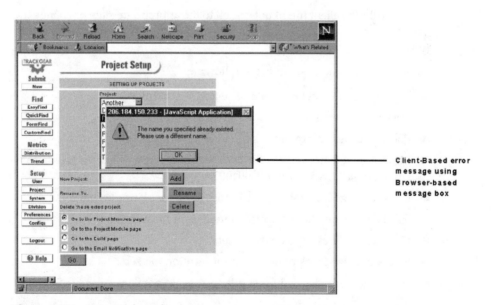

Client-Based error message using Browser-based message box

Figure 9.14 Browser-based error message.

Source: © 1999 LogiGear Corporation.

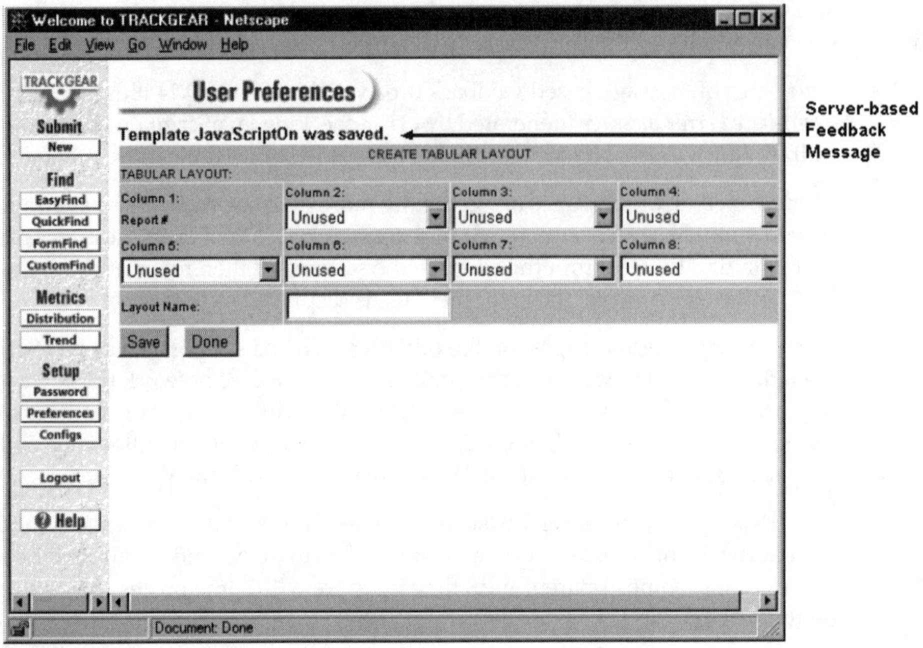

Figure 9.15 Server-based feedback.

Source: © 1999 LogiGear Corporation.

Additionally, the client might not switch to the appropriate state or change the affected data items in the right way unless it understands the error condition reported by the server.

Some errors to look for include the following:

- Displaying incorrect error message for the condition.
- Missing error messages.
- Poorly worded, grammatically incorrect, and misspelled errors.
- Messages were not written for the user and, therefore, are not useful to the user. For example, "Driver error 80004005."
- Error message is not specific nor does it offer a plausible solution.
- Similar errors are handled by different error messages.
- Unnecessary messages distract users.
- Inadequate feedback or error communication to users.
- Handling methods used for similar errors are not consistent.

Ask yourself these questions:

- Does the UI cause deadlocks in communication with the server (creating an infinite loop)?

- Does the application allow users to recover from error conditions, or must the application be shut down?

- Does the application offer users adequate warning and options when they venture into error-prone activities?

- Are error messages neutral and consistent in tone and style?

- Is there accompanying text for people who are hearing-impaired or have their computer's sound turned off?

- If video is used, do picture and sound stay in sync?

Data Presentation (Data Output)

In Web applications, information can be communicated to users via a variety of UI controls (e.g., menus, buttons, check boxes, etc.) that can be created within an HTML page (frames, tables, simulated dialog boxes, etc.).

Figures 9.16, 9.17, and 9.18 illustrate three data presentation views that are available in the sample application. Each view conveys the same data through a different template built using HTML frames and tables.

In this sample application example, there are at least three types of potential errors: (1) *data* errors (incorrect data in records caused by write procedures), (2) *database query* errors, and (3) *data presentation* errors. A data error or database query error will manifest itself in all presentations, whereas a presentation error in server-side scripts

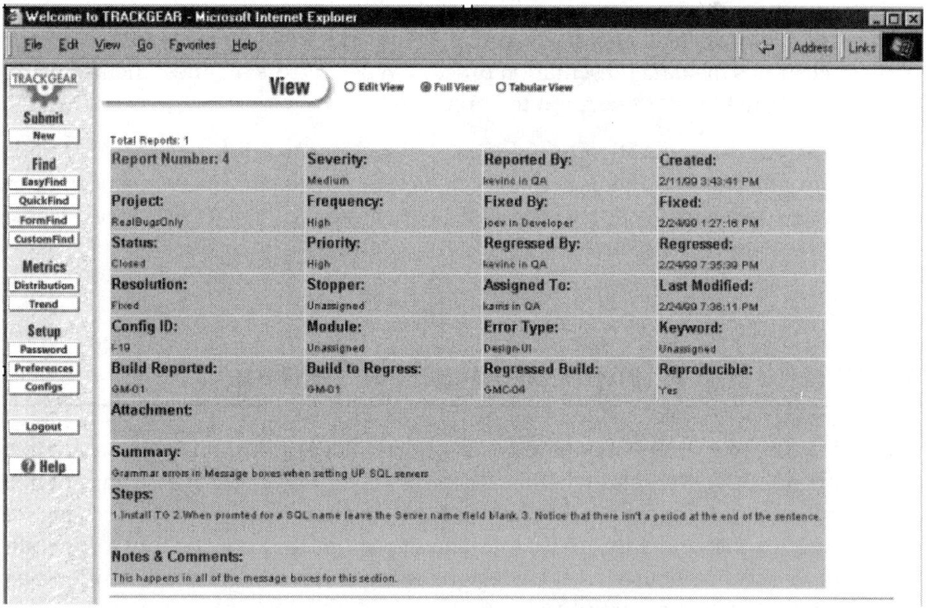

Figure 9.16 Single issue report presented in Full View.

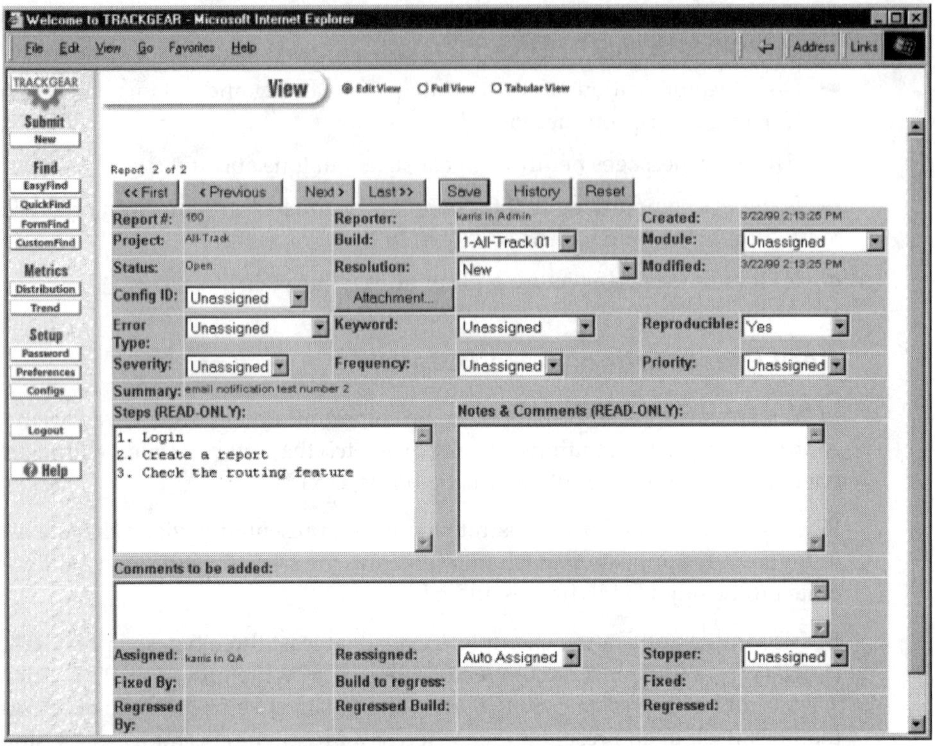

Figure 9.17 Same issue report presented in Edit View.

will manifest itself only in the presentation with which it is associated. Figure 9.19 illustrates the data presentation process. Where errors manifest themselves depends on where the errors occur in the process.

Analyze the application to collect design architectural information. One of the most effective ways to do this is to interview your developer. Once the information is collected, use it to develop test cases that are more focused at the unit level, as well at the interoperability level.

User Interface Implementation Testing

User interface implementation testing examines applications with an eye toward their operation. It evaluates whether UI features work properly. If a UI control does not operate as designed, it will likely fail to deliver accessibility to underlying features, which, independently, may be functioning properly. Functionality testing often takes place simultaneously with UI design testing, but it is helpful to consider the two types of testing separately.

Figure 9.18 Multiple issue reports presented in Tabular View.

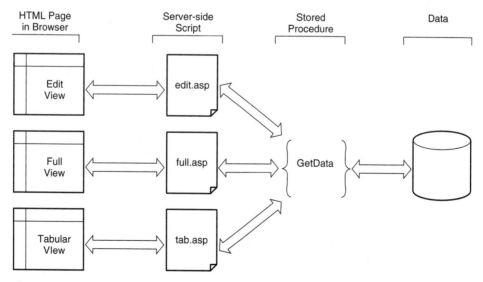

Figure 9.19 Data presentation diagram.

NOTE This section includes some overlap in information with functionality tests that are run specifically on UIs, and functionality tests that are run on all other features of an application. The TOFT section of Chapter 10, "Functional Tests," includes more complete information on the execution of functional tests. The content of this chapter is useful only in supporting functional testing efforts that are specific to UI.

The line between design consistency and design functionality is not always a clear one. An example that illustrates such a gray area is a text link of a certain color that remains consistent from one screen to the next while the background on which the text is displayed changes. As the background changes, the text becomes illegible on certain screens. Although the text is consistent in such an example, the color of the text should be adjusted to improve legibility.

Miscellaneous User Interface Elements

Table 9.4 lists miscellaneous interface elements that require testing.

Complications Specific to Web Applications

- Web browsers present their own unique set of challenges in functionality testing. Most significantly, the marketplace is crowded with a number of browser brands and versions. If the goal is to support most browsers out there, developers often must code for the lowest-common-denominator Web user—meaning those users who have the slowest modems and the least sophisticated, most outdated browsers. Even with careful HTML development, variations in graphical presentation are nearly inevitable between browsers. For example, when viewing an identical table with both Microsoft Internet Explorer and Netscape Navigator, a user may see different results.

- Browser-server communication is explicit-submission–based, meaning that data entries and updates are not written to the server until the user initiates an action. For example, input data will be lost if a user shuts down a Web application before clicking a submission button, such as Save or Submit.

- Scripting languages, such as JScript, JavaScript, and VBScript, can be used to simulate limited browser-side, submission-driven event handling. Without browser-side scripting, error handling must be done on the server side, which is not always effective. For example, someone in Ireland is interacting with a server in California. If the user submits data in an incorrect format, the user will be notified immediately only if the scripting is handled on the client side. If the error is han-

Table 9.4 Miscellaneous UI Elements

ELEMENT TYPE	ISSUES TO ADDRESS
Instructional and technical information	Accuracy of information and instructions.
Fonts	Consistency of style.
	Legibility of text.
	Difficulty of reading italic and serif fonts.
	Visual clutter resulting from multiple font faces on a single document, as well as the availability of font faces on the targeted platforms.
Colors	Suitability of background colors.
	Suitability of foreground colors.
	Suitability of font colors.
	Haphazard use of color can be negative and confusing.
	Subtle, complementary color choices are generally more pleasing than saturated, contrasting colors.
Borders	Three-dimensional effects on command buttons can be effective visual cues for users.
	Use of three-dimensional effects on noninteractive elements can be confusing.
Images	Large images may increase load time.
	Visual cues and design details should blend with background, not compete with it.
	Suitability of background.
	Legibility of labels.
	Legibility of buttons.
	Suitability of size of images.
Frames	Some older browsers cannot display frames.
	Display settings and browser types can affect how frames are displayed.
	Back buttons often have unexpected results.
Tables	Nested tables (tables within tables) slow down HTML load time.
	Presentation may vary depending on display settings and browser type (improper scaling or wrapping may result).
	Testing should include all browsers and display settings and browser window sizes.

dled on the server side, the data will have traveled to California and back to Ireland before the user learns of the client-side error.

- Web applications use a single-page paradigm. Therefore, they do not have the benefits of hierarchical organization that GUI-based applications (such as Windows applications) have. Web applications have no provision for the modal dialog box paradigm that is so common in other GUI-based environments; when modal dialog boxes are used to present error messages to users in a Windows environment, they require the user to take an action before control of the application or operating system is returned to the user.

- The browser Back button can complicate the dependent relationship between pages in Web applications. Clicking the Back button, rather than an appropriate explicit-submission button, is a common cause of loss of uncommitted data.

- Changes to monitor color depth settings (16 colors, 24 bit color, 32 bit color, etc.) often creates unexpected display results, as do changes to screen resolution (640 × 480, 800 × 600, 1280 × 1024, etc.) and font size. It is recommended that all such combinations of color depth, screen resolution, and font size be addressed in browser-based application testing.

- Different brands and versions of browsers on different platforms (Windows, Solaris, Macintosh, etc.) may display HTML elements differently. Depending on display settings, even a single browser can display elements in multiple ways. Additionally, resetting the size of a browser's window can lead to unexpected table and frame presentation. It is recommended that Web applications be tested with all common browser brands and versions.

Figures 9.20 and 9.21 illustrate UI errors that are the result of browser incompatibility. The HTML tags for these examples are specific to one browser. They are not designed to be compatible with other browsers. These errors are a result of the different manner in which the two browsers read standard HTML tables and controls. The browser in Figure 9.21 does not accurately display the scrolling text box and pull-down menu as the browser in Figure 9.20 displays. Both browsers present the same HTML page with different results.

Display Compatibility Matrix

Appendix G, "Display Compatibility Test Matrix," lists variations in display settings that should be considered during browser-based application testing.

Testing Considerations

USER INTERACTION TESTING CONSIDERATIONS

- How is information presented to the user?
- Is there a central workspace? If so, does it remain consistent from screen to screen?
- Is data presented in frames? If so, is there a choice for nonframe browsers?

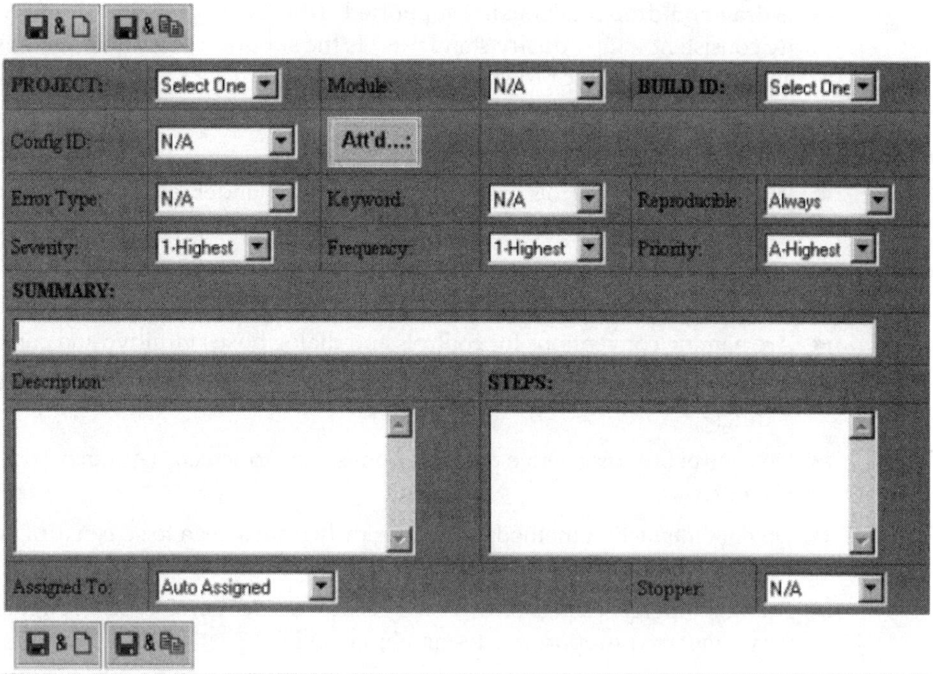

Figure 9.20   Browser incompatibility—Browser A.

- What means of data manipulation are included in the application under test?
- Are data manipulation methods presented intuitively and consistently?
- Are data manipulation methods consistent with Web application standards (possibly platform-specific)?
- Are data manipulation methods consistent with industry standards (possibly product-specific)?

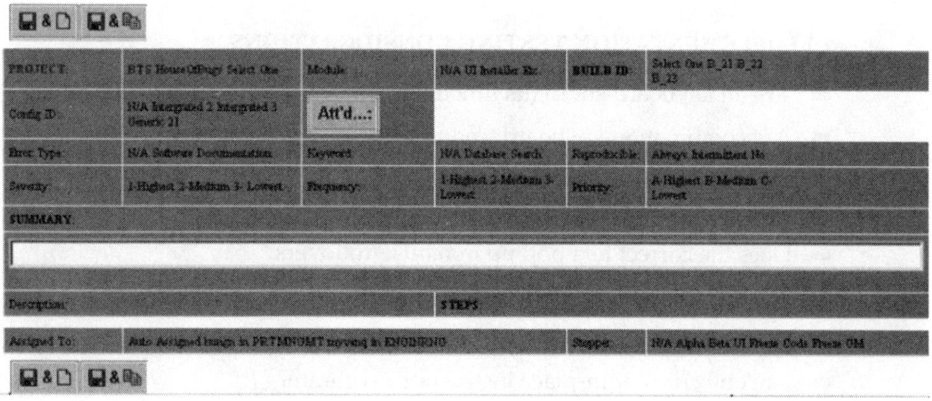

Figure 9.21   Browser incompatibility—Browser B.

- Is drag-and-drop functionality supported? If so, is the drag-and-drop functionality consistent with industry standards? Is the support compatible across vendors and platform-specific browsers?

UI CONTROL TESTING CONSIDERATIONS

- What are the UI controls used by the application under test: dialog boxes, radio buttons, drop-down menus?
- Are the layout and implementation of UI controls intuitive and consistent throughout the application?
- Are naming conventions for controls and dialog boxes intuitive and consistent?
- Are the default settings for each control the most commonly used and least risky settings?
- Do control buttons change position from screen to screen? (Are they consistently placed?)
- Do data interaction methods vary illogically from screen to screen (drag-and-drop, text entry, queries, etc.)?
- Do the property settings of UI-based HTML tags (color, size, ʋtyle, alignment, wrapping, etc.) support the design objectives?
- Are properties consistently applied to all HTML elements?
- Are the interface components unusual or confusing in any way?
- What dynamic UI elements (scripts, Java applets, ActiveX controls, SSIs, CSS, DHTML, etc.) are utilized by the application? Consider testing with all supported browsers to uncover vendor- or platform-specific errors?
- Do the dynamic UI elements fit with the overall design approach?
- Are dynamic UI elements implemented intuitively and consistently?
- Are third-party plug-ins, such as QuickTime, ShockWave, RealPlayer, and Adobe Acrobat, included? Which versions of these components does the product claim to support?

UI IMPLEMENTATION TESTING CONSIDERATIONS

- Are all keyboard shortcuts functioning for ActiveX and Java applet components?
- Are combination keyboard/mouse functions operating properly for ActiveX and Java applet components?
- Do all mouse-rollovers (ALT text) operate properly? Any missing ALT?
- Does the correct text pop up in mouse-rollovers?
- Are appropriate command buttons default-highlighted?
- Do command buttons perform the actions they purport to?
- Are on-screen or in-place instructions accurate?
- Do graphics and text load as required?
- Do links and static text support the intended design?

Bibliography and Additional Resources

Bibliography

Cluts, Nancy Winnick. *Programming the Windows 95 User Interface.* Redmond, WA: Microsoft Press, 1995.

Goodman, Danny. *Dynamic HTML: The Definitive Reference.* Sebastopol, CA: O'Reilly and Associates, Inc., 1998.

Holzner, Steven. *Web Scripting with VBScript.* New York: M&T Books, 1996.

Meyer, Jon, and Troy Downing. *Java Virtual Machine.* Sebastopol, CA: O'Reilly and Associates, 1997.

McKay, Everett N. *Developing User Interfaces for Microsoft Windows.* Redmond, WA: Microsoft Press, 1999.

Microsoft Corporation. *The Windows Interface Guidelines for Software Design.* Redmond, WA: Microsoft Press, 1995.

Powell, Thomas A. *HTML: The Complete Reference, Second Edition.* Berkeley, CA: Osborne/McGraw-Hill, 1999.

Simpson, Alan. *Official Microsoft Internet Explorer 4 Site Builder Toolkit.* Redmond, WA: Microsoft Press, 1998.

Recommended Reading

About Face: The Essentials of User Interface Design
By Alan Cooper, IDG Books Worldwide (1995).

Web Style Guide: Basic Design Principles for Creating Web Sites
By Patrick J. Lynch and Sarah Horton, Yale University Press (1999).

Microsoft Windows User Experience (Microsoft Professional Editions)
By Microsoft Corporation, Microsoft Press (1999).

Handbook of Usability Testing: How to Plan, Design, and Conduct Effective Tests
By Jeffrey Rubin, John Wiley & Sons (1994).

Useful Links

QA City—More information on Web testing and other software testing–related subjects
www.qacity.com

Microsoft MSDN UI page
http://msdn.microsoft.com/ui

Web Content Accessibility Guidelines
www.w3.org/TR/WAI-WEBCONTENT/

Yale University—Online style guide
http://info.med.yale.edu/caim/manual/

CHAPTER 10

Functional Tests

The purpose of this chapter is to point out several test types and techniques used in functionality testing, whether we have specifications or not. The premise of this testing is to find errors in the process of checking if the product is useful for its intended users and if it would do what a target user reasonably expected it to do. This chapter analyzes a variety of functional tests with an eye on their use during the testing process.

Introduction

Functional testing is a broad category of testing. It includes a variety of testing methods such as FAST, TOFT, Boundary, FET, exploratory testing, and other attacking techniques. This chapter details some of these functional test types and relates them to Web-testing examples.

Topics Covered in This Chapter

- Introduction
- An Example of Cataloging Features in Preparation for Functional Tests
- Testing Methods
- Bibliography

To better define the scope of functionality tests, look at various degrees of the functioning of an application:

- *FAST.* Does each input and navigation control work as expected?
- *TOFT1.* Can the application do something useful as expected?
- *Boundary.* What happens at the edge of specified use?
- *Forced-error.* What happens when an error condition occurs?
- *Exploratory.* What does experience tell about the potential problematic areas in the application? This involves simultaneous learning, planning, and executing tests.
- *Software attacks.* Why does software fail? How do you turn lessons learned into a series of attacks to expose software failures?

An Example of Cataloging Features in Preparation for Functional Tests

Following is an example of how the features in the Sample Application (described in Chapter 7, "Sample Application") are cataloged.

Testing the Sample Application

We will use the sample project's chart generation feature to detail some specific test cases for the varieties of functional testing. Chapter 7, "Sample Application," describes this feature as a single Java applet running on the client browser to display bug metrics.

For the purpose of example, bug metrics measure bug-report activity or resolution at any one time (distribution metrics) or over time (trend metrics) to support test project status monitoring. In the sample application, these metrics can be displayed as tables and charts.

This feature under test allows users to generate trend metrics based on a variety of criteria. The function works by choosing (1) a template to specify the type of data or comparisons to graph; (2) the period (daily, weekly, or monthly); and (3) the Start and End dates.

Figure 10.1 shows the trend metrics generation page from the Sample Project. Figure 10.2 illustrates the result table and chart from the criteria chosen in Figure 10.1. Figure 10.3 shows a matrix that lists test cases to target the functionality of the sample project's chart generation feature.

Testing Methods

Several common black-box testing methods that can be applied to functional tests will be discussed in this section.

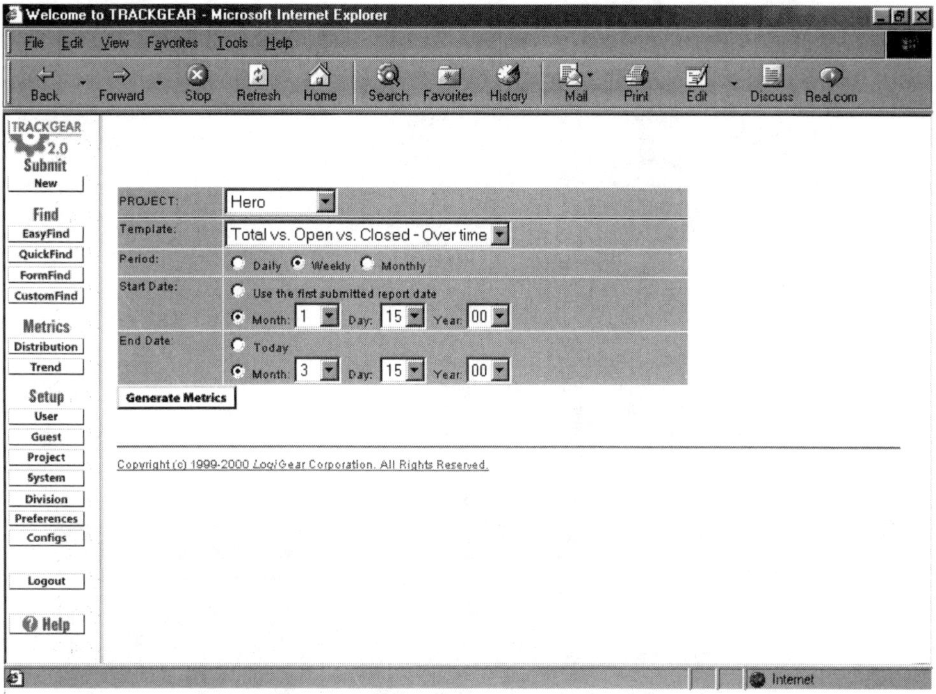

Figure 10.1 Trend metrics generation page.

Functional Acceptance Simple Tests

Functional acceptance simple tests represent the second level of acceptance testing [relative to the release acceptance test (RAT), which was discussed in Chapter 3, "Software Testing Basics"]. Rather than including only a small sampling of a program's functionality (as in RAT), functional acceptance simple test (FAST) coverage is wide in breadth, but shallow in depth. The FAST exercises the lowest level of functionality for each command of a program. The combinations of functions, however, no matter how firmly integrated, are not tested within the scope of FAST. Such issues are considered in task-oriented functional testing (TOFT), which is discussed later in this chapter.

A test team can reject a build after it has been accepted into FAST. However, this is rare. The rejection expresses a determination by the test team that further testing of this build would be a waste of time, either because so many tests are blocked or because the build itself is invalid. More often, the test team continues testing a buggy build but reassigns some testers to other work if their tests are blocked by bugs.

One of the objectives of FAST is to check for the appropriate behaviors of user interface (UI) controls (i.e., text box, pull-down list, radio button, etc.) based on the intended designs. This entails checking for the existence of UI controls on each page, window, or dialog box; checking if the default state (such as enable, disable, high-

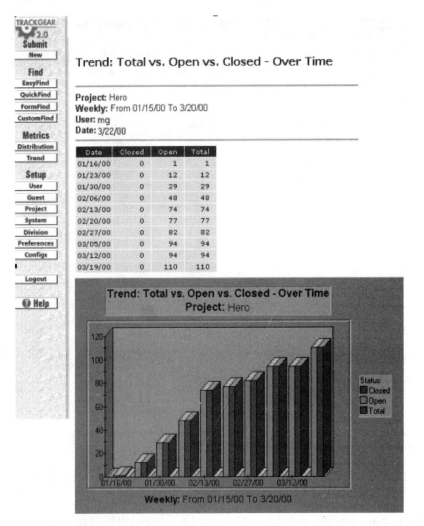

Figure 10.2 Result table and chart.

lighted, etc.) is as intended; checking if the default value or selected mode is as intended; checking if the tab order is as intended; and if the behavior of shortcuts (e.g., Ctrl-X, Ctrl-V, etc.) and other access keys (e.g., Alt-O for Open) is as intended. Additionally, in this process, you learn about the developer's thoughts and implementation logic in crafting the functionality delivered to the end user. You use this information later to design test cases that poke into the flaws of the design logic.

In a Web environment, things to check for in FAST include:

- Links such as content links, thumbnail links, bitmap links, and image map links.
- Basic controls, such as backward and forward navigating, zoom-in and zoom-out, other UI controls, and content-refreshing checks.

No.	Template	Period	Start Date	End Date	P/F/B	Comments
		P: Passed	F: Failed	B: Blocked		
		Note:				
		Watch for date boundary conditions such as First/Last Day of Month, Day-of-Week and Minute-of-Day.				
		Watch for sorting order of attributes such as Priority, Severity, Frequency, etc.				
		Watch for multiple dimension table				
		Watch for one or more of the attributes have no records				
1	1	Daily	Submitted Date	Today		
2			Submitted Date	Same Date		
3			Spec. Date	Today		
4			Spec. Date	Spec. Date		
5			Spec: Same Date	Spec: Same Date		
6			*No Record-Date*	*No Record-Date*		
7		Weekly	Submitted Date	Today		
8			Submitted Date	Spec. Date		
9			Spec. Date	Today		
10			Spec. Date	Spec. Date		
11			Spec: Same Date	Spec: Same Date		
12			*No Record-Date*	*No Record-Date*		
13		Monthly	Submitted Date	Today		
14			Submitted Date	Spec. Date		
15			Spec. Date	Today		
16			Spec. Date	Spec. Date		
17			Spec: Same Date	Spec: Same Date		
18			*No Record-Date*	*No Record-Date*		
. . .	. . .	. . .	. . .	. . .	. . .	. . .

Continues

Figure 10.3 Functionality test cases for the trend-charting feature.

87		Monthly	Submitted Date	Today		
88			Submitted Date	Spec. Date		
89			Spec. Date	Today		
90			Spec. Date	Spec. Date		
91			Spec: Same Date	Spec: Same Date		
92			*No Record-Date*	*No Record-Date*		

Figure 10.3   *(Continued)*

- Action command checks such as add, remove, update, and other types of data submission; create user profiles or user accounts including e-mail accounts, personal accounts, and group-based accounts; and data-entry tests.

Other key features such as log in/log out, e-mail notification, search, credit card validation and processing, or handling of forgotten passwords.

Some of the simple errors you may find in this process include the following:

- Broken links
- Missing images
- Wrong links
- Wrong images
- Correct links with no or outdated contents
- Errors in ordering/purchasing computation
- Ignoring credit card classifications
- Accepting expired credit
- Accepting invalid credit card numbers
- Incorrect content or context of automated e-mail reply
- No intelligence in address verification
- Server not responding (no server-updating message to user) to Domain Name Service (DNS) errors
- Inability to validate invalid user's e-mail addresses

Task-Oriented Functional Tests

Task-oriented functional tests (TOFTs) check whether the application can do useful tasks correctly. They are positive tests that check program functions by comparing the

Testing the Sample Application

"Functional Acceptance Simple Test Matrix—Trend Metrics" checks whether a chart is generated when the tester selects the specified criteria. The FAST does not necessarily check whether the generated chart presents accurate data. The tests are passed even if the content of a metric generated by one of these test cases is incorrect—though an issue report should be written up to track the problem. The FAST, in this scenario, simply ensures that something is drawn—regardless of accuracy. The accuracy or the output would be the focus of TOFT, which is discussed in the next section. For "Functional Acceptance Simple Test—Trend Metrics," we choose test cases to exercise a combination of functional choices.

results of performed tasks with product specifications and requirements documents, if they exist, or to reasonable user's expectations. The integrity of each individual task performed by the program is checked for accuracy. If behavior or output varies from what is specified in product requirements, an issue report is submitted.

The TOFTs are structured around lists of features to be tested. To come up with a features-to-be-tested list, the product specification should be carefully dissected. The product itself must also be examined for those features that are not well defined or that are not in the specification at all.

Every function and feature becomes an entry on the features-to-be-tested list. Consideration should also be given to competitive influences and market demands in developing the details of the list. For example, if competitive pressures dictate that a certain function should execute in less than 2 seconds, then that requirement should be added to the features-to-be-tested list. Once your features-to-be-tested list is complete, each entry on it should be used to define a test case that checks whether the feature's requirements have been met.

Testing the Sample Application

The "Task-Oriented Functional Test Matrix—Trend Metrics" would include the entire test suite detailed in Figure 10.3 to completely exercise this aspect of the sample project's trend metrics feature. Note that it would take a lot more than this simple matrix to completely exercise this part of the program. Beware of words like *complete*.

These test cases check whether output data (the trend metrics and charts) accurately reflect input parameters (in this scenario, a data set that incorporates daily bug-tracking activity). The sample data set includes the number of new reports opened versus the number of reports closed over a given period. The TOFT test cases check whether output metrics mirror the particulars of the input data set.

Forced-Error Tests

Forced-error tests (FETs) intentionally drive software into error conditions. The FET's objective is to find any error conditions that are undetected and/or mishandled. Error conditions should be handled gracefully. That is, the application recovers successfully, the system recovers successfully, or the application exits without data corruption and with an opportunity to preserve work in progress.

Suppose that you are testing text fields in an online registration form and the program's specification disallows nonalphabetical symbols in the name field. An error condition will be generated if you enter 123456 (or any other nonalphabetic phrase) and click the Submit button. Remember, for any valid condition, there is always an invalid condition.

A complete list of error conditions is often difficult to assemble. Some ways of compiling a list of error conditions include the following:

- A list of error messages from the developers
- Interviewing the developers
- Inspecting the string data in a resource file
- Information from specifications
- Using a utility to extract test strings out of the binary or scripting sources
- Analyzing every possible event with an eye to error cases
- Using your experience
- Using a standard valid/invalid input test matrix (such as the one in Appendix F)

Once you have a complete list of error conditions, each error condition should be run through a the following testing process:

1. *Force the error condition.*   Direct the software into the error condition specified in the test case.

2. *Check the error detection logic.*   Error handling starts with error detection. If an error goes undetected, there is no handling. From the developer perspective, detection is done through validation. For example, in the code, an input value is validated using some constraints. If the value does not satisfy the constraints, then do something about it (i.e., disallow the input). Test cases should be designed to poke into the flaws of the validation logic.

3. *Check the handling logic.*   Now that the detection is in place, we need to check how each detected error condition is handled from the following dimensions:

   - Does the application offer adequate forgiveness and allow the user to recover from the mistakes gracefully? For example, if one of the inputs in a 20-field form is invalid, does the application allow the user to reenter valid data to that one field, or does it force the user to start it all over again?

   - Does the application itself handle the error condition gracefully? If the program terminates abnormally (e.g., due to a critical error, the application exits without going through the normal exit routines), a variety of cleanup activities might not have been done. For instance, some files might have been left often, some variables might have incorrect data, or your database is in an inconsistent state.

- Does the system recover gracefully? Does the system crash or continue operating with erratic or limited functionality, or compromised security? For example, in a Web-based system, critical errors should be predicted, examined, and handled so that system crashes can be avoided. However, a system crash caused by an error condition might be a better outcome than having the system continue running but produce wrong results or compromise security.

  Keep in mind that if one of the physical servers must reboot itself for any reasons, when the system is restarted, it is possible that not all services (e.g., SMTP service, database services, etc.) will restart successfully. You should check to make sure that the restart routine does what you expect it to do.

4. *Check the error communication.*

- Determine whether an error message appears. If an error message appears, then this part of the test is passed (the accuracy of the message is secondary to the fact that a message has been generated).

- Analyze the accuracy of the error message. Does the message tell the user what's wrong? Can the user understand it? Do the instructions match the error condition? Will the instructions help users successfully escape the error condition? You also need to ask yourself if the application offers adequate instructions so that the user can avoid an obvious error condition in the first place.

- Note that the communication does not have to be in error messages. It can be in another medium such as an audio cue or visual cue. Use your judgment to assess which medium is the most appropriate and voice your concern accordingly.

5. *Look for further problems.* Are any other related issues uncovered in generating this error condition? For example, there might be a memory leak, a stack corruption, a partially updated data structure or table entry, or a wild pointer. A calculation might have been incorrectly completed. You might use data collected from logging tools to analyze the state of the servers, thereby detecting the implication associated with error messages.

Figure 10.4 walks you through an example of a Web system to demonstrate the error-handling process. First, the user takes certain action and puts the system or application in an error state. This can be done in a variety of ways, simply from invalid keyboard input, disconnecting from an ISP, removing a network connection cable, or attempting to follow an incorrect path through the application.

The error must then be detected. There may be code to handle an error, but it's useless if the application did not detect the error. As illustrated in Figure 10.4, the error might be detected at any component in the communication chain involved in executing the request. Does a message go back to the client at all? If not, was there proper silent error handling? Could there be improper silent error handling? What test

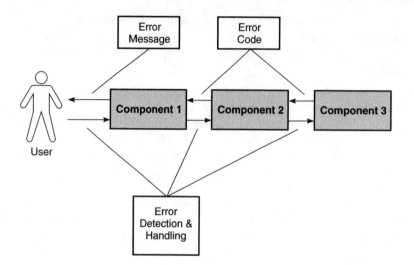

Figure 10.4 Error detection and handling path.

would have to be created to generate an error behind the client that the client will not be advised of but that will be persistent?

The detected error must then be handled. Will the application fix the error itself? In most cases, some components may return an error code or message. The error condition is usually communicated back to the user in the form of an error message. This can be done either on the client side (if that is the expected behavior) or on the server side (after the user sends a request to the server).

For example, the user enters a request. The request is sent to the Web server, which then passes it along to the database server. If the database server experiences an error condition, it will then return an error code. The Web server either generates an error message that is based on the error code, or it forwards the error code back to the client. (For more information, see Chapter 9, "User Interface Tests," for an example of client- and server-side error message handling).

In this error-handling scheme, consider the following issues:

- An error condition might occur anywhere in the chain transaction processing.
- Each component within the chain might fail to detect or interpret an error condition correctly.
- Each component within the communication chain might fail to forward an error code to the next component.
- An error condition (code) needs to be translated into an understandable message so that the user will know what happened. For example, "Exception 80065" does not mean anything to the user.
- The user does not know or care where the error happens. One only needs to know what the error is (from the human perspective) and how to correct the situation.

■ The goal of forced-error tests is to put the application in an error condition. The first level of the test is to make sure an error message is received by the client. Second, test that the error message is correct. That is, it should convey the description of the error and tell the user how to resolve the error.

The next step is to check if the error condition was properly handled. This may be instantly apparent, but in most cases, we may not know what has resulted from the error condition. A key for testers is to keep good notes of what action is taken, and in what order, so that bugs can be better investigated and reproduced.

As discussed earlier, there are numerous ways to collect error condition information. The most systematic way of generating a preliminary error condition test is to get a list of all error messages from the program's developers. Additional error conditions can be uncovered through guesswork based on past testing experience. You may also discover bugs accidentally while performing other kinds of testing.

A full cycle of FET may require two to three builds to complete. That is because testers have to perform countless error-generating activities that, in an ideal world, users would never do. Only by creating unexpected situations (e.g., entering special characters into fields that are designed for numerals and by requesting page margin settings that are impossible) can you generate error conditions that are unrelated to the known error conditions.

Boundary Condition Tests and Equivalent Class Analysis

Boundary tests are similar to FETs in that they are the boundaries of each variable. For example, in testing an online registration form, you need to check if a text field with a specified character limit from two to seven characters is, in fact, functioning as expected. Does the field accept two, three, six, and seven characters? What about one character? Or eight? Can the field be left empty? Boundary and equivalence class test-case design techniques are discussed in Chapter 3, "Software Testing Basics."

Boundary tests are an extension of TOFTs and FETs. There is some overlap between the test types. See Table 10.2 at the end of this chapter for a visual representation of the differences and overlap between TOFT, FET, boundary, and FAST.

Exploratory Testing

Exploratory testing* is a process of examining the product and observing its behavior, as well as hypothesizing what its behavior is. It involves executing test cases and creating new ones as information is collected from the outcome of previous tests. Test execution includes setting up an environment, creatively coming up with input data to attack the program, observing the program's response, evaluating what has been

---

* "In operational terms, exploratory testing is an interactive process of concurrent product exploration, test design and test execution." —*James Bach*

Testing the Sample Application

An example of an FET using the sample project includes requesting a metric (or chart) that has a start date that is later than its end date. In effect, this test case requests the impossible. Such a chart cannot exist. Yet, the sample project enables users to request such a chart, so the scenario must be tested.

The intent of this test case is not to ensure accuracy of output, but to examine how the program responds to the error condition. Does the system crash? Is the user given a chance to amend their request? Is an error message presented to the user (regardless of the error message's accuracy)?

Getting a list of all error messages is an effective means of generating test cases for FET. Figure 10.5 shows a straightforward FET with a start date for a chart of September 31. We all know "30 days has September." A "Start Date Not Found or Invalid" error message is returned.

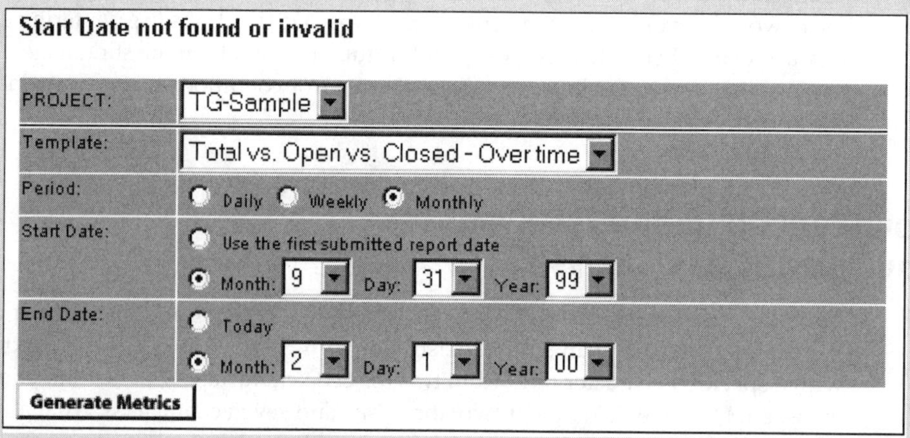

Figure 10.5 Metrics submit screen for incorrect date.

learned, and then starting the next test. Exploratory testing has many names and can take many forms. It is also referred to as *unstructured* or *ad hoc* testing and is, contrary to some beliefs, a methodical testing strategy. It involves "thinking outside the box," testing behavior that we may not expect but that any user may, mistakenly or intentionally, do.

You do exploratory testing by walking through the program, finding out what it is, and testing it. It is called *exploratory* because you explore. According to Bach, exploratory testing means learning while testing. It's the opposite of pre-scripted testing—just like playing twenty questions. If we had to specify all our questions in advance, the game would be nearly impossible, because with each question we learn more about what the next test should be. The elements of exploratory testing include:

Testing the Sample Application

Using the sample project's trend metrics feature as an example, boundary tests can be used to check if the program responds appropriately to user requests at the boundaries of the data set. For example, we make a data set in which report data begins on April 1, 1999, and ends on April 30, 1999. The specified limits of this data set are therefore 4/1/99 and 4/30/99. Any user requests that specify start and end dates between 4/1/99 and 4/30/99 should not generate errors. Any user requests that specify start dates before 4/1/99 or after 4/30/99 should generate errors.

In this example, the boundary test requires three values for each end of the limits—3/31/99, 4/1/99, and 4/2/99 for the start date; and 4/29/99, 4/30/99, and 5/1/99 for the end date. Each boundary test must confirm that accurate trend metric data is returned for requests that specify start and end dates between 4/1/99 and 4/30/99; and that error conditions are handled gracefully for requests that specify start and end dates before 4/1/99 or after 4/30/99. Table 10.1 shows combinations of values that are to be tested in boundary testing for the sample project's trend metrics.

Table 10.1 Combinations of Values to Be Tested in Boundary Testing for the Sample Project's Trend Metrics

BOUNDARY TEST CASE NO.	START DATE	END DATE	EXPECTED RESULT
1	4/1/99	4/30/99	Nonerror (TOFT)
2	3/31/99	4/30/99	Forced-error (FET)
3	4/2/99	4/30/99	Nonerror (TOFT)
...	...	...	Forced-error (FET)

- Product exploration
- Test design
- Test execution
- Heuristics
- Reviewable results

See Bach's paper at www.satisfice.com.

Software Attacks

Particularly useful for designing test cases are the 21 attacks on software described by James A. Whittaker in his paper, "How to Break Software," http://se.fit.edu/papers .htm. According to this paper, software attacks fall into at least one of three general categories: (1) input/output attacks, (2) data attacks, and (3) computation attacks.

Table 10.2 Special Characters and Example Boundary Test Input

CHARACTERS TESTED	CORRESPONDING TEST TYPE
0	Boundary, special-case, or forced-error?
2–7	Task-oriented functional testing?
1 or <2	Boundary or forced-error?
8 or >7	Boundary or forced-error?
?, +, (, #, !, <	Forced-error?
%n, $name, etc.	Forced-error or special cases that are meaningful (used as keyword in that programming environment) to the application under test?

What Method Is It?

Definition of test *types* or *methods,* by itself, is not important. What is important is to make sure that relevant test cases (and their probability of revealing failures) are used to exercise a feature in search for errors.

As illustrated in Table 10.2, the lines between boundary tests, TOFTs, and FETs are not always clear. Using the text field example given above, you can perform any of these three test types, depending on what character you enter into the field with the two- to seven-character limits.

It does not matter which method it is. It's important that a test case would have a high probability of finding errors.

Bibliography

Bach, James. *General Functionality and Stability Test Procedure for the Certified for Microsoft Windows Logo.* Redmond, WA: Microsoft, 2000.

Kaner, Cem, et al. *Testing Computer Software,* second ed. New York: John Wiley & Sons, Inc., 1999.

LogiGear Corporation. *QA Training Handbook: Testing Web Applications.* Foster City, CA: LogiGear Corp., 2000.

LogiGear Corporation. *QA Training Handbook: Testing Windows Desktop and Server-Based Applications.* Foster City, CA: LogiGear Corp., 2000.

LogiGear Corporation. *QA Training Handbook: Testing Computer Software.* Foster City, CA: LogiGear Corp., 2000.

Whittaker, James A. "How to Break Software." SQE STAR East Conference Proceedings, May 2000.

Whittaker, James A., and Alan Jorgensen. "Why Software Fails." *ACM Software Engineering Note* 24 (1999): 4.

CHAPTER 11

Database Tests

Why Read This Chapter?

All Web-based data access applications require database servers. To effectively plan for database testing and the analysis of database-related errors, it is useful to understand key database technology concepts, how Web server components interact with the database components, and other testing issues.

Introduction

This chapter offers an introduction to database components, application-database interaction, data warehouses, and data marts. Technical terms and examples that are useful in improving test planning and bug-report communication are also discussed.

Topics Covered in This Chapter

- Introduction
- Relational Database Servers
- Client/SQL Interfacing
- Testing Methods
- Database Testing Considerations
- Bibliography and Additional Resources

Databases play an important role in Web application technology. They house the content that Web applications manage—fulfilling user requests for data storage and record queries. Understanding how databases operate within Web applications is essential to effective database testing. Databases are repositories that are organized in such a way that it is easy to manage and update the data they contain. One of the database technologies commonly used in Web-based applications is the *relational database*. Relational databases are tabular databases that can be easily reorganized and queried. Additionally, in a Web environment, the term *distributed database* is used to refer to databases that are dispersed over multiple servers on a network.

Two common approaches used to address the needs of target users are *online transaction processing* (OLTP) and *online analytical processing* (OLAP). Online transaction processing is transaction-oriented. The design objective is to support users who need access to systems to process sales or other types of transactions. An example of an OLTP-type of application is an e-commerce system where sales transactions are processed between buyers and merchants. In contrast, OLAP is intended for users who need access to systems such as data warehouses and data marts to obtain various types of metrics or analytical reports. Figure 11.1 shows an example of OLTP versus OLAP design.

Three databases containing operational information are used for product sales, training registration, and purchasing (OLTP).

A data warehouse collects and transforms the raw data from the operational databases and stores it in a read-only informational database. This information is used to support decision-making processes (OLAP). Data replication executes every hour 24/7/52.

Data warehouse information is further parsed and distributed to data marts that are designed for sales and fulfillment departments to help in marketing expenditure and inventory control decisions.

Data warehouses are large databases that aggregate and process information from multiple databases. The data is stored in a format that supports various analytical needs. Data marts are customized databases normally derived from a data warehouse that has been formatted to meet the needs of specific workgroups. Data warehouses are structured around data. Data marts are structured around user needs. Data warehouses also allow Web sites to catalog large amounts of user profile data, e-commerce purchases, use and session data information, trends, and statistics. Data warehouses are large databases that aggregate information from multiple databases. Raw data is transformed via a filtering process and stored in a format that accommodates the database designer's informational needs. Generally, the data warehousing process supplies data marts (see following) or users with the data they require. Data warehouses are commonly referred to as *informational* databases.

Data marts are informational databases that have been custom formatted to meet the needs of specific workgroups. They differ from data warehouses, which are structured around data, in that they are built around the needs of users. Generally, both database types are read-only. They may be used to collect database activity statistics, such as numbers of calls, page hits, sources of hits, MIME types, header names, and so on.

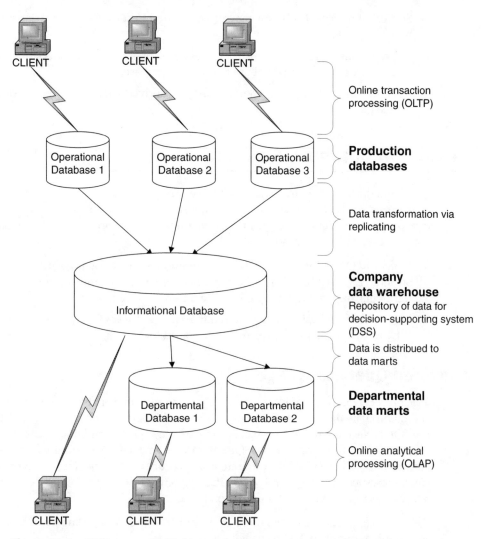

Figure 11.1 OLTP versus OLAP (data warehouse and data mart) example.

There are two ways to copy and update databases. With *synchronous updates,* changes in the operational database immediately affect the informational database. With *asynchronous updates,* changes in the operational database are uploaded to the informational database at regular time intervals.

Data warehouses can be designed to selectively collect data about operational activities in an OLTP system. The data can then be transferred to an OLAP system where it can be used for reporting, analysis, and decision support. Information stored in data warehouses is typically summarized, historical, read-only data. The goal of such a design is to improve query performance for decision-supporting systems (DSSs).

Several different data extraction processes may be implemented:

- Subsets of rows and columns may be configured to copy data from a source database to a target database.

- Aggregations of data, such as summaries or number of hourly transactions, may be copied from a source database to a target database.

- Data that are sent to target databases may be derived via calculations on raw-source data.

Relational Database Servers

Relational databases organize data into tables, records, and fields. They provide data storage and data access to clients upon request. Typical services include table and record creation, deletion, modification, data filtering, and sorting. Relational database servers consist of two components:

1. *Structured Query Language (SQL)* (see definition in the following subsection). Structured Query Language offers front-end query commands used for writing, retrieving, and manipulating data in two-dimensional table formats.

2. *Physical data.* Physical data is stored in *relational database management systems* (RDBMSs), which offer powerful storage access schemes.

Structured Query Language

Structured Query Language is a programming language that enables users to access and manipulate data at runtime. Application developers and database administrators use SQL to design data tables, objects, indexes, views, rules, and data access controls. Using English-based commands, SQL can maximize database flexibility and system performance while enforcing certain required security measures. Other programming languages, such as C, C++, and Visual Basic, can integrate SQL commands to enable data connectivity and data manipulation features.

Web-based applications offer users a browser-based interface through which they can access and manipulate data records.

Database Producers and Standards

The key players of the SQL server application market are Sybase, Microsoft, Oracle, IBM, and Informix. Most SQL server applications support features that are based on one or more of the following standards: ANSI SQL89, SQL92, and SQL99. Although an in-depth analysis of these standards is beyond the scope of this book, brief descriptions of each follow.

SQL89. Published in 1989, this is a revised version of the original SQL standard that was published in 1986 by ANSI and ISO. SQL89 supports the creation of tables, indices, views, and referential integrity (the ability to add constraints using PRIMARY KEY, FOREIGN KEY, and REFERENCE clauses within table and column definitions). Support for Embedded Static SQL was also added with this standard.

SQL92. SQL92 introduced many new features such as support for embedded SQL in additional languages, additional data types, advanced error handling, and so on.

SQL99. This standard added many new features to the existing one.

Database Extensions

Database extensions are proprietary features that increase database functionality. Stored procedures, triggers, and rules are examples of database extensions. Most SQL servers support database extensions of one sort or another. Unfortunately, the extensions supported by one vendor are often incompatible with the extensions supported by other vendors.

Stored procedures are compiled SQL statements. Stored within databases, these procedures can be called upon by name as needed. They also accept input parameters. They are analogous to *subroutines* or *functions* in traditional programming terminology. To improve programming productivity (and, sometimes, to intentionally introduce incompatibility), database vendors often include stored procedures that perform common database services.

A *trigger* is a type of stored procedure that is executed when an event occurs. For example, a trigger may be executed when a certain table is modified.

Rules define restrictions on values of table fields and columns. Rules are used to enforce business-specific constraints. Entered data that do not meet predefined rules (e.g., values that do not fall within an acceptable range) are rejected or handled appropriately.

Defaults are defined values that are automatically entered into fields when no values are explicitly entered.

Example of SQL

Following is a data insertion example that includes data entry for a specific database field. The example includes a subsequent query for the same data, illustrating how SQL databases are created and later utilized.

1. First, create a table to store information about company sales staff. Avoid creating duplicate IDs within the same table.

```
CREATE TABLE staff
(id INT, city CHAR(20), state CHAR(2), salary INT, name CHAR(20))
```

2a. Populate the STAFF table using INSERT statements.

```
INSERT INTO staff (id, city, state, salary, name) VALUES
(13, 'Phoenix', 'AZ', 33000, 'Bill')
INSERT INTO staff (id, city, state, salary, name) VALUES
(44, 'Denver', 'CO', 40000, 'Bob')
INSERT INTO staff (id, city, state, salary, name) VALUES
(66, 'Los Angeles', 'CA', 47000, 'Mary')
```

2b. An alternate to creating the table directly (as in example 2a), you can populate the STAFF table using a stored procedure.

```
/* Create stored procedure that accepts parameters for inserting records
*/
CREATE PROCEDURE add_staff (@P1 INT, @P2 CHAR(20), @P3 CHAR(2), @P4
INT, @P5 CHAR(20))
AS INSERT INTO staff
VALUES (@P1, @P2, @P3, @P4, @P5)
/* Inserting 3 records with created stored procedure */
add_staff 13, 'Phoenix', 'AZ', 33000, 'Bill'
add_staff 44, 'Denver', 'CO', 40000, 'Bob'
add_staff 66, 'Los Angeles', 'CA', 47000, 'Mary'
```

3a. Query for all entries in the STAFF table. SQL statements (see Figure 11.2).

```
SELECT * FROM STAFF
```

ID	CITY	STATE	SALARY	NAME
13	Phoenix	AZ	33000	Bill
44	Denver	CO	40000	Bob
66	Los Angles	CA	47000	Mary

Figure 11.2 Query results.

3b. Query for all entries in the STAFF table using the stored procedure (Figure 11.3).

```
/* Create a stored procedure that does not use parameters */
CREATE PROCEDURE all_staff
AS SELECT * FROM staff
/* Query for all entries in the STAFF table */
all_staff
```

ID	CITY	STATE	SALARY	NAME
13	Phoenix	AZ	33000	Bill
44	Denver	CO	40000	Bob
66	Los Angles	CA	47000	Mary

Figure 11.3 Query results (comparative selection).

4. Query staff with salaries higher than $35,000 (selecting only certain rows that meet the query criteria). SQL statements (Figure 11.4).

```
SELECT * FROM staff WHERE salary > 35000
```

ID	CITY	STATE	SALARY	NAME
44	Denver	CO	40000	Bob
66	Los Angles	CA	47000	Mary

Figure 11.4 Query results (column-based selection).

5. Query only ID, CITY, and STATE columns for all entries (selecting only certain columns) (Figure 11.5).

```
SELECT id, city, state FROM staff
```

ID	CITY	STATE
13	Phoenix	AZ
44	Denver	CO
66	Los Angles	CA

Figure 11.5 Query results (column and comparative selection).

6. Query only ID, CITY, and STATE of staff with salary higher than $35,000 (Figure 11.6).

```
SELECT id, city, state FROM staff
WHERE salary > 35000
```

ID	CITY	STATE
44	Denver	CO
66	Los Angles	CA

Figure 11.6 Query results.

7. Create a trigger to notify when there is a change to the table.

```
/* Create a trigger to send an email to a Sales Manager
alias when there is a change in the staff table. */
CREATE TRIGGER DataChangeTr
ON staff
FOR INSERT, UPDATE, DELETE
AS
/* Send an email to the address SALESMGR with change status message
*/
EXEC master..xp_sendmail 'SALESMGR', 'Data in the staff table has
been changed.'
GO
```

8. Create and bind (associate) defaults.

```
/* Create a default to be bound (associated) to the name column. It
means that the default value for the name column in the staff table
will be "Unassigned" */
CREATE DEFAULT name_default as 'Unassigned'
GO
sp_bindefault name_default, 'staff.name'
GO
```

9. Create and bind rules.

```
/* Create a rule to be bound to a new user-defined data type
age_type. By binding the age_rule to the age_type data type, the
entered value will be constrained to > 18 and < 65. */
sp_addtype age_type, int, 'not null'
GO
CREATE RULE age_rule
AS @age_type > 18 and @age_type < 65
GO
sp_bindrule age_rule, age_type
```

Client/SQL Interfacing

Client applications may be built from one of several different programming languages. There are two main approaches to integrating these programming languages with the execution of SQL queries: (1) embedded SQL (ESQL) and (2) SQL call-level interface (CLI).

Embedded SQL statements must be precompiled for the target programming language and target database (using vendor-specific precompilers). Structured Query Language statements must be recompiled for each supported SQL vendor. Every change made to source code requires recompilation of all vendor-specific SQL statements. Therefore, embedded SQL statements complicate application installation and deployment. They make the development of commercial-off-the-shelf (COTS) products more challenging.

With SQL CLI (as opposed to ESQL), applications execute SQL statements and stored procedures to access data.

Microsoft Approach to CLI

Open Database Connectivity (ODBC) is a Microsoft version of SQL CLI. As illustrated in Figure 11.7, it is used for accessing data in heterogeneous environments of relational and nonrelational database management systems (DBMSs). Think of ODBC as a transfer protocol that is used to move data between Web applications and SQL servers. Open Database Connectivity is based on the CLI specifications of the SQL access group. In theory, it provides an open, vendor-neutral means of accessing data that is stored in disparate PC and mainframe databases. With ODBC, application developers may enable an application to simultaneously access, view, and modify the data of multiple database types.

As illustrated in Figure 11.8, Microsoft's object-oriented approach to CLI is through OLE DB's ActiveX Data Objects (ADO). OLE DB is Microsoft's application program interface (API). It offers applications access to multiple data sources. OLE DB offers Microsoft SQL ODBC capabilities and access capabilities to data types other than MS SQL.

ActiveX Data Objects is an object-oriented interface that provides data access features to applications via object and class interfaces instead of procedural APIs. The data

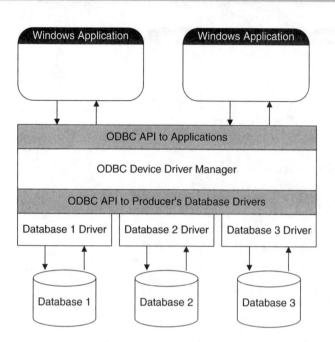

Figure 11.7 ODBC layers.

request process runs as follows: initialize OLE, connect to a data source object, execute a command, process the returned results, release the data source object, and uninitialize OLE. For example, if the Web application under test supplies data to users with an Oracle database, you would include ADO program statements in an Active Server Page–(ASP-) based HTML file. When a user submits requests for a page

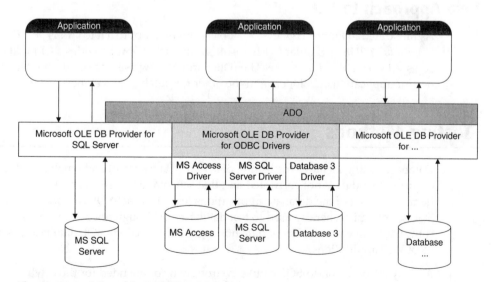

Figure 11.8 Microsoft ADO/OLE DB layers.

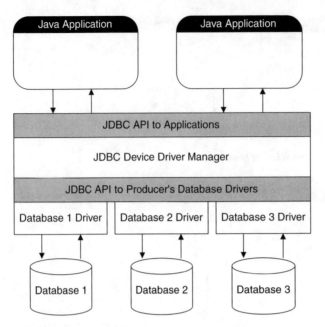

Figure 11.9 JDBC layers.

with data from the database, the requested page would include appropriate data returned from the database, obtained using ADO code. To make this work, Microsoft and database suppliers provide a program interface layer between the database and Microsoft's OLE DB. OLE DB is the underlying system service of ADO that a developer uses.

Java Approach to CLI

As illustrated in Figure 11.9, the Java object-oriented approach to CLI is *Java Database Connectivity* (JDBC). Similar to Microsoft's approach, JDBC provides a CLI that can be accessed via an object interface. The JDBC provides two sets of standard interfaces: one for application developers and the other for database developers.

Testing Methods

Database testing includes the testing of actual data (content) and database integrity—ensuring that data is not corrupted and that schemas are correct; as well as the functionality testing of the database applications (e.g., Transact-SQL components). The SQL scripting is generally used to test databases. Although not all databases are SQL-compliant, the vast majority of data hosting is supported via SQL databases, as are most Web applications.

A 2-day introduction-to-SQL course is strongly recommended for those who do not have enough basic SQL experience to properly test databases. The SQL testing typically considers the validation of data (i.e., ensuring that entered data shows up in the database). Accessing structured data with SQL is quite different from Web document searches, which are full text searches. Structured data in the relational DBMS model implies that data is represented in tables of rows and columns. Each row in a table represents a different object, and columns represent attributes of row objects.

Because column values are named and represented in a consistent format, rows can be selected precisely, based on their content. This is helpful when dealing with numeric data. Data from different tables can be joined together based on matching column values. Useful analysis can be performed in this way—for example, listing objects that are present in one table and missing from a related table. Rows can be extracted from large tables also, allowing for regrouping and the generation of simple statistics.

Testing can be applied at several points of interaction. Figure 11.10 shows that failures may occur at several points of interaction: client-side scripts or programs, server-side scripts or programs, database access services, stored procedures and triggers, and data stored in the database table. Therefore, testing can and should be applied at several points of interaction. Although client-side and server-side scripts are independent to the stored procedures and actual data, the scripts or programs that interact with them play a very important role. They are used to validate and handle errors for input and output data.

Common Types of Errors to Look For

Two common classes of problems caused by database bugs are *data integrity errors* and *output errors.*

Data is stored in fields of records in tables. Tables are stored in databases. At the programming level, a data integrity error is any bug that causes erroneous results to be stored or data corruptions in fields, records, tables, and databases. From the user's perspective, it means that we might have missing or wrong data in records (e.g., wrong social security number in an employee record); we might have missing records in tables (e.g., an employee record missing from the employee database); or data is outdated because it was not properly updated; and so on.

Output errors are caused by bugs in the data retrieving and manipulating instructions that occur, although the source data is correct. From the user's perspective, the

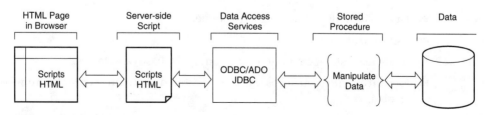

Figure 11.10 Several points of interactions.

symptoms seen in the output can be similar to data integrity errors. In doing black-box testing, it's often a challenge to determine if a symptom of an error is caused by data integrity errors or output errors. See Chapter 9, "User Interface Tests," Figure 9.19, for a discussion on this topic.

Instructions for manipulating data in the process of producing the requested output or storing and updating data are normally in SQL statements, stored procedures, and triggers. Bugs in these instructions will result in data integrity errors, output errors, or both.

Generally, database operations involve the following activities:

- First-time activities (e.g., the setup process)
  - Connect to the database server.
  - Create new databases.
  - Create tables, defaults, and rules; populate default data.
  - Compile stored procedures and triggers.

After the setup process is completed successfully, using the database consists of the following activities:

- Connect to database.
- Execute SQL statements, stored procedures, and triggers.
- Disconnect from the database.

The common types of errors uncovered in database activities include:

- Failures in connecting to the database. Several potential problems that cause this type of failure include the following:
  - Invalid user name, password, or both.
  - User has inadequate privileges required for certain data activities such as creating tables and stored procedures.
  - Invalid or wrong DSN (Microsoft Windows platform—See examples in Figures 11.22 through 11.25 for more information).
  - Failure to connect to the server that has the needed file DSN.

Several potential problems that can cause failures in creating databases, tables, defaults, rules, stored procedures, and triggers, as well as failures in populating default data include:

- Unable to write to the specified volume.
- Fail to create files.
- Inadequate storage required for creating databases and tables.
- Resource contention keeps one or more stored procedures or tables from being created.

Some of the common errors in the instructions (stored procedures, triggers, etc.) include:

- The database is configured to be case-sensitive, but the code is not.
- Using reserved keywords in the SQL statement. For example:

  SELECT **user** FROM *mytable.*

  Since **user** is the reserved keyword, this can cause a problem.
- NULL is passed to a record field that does not allow NULL.
- Mishandling single quote (') in a string field. See Figure 11.15 for an example.
- Mishandling comma (,) in an integer field. See Figure 11.18 for an example.
- Mishandling wrong data type. For example, if a field such as `employee_salary` in a record expects an integer, but receives $500 instead, it will complain because 500 is an integer but $500 is not. See Figure 11.18 for more examples.
- A value is too large for the size the field.
- A string is too long for the size the field. See Figure 11.17 for an example.
- Timeout—The time it takes the database to complete executing the procedure is longer than the timeout value set in the script (e.g., ASP script).
- Invalid or misspelled field or column, table, or view name.
- Undefined field, table, or view name.
- Invalid or misspelled stored procedure name.
- Calling the wrong store procedure.
- Missing keyword. An example would be the code written as follows:

```
...
create view student_view
select * from student_tbl
...
```

  instead of

```
...
create view student_view as
select * from student_tbl
...
```

  Notice that *as* was omitted.
- Missing left parenthesis. For example:

```
...
INSERT INTO staff id, city, state, salary, name) VALUES
(13, 'Phoenix', 'AZ', 33000, 'Bill')
```
- Missing right parenthesis. Example:

```
...
INSERT INTO staff (id, city, state, salary, name VALUES
(13, 'Phoenix', 'AZ', 33000, 'Bill')
...
```
- Missing comma. For example:

```
...
INSERT INTO staff (id, city, state, salary, name) VALUES
```

```
(13, 'Phoenix', 'AZ', 33000 'Bill')
...
```

- Missing keyword

- Misspelled keyword

- Missing opening or closing parenthesis before the keyword

- Certain functions are disallowed to be used with group by. For example, the following statement can cause error:

```
...
group by count (last_name), first_name, age
...
```

- Missing arguments for a function.

- Missing values. For example:

```
...
/* Create stored procedure that accepts parameters for inserting
records */
CREATE PROCEDURE add_staff (@P1 INT, @P2 CHAR(20), @P3 CHAR(2), @P4
INT, @P5 CHAR(20))
AS INSERT INTO staff
VALUES (@P1, @P2, @P3, @P4, @P5)
/* Inserting 3 records with created stored procedure */
add_staff 13, 'Phoenix', 'AZ', 'Bill'
...
```

- Insufficient privilege to grant permissions.

- Invisible invalid characters such as ESC.

- Errors in implementing COMMIT TRANSATION and ROLLBACK TRANSAC-TION. The COMMIT TRANSACTION statement saves all work started since the beginning of the transaction. The ROLLBACK TRANSACTION statement cancels all the work done within the transaction. COMMIT and ROLLBACK errors cause partial data to be undesirably saved.

There are several approaches to database functionality testing. We'll discuss these approaches in the following sections.

White-Box Methods

Although white-box testing is beyond the scope of this book, it's worth a discussion because several of these methods are quite effective for database testing. More important, the discussions offer knowledge that can be useful for black-box testers in designing powerful test cases.

Code Walk-through

Code walk-through is a very effective method to find errors at the source level. This method is not unique to database testing. It has been used for many programming languages. This is a peer-review process in which the author of the code guides other developers through her code, one line at a time. Along the way, reviewers are encouraged to point out any inefficiencies, redundancies, inconsistencies, or poor coding practices they see. The goal of the reviewers should be to carefully examine the code under review and identify as many potential errors as possible (but not necessarily to determine how to fix the identified errors in these sessions). Walk-throughs are effective when black-box testing is impractical for testing stored procedures at the unit level and when debugging programs are unable to track down logic errors in code.

Code walk-throughs tend to work better when they are limited to just a few developers and last no more than a couple of hours. If the reviewed objects require further review, a follow-up walk-through should be scheduled. Although as a black-box tester, one might not have the coding skill to contribute, participating in the walk-through is still extremely useful for at least three reasons:

1. A black-box tester can gain a great deal of knowledge about how the code works internally. This knowledge becomes of great value in designing black-box test cases.

2. As a tester, one is often very good at asking what-if questions (what if the data type passed to the parameter is an invalid one?) These questions, in turn, reveal many bugs, as well as information for designing good error-handling mechanism.

3. The tester can learn to become a good facilitator and record keeper. This helps the group to be better focused on identifying issues rather than on figuring out the fixes for the identified issues. This also helps in tracking the identified issues for later checking to make sure problems are adequately addressed.

As discussed earlier, SQL extensions such as Transact-SQL (supported by Microsoft and Sybase Server database product) and PL/SQL and SQL*Plus (supported by Oracle Server database product) are similar to other programming languages. Therefore, there will be syntactic as well as logic errors to be found in using expressions, conditions, and operators, along with functions such as date and time functions, arithmetic functions, data conversion functions, and so on.

Redundancy Coding Error Example

This is a simplified example of a redundancy error in the ASP code that can be caught using the code walk-through approach. This error will cause performance degradation. However, it will not expose any visible error at runtime. Therefore, from the black-box testing perspective, we will not see this bug.

```
'Send a query to the SQL database from an ASP
Set RS = Conn.Execute ("Select * from STAFF")
'Now, loop through the records
If NOT RS.EOF Then
'Notice that the If statement is redundant because
'the condition is already covered in the Do while loop.
'From the black-box testing perspective, this error
'will not cause any visible failure.
Do while Not RS.EOF
```

```
'The code that manipulates, formats and displays
'records goes here
...
      Loop
End If
```

Inefficiency Coding Error Example

Here is a simplified example of an inefficiency error. This error will cause performance degradation. However, it will not expose any visible error at runtime. Therefore, from the black-box testing perspective, we will not see this bug.

Using data in the staff table similar to one shown in Figure 11.11, we will be querying the data and displaying results in an HTML page.

ID	CITY	STATE	SALARY	NAME
13	Phoenix	AZ	33000	Bill
44	Denver	CO	40000	Bob
66	Los Angles	CA	47000	Mary

Figure 11.11 Query results.

Now, suppose that the application under test offers two views, a complete view showing all fields and records, and partial view showing all fields except CITY and all records.

For the complete view, the SQL statement to query data should look something like this:

```
SELECT * FROM staff
```

This query statement will be sent to the database. After the database server returns the record set, the application will then format and display the results in an HTML page. The complete view in the Web browser would look like the illustration in Figure 11.12.

For the partial view, instead of sending this SQL statement to query data:

```
SELECT id, state, salary, name FROM staff
```

The application sends the same SQL statement as one in the complete-view case.

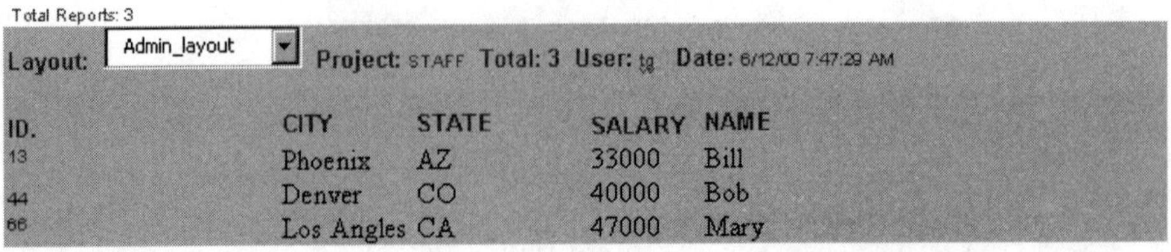

Total Reports: 3

Layout:	Admin_layout		Project: STAFF Total: 3 User: tg Date: 6/12/00 7:47:29 AM

ID.	CITY	STATE	SALARY	NAME
13	Phoenix	AZ	33000	Bill
44	Denver	CO	40000	Bob
66	Los Angles	CA	47000	Mary

Figure 11.12 The complete view.

After the database server returns the record set, the application will then format and display the results in an HTML page. The partial view in the Web browser would look like the illustration in Figure 11.13. Notice that there is no failure from the user or black-box tester perspective. This type of error only causes the database to do unnecessarily extra work. Hence, the overall performance might be affected.

Executing the SQL Statements One at a Time

It is possible to test stored procedures by executing SQL statements one at a time against known results. The results can then be validated with expected results.

This approach is analogous to unit testing. One benefit of this approach is that when errors are detected, little analysis is required to fix the errors. However, this approach is tedious and labor intensive.

Executing the Stored Procedures One at a Time

Stored procedures often accept input parameters and contain logic. Sometimes, they call other procedures or external functions. Therefore, logic and input dependencies must be taken into account when testing stored procedures. This testing approach is then similar to the testing of functions. For each stored procedure, analyze the data type and constraint of each input parameter: the user-defined return status value and conditional logic code within the stored procedure.

Design test cases that cover both valid and invalid data types. In addition, apply equivalent class-partitioned values and boundary conditions in designing input parameters. (See the section entitled "Test-Case Development" in Chapter 3, "Software Testing Basics," for more information.) Consider exercising various possible paths based on the conditional logic.

Execute the stored procedure by passing various input parameters into the procedure. Validate the expected results, as well as the user-defined return values, and the handling of error conditions (by rule enforcement, as well as business logic).

For example, we want to test the add_staff stored procedure created in example 2b earlier. Using Microsoft SQL 7.0, we launch the SQL Server Query Analyzer. We execute the following statement to call the add_staff stored procedure and pass in the parameters:

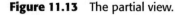

Total Reports: 3

Layout:	NoCity_Layout	Project: STAFF Total: 3 User: tg Date: 6/12/00 8:22:58 AM	
ID	STATE	SALARY	NAME
13	AZ	33000	Bill
44	CO	40000	Bob
66	CA	47000	Mary

Figure 11.13 The partial view.

```
add_staff 13, 'San Francisco', 'CA', 33000, 'Joe'
```

As shown in Figure 11.14, because the input data is valid, it confirms that the record is added successfully.

Let's try a test case with potential problematic input data. In this case, we will pass 'Mary's' to the name parameter (the fifth parameter of this stored procedure). Because it's known that a single quote (') is used by SQL to mark the beginning and end of a string, the extra single quote in Mary's is expected to create a problem if it's not handled properly. We execute the following query to call the add_staff stored procedure and pass in the parameters:

```
add_staff 13, 'San Francisco', 'CA', 33000, 'Mary's'
```

As shown in Figure 11.15, a SQL syntax error results.

Now, we run the same stored procedure, this time escaping the single quote character by placing an additional single quote character.

```
add_staff 14, 'San Francisco', 'CA', 33000, 'Mary''s'
```

Notice that the record is now added successfully without error as shown in Figure 11.16.

What this tells us is that we must check all the text parameters passed to this procedure to make sure that single quotes are escaped with other single quotes. This can be done through the scripting or the programming language of your choice.

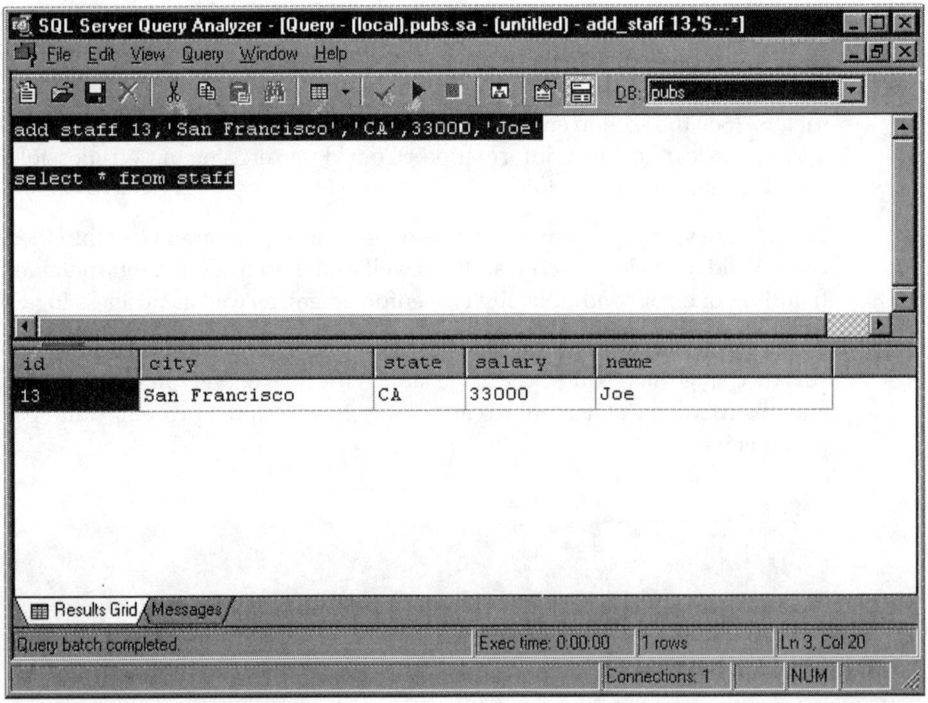

Figure 11.14 Valid input data.

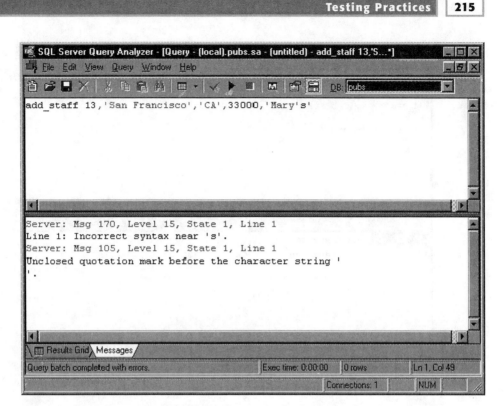

Figure 11.15 A SQL syntax error.

Let's look at what happens when a string passed in exceeds the limit of the maximum number of characters. In this case, the size of State field is two characters (See example 1 of the section entitled "Example of SQL," earlier in this chapter.)

```
add_staff 15, 'Albany', 'New York', 33000, 'John'
```

Now, we check the contents of the staff table.

Notice that in the State field, as shown in Figure 11.17, "New York" is truncated, becoming "NE" (Nebraska). We can fix this by ensuring that only two characters are allowed in the Web form that the user uses to submit to the database. We can do this via client-side scripting with JavaScript or use server-side validation with the scripting or programming language for our application (e.g. Asp, perl, Jsp, C++, VB, etc.).

Figure 11.18 shows an example of mishandling a comma. Here, we pass in a supposed integer with a comma (,) used as a thousand separator.

```
add_staff 15, 'Albany', 'New York', 33,000, 'John'
```

Running this query will produce an error. Note that the comma is interpreted as a field delimiter. The comma in 33,000 causes the parser to think that there is an extra parameter. Therefore, the "Too many arguments" error is raised. Similar to other cases, we must check our Web form that passes the data to the stored procedure to make sure that the data is valid and the error condition should be handled.

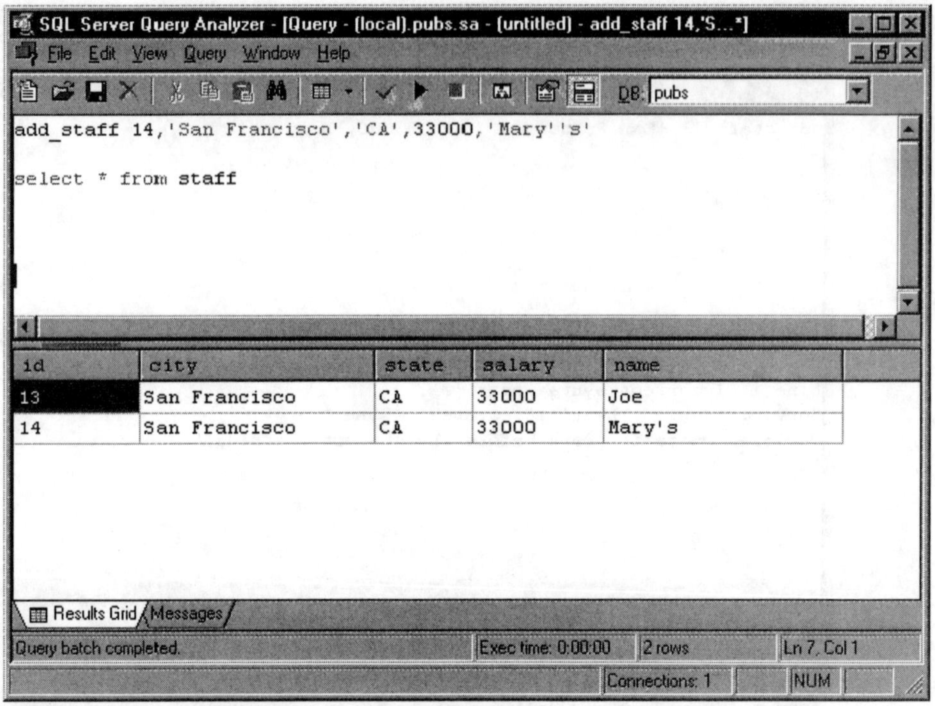

Figure 11.16 Single quote (') is properly handled.

Finally, we look at an example of wrong data type passed into the stored procedure. Here, we pass a string data type to the Salary field.

```
add_staff 15, 'Albany', 'New York', '33,000', 'John'
```

Running this query will produce an error. As shown in Figure 11.19, the stored procedure was expecting an integer data type; instead, it received a string.

Testing Triggers

Triggers are executed when certain events such as INSERT, DELETE, and UPDATE are applied to table data. Trigger implementation can be very powerful. For example, a trigger can call itself recursively or call other stored procedures.

We need to identify all the triggers that are part of the application. We then analyze and catalog the conditions under which a trigger will be executed. We try to understand the tasks that each trigger carries out. We then write and execute SQL statements or stored procedures to induce the conditions and validate the expected results.

The testing objectives should include the following:

■ Does the stored procedure or trigger meet the design objectives?

■ For each conditional statement, does the handling of the condition execute properly?

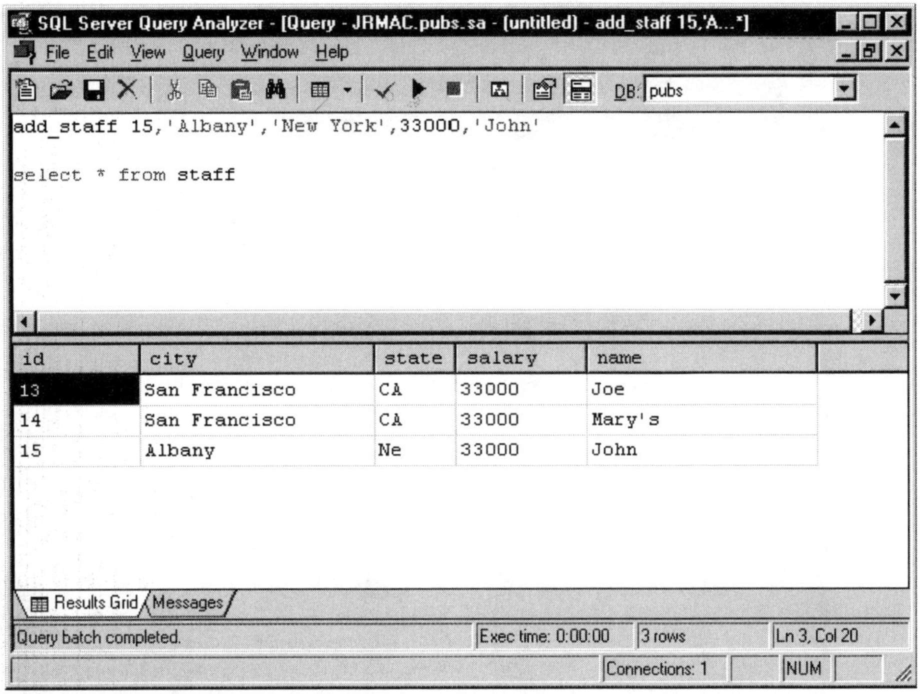

Figure 11.17 The string is too long.

- For each predefined input, does the procedure produce correctly expected outputs?
- Have all input cases identified in the equivalence class and boundary condition partitioning process been executed (either by walk-through, executing the stored procedure, or calling the stored procedure from other procedures)?
- For each possible error condition, does the procedure detect such condition?
- Is the handling of each detected error reasonable?

External Interfacing

In this method, the analysis of test case design is similar to the white-box and black-box testing approaches. However, instead of executing a stored procedure individually, stored procedures are called from external application functions. Whether an application is implemented with compiled programming languages such as C++ or Visual Basic, or with scripting languages such as perl, JSP (Java Server Page), or Microsoft ASP (Active Server Page), this method addresses both the testing of the functionality of stored procedures, and the interoperability between the application and the stored procedures. Additionally, this method also addresses the testing of proper application-database connectivity and authentication. Several automated testing tools such as Segue SILK and Mercury Interactive WinRunner also provide scripting features that allow for database connection and stored-procedure execution.

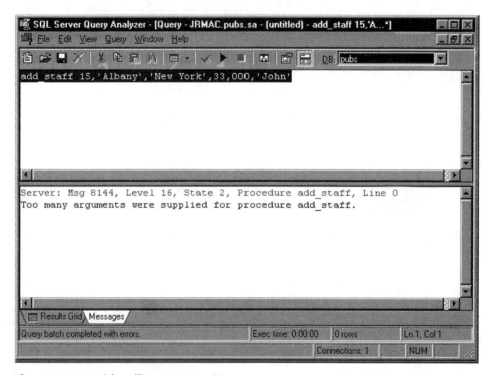

Figure 11.18 Mishandling a comma (,).

Black-Box Methods

In applying black-box testing methods, we will discuss test-case design, preparation for database testing, and setup/installation issues.

Designing Test Cases

Using the traditional black-box testing approach, test cases are executed on the browser side. Inputs are entered on Web input forms and data is submitted to the back-end database via the Web browser interface. The results sent back to the browser are then validated against expected values. This is the most common method because it requires little to no programming skill. It also addresses not only the functionality of the database's stored procedures, rules, triggers, and data integrity, but also the functionality of the Web application as a whole. There are two drawbacks to this method. One is that sometimes the results sent to the browser after test-case execution do not necessarily indicate that the data itself is properly written to a record in the table. The second drawback is that when erroneous results are sent back to the browser after the execution of a test case, it does not necessarily mean that the error is a database error. Further analysis will be required to determine the exact cause of the error.

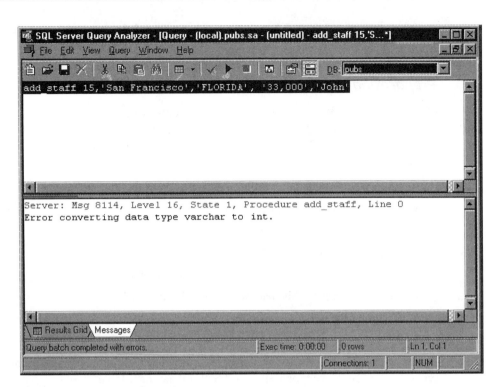

Figure 11.19 Wrong data type.

As it turns out, several examples shown in "Executing the Stored Procedures One at a Time" earlier in this chapter, are not realistic. For instance, if we already know that a single quote (') will cause the SQL parser to think that it's the end of the string, when the single quote is not handled properly, SQL will fail. So what's the point of trying something that you already know will fail?

There are at least four important lessons learned in these exercises:

1. There are input/output (I/O) validations and error handlings that must be done outside of the stored procedures. These areas (both client and server sides) should be thoroughly analyzed and tested.

2. Based on the acquired knowledge about things that would cause SQL to break, we should do thorough analysis to design black-box test cases that produce problematic inputs that would break the constraints; feed in wrong data type; pass in problematic characters, such as comma (,) and single quote ('); and so on.

3. Testing the interaction between SQL and other components such as scripts is an equally important task in database testing.

4. Understanding how to use database tools to execute SQL statements and stored procedures can significantly improve our ability to analyze Web-based errors. For

instance, it can help us determine whether an error is in the stored procedure code, the data itself, or in the components outside of the database.

Preparation for Database Testing

Generate a list of database tables, stored procedures, triggers, defaults, rules, and so on. This will help us to have a good handle on the scope of testing required for database testing. Figure 11.20 illustrates a list of stored procedures in a Microsoft SQL 7.0 database.

1. Generate data schemata for tables. Analyzing the schema will help us determine:

   - Can a certain field value be NULL?
   - What are the allowed or disallowed values?
   - What are the constraints?
   - Is the value dependent upon values in another table?
   - Will the values of this field be in the look-up table?
   - What are the user-defined data types?
   - What are the primary and foreign key relationships among tables?

Figure 11.21 shows a screen shot of a table design that lists all the column names, data types, lengths, and so on, of a Microsoft SQL 7.0 database table.

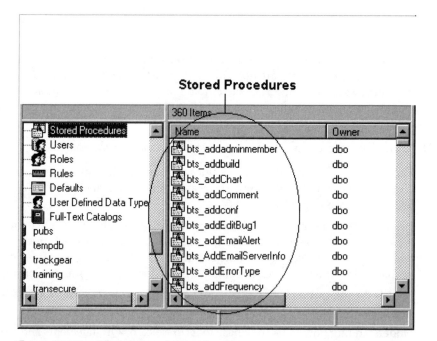

Figure 11.20   A list of stored procedures.

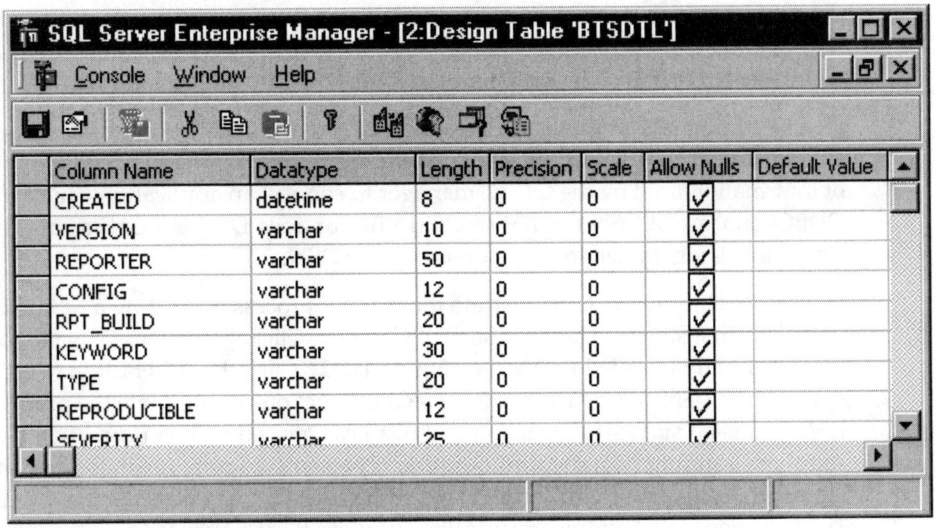

Figure 11.21   Table design view.

2. At a high level, analyze how the stored procedures, triggers, defaults and rules work. This will help us determine:

   ■ What is the primary function of each stored procedure and trigger? Does it read data and produce outputs, write data, or both? Pay particular attention to procedures that have keywords such as INSERT, DELETE, and UPDATE because they might have effects on data integrity.

   ■ What are the accepted parameters?

   ■ What are the returned values?

   ■ When is a stored procedure called, and by whom?

   ■ When is a trigger fired?

3. Determine what the configuration management process is. That is how the new tables, stored procedures, triggers, and such are integrated in each build. In other words, how can you determine if stored procedures are added, removed, or updated? This will help us determine the effects on our testing.

Setup/Installation Issues

During the installation process, the installer often needs to establish connectivity with the database server. This process requires authentication, which means that the installer needs to have a proper database-user ID and password to connect to the database. Generally, the user ID and password are entered into the installer screen and passed to the database during the authentication process. The user ID must be one that has adequate rights to create data devices (the physical files that store data), databases, and tables. The ID must also have rights to populate data and defaults, drop and generate stored procedures, and so on. This process is prone to errors. Each step within the process is susceptible to failure. It is quite possible that out of 100 tables created, 1 or 2 tables will not be created correctly due to a failure.

Here is an example of data source creation during the installation process. The *data source name* (DSN) used in Microsoft ODBC technology is a reference to the collection of information used by the ODBC manager to connect an application to a particular ODBC database. A DSN can be stored in a file, or a file DSN. A DSN can also be stored in a User/System registry or a machine DSN.

Figures 11.22 through 11.25 illustrate the manual process of creating a MS-SQL server DSN. The first step is to launch the ODBC applet. Click the system DSN tab to view a list of currently installed DSNs. (See Figure 11.22). Click the Add button to create a new system DSN and follow the on-screen instructions to complete the process. If a DSN is created successfully, dialog will display. Once all of the information has been supplied, a summary of the configuration is presented. From the dialog box shown in Figure 11.23, test the data source to see if it has been set up correctly. (See Figure 11.24.) Suppose that, in this process, the supplied ID or password is incorrect; an error message will display (as shown in Figure 11.25).

Now, consider that the preceding manual process can be implemented (coded) in the installation program—the complete DSN creation procedure being executed programmatically. Any errors that arise during this process can cause an invalid DSN. An invalid DSN will cause a failure in connecting to the database server. If the

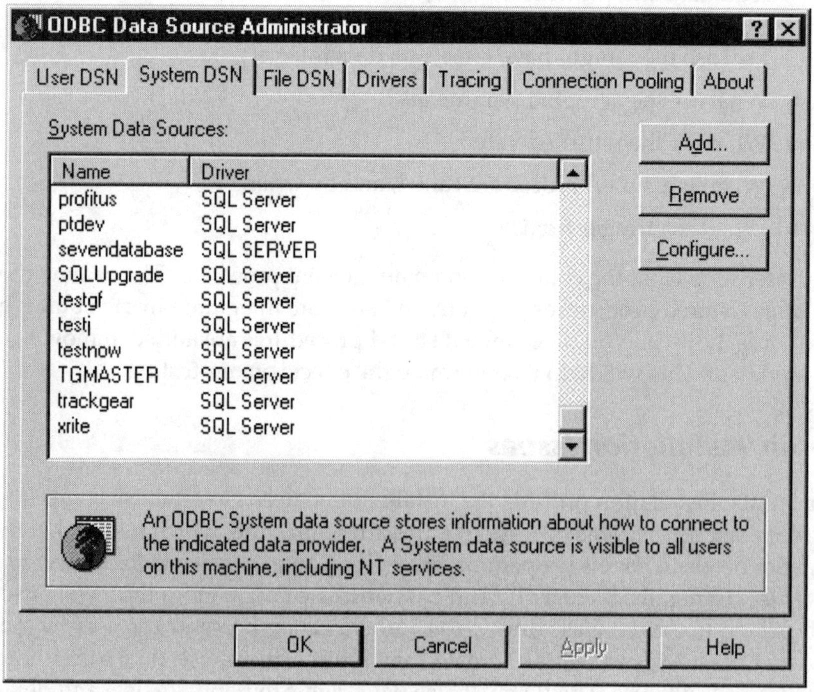

Figure 11.22   ODBC data source administrator.

```
ODBC Microsoft SQL Server Setup                              [X]

        A new ODBC data source will be created with the following
                            configuration:

 Microsoft SQL Server ODBC Driver Version 03.70.0623          [▲]

 Data Source Name: trackgear
 Data Source Description:
 Server: (local)
 Database: trackgear
 Language: English
 Translate Character Data: Yes
 Log Long Running Queries: No
 Log Driver Statistics: No
 Use Integrated Security: No
 Use Regional Settings: No
 Prepared Statements Option: Drop temporary procedures on
 disconnect
 Use Failover Server: No
 Use ANSI Quoted Identifiers: Yes
 Use ANSI Null, Paddings and Warnings: Yes

                                                             [▼]

  [ Test Data Source... ]          [  OK  ]      [  Cancel  ]
```

Figure 11.23   Configuration summary.

installer cannot establish a connection to the database server and it did not check for such an error, all the code used to create devices, databases, tables, stored procedures, and triggers will fail.

Database Testing Considerations

- Using a call-level interface such as Microsoft ODBC, in theory, applications are not involved with the types of back-end databases because they only interact with the ODBC layer. In practice, however, there are incompatibility issues among different types of back-end databases. Therefore, we should test each supported database individually to ensure that errors specific to incompatibility can be isolated more easily.

- Applications that use Microsoft ASP technology generally rely on DSN to make connections to SQL servers. An invalid DSN will cause a connectivity failure.

- Structured Query Language databases may not be able to accept special characters (', $, @, &, etc.) as valid inputs.

- Data sent to a database server may be corrupted due to packet losses caused by slow connections.

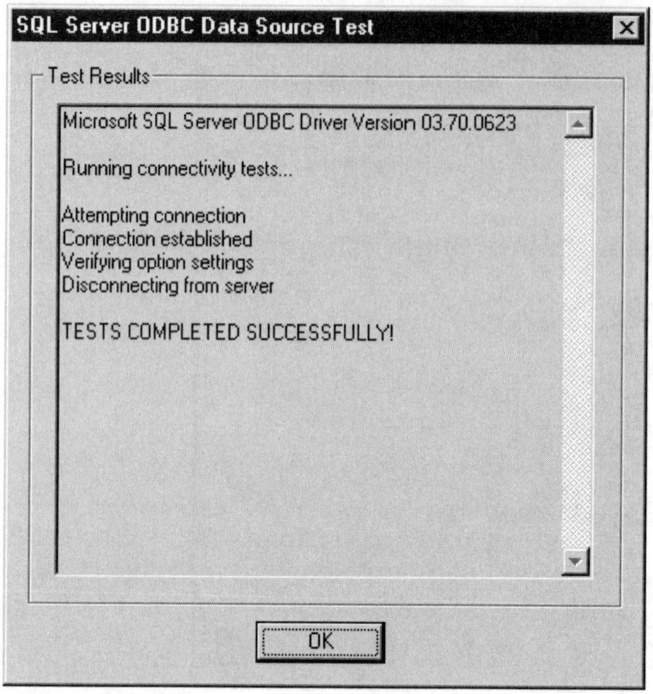

Figure 11.24 Data source test confirmation.

- Script time-out issues may cause data corruptions or erroneous outputs. For example, the time it takes the database to complete executing the query is longer than the time-out value set in the script.

- Local browser caching and Web server caching may cause problems in an application's interaction with the database server.

- Do the automatic database backup recovery procedures need to be tested?

- Database rollback logic, if not properly implemented, can cause data corruption. Identify where and how rollback logic is implemented. Design test cases to exercise those areas.

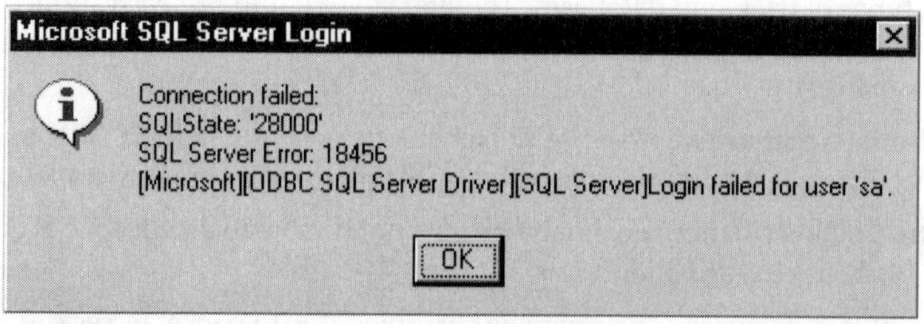

Figure 11.25 Invalid ID or password error message.

- Running out of hard disk space can cause serious problems to data in a SQL database. What happens when your server runs out of disk space?

- Localized support may require the support of the native version of the operating system, Web server, database server, application server, and browsers. Consider testing the Web application from different countries, using various browsers with language settings.

- The SQL Server Performance Monitor is available as a selection from the MS-SQL Server program group.

- With MS-SQL Server, verify that all DSNs correctly point to the appropriate servers; otherwise, changes may undesirably apply to the wrong database.

- Ensure that new/closed files are assigned correct permissions, owners, and groups. This is a necessity for Unix and may apply to Windows NT.

- Check for proper permissions on file-based directories. Check for the existence of and proper permissions for the source and target directories.

- Check for accessibility to the machine on which the target directory resides.

- Test for proper error handling when the logs have incorrect permissions. This is a necessity for Unix and may apply to Windows NT.

- Check for proper loading of all tables in the database.

- Check for proper error handling when database files fail to load.

Bibliography and Additional Resources

Bibliography

Branchek, Bob, et al. *Special Edition Using Microsoft SQL Server 6.5.* Indianapolis, IN: Que Corporation, 1995.

Bourne, Kelly C. *Testing Client/Server Systems.* New York: McGraw-Hill, 1997.

Coffman, Gayle. *SQL Server 7: The Complete Reference.* Berkeley, CA: Osborne/McGraw-Hill, 1999.

Holmes-Kinsella, David, et al. *Special Edition Using Gupta SQL Windows 5.* Indianapolis, IN: Que Corporation, 1995.

Kaner, Cem, et al. *Testing Computer Software,* second edition. New York: John Wiley & Sons, 1999.

LogiGear Corporation. *QA Training Handbook: Testing Web Applications.* Foster City, CA: LogiGear Corporation, 2000.

LogiGear Corporation. *QA Training Handbook: Testing Windows Desktop and Server-Based Applications.* Foster City, CA: LogiGear Corporation, 2000.

Orfali, Robert, et al. *Client/Server Survival Guide, Third Edition.* New York: John Wiley & Sons, 1999.

Stephens, Ryan, et al. *Teach Yourself SQL in 21 Days.* Indianapolis, IN: Sams Publishing, 1997.

Additional Resources

Articles and information for Microsoft SQL Server
www.swynk.com/sysapps/sql.asp

The Development Exchange's SQL Zone
www.sql-zone.com/

Microsoft site for information about SQL Server
www.microsoft.com/sql

Microsoft site for information about OLAP Services
www.microsoft.com/sql/olap

Microsoft site for information about English Query
www.microsoft.com/sql/eq

Microsoft Worldwide SQL Server User's Group
www.sswug.org/

SQL Server Magazine
www.sqlmag.com/

CHAPTER 12

Help Tests

Why Read This Chapter?

Having an understanding of the technologies that are used in the implementation of Web-based help systems (and the potential errors associated with those technologies) is critical to successful test planning.

Introduction

Web-help testing is a two-phase process. The first phase of testing involves the analysis of the system undergoing testing—determining its type, intended audience, and design approach. Once the particulars of the system have been identified, the second phase of the process begins—the testing phase. The testing phase itself is a two-part process that includes:

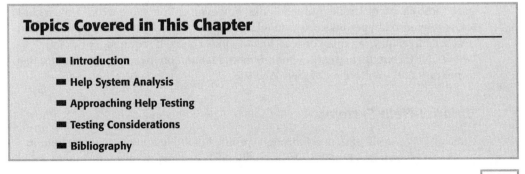

Topics Covered in This Chapter

- Introduction
- Help System Analysis
- Approaching Help Testing
- Testing Considerations
- Bibliography

1. Testing the system as a stand-alone component.
2. Testing the interaction of the system with the application.

Help System Analysis

Before beginning the testing of a Web-based help system, you should understand the system's intended purpose, the design approach, the technologies used, and the potential errors associated with those technologies. The following sections offer analyses of Web-help design approach, technologies, and potential errors.

Types of Help Systems

There are several types of Web-based help systems. Each type involves unique objectives and benefits. By clearly identifying the type of help system under test, you can apply appropriate testing practices. Note that this chapter looks only at the testing of Web-based help systems, not printed documentation or PDF-based help systems.

Application-Help Systems

Application-help systems reside within and support software applications. They commonly support users in operating applications by offering context-sensitive assistance. Context-sensitive help gives users instruction that is relevant to the activities they are actively engaged in. An example of context-sensitive help includes clicking a Help button while a credit card billing information form is displayed. Clicking the Help button in this context generates help content that explains the controls and functionality associated with the billing form. Sometimes, you also get explanations of the intent of the form and the place of the form in a long transaction chain—that is, sometimes, you get help that explains the application, not just its buttons.

Reference-Help Systems

Reference-help systems offer in-depth information about specific subjects, such as building a Web site or digital photography basics. They do not act as how-to guides for specific applications. Web-based reference systems are organized around the subject matter they present in a way that is similar to how printed reference books are organized into chapters. Unlike printed books, however, online reference systems include cross-referenced hyperlinks between related topics. Although they are generally context sensitive, they can often be read linearly like a book, if required. For example, www.CNBC.com has a great deal of reference material on investing and finance that is not part of the feature set of their Web site.

Tutorial-Help Systems

Tutorial-help systems walk users through specific how-to lessons in an effort to train them in a given subject matter. Occasionally, such systems are used in tandem with books (possibly in a school setting). Tutorial-help systems are often interactive, encouraging user input and offering feedback. This type of help system generally lacks context sensitivity. See www.cnet.com in their section, "Tech Help How-Tos and Tips," for examples of tutorials and how-tos.

Sales and Marketing–Help Systems

Sales and marketing tools convey product benefits to potential customers. The goal of *sales and marketing–help systems* is to get users to buy certain products or take an action of some kind, such as filling out a Web-based questionnaire or requesting information from a manufacturer via an online form. These systems may include live demonstrations and interactivity. The products being presented may or may not be software applications. This type of help system generally lacks context sensitivity.

Evaluating the Target User

There are four primary skill types that should be tracked when evaluating target users: (1) computer experience, (2) Web experience, (3) subject matter experience, and (4) application experience. (See Chapter 9, "User Interface Tests," for detailed explanations of target-user skill types.) Considering your application, English skill or grade level may also need to be evaluated. A help system should be evaluated by how closely its characteristics match the experience and skills of its intended users. Discrepancies in experience level between target user and system indicate the potential for error conditions and poor usability. The key question is whether the help system communicates the information that the reader needs, in a way that the reader can understand.

Evaluating the Design Approach

Web-based help system design entails the same testing challenges that are involved in UI testing. Look and feel, consistency, and usability tests all come into play. Means of navigation, UI controls, and visual design (colors, fonts, placement of elements, etc.) should be intuitive and consistent from screen to screen. Please refer to Chapter 9, "User Interface Tests," for detailed information regarding design approach, consistency testing, and usability testing. However, the mission is different. Here, the entire point of the application is to present content in a way that is easy to find and easy to understand, but with a slick display.

Evaluating the Technologies

Some of the authoring technologies used for Web-based help systems are:

Standard HTML (W3 Standard)

Standard HyperText Markup Language (HTML) page technology can be used to build help systems that combine framesets, multiple windows, and hyperlinks. As with any HTML-based system, hyperlinks must be tested for accuracy.

Context sensitivity presents complications in HTML-based systems. The correct help page ID must be passed whenever the Help button is clicked. However, HTML does not allow for the same hierarchical architecture that Windows-based applications are built upon. Thus, users may advance to other screens while viewing help content that is no longer applicable, the help browser window might become hidden by the application window, or the wrong page ID might be passed, resulting in incorrect help content.

Some applications, such as eHelp's (formerly Blue Sky Software) WebHelp, support the authoring of Web-based help systems that have Windows-styled help features such as full-text browsing and pop-up windows. WebHelp uses Dynamic HTML and supports both Internet Explorer and Netscape Navigator. To learn more about the functionality of WebHelp and read white papers on many help-authoring subjects, visit:

http://robohelp-resources.helpcommunity.com/resources/ArticlesFiles/articles.htm

www.ehelp.com

www.helpauthoring.com/webhelp/webhelp.htm

www.wextech.com/ts4whitepr.htm

Refer to Figure 12.1 for an example of RoboHelp's HTML-based WebHelp.

Java Applets

Java-based help systems can be run from servers while UI is displayed through Web browsers. Sun Microsystem's JavaHelp (supported by eHelp's RoboHelp, Figure 12.1) combines HTML and XML with 100 percent Pure Java. JavaHelp is a platform-independent authoring environment that enables developers to create online help in Web-based applications and Java applets. For more information about JavaHelp, go to:

http://robohelp-resources.helpcommunity.com/resources/ArticlesFiles/articles.htm

www.ehelp.com

www.helpauthoring.com/javahelp/javahelp.htm

http://java.sun.com/products/javahelp/

Also, see Figure 12.2 for an example of JavaHelp's Java-based help system.

Netscape NetHelp

NetHelp is a HTML-based, cross-platform, online help-authoring environment. It is based on technology that is built into the Netscape Communicator suite. It is compatible only with Navigator. Figure 12.3 shows an example of Netscape's NetHelp help system. For more information about Netscape NetHelp, visit http://home.netscape .com/eng/help

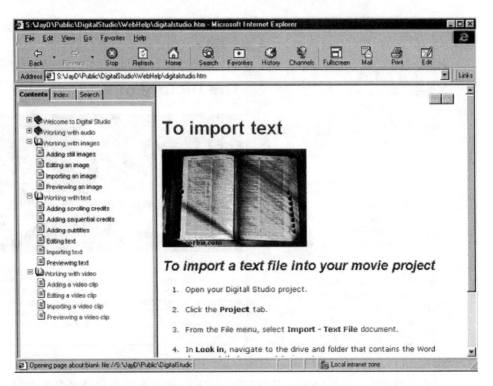

Figure 12.1   RoboHelp's HTML-based WebHelp.

Source: Graphics from *Demystifying Help,* a white paper produced by eHelp Corporation. Reproduced with permission from eHelp Corporation.

ActiveX Controls

Microsoft's HTML Help ActiveX control allows for the creation of Web-based help systems that have tables of contents, cross-referencing links, indices, and a splash window that accompanies the HTML Help Viewer. It is compatible only with Internet Explorer. See Figure 12.4 for an example of Microsoft's HTML Help ActiveX control.

Help Elements

Web-based help systems are commonly made up of the following elements. Help systems created with authoring programs such as WebHelp have many design elements that mimic the features of Windows-based help systems. Such elements include the book-and-page metaphor for help topic organization.

Elements to test include:

Contents tab (optional)

- Book links
- Page links

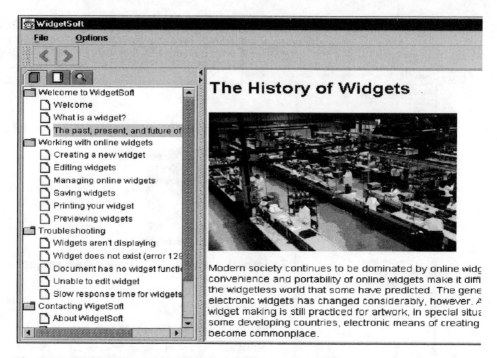

Figure 12.2 JavaHelp Java-based help system.

Source: Graphics from *Demystifying Help,* a white paper produced by eHelp Corporation. Reproduced with permission from eHelp Corporation.

- Topic page names
- Topic displayed in main window
- Topic displayed in secondary window

Index tab
- Single-level
  - With sublist
  - Without sublist
- Multilevel
  - With sublist
  - Without sublist

Find tab (optional)
- Full-text search
- Associative links

Other custom tabs (optional)
- Favorites

Glossary
- Self-defining terms
- Browse sequences

Figure 12.3 Netscape NetHelp help system

Rich topics
- Video
- Sound
- Links
- Text
- Graphics

Dynamic content
- Scripting
- ActiveX controls

Figure 12.4 ActiveX-based Microsoft HTML Help.

- DHTML
- XML
- Java applets

Context-sensitive help

Pop-up windows (self-sizing)

Secondary windows (self-sizing)

Buttons

Expanding text (DHTML)

Pull-down text (DHTML)

Approaching Help Testing

Once the technological particulars of the system have been identified, you can begin the testing process.

Testing the Sample Application

The help system of the sample application is built with standard HTML. It can be accessed from any screen in the application by clicking the Help button, so it is an application-help system. An example is shown in Figure 12.5.

Table of Contents

Adding configuration profiles		
Overview		

To add a hardware/software configuration profile, enter information that describes the profile into any or all of the following fields:

Config ID	ROM	DVD
Model	Video Card	Printer
Brand	Video Memory	Modem
O.S.	Hard Disk	Scanner
CPU Brand	Disk Size	CD-ROM
CPU Speed	Sound Card	RAM
Other HW	Other SW	Network Cards

Click the Save button when finished to save the configuration profile. Click the Reset button to reset the profile to its last saved state. Click the Done button to return to the Setting Up Hardware/Software Configuration Profile screen.

Figure 12.5   Sample application's standard HTML help system.

Looking at the design approach of the help system, you see that the system is context sensitive; clicking the Help button at any time while using the application links users directly to help content that supports the current activities and on-screen options. Each help screen includes a table of contents hyperlink. Users click this link to access the system's table of contents, from which they can access related content and, if they wish, read the entire system's contents from start to finish like a reference book. Also, hyperlinked keywords within the text link users to related content.

Though client-side users (end users and administrators) have access to differing privileges and UI controls in the sample application, both user types are referred to the same help system. This approach has positive and negative implications. End users may be exposed to administrator-level content that they do not expect or understand.

Two-Tiered Testing

The testing phase is a two-tiered process that includes testing the help system as a stand-alone system and testing the help system's interaction with the application.

Stand-alone Testing

Web-based help systems are subject to the same compatibility and functionality issues as are all applications. They need to be evaluated as stand-alone applications in accordance with the technologies that created them—Java-based systems, for example, should be tested in the same way that any stand-alone Java application would be tested. ActiveX-based systems, like all ActiveX components, should be evaluated for compatibility issues (they should support all the relevant versions of browsers).

Interaction between the Application and the Help System

The help system must be tested in combination with the application to ensure that all context-sensitive IDs are passed and that correct help content is displayed throughout all states of the application. Issues to consider include the *map* file:

- Names of help files
- Topic IDs for Help buttons on dialog boxes
- Accessing help through F1, shortcut keys, buttons, and so on

Types of Help Errors

Following are a number of help-related testing issues and error examples.

UI DESIGN

- Functional testing of a help system checks whether everything is operating as intended. Each link should be operational and lead users to their intended destination. All graphics should load properly.
- Web systems are vulnerable to environmental conditions surrounding platform compatibility, display resolutions, and browser types.
- As with all Web content, help systems should operate consistently across multiple screen resolutions, color palette modes, and font size settings. This is a particularly important issue for help because these types of legibility errors are common. For information regarding testing of display settings and fonts, see Appendix G "Display Compatibility Test Matrix." This matrix shows lists of display settings to use during your help testing. It is good practice to change your display settings regularly during the course of your testing, and it is particularly important during help testing as help probably uses different technology to be displayed; formatting and readability issues are key to a useful help system.

CONSISTENCY OF THE HELP SYSTEM

- Help system implementation should be consistent throughout; otherwise, user confusion may result.

- Consistency issues to test for include:

  - *Organization.* Is the system structured in a way that makes sense? Are available options clearly laid out for users? Is the system easy to navigate?

  - *Design approach.* Applications are often designed around familiar structures and patterns to enhance their usability. Many help systems are organized hierarchically; some are context sensitive. Is the metaphor used by your system consistent from screen to screen? Do methods of searching and navigation remain consistent?

  - *Terminology.* Is there consistency of language throughout the system? A command or term referred to in one context should be referred to in the same way in all other contexts. See the section entitled "Testing for Consistency" in Chapter 9, "User Interface Tests," for a list of synonymous commands that are often mistakenly interchanged.

  - *Fonts and colors.* Are font sizes and styles used consistently throughout the system? Are links, lettering, backgrounds, and buttons presented consistently?

  - *Format.* Text should be formatted consistently.

HELP SYSTEM USABILITY

- Usability concerns how well a help system supports its users. Usability issues are often subjective. Ideally, users should be able to easily navigate through a help system and quickly get to the information they need.

- Does context-sensitive assistance adequately support users from screen to screen?

- Is the system appropriately designed for the skill levels of the target user?

- What about user perception—will users consider the system to be useful, accurate, and easy to navigate?

- How many clicks does it take users to get to the information they are looking for?

- Please refer to Chapter 9, "User Interface Tests," for more information on consistency and usability testing.

HELP SYSTEM CONTENT

- A help system is only as valuable as the information it conveys. Inaccuracies in procedural instruction lead to confusion. In some instances, technical inaccuracies in help systems can lead to serious data loss.

- Every fact and line of instruction detailed in a help system should be tested for accuracy.

- Content should be tested for correct use of grammar and spelling.

- Has important information been omitted?

FUNCTIONAL ERRORS

- Functional testing of a help system ensures that everything is operating as intended. Each link should be operational and lead the user to the intended destination. All graphics should load properly. The table of contents links should be working.

- Help elements to be tested for proper functionality include:
  - Jumps
  - Pop-ups
  - Macros
  - Keyword consistency
  - Buttons
  - Navigation
  - Context-sensitive links
  - Frames/no frames

TECHNOLOGY-RELATED ERRORS

- Compatibility
- Performance
- Look for and research errors that are common to each technology type, then design test cases that look for those errors.
- Visit online technical support and issue databases that are specific to each technology type. Such sites list bugs that users have dealt with in the past. They are a great place to begin research for test-case design. For an example, visit eHelp's technical support knowledge base at www.helpcommunity.com.

Testing Considerations

APPLICATION-HELP SYSTEMS

- Are there multiple methods available for accessing help from within the application (UI button, navigation bar, menu, etc.)? If so, each method should be tested for proper functionality.

- Does context-sensitive information meet the needs of the intended audience in every situation? Different users have different needs; depending on their skill level and where they are in a program, users will require different information from the help system.

- Does the system include graphics? If so, do the graphics load properly?

REFERENCE-HELP SYSTEMS

- Is the system designed to link to other online resources? If so, are the links working properly? Are the other resources active and available?

- Is the subject matter compatible with the knowledge and skill levels of the system's target audience?

- Is the information design of the system intuitive?

TUTORIAL-HELP SYSTEMS

- How are users directed through the content? Are the intended navigation paths clearly marked?

- Is appropriate user feedback delivered?

- Does the system respond accurately to user input?

SALES AND MARKETING–HELP SYSTEMS

- How will the presentation be delivered? Is the system working properly on all delivery mediums?

- Is the system compatible with the computing skills of the target audience?

ONLINE HELP VERSUS PRINTED HELP

- Though online help systems and printed help serve effectively the same purpose, their testing differs in a few important ways:

  - Online help systems are interactive. Links, navigation, software functionality, and browser settings are complexities not found in traditional printed documentation.

  - Formatting can be dynamic. The diversity of browser types and browser versions leads to variations in content display. Where one browser may display content accurately, another browser may display content with inaccurate font size, unintended background color, and wrapping text.

ENVIRONMENTAL-CONDITION TESTING

- Web systems are vulnerable to environmental conditions surrounding platform compatibility, display resolutions, and browser types.

- Environmental variables to pay attention to include:

  - Cross-platform compatibility: Mac, Windows, and Unix

  - Graphic hotspots

  - Display color (i.e., compiled with 16.8 million–color palette, displayed with 16-color palette)

  - Display resolution (i.e., compiled at 1024×768, displayed at 640×480)

Bibliography

Deaton, Mary, and Cheryl Lockett Zubak. *Designing Windows 95 Help: A Guide to Creating Online Documents.* Indianapolis, IN: Que Corporation, 1997.

Horton, William. *Designing and Writing Online Documentation: Hypermedia for Self-Supporting Products.* New York: John Wiley & Sons, 1994.

CHAPTER 13

Installation Tests

Why Read This Chapter?

To be effective in testing installation programs, we need to analyze the functional roles of both the installation and uninstallation programs from the designer's perspective. Knowledge of potential issues and common errors that are specific to the operating system and environment in which the installation program will be running contributes to effective test-case design. It is also helpful to learn about available tools and techniques that can be used to track changes to the environment, both before and after installations and uninstalls.

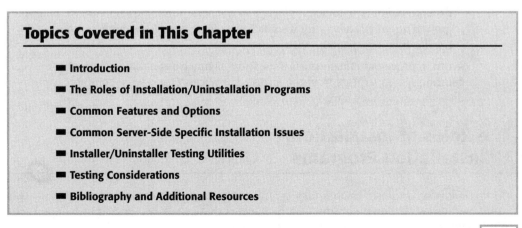

Topics Covered in This Chapter

- ■ Introduction
- ■ The Roles of Installation/Uninstallation Programs
- ■ Common Features and Options
- ■ Common Server-Side Specific Installation Issues
- ■ Installer/Uninstaller Testing Utilities
- ■ Testing Considerations
- ■ Bibliography and Additional Resources

Introduction

This chapter looks at the functional roles of installation and uninstallation programs. Common errors and issues that are associated with these programs in Web environments are discussed. Installation methods for both client-side and server-side installations are explored. Test-case design and test considerations for testing installation and uninstallation programs are covered. Tips and tools related to tracking changes to the environment (such as the InCtrl utility shown in Figure 13.6) are also discussed.

In an installation process, undetected errors—either server-side or client-side—can prevent robust applications from functioning properly. Web applications involve a server-side software installation of one sort or another. Occasionally, Web applications, even those that utilize Web browsers for their user interface (UI), also involve client-side software installations (installing plug-in components, ActiveX controls, etc.). Some Web applications install platform-specific TCP/IP clients that are used in place of regular browsers.

Effective installation testing requires solid knowledge of the operating system and the environment on which the installer will be running and the application will be installed. Environmental dependencies involving software/hardware configurations and compatibility need to be clearly understood so that failure symptoms can be quickly identified as either software errors or user errors.

Installation program bugs may originate from several sources:

- The detection and interpretation of environment variables (e.g., How much disk space is available? Which browser is installed and where is it installed?).
- The copying of files. For Web installations, a common source of error is having an intermittent network connection.
- The configuration of the system and the environment.
- Software and hardware incompatibility.
- The user might install the wrong application or the wrong version or might terminate operation prematurely or do other things that interfere with the installation.
- Background noise—for example, the virus checker that the user runs in the background might interfere with installation in several ways. Sometimes, the installation itself will propagate a virus.

We can improve our effectiveness if we learn as much as possible about what the operating system expects from the installed application and what common application setup errors have already been discovered.

The Roles of Installation/ Uninstallation Programs

Following are descriptions of the typical activities that are associated with installation and uninstallation programs. Common errors that installation and uninstallation programs are associated with are also discussed.

Installer

An installer often begins an installation by retrieving user operating environment information. In this process, installers learn about user hardware/software configurations and memory information, such as RAM and disk space availability. Based on its interpretation of collected information, the installer will then create new directories, install files, and configure the system so that the application will run successfully. Typically, the copying of data files includes moving executables (.EXEs), software components such as Java classes (.JAR), dynamic link libraries (DLLs), and so on into appropriate directories on the user's hard disk. Sometimes, compressed files (such as .ZIP or .TAR) need to be uncompressed before application files can be copied to the directories. After the copying process is complete, the installer will configure the *application operating environment* by adding or modifying configuration data files and (in Windows-based environments) registry entries.

Here is an example series of activities performed by an installation program:

- Execute the installer from the source host.
- Log in the destination host.
- Interrogate the destination host to learn about its environment.
- Install software components based on the information collected from the user environment and install option selected by the user (such as Full, Compact, or Custom).
- Uncompress the ZIP or TAR files.
- Search for or create directories.
- Copy application executables, DLLs, and data files, preferably checking for each file whether a more recent copy is already on the destination system.
- Copy shared files (shared with other applications). For example, in Windows environment these files are copied to the \Windows\System or \Winnt\System directory.
- Copy shared files (shared within company-only applications). For example, in Windows environment these files are copied to the \MyCompany\SharedDLLs\.
- Create registry keys (Windows only).
- Validate registry key values (Windows only).
- Change registry, .INI files, and/or .BAT files (Windows only).
- Reboot the system (Windows only).
- Populate database tables, stored procedures, triggers, and so forth.
- Create or update configuration files.

Following are descriptions of several classes of installer errors along with examples of those errors.

Functionality errors.   Installer functionality errors are miscalculations or failures in an installer's tasks (collecting data, creating folders, installing files, etc.). Examples include an installer not checking for available disk space or failing to complete an installation due to a forced reboot in the middle of the install script.

User interface design errors. User interface design errors are failures in conveying information to the user. Examples include incorrect, incomplete, or confusing instructions; surprising functions for controls; nonstandard menus; and inappropriate error messages.

User interface implementation errors. User interface implementation errors are failures in the installation of UI controls and UI functionality. Examples include incorrect behavior of common function keys (such as ESC, ENTER, F1, etc.) and improper UI updating and refresh during dialog box interaction.

Misinterpreting collected information. Errors in an installer's interpretation of collected information about the user environment include any misidentification of user hardware or software. Examples include an installer not correctly identifying the user's software platform and failing to detect the preexistence of a browser.

Operating system errors. Operating system errors are failures in user environment settings and file copying. Examples include the installer failing to add a shortcut to the Start menu, inaccurate registry settings, and application fonts being placed in an incorrect folder.

Dynamic link library—specific errors. The DLL-specific errors include failures in the detection and copying of correct DLLs. Examples include the installation of incorrect versions of DLLs and the failure to check for preexisting required DLLs. Another common one is trouble installing a DLL that is currently in use (already loaded in memory).

Uninstaller

The role of an uninstaller is to reverse the installation process (reversing the file copying and configurations that were executed by the associated installation program). Uninstallers often remove all data files—including application executables and DLLs—that have been installed by the installer.

Uninstallers generally offer users options for keeping and removing user data. They recover an application environment to the state it was in prior to the software installation. In Windows environments, this process involves modifying files, modifying registry entries, and removing entries that were created by the installer.

Here is an example series of activities performed by an uninstallation program:

- Remove directories.
- Remove application files.
- Remove application EXE and private DLL files.
- Check whether certain files are used by other installed applications.
- Remove shared files (shared with other applications) if no other installed application needs to use it.
- Remove shared files (shared within company-only applications) if no other installed application needs to use it.
- Remove registry keys (Windows only).

- Restore original registry key validations (Windows only).
- Execute the uninstaller via links or command lines.
- Execute the uninstaller via Add/Remove programs (Windows only).

Any of these uninstallation activities may introduce errors. Potential errors include the uninstaller not completely removing files (including program folders, directories, and DLLs) or removing files that shouldn't be removed (such as data files that were created by the application but that the user wants to keep; graphics files that came with the application that the user wants to keep; and files that are not marked as shared system files but are, in fact, used by more than one application and system DLLs).

Common Features and Options

The primary measure of success for an installation program is the installed application functioning as expected under all setup options and supported software/hardware configurations. The secondary measure of success is the quality of the installation program itself—its functionality, accuracy of instruction, UI, and ease of use. Following is an examination of common features and options that are supported by installation programs. An understanding of these functions assists us in identifying and executing adequate test coverage.

User Setup Options

Installation programs often allow users to specify preferred setup options. Here is a sample list of setup options that might be supported by an installer (each option should be fully tested).

Full, typical, or expanded setup. *Typical* is usually the default option. It installs most but not all application files and components. *Full* might install all files and components. *Expanded* might install all files and components, and additionally install files or components that would normally be left with the vendor or on the CD.

Minimum setup. This installs the fewest possible number of files required to operate the application. This option helps conserve disk space.

Custom setup. This offers users the option of specifying only the exact components they wish to have installed (such as additional utilities and certain application features).

An example of server-side custom setup options include:

- Application server only
- Database server setup only
- Initialize database only
- Create and initialize database

Command-line setup. This option uses batch scripts to run the setup without user interaction via the UI.

Testing should start with the typical setup option, because this is the most commonly selected option. Once this setup option is considered to be stable, testing of the other setup options may begin. In theory, the functionality within the code remains unchanged from option to option; based on the setup conditions specified by the user, a subset of the standard functions will be called in a particular sequence to carry out the desired result. Errors are often introduced in the implementation of this conditional logic, however. Typical errors in this class range from missing files that should have been copied, skipping a configuration procedure that should have been executed, and missing error detection code that warns users of fatal conditions (such as "not enough disk space to install"). These errors may ultimately prevent an installer from executing successfully or the installed application from functioning properly.

Installation Sources and Destinations

The following sections explore the complexities of installing software over distributed-server systems. Source and destination media types (CD-ROM, Web, hard disk) and branching options within installation programs are also covered.

Server Distribution Configurations

In the testing of Web-based applications, all supported server-side installations should be identified and fully tested. Figures 13.1 through 13.3 are examples of possible server distribution configurations. Just because the installation process successfully executes with one server distribution configuration does not mean that the installation process will successfully execute with all other server distribution configurations.

Server-Side Installation Example

In a server-side installation, the user (usually an administrator) must, at a minimum, be able to specify the following:

- The ID of the host (the physical server) where the software is to be installed
- The ID and password (with adequate login privileges) for the host, so that the installation can successfully complete its tasks
- The ID and password for the Web server
- The path to the Web server
- The ID and password (with adequate login privileges) for the database server residing on the host, so that database setup procedures can be completed
- The path where the software components are to be installed and the database is to be created

Installers offer the following functionality through the UI:

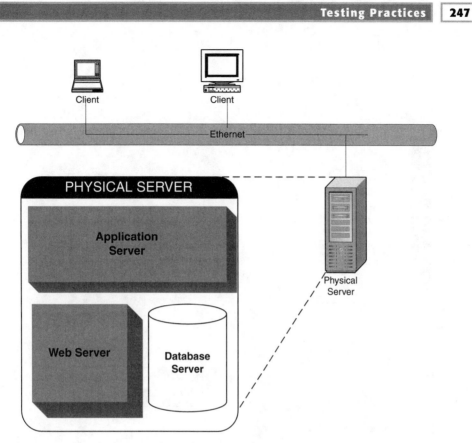

Figure 13.1   One-host configuration.

- A clickwrap software license agreement. If you choose not to agree with the terms, the installation software will normally stop installation.
- An input field for the host ID.
- Two input fields for the user ID and password that are used to log in to the host.
- Two input fields for the user ID and password that are used to log in to the database server.
- An input field used to specify the application path.

As an example (see Figures 13.1 through 13.3), under a one-host configuration (where both the Web server and the database server reside in the same hardware host) the installation completes successfully. However, under a two-host configuration (where the Web server lives on one host and the database server lives on another host), the installation program no longer works. To understand why this installer error has occurred, one should examine the installer's functionality:

- The installer only allows one input field for the host ID and a set of input fields for the user ID and password on that host. Under a two-host configuration, this

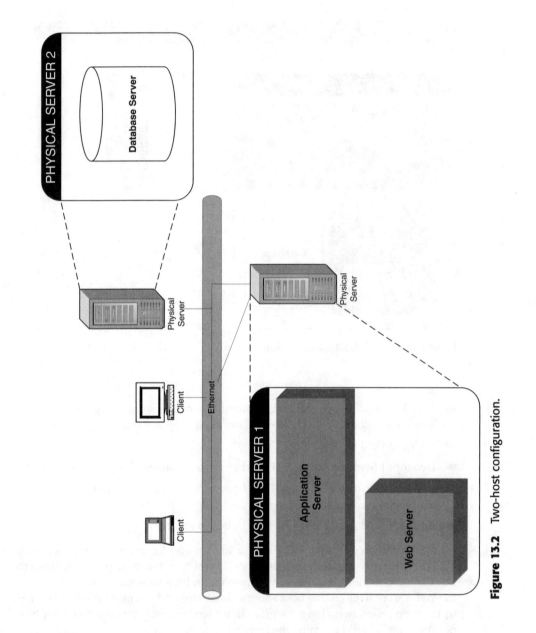

Figure 13.2 Two-host configuration.

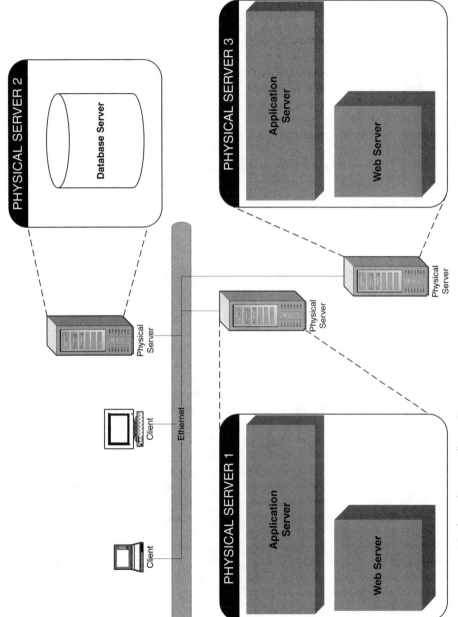

Figure 13.3 (*a*) Three-host configuration.

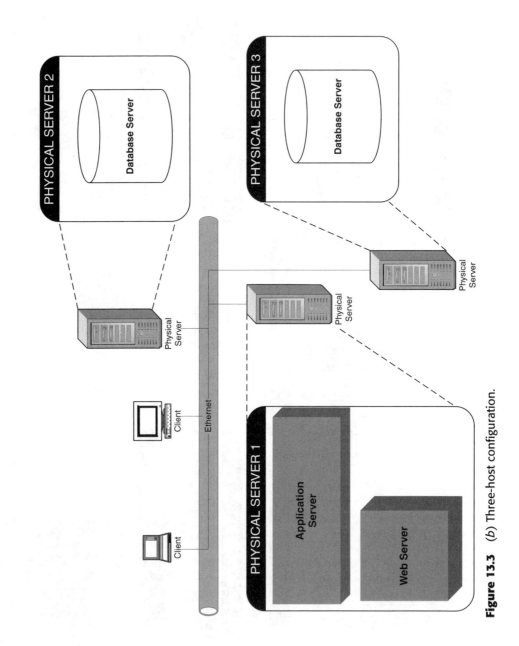

Figure 13.3 (b) Three-host configuration.

does not work because another set of input parameters is required to log on to the second host.

- Misinterpretation may result in a two-host configuration when the application path is set to C:\MYAPP. Does C:\MYAPP apply for host 1 or host 2?

Media Types

Installation programs may be run from several different media types, and applications may be installed on several different media types (as well as hosts). Each unique condition should be identified and thoroughly tested:

- Floppy disk installation from a local or remote drive: 1.44Mb, 120Mg, 233Mb
- CD-ROM installation from a local CD-ROM or a remote shared CD-ROM
- DVD-ROM installation (CD from a DVD player)
- Web installation (purchasing a product over the Web, using secure-server technology to get a code that unlocks the software)
  - Downloading and installing over the Web without saving the downloaded file
  - Downloading and saving the file, then executing the installer from the local or remote host
- Installing off a hard disk (includes downloadable installers)
  - Local or shared volume, in general
  - Local or shared FAT hard drive
  - Local or shared NTFS hard drive
  - Local or shared compressed NTFS hard drive
  - Local or shared Novell NetWare hard drive
  - Local or shared removable drives (such as Iomega, Zip, and Jazz)

Many installation errors are the result of running installers from, or installing to, different media types. For example, an installer might not autorun off a CD-ROM.

Branching Options

Installation programs typically include numerous branching options, which require users to make decisions about such things as continuing the installation, deciding where software should be installed, and deciding which type of installation should be performed. Figure 13.4 (*a*) through (*d*), which spans the next several pages, details a typical software installation process that might be executed on either the server side or the client side. It is a good idea to create a flow chart that depicts the branching options and use it to guide the creation of test cases.

This flow chart (Figure 13.5) presents the branching options that are illustrated in the preceding installation program example [Figure 13.4 (*a*)–(*d*)]. Charting the branching

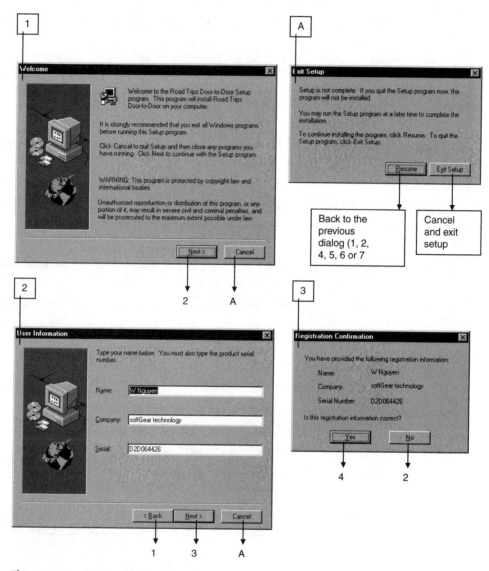

Figure 13.4 (*a*) Branching example.

options of an installation program under test is an effective means of guiding testing and determining required test coverage.

Common Server-Side-Specific Installation Issues

All Web applications require some form of server-side software installation. Although there are some Web applications that provide client-side functionality by installing

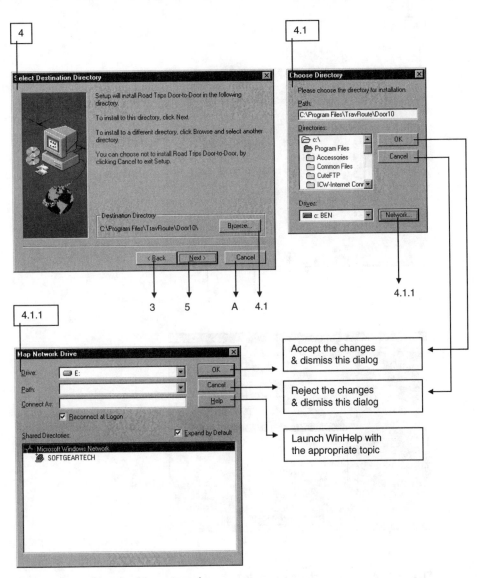

Figure 13.4 (*b*) Branching example.

software on the client side, most do not because their UI functions are supplied via Web browsers (the sample application is an example of this sort of application). Table 13.1 lists a number of common server-setup issues that may come up during installation testing.

Some common problems in Web application installations include:

- Database rules and permissions.
- Security.
- Server software version issues.

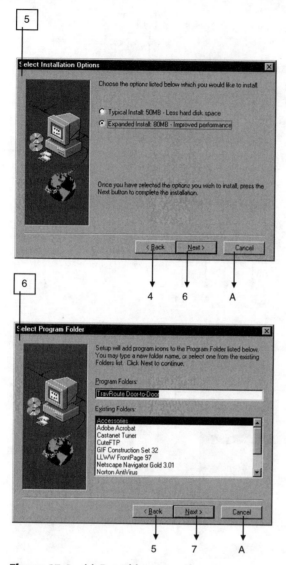

Figure 13.4 (c) Branching example.

- Time-out/waits.
- Application files being installed on the wrong server (with multiple server systems).
- Drive and path names.
- Unix paths use / such as Unix/MyDir/.
- Windows paths use \ such as Windows\MyDir\.
- Unix file name is case sensitive.
- Windows file name is not case sensitive.

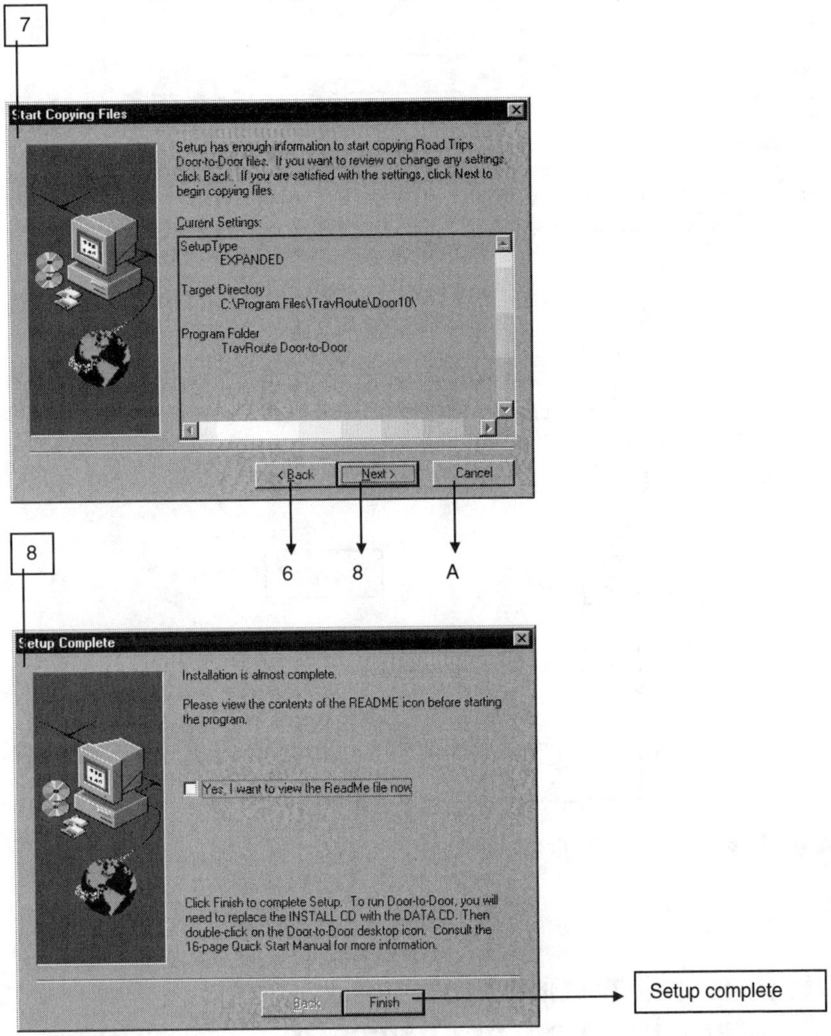

Figure 13.4 (*d*) Branching example.

- Unix file name does not allow space.
- Windows long file name does allow space.
- Problems related to installations occurring while other server software (such as .DLLs) is in use by other applications.

Installer/Uninstaller Testing Utilities

Here are some tools that you should consider for the installation and uninstall phase of your testing project. These comparison-based testing tools compare system attributes and files both before and after installation and uninstalls.

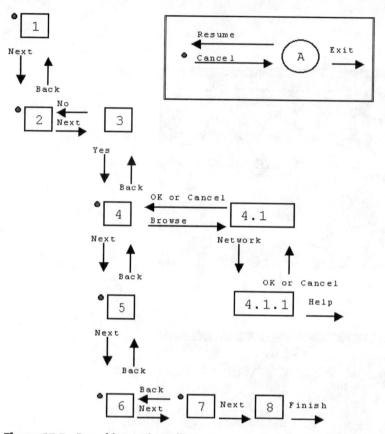

Figure 13.5 Branching options diagram.

Comparison-Based Testing Tools Look for the Addition, Deletion, or Change Of

- Directories and files
- Configuration data in specific files (.ini, .cfg)
- (Windows specific) Registry information in registry database

InControl3 and InControl4

InControl3 and InControl4 track all environment changes that are performed by an installer. They track changes made to the hard disk, registry, and other configuration files (such as WIN.INI and SYSTEM.INI). Figure 13.6 shows InControl4. InControl4 can be downloaded for free from www.zdnet.com/pcmag/pctech/content/18/02/ut1802.001.html.

Table 13.1 Server-Side Installation Issues

SERVER-SETUP COMPONENT	DESCRIPTION	ISSUES TO ADDRESS
Server ID	ID used by servers/processes to access services or components that reside on a server (local or remote host).	Name IP Local | Name | IP (if the target server is local)
Physical server	Often referred to as a host. This host (physical hardware box) has an OS installed on it and is configured to communicate with other hosts on a network.	Minimum versus maximum configuration issues Service packs Hardware compatibility issues
Server-software component	Server software or component installed on a physical server.	Web server Database server Application server POP server SMTP server Proxy server Firewall
Accessing services	The process of logging into, interacting with, and accessing resources on a server.	Server name Server IP Local | Name | IP (if the target server is local)
Web server	Server that hosts HTML pages and other Web service components. It receives and processes requests from/to clients and other services.	Distributed servers Vendor/OS/Version Server configuration for operability and security Account ID, password, and privileges Manual versus automated configuration
Database server	Typically a SQL DBMS that hosts system and user data. It may host stored procedures and/or triggers used by the application server or related services.	Distributed servers Vendor/OS/Version Server configuration for operability and security Manual versus automated configuration
ODBC	Object Database Connectivity: A Microsoft application interface that enables applications to access data from a variety of data sources.	Datasource name (DSN) Server name Login ID and password Account privileges Authentication methods (e.g., NT versus SQL server) Driver version incompatibility issues Target database driver incompatibility issues

Continues

Table 13.1 *(Continued)*

SERVER-SETUP COMPONENT	DESCRIPTION	ISSUES TO ADDRESS
Application server	Typically consists of code packaged in both binary objects (such as .EXEs, .DLLs, .COMs, JavaClass, and scripts) and integrated third-party components. These pieces work in concert with one another (and with other servers) to provide end-product functionality.	Distributed servers Vendor/OS/Version Server configuration for operability and security Manual versus automated configuration

InControl2

InControl2 is similar to InControl3, except that it is designed for 16-bit environments. InControl2 can also be downloaded from ZDNet.

Norton Utilities' Registry Tracker and File Compare

These tools provide similar functionality to that of InControl3. However, these products are not shareware.

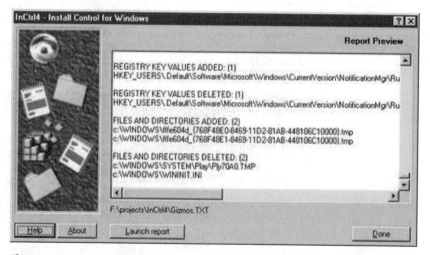

Figure 13.6 InControl4.

Testing Considerations

SOME OBJECTIVES OF INSTALLATION TESTING

- Test the functionality and UI of the installer.
- Test the functionality of the application that is installed and set up.
- Test the known error conditions and error handling of the installer and uninstaller.
- Test the impact that the installer and uninstaller have on existing system environments.
- Test software and hardware compatibility.
- Test the installer functionality on multiple server configurations.
- Test the installer functionality using multiple installation options and conditions.
- Test the configurations and modifications that the installer makes to existing files and registry entries.
- Test the uninstall program to see that it removes all data files—including application executables and .DLLs—that are installed by the installer.
- If your company markets multiple products with independent installers, test for installer compatibility between products. For example, can you install both products without conflicts? Can you uninstall individual products without affecting the others?

AREAS OF CONCERN THAT SHOULD BE CONSIDERED DURING INSTALL/UNINSTALL TESTING

- The functionality of the installed application.
- The functionality of the install and uninstall programs.
- The error handling of the install and uninstall programs.
- The UIs of the install and uninstall programs.
- The environment conditions in which the install and uninstall programs (and, ultimately, the installed application) will operate. Test coverage should include application-specific and environment-specific variables (including both dynamic and static conditions).
- Application-specific conditions—all supported user-setup options, all supported upgrade options, and all reinstallation conditions.
- Environment-specific conditions—all supported software and hardware conditions (especially when the installer relies on the existing configuration in determining which setup options to run).
- Does your product require administrative (Admin) privileges to install it? If so, is an explicit error message to this effect given if you try to install it without Admin rights?

TEST SCENARIOS THAT SHOULD BE CONSIDERED

- Installation under minimum configuration.
- Installation and running of application on a clean system (a clean environment consists of only the required components of an operating system).
- Installation and running of an application on a dirty system (a dirty environment consists of the operating system components and other commonly used software such as various versions for browser, productivity applications, virus checkers, etc.).
- Installation of upgrades that are targeted toward an operating system (e.g., Windows 98 to Windows 2000).
- Installation of upgrades that are targeted toward new application functionality—Did the installer remove the dated files? Did any other applications depend on the dated files?
- Installation of software over multiple operating systems.
- Reducing the amount of free disk space during installation to see if the installer can respond gracefully to an unexpected lack of sufficient space after the installation has begun.
- Canceling the installation midway through to see how well it restores the system to the base state.
- If you change the default target installation path to a different drive, will all the files really be installed in the specified path? For example, changing C:\program files\targetdir to D:\program files\targetdir. Some programs will still place some files in the C:\program files\targetdir path without warning, thus spreading the installation between two or more drives.

FUNCTIONAL INSTALLATION-TESTING CONSIDERATIONS

- Execute the test cases in Appendix F (Input Validation Matrix).
- Test a mix of UI navigation and transition paths.
- Look for user-level logic errors. For example, run the installer by following all on-screen instructions and user guide instructions; look for software-to-documentation mismatches.
- Consider test cases for error detection and error handling.
- Make sure that the installer does not prompt inaccurate or misleading error messages.
- Consider whether the installer might obtain incorrect path information and thereby install shared files in the wrong place or update registry keys with the wrong information.
- Consider incorrect default path errors. For example, the default system directories for NT 3.51 and NT 4.0 are not the same.
- Test with full, compact, and custom installation options.
- Test with various installation branches.

SOME COMMON INSTALLATION-FUNCTIONALITY ERRORS

- The main application does not successfully operate in all setup options.
- The installer fails to operate under the minimum configuration.
- The installer fails to operate under the maximum configuration. For example, if the size of the variable used to store the value of free disk space is too small for the actual amount of free disk space, that variable will be overflowed. This error often leads to a negative value reported for free disk space. In turn, it might prevent the installer from executing.
- The installer assumes (via a hard-coded path) that some source files are on floppy drive A. Therefore, installation fails if the user installs from floppy drive B or over the network or from any other drive whose name is not A.
- The installer fails to provide the user with default options.
- The installer does not check for available disk space.
- The installer fails to check whether certain key components (such as Internet Explorer or Acrobat) are already present on the user's system. Instead, it installs a new version (which might be older than the copy on the user's disk) and sets a path to that newly installed version.
- The installer fails to inform the user of how much space the installation requires.
- The installer fails to operate on a clean system.
- The installed application fails to operate after the completion of an install on a clean system.
- The installer fails to complete due to a forced reboot in the middle of the install script.
- The uninstaller fails to remove all program files.
- The uninstaller removes files that the user created without informing the user or offering an alternative.
- The uninstaller moves user files stored in the user directory to a new location without informing the user or offering an alternative.
- The uninstaller fails to remove empty directories left behind by the application.

USER INTERFACE INSTALLATION TESTING CONSIDERATIONS

- Execute the test cases in Appendices D and E (the mouse and keyboard action matrices).
- Test the default settings of the UI controls.
- Test the default command control for each dialog and message box. Does it lead to a typical installation?
- Check the behavior of common function keys such as ESC, ENTER, F1, Shift-F1, WINDOWS, etc.
- Check for proper UI updating and refresh during dialog box interaction. Also check navigation between dialog boxes (using Back and Next buttons).

- Test the default click path that is generated by clicking the Tab button repeatedly. Is the path intuitive?

- Test the default click path that is generated by clicking the Tab button repeatedly while holding down the Shift button. Is the path intuitive?

- Test the implementation of accelerator keys (underscores beneath letters of menu-selection items). Are the keys functional? Have intuitive character selections been made (N for Next, B for Back, etc.)?

- Are there conflicts between accelerator commands? If so, is the most commonly used command given preference?

- If a common command is not given an accelerator shortcut, is a symbolic alternative offered (for example, Ctrl-X for Cut, and Ctrl-W for Close)?

- Is a quick-key or accelerator key (one-handed) interface possible?

COMMON UI CONVENTION FOR DIALOG BOX COMMANDS

- The X button in the top right corner of Windows means "close the current window" or "close the current window and cancel the current operation."

- *Next* means "go to the next dialog box and close the current dialog box."

- *Back* means "go to the previous dialog box and close the current dialog box."

- *Cancel* means "cancel the current operation and close the current dialog box."

- *Resume* means "resume the current application and close the current dialog box."

- *Exit Setup* means "exit the setup program and close the current dialog box."

- *Yes* means "yes to the question being posed and close the current dialog box."

- *No* means "I choose No to the question being posed and close the current dialog box."

- *Finish* means "finish the installation and close the current dialog box."

COMMON ERRORS IN MISINTERPRETATION OF COLLECTED INFORMATION (WINDOWS SPECIFIC)

- The installer misidentifies the existence (or nonexistence) of a certain application (e.g., a browser) or shared file (e.g., a DLL) because it refers to an unreliable source—for example, a wrong key in the registry database.

- The installer misidentifies the software platform and configuration (OS, drivers, browsers, etc.).

- The installer misidentifies the hardware configuration (CPU type, CPU clock speed, physical or virtual memory, audio or video player settings, etc.) because it misinterprets the return values of an API call.

COMMON INSTALLATION ERRORS RELATED TO OPERATING SYSTEM ISSUES (WINDOWS SPECIFIC)

- The installer fails to register basic information (per Microsoft logo guidelines) such as company name, application name, or version in the registry.

- The installer copies files other than shared DLLs to \WINDOWS or \SYSTEM directories.
- The installer fails to register OLE objects in the registry.
- The installer places application fonts in a folder other than the Fonts folder.
- The installer fails to use a progress indicator.
- The installer fails to add shortcuts to the Start menu.
- The installer fails to register document types.
- The installer fails to support universal naming convention (UNC) paths.
- The installer does not autorun from a CD.
- The name of the installation program is not SETUP.EXE.
- The installer fails to configure the Context menu.
- The uninstaller fails to remove all information from the registry.
- The uninstaller fails to remove shortcuts from the desktop.
- NTFS compression—Some applications have problems and display erroneous I/0 error messages when they detect NTFS compression.

COMMON DLL-RELATED ERRORS (WINDOWS SPECIFIC)

- The installer fails to copy required DLLs (perhaps the files are not even included in distributed media).
- The installer fails to install the correct versions of DLLs (MFC DLLs, IFC DLLs, and other shared DLLs).
- The installer fails to check for the existence of DLLs needed by the application.
- The installer fails to correctly reference count sharable DLLs in the registry. Shared DLLs that are to be installed in the Windows\System or Program Files\Common Files directories (that are not part of a clean install of Windows 9x) need to register, increment, and decrement the reference count in the registry.
- The application fails to operate correctly due to the existence of several incompatible versions of DLLs that are shared by multiple applications.
- The application fails to operate properly due to the existence of several incompatible versions of DLLs that are produced or supported by a specific vendor.
- The installer fails to copy system-wide shared files (e.g., VBRUN40O.DLL) to the Windows\SYSTEM or WinNT\SYSTEM directories.
- The uninstaller fails to correctly reference count sharable DLLs in the registry.
- After decrementing a DLL's usage count that results in a usage count of zero, the uninstaller fails to display a message offering to delete the DLL or save it in case it might be needed later.
- The uninstaller fails to completely remove files, including program folders (unless there is user data in them), LNK files, non-system-shared files (if no longer used), directories, and registry keys.
- The uninstaller mistakenly removes system DLLs.

Bibliography and Additional Resources

Bibliography

Agruss, Chris. "Automating Software Installation Testing." *Software Testing and Quality Engineering* (July/August 2000). (See www.stqemagazine.com.)

Chen, Weiying, and Wayne Berry. *Windows NT Registry Guide.* Menlo Park, CA: Addison-Wesley Developers Press, 1997.

Microsoft. *The Windows Interface Guidelines for Software Design.* Redmond, WA: Microsoft Press, 1996.

Cluts, N. *Tips to Ensure Your Windows 95 Application Runs Under Windows NT 4.0* (May 1996). (See www.microsoft.com.)

Nyman, N. *Problems Encountered by Some Windows 95 Applications on Windows NT* (October 1996). (See www.microsoft.com.)

Wallace, Nathan. *Windows 2000 Registry: Little Black Book.* Scottsdale, AZ: Coriolis Technology Press, 2000.

Additional Resources

Jasnowski, M. "Installing Java with the Browser." *Java Developer's Journal* (March 2000). (See www.javadevelopersjournal.com.)

Microsoft Windows 9x/NT/2000 Logo Guidelines (See www.microsoft.com.)

CHAPTER 14

Configuration and Compatibility Tests

One of the challenges in software development is not only to ensure that the product works as intended and handles error conditions reasonably well, but also to ensure that the product will continue to work as expected in all supported user environments. In the PC stand-alone environment, this testing effort has proven to be a daunting task. Web application's client-server architecture further multiplies the testing complexity and demands. This chapter offers an analysis and guidance on configuration and compatibility testing. It discusses the needs of testing on both server and client sides. It also offers examples of configuration and compatibility specific errors to suggest testing ideas that can be applied to your testing and bug analyzing.

Topics Covered in This Chapter

- Introduction
- The Test Cases
- Approaching Configuration and Compatibility Testing
- Comparing Configuration Testing with Compatibility Testing
- Configuration/Compatibility Testing Issues
- Testing Considerations
- Bibliography

Introduction

It's not possible to have complete test coverage [see Chapter 2 in *Testing Computer Software,* second edition (Kaner et al., 1999)], nor is it cost-effective. The goal of Web configuration and compatibility testing is to find errors in the application while it operates under the major real-world user environments. Performance and minimum-system requirements—determined at the beginning of product development—are used as a baseline in the design of configuration and compatibility test cases.

The strategy in both configuration and compatibility testing is to run functional acceptance simple tests (FASTs), subsets of task-oriented functional tests (TOFTs), and modified sets of forced-error tests (FETs) to exercise the main set of features. These tests focus on data input and output, settings dependencies, and interactions on a wide range of software and hardware configurations in an effort to uncover potential problems.

These tests focus on problems that an application may have in running under a certain condition that is not covered under standard functional testing. Testing covers the expected user-installed base, in addition to other machines, configurations, connectivity, operating systems (OSs), browsers, and software that may be identified by the development or marketing team as problematic.

Configuration and compatibility testing are potentially more labor-intensive for Web systems compared with the PC stand-alone system due to both their component-based and distributed architectures. The configuration and compatibility testing of a Web system must take servers, databases, browsers, and connectivity devices into account.

Configuration and compatibility testing generally covers the following:

SERVER SIDE

- Application server
- Web server
- Database server
- Firewall
- OS
- Hardware
- Concurrent applications

CLIENT SIDE

- Browser type and version
- OS
- Minifirewall
- Childproof blocking
- Concurrent applications (instant messaging, virus checkers, etc.)
- Client-side hardware such as local printers, video, and storage

- Minifirewalls—childproof blocking
- Transmission Control Protocol/Internet Protocol (TCP/IP) stack
  - AOL stack
  - Microsoft Networking stack
  - Other third-party TCP/IP stacks

NETWORK DEVICES AND CONNECTIVITY

- Bridges, routers, gateways, and so forth
- Internet/Intranet
- 10/100 Base-T, modems, T1, ISDN, DSL, and so forth

The Test Cases

The goal of configuration and compatibility test cases is to evaluate end-to-end functionality from a high level for most features and from a lower level for any feature that is expected to be problematic.

There is usually a time element involved in developing compatibility and configuration tests. It is not practical to execute the entire set of tests on every environment. Time considerations may only allow a very short time of testing per environment. If you run 4 hours of tests on 20 OS, hardware, and browser combinations (not really that many), you have already spent 2 weeks just testing. This does not take into consideration time for bug submission, research, or system setups.

Choosing the right set of configuration and compatibility test cases requires experience and team input. The best approach is to target troublesome areas, as well as to ask developers about particularly vulnerable configuration or incompatibility scenarios. For example, if DHTML (Dynamic Hypertext Markup Language) is heavily used, incompatibility issues are expected among browser types and versions.

Approaching Configuration and Compatibility Testing

Choose the test configurations and test cases wisely. Tests should focus on the types of things that can go wrong when you change from one configuration to another. A good strategy for configuration and compatibility test planning is to model it after the seven steps to good configuration testing, as outlined in Chapter 8 of *Testing Computer Software,* second edition (Kaner et al., 1999).

1. *Analyze the market share.* If you can only support four major releases of browsers or database servers, which ones do the majority of your target audience use? Focus the testing and fixing of configuration and incompatibility on those platforms.

2. *Analyze the software on both the client side and the server side.* For example, you need to fully understand how the browser works to come up with useful test cases. That is, to understand how the various settings on the browser will affect the application, how various releases of the browser will affect the application, how various releases of the Web servers will affect the application, and so on. How will various settings on server side affect the behavior of the application or the security of the overall system? (These topics are discussed throughout this book.)

3. *Analyze the ways in which the server generates contents and in which the browser interprets, then formats and displays the contents.* For example, if the application is browser based (supporting the major commercial releases of browsers such as Netscape Navigator and Internet Explorer), you might not have to worry about dealing with incompatibility among various printer, display, audio, and other input/output (I/O) devices. However, you will have to test with various releases of each major browser because the understanding is that there will be an incompatibility issue in interpreting HTML, style sheet information and scripts, executing Java applets or ActiveX control, and so on.

4. *Save time.* Work in equivalent classes and go for broad and then deep coverage. For example, start testing with the major release of each supported browser. Look for functionality and configuration-specific issues first. Have those issues resolved before moving on to testing various minor releases.

5. *Improve efficiency.* Always look for ways to automate repetitive tasks. Keep good records so that you won't have to waste time testing redundant test cases and configurations.

6. *Share your experience.* Archive configuration lists, test cases, and other test documentation for later reuse. Build a knowledge base of configuration and incompatibility issues to share with other testers or to use in the next project.

7. *How do software and hardware components interact with each other?* Chapter 3, "Web Application Components," discusses how the various components potentially interact with each other on both the client side and the server side. In this chapter, the section entitled "Distributed Server Configurations" also demonstrates an example of how a physical server configuration might affect the functionality of the application. Focus your thinking around those issues in deciding the configurations with which the application needs to be tested.

Although it is not feasible to test for every conceivable combination of hardware and software, compatibility testing can deliver reasonable risk assessment by testing a cross-section of available hardware and software. Representative models from each class of hardware and software is tested in combination, thereby offering significant insight into major risk issues.

Equivalence class analysis requires experience, research, knowledge, and careful thought. To partition various operating environments, you must have knowledge of the technologies used in the Web site or application. This includes technologies like Java applet, ActiveX control, QuickTime, or Windows Media Player, along with an understanding of how these components work in various browsers. The general idea is to cluster like components into classes—so that the testing of any one member of a class is representative of all other members of the class. Components that are under test should be grouped into a common class when it is expected that their testing will generate identical results.

For example, the browser-based application under test supports report printing. It relies on the browser to render the page and send it to the printer. We know that in this application, most of the HyperText Markup Language (HTML) pages sent to the browsers are pure HTML. Only a few of them contain Java applets that are visible in the browser. Analyzing this application, we discover two classes of content in the Web pages: (1) pure HTML and (2) HTML mixed with visible Java applets. For the pure HTML class, we would not expect to find any errors in the outputs sent to the printer because pure HTML printing is well tested by the browser vendor. When we see a Java applet displayed in the browser, however, that applet might not show up when the page is sent to the printer. This is an incompatibility issue in the browser. Therefore, printing tests should be exercised for all pages with Java applets. This type of analysis helps determine the configurations to focus on, and other configurations that can be overlooked for the interest of time.

Before testing begins, it's recommended that the test team present the results of their equivalence class analysis to the project team. The results should be in the form of a test matrix that clearly details which equivalent classes have been identified and which hardware and software components represent the various classes. [For more information on equivalent class partitioning, read *Testing Computer Software* (Kaner et al., 1999), pages 7–11, 126–133, 399–401.]

Considering Target Users

The system under test should be analyzed against the target-user installed base. For example, a company's internal Web-based application may be used almost exclusively with Netscape Navigator 4.73 on laptops of a particular brand or variety. In such a scenario, testing should focus primarily on the application's performance on laptops.

Remember to also test the not-so-common configurations. Testing that is limited to only the most popular or common configurations might miss important errors and may give you a false sense of security that you have covered your bases and know the risk.

User-installed base analysis may indicate that the application:

- Must run on certain current browsers
- Must run on certain current hardware
- Must run on certain types of Internet connections (with and without proxy servers, firewalls, modems, and direct connections of various bandwidths)

When to Run Compatibility and Configuration Testing

Compatibility and configuration testing should begin after the first round of functional tests has been completed and, hopefully, after many functional errors have been discovered. Otherwise, it may be difficult and time consuming to differentiate configuration errors from functionality errors. If there are suspected problem areas, limited configuration testing may be run during the functionality testing phase; this may also be done to validate functionality on specific devices.

Potential Outsourcing

With the rapid advances in hardware manufacturing, OS development, software component development, and browser releases, it is not always feasible for software development organizations to maintain an array of system configurations preserved for in-house compatibility testing. Testing labs that can handle most configuration and compatibility testing needs are available.

Visit LogiGear Corporation at www.logigear.com or Brian Marick's Corner at RST Corporation's www.rstcorp.com/marick/root.htm for information regarding organizations that can help with software testing outsourcing.

Comparing Configuration Testing with Compatibility Testing

The line between configuration and compatibility testing is often misunderstood. *Configuration testing* is designed to uncover errors related to various software and hardware combinations, and *compatibility testing* determines if an application, under supported configurations, performs as expected with various combinations of hardware and software flavors and releases. For example, configuration testing might validate that a certain Web system installed on a dual-processor computer operates properly; compatibility testing would thereafter determine which manufacturers and server brands, under the same configuration, are compatible with the Web system.

Configuration testing of Web systems involves the testing of various supported server software and hardware setups, browser settings, network connections, TCP/IP stack setups, and so on. The goal is to ensure that the application is thoroughly exercised with as many configurations as possible. With each supported configuration, it is expected that the features will operate as a reasonable user would expect. Should there be an error condition, the error should be detected and gracefully handled by the application.

Due to the complexity of the client-server architecture, environmental-specific errors are more difficult to reproduce in client-server systems than they are in the single-PC model. In Web application environments, we often do not know the actual cause of failure conditions. When experiencing failures, a Web application might present an incorrect error message because it's not capable of recognizing the main causes of the failure. Test partitioning is effective in weeding out such elusive environment-specific errors—commonly caused by session time-outs, lack of disk space, downloading activities, or security settings that prevent ActiveX controls from being downloaded. (See Chapter 3, "Web Application Components," for more information regarding test partitioning.)

Testing the Sample Application: Configuration Issues

This example illustrates the challenge of differentiating configuration issues from actual software errors. Figure 14.1 shows a failed login error message that has been generated by the sample application. By simply looking at this error message, it is impossible to determine whether this error is the result of a software bug, a server-side configuration issue, a compatibility issue, a browser configuration issue, or all of these.

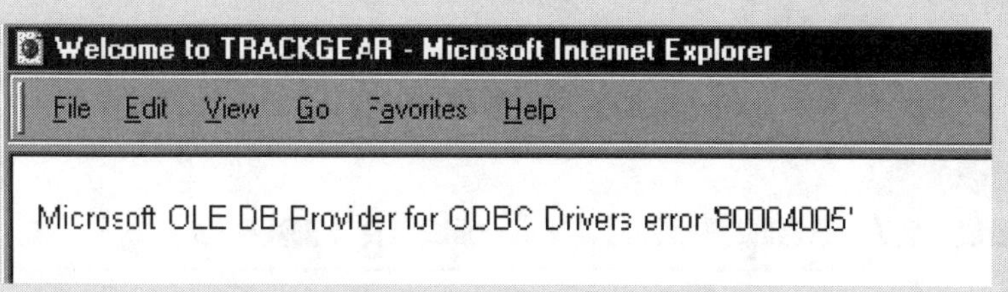

Welcome to TRACKGEAR - Microsoft Internet Explorer

File   Edit   View   Go   Favorites   Help

Microsoft OLE DB Provider for ODBC Drivers error '80004005'

Figure 14.1   Failed login error message.

Possible conditions that might generate this error message include:

SERVER-SIDE CONFIGURATION ISSUES

IIS (Web server) virtual directory has not been set up properly.
- This is a server configuration issue. However, if the installation program failed to programmatically configure the Web server according to specification, then this is a software error. If the system administrator fails to properly configure the Web server according to specification, then this is a user error.

Application directory has not been configured properly to execute scripts.
- The issue is similar to that described previously.

Default Web page has not been set up properly.
- The issue is similar to that described previously.

SQL server is not running.
- The SQL server must be running for the application to work properly.

DLL/COM objects are missing or were unsuccessfully registered.
- This problem is often caused by software errors in the installation program. If the components must be manually registered, then this is a configuration issue.

CLIENT-SIDE CONFIGURATION ISSUES

JavaScript has been disabled.
- Because the application requires the browser to have JavaScript enabled, this is a client- or browser-side configuration issue.

Continues

Testing the Sample Application: Configuration Issues *(Continued)*

JavaScript has been disabled.
- Because the application requires the browser to have JavaScript enabled, this is a client- or browser-side configuration issue.

High-security settings.
- High-security settings prevent the application from downloading and running certain unse- cured active contents (e.g., ActiveX controls, Java applets, etc.) required by the application.

Configuration/Compatibility Testing Issues

The following sections explore some of the many issues that may be encountered during configuration and compatibility testing. Some error examples are also included.

COTS Products versus Hosted Systems

The testing of commercial-off-the-shelf (COTS) products is potentially more labor intensive than the testing of hosted Web systems. With a hosted Web system, your development team has a lot more control over the server environment. Occasion- ally, your hosted system might be pulling some contents (e.g., stock quotes infor- mation, news, weather information, etc.) from your partner, but for the most part, this system is considered a controlled environment. The system is overseen by an information services staff and system developers. The testing of this type of system is run on only the few configurations that are specified by the system's designers and network administrators (specific server, specific amount of memory, specific connectivity, etc.). In contrast, COTS systems should be exercised with all configu- rations claimed by their product data sheets. Commercial-off-the-shelf products commonly have to integrate well with the buyer's environments, and certainly, you don't have much control over the server-side configurations of your customer.

Testing the Sample Application: Incompatibility Issues

Figures 9.20 and 9.21 in Chapter 9, "User Interface Tests," illustrate an incompatibility issue between two browsers. This example demonstrates that the same HTML page served by a Web server can be interpreted or formatted very differently by different browsers.

Distributed Server Configurations

On the macrolevel, a Web system may work correctly with some distributed server configurations while not working correctly with others. Figures 14.2 and 14.3 illustrate two possible distributed server configurations that comprise identical server-software components. Any errors generated by altering server distribution should be classified as configuration errors.

A typical system under test may utilize any of the following:

- Application servers
- Database servers
- E-mail servers
- Web servers
- Proxy servers

Client-Side Issues

The client side of Web systems may be responsible for numerous types of compatibility and configuration issues. To determine which client-side tests a Web application requires, identify the components that make up the client side of the Web application.

The system under test may include the following client-side components:

Possible OSs

- Windows (95, 98, 2000, NT)
- Various flavors of Unix
- Macintosh
- Linux
- Palm OS, CE, and other mobile-based devices

Communication components

- Browser
- E-mail
- Chat
- FTP

Client-side UI components

- ActiveX
- Java applets

Plug-ins

- QuickTime
- RealPlayer
- Flash
- Windows Media Player

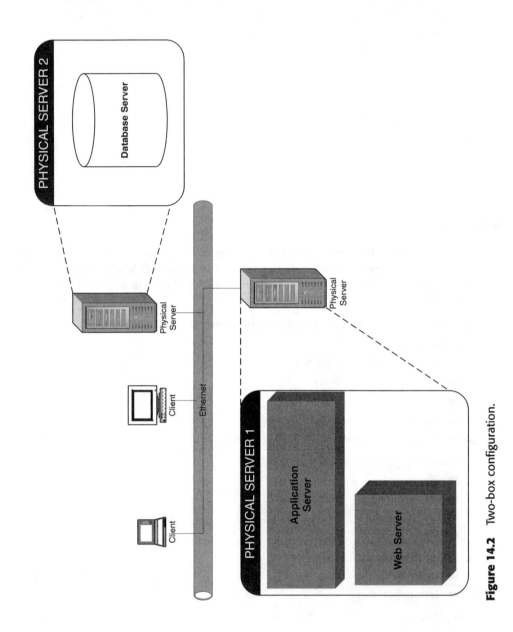

Figure 14.2 Two-box configuration.

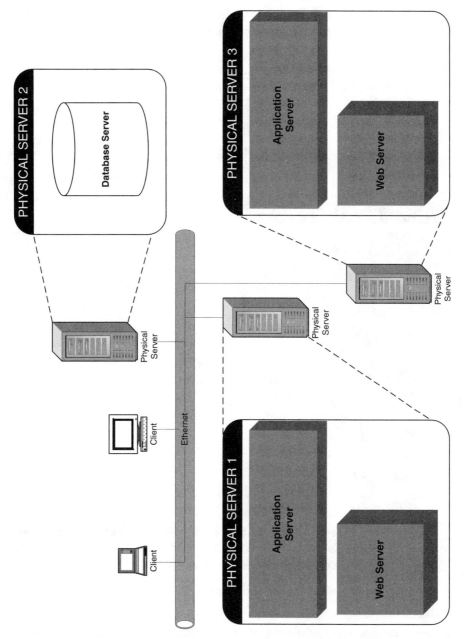

Figure 14.3 Three-box configuration.

Testing the Sample Application

Configuration may occur at any point within a Web system: client, server, or network. Here is an example that involves distributed server configurations. Figures 14.4 and 14.5 show two possible physical server configurations: *one-box* and *two-box* configuration.

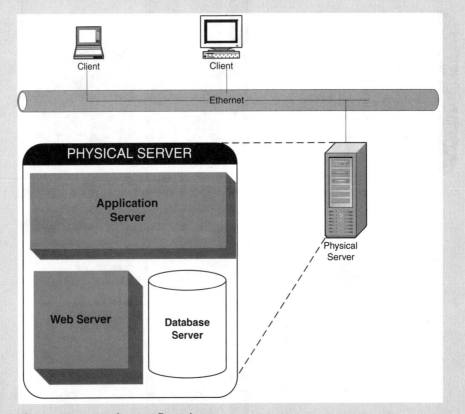

Figure 14.4   One-box configuration.

The application under test has some charting capabilities that enable a user to generate metrics reports, such as bar charts and line charts. When a user requests a metrics report, the application server pseudocode runs as follows:

1. Connect to the database server and run the query.

2. Write the query result to a file name c:\temp\chart.val

3. Execute the chart Java Applet. Read from c:\temp\chart.val and use the data to draw a graph.

4. Send the Java applet to the browser.

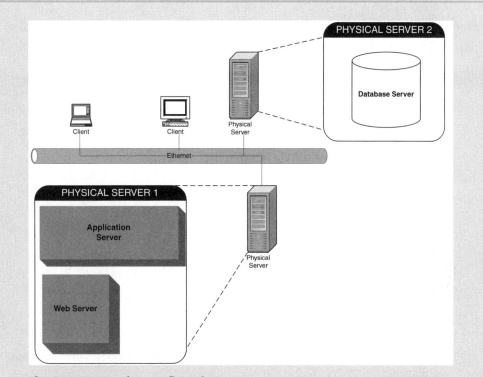

Figure 14.5 Two-box configuration.

During testing for this application, it's discovered that the charting feature worked on one of the preceding configurations, but not the other. After further investigation, we learned that the problem only occurred in the two-box configuration. After examining the code, we realized that the problem is in steps 2 and 3. In step 2, the query result is written to c:\temp\chart.val of the database server local drive. In step 3, the Chart Java applet is running on the application server that is not in the same box with the database server. When it attempts to open the file c:\temp\chart.val on the application server local drive, the file is not there. Does it mean that we read the code every time we come across an error? No, we can leave the debugging work for the developers. The key is we need to clearly identify which server configurations are problematic and include such information in bug reports. It's also recommended to have a cursory suite of test cases to be executed on all distributed configurations that are supported by the application server under test to ensure that configuration-specific errors are uncovered.

Connectivity

- Dial-up
- Leased line
- ISDN
- DSL

Hardware

- Manufacturer
- CPU
- RAM
- Graphic display card
- Video capture card
- Sound card
- CD-ROM drive
- Monitor
- Printer device
- Input device (mouse, tablet, joystick, etc.)
- Network card, modem card

Client-side compatibility differences may additionally include the following:

- Input/output device drivers (mouse, sound, graphics display, video, memory manager)
- Extensions running in the background
- Applications that provide input to the application under test, such as a word processor that creates files or a graphics program that creates images that the application is expected to use
- Applications running concurrently
- Network software
- Online services

Web Browsers

Web browsers are the central client-side component of most Web applications. A browser acts as an application shell in which a Web application runs. The behavior of different browser brands can vary, as can their support for Java commands, implementation of security settings, and other features. Each browser (and its relative release versions) may also have one or more interpreters—which may not be compatible with one another.

One of the primary challenges of browser testing is that there are more browser versions in use today than can feasibly be managed in functionality testing. The myriad browser settings that are available within each browser complicate things further. It is a good idea to include browser and browser settings testing in the compatibility test phase, rather than in the functionality test phase.

The number of browsers that are available in the marketplace increases at a rapid rate. For a list of browsers and the technologies that they support, check out www.browsers.com and http://websnapshot.mycomputer.com/browsers.html.

It is a good idea for the test team to meet with project management and developers to determine which browsers and browser settings will be included in test matrices. If the versions of supported browsers are not identified, test for compatibility with at least the two most recent releases of all supported browsers.

As with all software, browser patches should be thoroughly tested. In Internet time, people are shipping now and patching later—*patches* are nothing more than bug fixes. Without current patches, software may include buggy components.

Create a Web compatibility matrix to test Web-based applications for compatibility issues related to scripting, Java applets, ActiveX controls, style sheets, HTML, and plug-ins. The goal of such tests is to hunt down browser configuration errors. Web application user interfaces (UIs) are heavily dependent on browser settings. The assigned-size values of tables, cells, fonts, and other elements can potentially distort a UI and/or printed reports.

Web applications should be tested under a combination of various browser settings:

- General settings
- Connection settings
- Security settings (including ActiveX controls, plug-ins, Java, scripting, downloads, user authentication, etc.)
- Content settings
- Programs settings
- Other advanced settings (including browsing options, multimedia options, Java VM options, printing options, and HTTP options)

Testing the Sample Application: Browser Settings

The sample application requires an ActiveX control to be downloaded for the charting feature to work. The browser security setting for ActiveX control is set to High. In this case, it means only signed ActiveX control (a control that comes from a traceable and trustworthy source) is allowed for downloading.

Testing with this security setting, we discover that the charting feature no longer works, because the ActiveX we use is unsigned. To support users that will require this particular security setting to High, we need to have the ActiveX control registered as a signed control. (For more information on getting control registered, see Chapter 15, "Web Security Concerns.")

Testing the Sample Application: Browser Incompatibility

Let's look at another example of a compatibility difference between Microsoft Internet Explorer and Netscape Navigator.

- The home directory path for the Web server on the host myserver is mapped to: C:\INETPUB\WWWROOT\

- A file name (mychart.jar) is stored at C:\INETPUB\WWWROOT\MYAPP\BIN

- The application session path (relative path) is pointing to C:\INETPUB\WWWROOT\MYAPP\BIN, and a file is requested from .\LIB.

- When a page is requested from http://myserver/, data will be pulled from C:\INETPUB\WWWROOT\

Using Internet Explorer version 4.x, the Web server looks for the file in C:\INETPUB\WWWROOT\MYAPP\BIN\LIB because the browser relies on relative paths. This is the intended behavior and the file will be found; this means that the application will work as expected using Internet Explorer 4.x.

Instead, if Netscape Navigator version 4.x (a browser that doesn't like .\) is used, the Web server defaults to C:\INETPUB\WWWROOT\LIB and tries to look for mychart.jar from there. This is a problem for this particular application because the file (mychart.jar) will not be found there—so the current implementation for this feature will not work with Netscape Navigator. This is not to say that Internet Explorer is better than Netscape Navigator; it simply means that there are incompatibility issues between browsers—and that the code should not assume that relative paths work for all browsers. More important, it suggests that when you experience an error in one environment, the same error may *not* appear in a different environment.

Testing Considerations

It is essential that the system under test be analyzed against the target-user installed base.

- What browsers will the users have?
- What related applications will the users have?
- What hardware will the users have?
- What types of Internet connections will the users have?

Issues involved in server configuration testing fall into the following categories:

- Distributed server configuration
- Server administration and configuration
- Software compatibility
- Hardware compatibility

- Server software running on top of the OS (IIS, SQL)
- Differences between database types (SQL, Oracle, Informix, Sybase, etc.) and versions (Oracle 7.x versus Oracle 8.x)
- Proxy servers
- Server OSs (Unix, Mac, PC)
- OS/browser combination
- Hubs
- Network cards
- TCP/IP stack

Commercial-off-the-shelf products, such as the sample application, require the following testing:

- Server-software configuration tests
- Hardware configuration tests
- Connection configuration tests
- Stack configuration tests

Compatibility testing considerations include the following:

- *Compatibility issues* involve the swapping of comparable elements within a properly configured system.
- Test only with supported configurations. Focus on how the application performs with alternate hardware and software components.
- Test multiple releases of supported components.

Software compatibility includes differences in the following:

- Operating system versions
- Input/output device drivers (mouse, sound, graphic display, video, memory manager)
- Extensions running in the background
- Applications running concurrently with tested application
- Network software supported by the tested application
- Online service supported by the tested application
- Firewall configuration
- Effects of the client living behind a proxy

Installation considerations include the following:

- *Server installation compatibility tests* look for system-specific problems that have not been uncovered during TOFT or installation functionality tests—not to confirm that the install functions as prescribed. See Chapter 13, "Installation Tests," for more detail regarding installation testing. The same is applicable to client installs, which should already have been functionality tested. *Client installation compatibility tests* evaluate the client installation over a variety of systems to see if there are any reboot problems or browser-specific issues.

- Server installation compatibility tests verify that the following installation functions operate correctly across all target OSs and possible system architectures:

  - Necessary directories are created in the proper locations.

  - System files—such as DLL files—are copied to the correct directories.

  - System files—such as registry keys—are modified as appropriate.

  - Error conditions are detected and handled gracefully.

  - Uninstall program removes all installed files and restores the operating environment to its original state.

Browser testing considerations include the following:

- The behavior of different browser brands can vary, as can their support for Java commands, implementation of security settings, and other features. Each browser (and its relative release versions) may also have one or more interpreters—which may not be compatible with one another. Browser testing should be thorough, and performed early in the functionality testing phase, so that as many browser-related bugs as possible can be identified early on.

- Does the application under test utilize a media player? Does the player (for example, QuickTime) need to be preinstalled with the application?

- Are ActiveX controls, Java scripts, or other scripting downloaded by the application?

- Create a *Web compatibility matrix* to test your Web-based applications for incompatibility issues related to scripting, Java applets, ActiveX controls, style sheets, HTML, and plug-ins.

Following are some other browser testing issues that may require attention:

- *Active desktop.* Different versions of Internet Explorer should be tested both with and without the use of the active desktop.

- *Encryption.* 40- versus 128-bit.

- Instant messaging.

- *Style sheets.* Not all browsers support style sheets. Of those browsers that do support style sheets, many do not necessarily support full style sheet implementation. For more information on cascading style sheets, visit the World Wide Web Consortium's site at www.w3.org/style/css/#browsers, or visit the following URL to access a style sheet compatibility chart: www.webreview.com/guides/style/mastergrid.html.

For browser statistics and information on which browsers support which technologies, visit www.browsers.com and http://websnapshot.mycomputer.com/browsers .html. Note that the functionality issues associated with browser technologies such as cascading style sheets, JavaScript, dynamic HTML, tables, links, and frames are discussed at length in Chapter 9, "User Interface Tests."

Bibliography

Kaner, Cem, et al. *Testing Computer Software,* second edition. New York: John Wiley & Sons, 1999.

LogiGear Corporation. *QA Training Handbook: Testing Web Applications.* Foster City, CA: LogiGear Corporation, 2000.

LogiGear Corporation. *QA Training Handbook: Testing Windows Desktop and Server-Based Applications.* Foster City, CA: LogiGear Corporation, 2000.

LogiGear Corporation. *QA Training Handbook: Testing Computer Software.* Foster City, CA: LogiGear Corporation, 2000.

CHAPTER 15

Web Security Concerns

Why Read This Chapter?

Hackers break into [your company name here] e-commerce site! This will not be your favorite headline. Can this be prevented? Whose responsibility is it? Attempting to answer these questions could be a challenge for a tester as well as the organization as a whole.

Security issues are of the highest concern to many company executives. Despite this fact, security testing is often the least understood and least well-defined test type. Security testing is a broad effort that requires domains of expertise beyond traditional software testing. This chapter contains a discussion of security issues and outlines how testing roles fit in the big picture of security testing. It also discusses security-related testing as it's applied to testing Web-based applications.

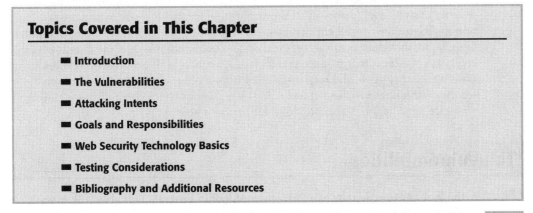

Topics Covered in This Chapter

- Introduction
- The Vulnerabilities
- Attacking Intents
- Goals and Responsibilities
- Web Security Technology Basics
- Testing Considerations
- Bibliography and Additional Resources

Introduction

For application producers and users to feel confident in a Web-based system, they must have a reasonable level of comfort that a system is secure. However, there is no 100 percent secure Web-based system! Web systems include too many variables to absolutely remove all of their vulnerabilities. Software is one of the key components in the Web system. Software can never be bug-free, because it's impossible for us to completely test the system. Bugs in software open up the vulnerability of the Web system. In addition, every time a new security tool comes out, many other tools follow with the sole purpose to defeat it. So, what's with the paranoia? Is there a point in trying to go after something that can't be done perfectly?

Security effort is an ongoing process of change, test, and improvement. Because it's impossible to have a perfectly secure system, the goal is to figure out the level of protection that is secure enough for an organization's needs. "Good enough," as narrowly defined, means that the security solutions will cost significantly less than the damage caused by a security breach. At the same time, the ideal solutions are ones that deter persistent intruders by making penetrating the system so difficult and time-consuming that it's not worthwhile as a reward even when their efforts succeed.

Security trade-offs consist of compromises between security and functionality/usability. If the security of the system is too rigid, it will be difficult to use the system or to get any work done effectively. If the security is too primitive, then the system is vulnerable and there is potential for intrusions.

Web security testing in a traditional sense means testing the effectiveness of the overall Web system security defenses. It requires a combination of knowledge in security technologies, network technologies, programming, and, often times, some real-world experience in penetrating security of network systems. This type of knowledge is normally beyond the reach of a software tester. It's a good idea, however, for us as testers to understand the scope of security issues better so we understand what tasks need to be done by ourselves and what other tasks should be done by other experts. In this discussion, my assumption is that software testers are responsible for testing the systems to uncover functionality, interoperability, configuration and compatibility errors as they are related to security implementation, and potential problems introduced by security design flaws (primarily at the application level). Software testers are not responsible for the overall effectiveness of Web security defenses. With that in mind, this chapter introduces various types of system vulnerabilities and the intents of several types of attacks to introduce you to security concerns. It progresses with discussions on security goals and responsibilities. It then offers an introduction to Web security technologies, followed by testing examples and considerations. Additional reference information is also provided for further research and reading.

The Vulnerabilities

In the Web environment or network environment in general, a security hole is an exposure on the hardware or software that allows unauthorized users to gain increasing access privilege without going through the normal authorization process to obtain such a level of access. Hackers attack the Web system by using numerous techniques to exploit various security holes in each component of the system. Some of the techniques are designed to allow unauthorized users to gain access to Web system resources or to disallow authorized users to access resources. Others are designed to create inconvenience and service degradation or to destroy data. Following are some of the common vulnerabilities.

Software Bugs

Many security vulnerabilities are the result of bugs in programs such as Web browsers and Web servers. These bugs, unfortunately, either went undetected during the testing process or were side effects of fixes, which, in turn, open up security holes. Some are easier to exploit than others. One of the commonly mentioned bugs is Buffer Overflow, which allows malicious code to be executed on the client machine. For example, entering a URL into a browser that is much longer than the buffer size allocated for a URL will cause a memory overwrite (buffer overflow) error if the browser does not have error detection code to validate the length of the input URL. A seasoned hacker can cleverly exploit this bug by writing a long URL with code to be executed that can cause a browser to crash or to alter its security settings (from High to Low) or, at worst, to corrupt user data.

As these bugs are discovered, software vendors will quickly design and apply fixes. However, as we already know, there is no such thing as bug-free software. Therefore, these programs will never be free of security vulnerabilities.

Java Script (and Other Scripting Languages)

Java script security holes often involve compromising a user's privacy or capturing a user's data. For example, a malicious script can be attached to a request you send to a Web server, such as a URL or a database query, while you are navigating to a link in a Web page from an untrusted site. When the Web server responds to your request, the unwanted script tags along. The malicious script is now on your browser. It is possible that confidential information such as your user ID and password will be captured and sent off to some place (a server on the Internet) that you would not know if the script were designed to do so.

Java

Although the Java security model is to restrict the behavior of applets or applications to a set of safe actions, it is possible to have malicious instruction sets in Java code embedded in HyperText Markup Language (HTML) pages. For example, a Java application can contain instructions to delete files or reformat a local drive. If a Java application is allowed to be downloaded and executed, the user is exposed with this type of attack. This illustrates one of several security holes caused by bugs in Java implementation. Certainly, many of the bugs in Java implementation have been detected and fixed. Undoubtedly, many others are still unexposed, and new ones keep appearing that can potentially compromise user security.

ActiveX

The key issue with ActiveX controls is that they are distributed as executable binaries and allowed to have functionality similar to an application that is run on a local drive. It means that a malicious control can easily delete files on a local drive or transmit the user's confidential information to an unknown server on the Internet.

The ActiveX security model is very different from Java. ActiveX has no restriction on what a control can do. Instead, each control can be digitally signed by its author. This model relies on the user to control security by configuring the browser settings. For example, a browser can be configured to allow download-signed ActiveX controls only. One potential problem is the signed control might be certified by an untrustworthy certifying authority. In such a case, how comfortable are you executing that control on your system?

Cookies

A *cookie* is data that are created and left on the client browser memory or machine to provide certain information about the client or user every time the Web server receives a request from the client. In this model, the user is the target and only the Web server that sends or creates the cookie can understand the cookie information. Cookies allow a client to maintain information about itself between HyperText Transfer Protocol (HTTP) requests. The information could be from simple preferences such as display preferences and last visited page, to personal information such as user ID and password, snail mail or e-mail address information. That's right! It means that if your cookie information is exposed to other Web applications or Web sites, others can use the information to do things such as accessing your Web-based mail account. For example, a recent (May 2000) security alert from Peacefire.Org reports that cookies that have been set in Internet Explorer can be read by any third-party Web site outside of the domain that set the cookie. One of the implications is intercepting a cookie set by a free Web-based e-mail site that uses cookies for authentication, the operator of a malicious Web site could break into a visitor's free mail account, such as a HotMail or YahooMail account, and read the contents of his or her Inbox. By the way, this bug has been fixed by Microsoft. For more information on this particular security alert, go to www.peacefire.org/security/iecookies/. For more information on cookies, go to www.cookiecentral.com. From the user's perspective, there are two classes of concern regarding using cookies: (1) Malicious Web sites can capture cookie information and use it in a way that may harm the user, and (2) there are privacy concerns of being tracked while using the Web.

Spoofing

Spoofing is the act of deceiving by assuming a different identity for the purpose of stealing information (such as intercepting a buyer-merchant transaction and pretending to be a merchant to steal a credit card number) or gaining access to unauthorized resources. There are many things that one can spoof: e-mail spoofing to pretend as if an e-mail is sent from someone else, Internet Protocol (IP) spoofing to pretend as if data are coming from a trusted machine, Web page spoofing to pretend as if the Web is coming from the trusted source, and so on.

Virus and Worm

A *virus*, as most of us are familiar with, is a computer program that is designed to cause unexpected events or activities, from displaying playful messages to damaging actions such as erasing data on your hard disk. A computer transmits or receives a virus by interacting with other computers, usually by sending e-mail messages, attachments in e-mail messages, moving files, or downloading files. When an infected program or the virus itself (as a program) is executed, the virus code is loaded and run often with two primary objectives: (1) Do whatever it's designed to do (erase your hard disk) and (2) affect other programs by appending itself to those programs so it can then be propagated. A *worm* is similar to a virus. One difference between a worm and a virus is that a worm can be self-propagating by sending a copy of itself to other machines (via e-mail, for example).

Denial-of-Service Attacks

Denial-of-service attacks involve bombarding servers with so many bogus requests or e-mail messages that the servers are not able to process any legitimate requests that come in. The attacks commonly involve hackers secretly placing software agents on servers that are not related to the target server. A master command activates the agents and identifies the target; the full-bandwidth capacity of the servers hosting the agents is then unleashed upon the target server. Denial-of-service agents are a challenge to find because they are placed via backdoor methods. For example, an attack could be initiated from a cheap computer connected through a pay telephone—in which case the attacker might never be tracked down. The attacks might also be initiated from foreign countries where prosecution might be more difficult or impossible.

A high-profile example that illustrates the need for better security measures across the Internet is the 3-day assault that was waged against a number of prominent Web sites beginning February 7, 2000. Some of the Internet's biggest sites (Yahoo!, Amazon .com, E*Trade, buy.com, CNN, eBay, and ZDNet) were either temporarily shut down or seriously impaired by a series of denial-of-service attacks.

Yahoo! was bombarded with server requests from about 50 different IP addresses (at rates of up to 1 gigabyte per second!). It was a surprise to many that Yahoo!'s servers proved to be vulnerable to attack. Many experts speculate that the attacks were intended to demonstrate the lack of security measures that are in operation at most content and e-commerce Web sites. It does not appear that the attacks resulted in its instigators gaining access to confidential user information or financial gain other than media exposure.

Physical Attacks

Low-tech intruders can always attack by rummaging through garbage cans to look for confidential information such as a list of user IDs and passwords, breaking into a facility to steal a computer to get to the data on the hard disk of that computer, or simply sitting in front of an already-logged-in computer while the owner is on break to access unauthorized resources.

Attacking Intents

Depending on the magnitude of a security hole, it can allow varying degrees of exposure. A security hole could allow anything from service disruption due to a denial-of-service attack to invalid full access from a remote host. Depending on the hacker, each attack is designed with a certain intent. Some of the common intents include the following:

To steal.   This can be stealing money by capturing credit card numbers or spoofing certain users to conduct financial transactions such as money transferring. It can mean stealing confidential data such as proprietary information, business plan and financial information, or private e-mail communication. Also, it can mean stealing intellectual property, including downloading software applications, source code, or product design information.

To gain information.   This means capturing user data such as address information, computer configuration information, or purchasing patterns for marketing and sales purposes or other financial gains.

To disrupt activities.   Attacks such as denial of service or buffer overflow are often designed to knock the victim's server(s) out of commission with the intent to disrupt or degrade the level of service, and perhaps to get media exposure in the process.

To embarrass.   Through spoofing or other attack methods, hackers may alter the content of a Web site with their own content. This type of attack is normally designed to embarrass the owner or operator of the site.

Goals and Responsibilities

Several common goals of Web system security measures—and therefore their associated testing considerations—follow.

These following goals are particularly appropriate for e-commerce systems:

- Interactions and transactions between buyers and your company's system should be confidential.
- Data integrity should be preserved.
- Buyers and your company's system should be able to verify each other's identities (at least, electronically).

- Transaction records should be in a form that can withstand scrutiny in a court of law.

As a producer of Web-based systems, your company should be protected from the following:

- Exposing private network access to unauthorized external and internal intruders
- Losing confidential data and proprietary technology through hacking activities
- Losing data due to hardware and software errors, natural disasters, and theft

Although many of the security protection measures via browser settings on the client side are designed to protect users, the users do take on the responsibility to protect themselves from vulnerabilities by properly controlling these settings. Users of Web-based systems can be protected from the following:

- Exposure to virus attacks via active contents, plug-ins, cabinet files (.CAB), executables (.EXEs), DLLs, ActiveX controls, and other components
- Exposure to offensive contents
- Exposure of private information to third parties, either in violation of the Web site's stated policy or as an unauthorized data capturing by a third party that is independent of the intent of the Web site owner

Often, there are numerous people within an organization who influence the security concerns and operational infrastructure; these individuals make up an organization's *security team*. A security team may include the following:

- Policy makers who define security requirements that enhance user and producer confidence in system security defenses.
- Network administrators who design and implement security measures to provide security at the operational level.
- Software developers who design and implement security defenses at the application level (to meet security requirements).
- Software testers who are responsible for testing the systems to uncover functionality, interoperability, configuration and compatibility errors as they are related to security implementation (primarily at the application level and perhaps at the operational level as well), and discovering potential problems introduced by security design flaws.
- Security experts and consultants who help test and maintain your security programs as well as handle security breach. Often, this group of people consists of reformed hackers for hire. As some are ex-hackers, they developed their domain of expertise through practices over the years. They are responsible for conducting penetration testing (tests designed to evaluate the effectiveness of Web system defenses through the use of a combination of attack tools, security and hacking expertise, and IT knowledge) prior to the deployment of system as well as on an ongoing basis. Unless you have someone in your organization who is an expert in or designated to handle penetration testing, it's not expected that a typical software tester or developer would have this responsibility.

Web Security Technology Basics

The most common security technologies that are employed for Web-based systems follow.

Encryption.   Ensures that confidential textual information transmitted over the Internet (user IDs, passwords, credit card numbers, etc.) is protected (from sniffing devices, for example). Encryption does not prevent the theft of information; it simply ensures that information cannot be read by anyone other than its intended recipient.

Authentication.   Verifies the identify of clients and servers so that sensitive information is not mistakenly sent to the wrong people (possibly criminals) and that resources on private networks cannot be accessed by intruders.

Digital certificates.   Verify the identity of people and organizations for the purpose of public/private key encryption and decryption.

Firewalls.   Protects private networks and intranets from unauthorized access and data transmission via the Internet.

Authorization.   Verifies the person performing the given task has the privilege granted to do so.

Cryptography

Cryptography is the science of encoding messages so that they cannot be read by anyone other than their intended recipients. Public and private key cryptography, as illustrated in Figure 15.1, is a method of securely transmitting messages between parties by using two types of keys, which are strings of numbers used to decode encrypted messages. As the names imply, *public keys* are published freely, whereas *private keys* are protected from public access. For example, Party A might send one of many public keys to Party B in anticipation of Party B transmitting a confidential message. Party B could use the public key sent by Party A to encrypt a message that is sent back to Party A. In theory, no one intercepting the message could decrypt the message because they would not have access to Party A's private key.

Digital certificates are a form of cryptography. They link the identity of certificate owners to public and private keys that are used for encryption and decryption. They are also used to verify the purported identity of senders and recipients.

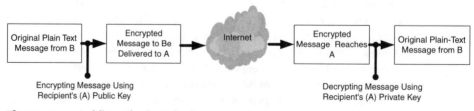

Figure 15.1   Public and private key cryptography.

Digital certificates should, at a minimum, contain the following information:

■ Owner's public key

■ Owner's name

■ Certificate expiration date

■ Certificate serial number

■ Name of the authority that issued the certificate

■ Digital signature of the authority that issued the certificate

Certificates may be obtained from certificate authorities (CAs) such as VeriSign (www.verisign.com). Available certificate types include site certificates, publisher certificates, and personal certificates. Personal certificates come in two classes. *Class 1 certificates* cover e-mail verification. *Class 2 certificates* cover standard consumer verification. Certificate authorities should provide the following functions:

■ Technology that ensures messaging security

■ Logistic infrastructure, such as secure facilities, IS, and customer support staff

■ Management infrastructure to monitor subscriber activities and handle disputes

Pretty Good Privacy

Pretty good privacy (PGP), using a variation of the public key system, is a program that allows files and e-mail messages to be encrypted and decrypted. Originally developed by Philip R. Zimmermann, PGP today is available both as freeware and in a commercial version, and it has become a widely accepted standard for e-mail security by individuals as well as corporations. For more information, downloading, or purchasing a commercial version, go to www.pgpi.com/ and www.nai.com.

Secure Multipurpose Internet Mail Extensions (S/MIME)

Secure Multipurpose Internet Mail Extensions (S/MIME), using the RSA (RSA Security, Inc.) encryption system, is a method that allows sending secured e-mail messages over the Internet. Both latest versions of the Microsoft and Netscape Web browsers have S/MIME included. RSA has proposed S/MIME as a standard to the Internet Engineering Task Force. For more information, go to www.rsasecurity.com/standards/smime/faq.html.

Security Protocols

Several commonly supported security protocols include *Secure Sockets Layer* (SSL), which operates at the session layer; *Secure-enhanced Hypertext Transport Protocol* (S-HTTP), which operates at the application layer; and *IP Security* (IPSec), which operates at the network or IP layer. IP Security is usually implemented in routers and switches. Figure 15.2 shows the supported security protocols.

For more information on S-HTTP, see the S-HTTP Request for Comments (RFC) draft that has been submitted to the Internet Engineering Task Force for consideration as a standard. RFC Internet draft 2660 describes S-HTTP in detail: www.ietf.org/rfc/rfc2660.txt.

Secure Sockets Layer is the security protocol that is most commonly supported by commercial Web browsers and servers. The SSL protocol provides the following; Figure 15.3 shows an example of the Secure Sockets Layer security protocol.

- Private client-server communication using encryption
- Data integrity for client-server communication via verification of contents within exchanged messages—ensuring that messages have not been altered or tampered with during transmission
- Client-server authentication via the exchange of digital certificate

Other supported security protocols that are comparable with SSL include Transport Layer Security (TLS) and Microsoft Private Communication Technology (PCT).

The SSL security protocol support is a two-sided operation—both client and server sides must be configured:

- A certificate with public/private keys must be obtained from a CA and installed on the *server side*.
- The Web server must support security protocols such as SSL or PCT.
- Support for protocols such as SSL and PCT must be enabled on the *client side*.
- HTTPs must be properly encoded in HTML pages to enable secure communication.

If the application under test will support both HTTP and HTTPS, then certificates will be required for the server and proper setup needs to be done for HTTPS communication on both server and client sides. If the HTTPS server is behind the firewall, port 443 should also be open for HTTPS traffic between client and server.

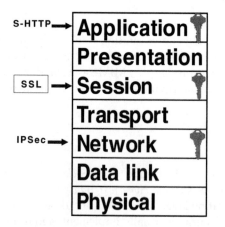

Figure 15.2 Security protocols.

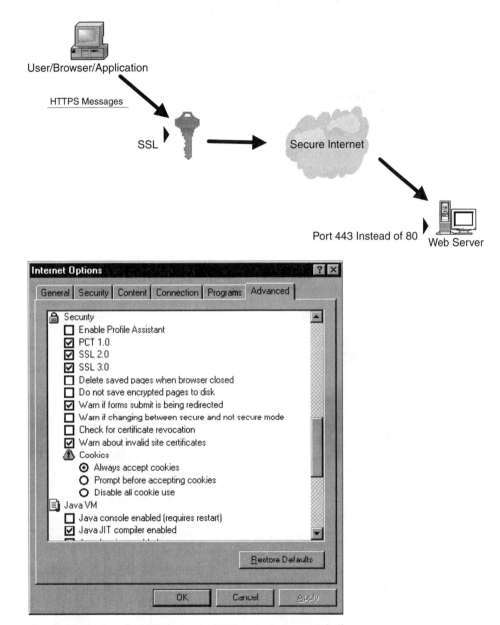

Figure 15.3 Secure Sockets Layer (SSL) security protocol.

Firewalls

Firewalls are shields that protect private networks from the Internet. They prevent unauthorized users from accessing confidential information, using network resources, and damaging system hardware—while allowing authorized users access to the resources they require. Firewalls are combinations of hardware and software—

making use of routers, servers, and software to shield networks from exposure to the Internet. There are two types of firewalls: *packet-filtering* firewalls (routers) and *proxy-based* firewalls (gateways). See Figure 15.4 for an example of a firewall.

Packet-Screening Firewalls (Routers)

The simplest firewalls block information by screening incoming packets. Packet filtering, typically implemented in routers, provides basic network security features at the IP level. Router tables can be configured to drop or permit packets based on communication protocols, application port numbers, and destination/source IP addresses. Routers inspect the headers of packets to determine where they are coming from, where they are going, and the protocol that is being used to send the data; routers can then block certain packets based on this information. Network administrators determine which types of information are allowed to pass through firewalls.

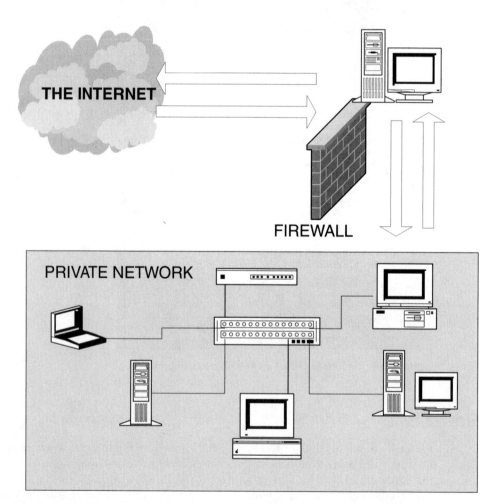

Figure 15.4 Firewall.

Proxy-Based Firewalls (Gateways)

Proxy servers are a more secure firewall technique than packet filtering. Proxy servers are software that runs on host computers in the perimeter of a firewall. Because proxy servers are located on perimeter networks, they are not part of corporate networks themselves. Proxy servers are designed to be a private network's only connection to the Internet. Because it is only the proxy server that interacts with the Internet—as opposed to many client computers and servers—security is easier to maintain. Proxy servers are also useful for logging traffic that passes between a network and the Internet.

As shown in Figure 15.5, routers can be used in combination with proxy servers to add an additional level of network protection; a router can take over in the event that a proxy server fails.

DMZ

A *DMZ* is a small network or a host sitting between a company's private network and the outside public network such as the Internet. It prevents outside users from

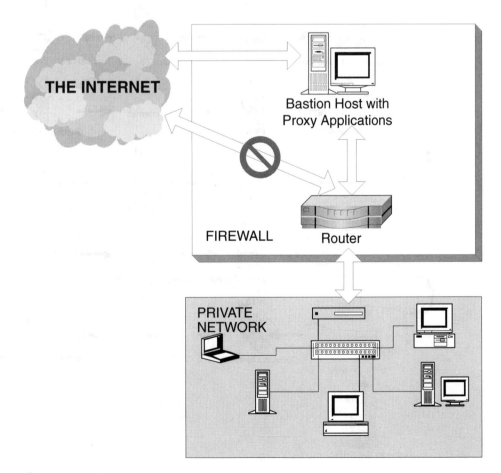

Figure 15.5 Proxy servers.

getting direct access to any server or host on a company private network. Normally, a DMZ host receives requests from users within the private network for access to Web sites or other data on the Internet. It will then create sessions for these requests on the Internet. However, the DMZ host is not able to initiate a session back into the private network. As to outside users on the Internet, they can only access a DMZ host or network. The DMZ host, typically, also contains the company's Web servers and FTP servers so the data can be served to the outside world. However, the DMZ provides access to no hosts within the private network because it cannot initiate any inward connections. In the event that the DMZ network is compromised, the data in those servers is compromised. Nevertheless, the private network will not be exposed.

An E-commerce Example

Figure 15.6 tracks a typical e-commerce transaction: from the client, to the vendor's servers, to the bank, and back to the client. Along the way, numerous databases, fire-

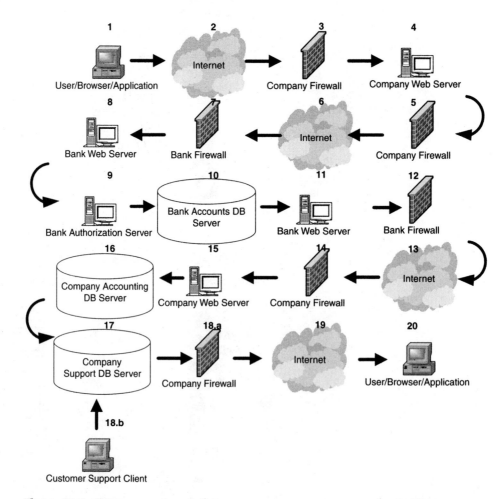

Figure 15.6 E-commerce transaction.

walls, and open Internet transmissions transpire. Note that steps 7 through 12 (detailed in the following list) occur beyond the bank's firewalls, and are therefore not accessible for testing.

1. User browses an e-commerce site and purchases a product by entering personal information and credit card data. Transaction is submitted.

2. User-submitted data are sent from the client to an e-commerce company Web server via the Internet (the public network).

3. When the submitted data hit the company firewall, the firewall examines the packet headers to determine the type of protocol used (e.g., HTTP, HTTPS, FTP, etc.). Depending on the firewall's configuration, the firewall might only allow packets that meet its security criteria (e.g., allowing only packets using HTTP and HTTPS and disallowing FINGER and FTP).

4. The company Web server receives, examines, and disassembles the packets into the appropriate data forms. Based on the information (data, function calls, redirection, etc.), the Web server will pass data to other processes such as ISAPI DLL, CGI, ASP programs, Java servlet, SQL stored procedures, and so forth. The verification server gets called by the Web server, receives user data for verification, and responds to the bank server with results. The Web server then redirects the data to the bank Web server for authorization.

5. Redirected data hit the company firewall. The firewall examines the packet header to determine if it should allow the data to pass through (e.g., the destination URL is a trusted URL and therefore the data are allowed to pass through).

6. Company-submitted data are sent to the bank via the Internet.

7. (Bank network) The bank's firewall examines the packet headers to determine the type of protocol used. Depending on the firewall's configuration, the firewall may or may not allow the packets to proceed.

8. (Bank network) The bank's Web server receives, examines, and disassembles the packets into appropriate data form. Based on the information (data, function calls, redirection, etc.), the Web server passes data to other processes such as ISAPI DLL, CGI, ASP programs, Java servlet, SQL stored procedures, and so on.

9. (Bank network) The authorization server gets called by the Web server, receives user data for authorizing the transaction (e.g., determining whether the account is valid by checking the address and user account name or determining whether the transaction amount is within the balance limit).

10. (Bank network) Assuming that the transaction is authorized, the user and merchant account databases are updated with appropriate debit and credit information.

11. (Bank network) Authorization information is sent from the bank Web server back to the company Web server.

12. (Bank network) The bank's firewall examines the packet headers to determine if they should be allowed to pass through.

13. Bank-submitted data are sent to the company Web server via the Internet.

14. The company firewall again examines the packet headers to determine the type of protocol used and whether the packets should be allowed to pass through.

15. The company Web server receives, examines, and disassembles the packets into the appropriate data forms. Based on the information, the Web server may pass data to other processes.

16. The Web server calls the company accounting database server. The accounting database is updated.

17. The company customer-support database is updated.

18.a. Data hit the company firewall. The firewall examines the packet headers to determine if the packets should be allowed to pass through.

18.b. Customer support/fulfillment staff access database for order-processing information.

19. Confirmation data are delivered to the user via the Internet.

20. User receives confirmation of purchase transaction.

First, we will use the diagram illustrated in Figure 15.6 to highlight all areas of the software that will be tested at each point and areas that we won't have control over. In this scenario, testing should focus on points 3 and 5 initially, and then advance to the testing of points 14 and 18.a (assuming that points 7 through 12 are processes that happen at the bank and that are treated as black-box activities that are beyond the reach of testing).

Testing should begin with a no-firewall environment, so that functionality-specific issues can be ironed out before firewall issues are explored. Issues to look for include application-specific errors that result from firewall software, configuration, and security defenses that cause packet dropping or splitting. For example, suppose your application will reply on port 25 to talk to the STMP server using SMTP protocol to support an e-mail notification feature. If your firewall is blocking out port 25, then the e-mail notification feature will fail. As another example, suppose your application will be deployed within an environment that uses DMZ. Your system is designed to have a Web and application servers separated from the database server. If you want the Web servers in DMZ but the database server inside the private network, the system will fail because the Web server cannot initiate requests to the database server that lives behind the private network.

Penetration Testing

Penetration testing evaluates the effectiveness of network system defenses. Penetration testing involves a series of tests that require a combination of attack tools, security expertise, and information technology (IT) knowledge. Penetration testing is an involved process that exceeds the skills and resources of many organizations. This type of testing is *not* normally done by software testers. Unless there is an in-house expert, it's common practice to bring in external expertise to help with this testing effort. Some issues to consider during penetration testing include the following:

- Penetration testing should be conducted before systems go live.

- Penetration testing must continue on a live system, particularly when any part of the system changes.

- Penetration testing activities often mimic the actions of real-life attackers.

- Penetration testing should consider the vulnerabilities of delivered data and intellectual property. For example, how easily might hackers be able to decrypt encrypted data, such as e-commerce transactions, or how easily might hackers be able to reverse-engineer a COTS application, and thereby steal proprietary source code?

- Have penetration testing requirements been established?

- Given the scope and knowledge that is required for penetration testing of a system, how can effective testing be implemented?

- Is there a penetration test plan with identified resources?

- Does the testing staff have the required time and skill to effectively run penetration testing? Can others within the organization help? If not, who will be responsible? Can the testing be outsourced?

- How effective are system router and firewall defenses?

- How easily might intruders be able to gain access to server or client hosts on a network?

- What are the open and closed ports on a server? If an intruder connects to the open ports, how far in the network system could they go? Given these vulnerabilities, what are the worst possible risks the system faces?

- Testing should be done from outside the network perimeter as well as from inside the perimeter (through limited-privilege accounts within the network).

- How effective are the system's security defenses as far as the delivery of data and applications go?

- Define objectives, scope, roles, and responsibilities for penetration testing.

- Develop a strategic test planning process.

- Define simple test metrics to evaluate severity and risk (e.g., database can be corrupted via a break-in).

- Consider evaluating and acquiring COTS testing tools to assist your organization in penetration testing.

For information on security tools currently available, go to:

CERT/CC site: www.cert.org/tech_tips/security_tools.html

Microsoft site: www.microsoft.com/technet/security/tools.asp

User Protection via Browser Settings

Browser settings that limit exposure to harmful Internet content can be set within Netscape Navigator and Microsoft Internet Explorer 4.x and 5.x browser. It's expected that the user will alter some of these settings. Furthermore, there is a major shift on the user side in terms controlling these settings. Web users are gradually more educated on using various settings to protect themselves. As a Web site or a Web application development team, you cannot force users to accept your settings. Therefore, you need to test with various combinations of the settings.

- For example, in Internet Explorer (IE) 4.x and 5.x, you can configure the browser to use one of the predefined zones. More important, in IE 5.x, the browser can also be configured to the security level for each zone. In some corporations, the IT department might specify the zone and security level settings on user browser. How do you think your application will be affected by a browser security setting of High? Make sure that you test with all browser security settings. For example, if the user has set a weak browser-security setting and the server can only handle strong encryption, errors will result.

- As part of each security level, the behavior of active contents will vary accordingly. One can customarily set the behavior of each type of active content (Java, ActiveX, scripting, cookies, etc.). How would the setting of type of content affect your application? For example, if cookies is disabled, would your application still work? If it would not, is it a software error, design error (unnecessary reliance on cookies), or is it a technical support issue?

- Is the third-party Java applet used in your application safe for your user to use?

- Is the third-party ActiveX control used in your application safe for your user to use?

- Note that most users never change these settings. Those who do restrict what they allow in and out of the browser.

Internet zone security settings on Internet Explorer are as follows:

High.   Active content that could potentially damage a user's computer is restricted.

Medium.   Users are warned before potentially damaging active content is run.

Low.   Users are not warned before potentially damaging active content is run.

Custom security settings for active content.   Enables users to define support options for specific active content types, including the following:

- ActiveX controls.
- Java applets and Java scripting.
- File types.
- Fonts.
- Active content downloading and printing.
- Installation and launching of desktop applications.
- Submission of nonencrypted form data.
- Downloading and installation options for software that comes from software distribution channels.
- Whether you use Netscape Navigator or Microsoft Internet Explorer, you need to test your Web application with various security configurations of various active content settings (Java, scripting, cookies, etc.) As discussed earlier, these settings enable users to protect themselves at the client site, because we have also established that the higher the security measurements, the lower the functionality and usability. How would these browser side settings affect the behavior of your application?

Additional browser-security settings include the following:

Do not save encrypted pages to disk. In a shared server environment, this will prevent people from seeing the user's secure information.

Warn if submitted forms are being redirected. Enables the browser to warn the user when information on a Web-based form is being sent to a location other than that of the Web page.

Warn if changing between secure and nonsecure model. Enables the browser to warn users when they are switching from a secure site to a nonsecure site. This is useful when testing an application in a supposedly secure mode.

Check for certificate revocation. Prevents users from accepting invalid certificates that have been revoked.

Warn about invalid site certificates. Enables the browser to warn a user when a URL in a certificate is invalid.

- *Certificate.* Should your application use certificates such as Site Certificate or Code Signing to allow users to identify active content such as Java applets and ActiveX controls before accepting, the installation of these certificates should be tested accordingly.

Accepting cookies: | Always | Prompt | Disable |. Enables users to specify whether cookies will be allowed to be stored on their system (with or without first alerting them), or disallowed altogether. A *cookie* is a file that is sent by an Internet site and stored on a user's machine. In theory, cookie files track information about user identity and preferences for a particular Web site.

- Does your application require the use of cookies? If yes, can the use of cookie be avoided?
- If your application requires the use of cookies, is your team prepared to lose sales to the population of users who will adamantly disallow their browser to accept cookies?
- If cookie is used:
  - What information is set in a cookie and how is the information used by the application?
  - Is the information in the cookie sensitive (such as ID, password, etc.)?
  - Is the information in the cookie personal (potentially violating the user's privacy)?
  - If the information in the cookie is sensitive and personal in nature, is it encrypted?
  - Does your application tell the user why it wants to use cookie—exactly what information your application collects, why, and how long does it intend to keep the information?
  - If the user chooses not to accept cookies, does your application still work?
  - When do cookies expire? What happens when a cookie is expired?

Enable and disable HTTP 1.1 support.   Many Web servers still support only HTTP 1.0. This feature enables users to specify which protocols their browser will use.

Certificate settings.   Enables the user to specify how certificates will be used to identify them, certificate authorities, and publishers.

Content settings.   Enables users to specify whether inappropriate contents will be restricted. If they are, users can specify which rating service will be used for blocking.the restricted content (for example, RSACi, the Recreational Software Advisory Council). Users can also set levels for restrictions on categories of objectionable content: offensive language, sex, and violence.

An Error-Handling Bug Example

Applications are often not aware of the actual causes of failure conditions they experience. Errors may be due to session time-outs, absence of available disk space, incomplete downloads, or browser security settings that prevent the downloading of active content (Java applets, ActiveX controls, etc.). An application might misinterpret an error condition and, in turn, present a misleading error message for all such error conditions.

Figure 15.7 shows the Internet Explorer 4.0 Safety Level setting screen. Note that an active content security setting of *Medium* has been selected—which means (among other things) that ActiveX controls cannot be downloaded. This application is a Web-based e-mail reader. It requires an ActiveX control to be downloaded before it can download attachments. Because of the medium security level setting, the ActiveX control cannot be downloaded. However, the application presents an erroneous error message in this scenario, such as that shown in Figure 15.8. Based on the advice given

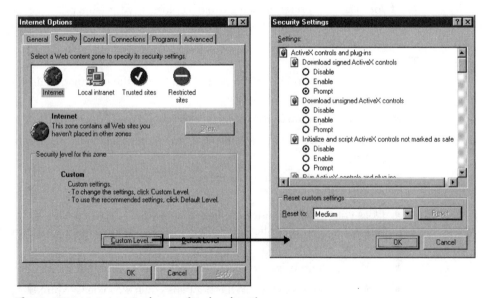

Figure 15.7 Internet Explorer safety level settings.

Figure 15.8 Inaccurate error message.

in the message, the user has two choices: (1) Continue to wait or (2) click on the Reload button to reload the control. Either choice will not download the ActiveX control because, in reality, the interference of the browser's security setting is the cause of this error condition.

Testing Considerations

General testing considerations include the following:

- Every component in a Web system involves its own security weaknesses. A security system is only as strong as its weakest link. The four usual places in which security defenses are imposed are

  - The client system (Web browser, other applications and components)
  - The server (Web, database and other servers)
  - The network
  - Online transactions

- An organization's *security team*, not the software testing team, determines policy on all security-related issues: user access, time-outs, content availability, database viewing, system protection, security tools, and more. Whether a company's security defense is secure enough is not a determination for the testing group to make. The role of a testing group is to test the existing system to look for errors in security implementation primarily at the application level.

- Usually the IT team holds most of the responsibility for network security. Staff other than the software testing team generally performs firewall testing, packet counting, traffic monitoring, virus protection, and server break-in testing.

- The IT team, not the software testing team, is responsible for installing IP address screening policies.

- Testing objectives should be to, in addition to looking for deficiencies in application-error detection and handling, gather configuration-related issues for the technical support knowledge base.

In terms of user-account password, login procedure testing considerations include:

- Does the Web system have an auto log-off feature (such as session time-out)? If so, does it work properly?

- Does the Web system implement and enforce frequent password changing? If so, does it work properly?

- If security is controlled at the application server level, rather than at the database server level, has the application's security logic been tested to see if user access is properly enforced? For example, to connect to a database server, a Web server needs to have an ID and password for such a database. It is possible for a Web server to use the same ID and password to log in a database regardless of who the end user is. The authorization process can then be done at the application level. In contrast, authorization can be done at the database level; that is, each end user would have an ID and password for the database account. Depending on who the end user is, the appropriate ID and password will be used.

- Have you tested the login logic enforced at the application level? Have you tested the login logic enforced at the database level? Have you tested the login logic enforced at both levels?

- Has any security-related testing been performed on third-party applications or components integrated with the Web system?

- How many consecutive failed logins are allowed (e.g., 3 times, 10 times, or an unlimited number of times)? Is this feature configurable by a user in a configuration file or a registry key? If yes, who has the privilege to make the change? Can the change be easily hacked?

- When the number of failed logins is exceeded, how does the application respond (e.g., by disallowing logins from that IP address until the security issue is reviewed or the security alert timer expires)?

- Which logics are applied to user names and passwords? Is it case-sensitive? Is there a minimum-number-of-characters rule? Is there a mixed rule that requires letter and number characters to be in combination? Does the implementation of these logics work?

- Are user names and passwords stored in the encrypted format (in user's registry database or configuration files, such as .INI files)?

- Have you tried to cut and paste user name and password?

- Have you tried to bypass the login procedure by using a bookmark, a history entry, or a captured URL? (For example, after you logged in a system successfully, try to capture the URL. Launch a new instance of the browser, then paste in the captured URL to see if you can get to the system.)

- Have you tested logging in using HTTP as well as HTTPS (assuming that your system supports HTTPS)?

- Are user name and password encrypted at the application level? If yes, has the feature been tested?

In terms of authorization procedure, testing considerations include:

- Are all authorized users able to access the system?

- Are unauthorized users blocked from the system? If an unauthorized login is attempted, how easily can it be done?

- When a new password is created for first-time login, is the default password deactivated if a new unique password is chosen?

- Do chosen passwords meet specified requirements (e.g., length, letters/numbers)? What happens if the requirements are not met?

- When the user must periodically change passwords, are old passwords deactivated when new ones are chosen?

- When there is a time restriction for logins, is transition between authorized and unauthorized periods handled correctly?

- Are outdated user account features removed and deactivated completely and correctly?

- Do expiration-based user accounts expire as expected?

In terms of database server security, testing considerations include:

- Are users granted excessive database privileges? In most database systems, users are given permission to access specific data that relate to their responsibilities. Additionally, certain users can often grant special access privileges to other users. Ensure that users are able to access appropriate data and that they are denied access to all other data. Can special access privileges be granted?

- Can special access privileges be granted to unauthorized users?

- Can special access privileges be limited to specific items?

- Can special access privileges be terminated?

- Do users in each group have appropriate access that meets, but does not exceed, their needs? Do all users get group assignments? Users are generally divided into groups of individuals who share the same access needs.

- Views are restricted tables that display portions of an entire table. Users can only access and edit fields that are visible to them within the view. Test to ensure that appropriate and intended information is accessible through individual views and that all other data is blocked. Also, test to ensure that views are protected from modification by unauthorized users, via both Graphical User Interface (GUI) management tools and SQL statements.

- Is the permission required to execute appropriate stored procedures granted to users?

- Do users have more access to the stored procedures than the requirements to perform their work? They should only have access to those stored procedures needed to perform their jobs.

- Can users other than the database administrator create, modify, or delete stored procedures? Ideally, only database administrators should have this type of privilege.

A Sample Security Test Planning Table

Here is an example of a security test planning table that I have used for analyzing security needs—implementation strategies, as well as testing requirements. Figure

Figure 15.9 Security test table.

Activities	Protection			Primary Target					Security Policies/Implementation					Testing Issues			
	User	Producer	Type	Client/Server Application	Database	Physical Server	Physical Client	The Network	Perimeter Security with Firewall [1]	Encryption [2]	Authentication [3]	Access Control [4]	Data Protection [5]	Requirement Testing [6]	Policy Implementation Testing [7]	Application Functional Testing [8]	System Functional Testing [9]
Offensive contents.	x	x	a	x			x										
Anti-virus	x	x	b	x		x	x		x			x		x	x	x	x
Blocking database from unwanted access		x	b		x						x	x		x	x		
Data loss due to disaster		x	b			x		x		x			x	x	x	x	x
Data loss due to hacking activities		x	b			x				x	x			x	x	x	x
Personnel security clearance		x	b			x						x		x	x		
Sabotage or theft of data		x	b		x	x						x		x	x		
Sabotage or theft of hardware		x	b			x						x		x	x		
Theft of credit-card numbers	x	x	b	x	x	x		x	x		x	x	x	x	x	x	x
Unauthorized access to private network data		x	b	x	x	x		x	x		x	x		x	x	x	x
Unauthorized release of personal information	x	x	b	x	x					x							
Intellectual property loss due to hacking activities		x	c	x	x	x								x		x	x
Spamming	x		d	x			x										
Unauthorized access to private network resources	x	x	e					x	x		x			x	x	x	x

[1] Perimeter security plan; firewall products used and their configurations; tasks and tools required for maintaining security.
[2] Encryption security plan and encryption technologies supported.
[3] Authentication security plan; authentication mechanism; tasks and tools required for implementation.
[4] Access control security plan; access implementation used for various platforms; access control configuration; task and tools required.
[5] Data backup and recovery plan.
[6] Examine the requirements to determine if they adequately meet the security objectives.
[7] Test the security policy implementation to find security holes in the plan.
[8] Test the application for security-enforced type of errors as well as application functional errors (side-effects).
[9] Test the Web system as a whole for functional errors that are specific to configuration, compatibility and performance issues.

a Children
b Data
c Intellectual property
d Privacy
e Network resource

15.9 illustrates the correlation among several key aspects of security issues including testing. To use it, first I identify the activities and issues with which we have security concerns. I enter the information in the first column, *Activities*. Next, for each activity, I identify whom we want to protect, what type of protection, and the primary or target area to focus upon. Information is then entered in the *Protection* and *Primary Target* columns, respectively. Next, I also identify the type of security measures applied to each activity and testing implementation. Information will then be entered in the *Security/Policies/Implementation* and *Testing Issues* columns accordingly. The table is complete. We now have a snapshot of a high-level security plan that can be used to track and communicate the security implementation throughout the project.

Bibliography and Additional Resources

Bibliography

Bourne, K. C. *Testing Client/Server System.* New York: McGraw-Hill, 1997.

Larson, E., and B. Stephens. *Web Server, Security, and Maintenance.* Upper Saddle River, NJ: Prentice-Hall PTR, 2000.

Orfali, R., et al. *Client/Server Survival Guide,* third edition, New York: Wiley, 1999.

Schneider, B. *Applied Cryptography: Protocols, Algorithms and Source Code in C,* second edition. New York: Wiley, 1996.

Tiwana, A. *Web Security.* Butterworth, Heinemann: Digital Press, 1999.

Additional Resources

CERT/CC Web site
  www.cert.org

Microsoft Web site on security
  www.microsoft.com/security

RAS Security Web site
  www.rsasecurity.com

Carnegie Mellon SEI Software Technology Review—A directed guide containing the latest information on several software technologies.
  www.sei.cmu.edu/str/

Carnegie Mellon SEI STR Glossary & Keyword Indexes—Glossary and keyword indexes for software technology review site
  www.sei.cmu.edu/str/indexes/

Computer System Security—An Overview, SEI STR
  www.sei.cmu.edu/str/descriptions/security.html

Firewalls and Proxies, SEI STR
   www.sei.cmu.edu/str/descriptions/firewalls.html

Cookie Central—This site is dedicated to offer information related to cookies.
   www.cookiecentral.com/

Cookie Managers Utilities—*PC Magazine* download page for cookie manager.
   www.zdnet.com/pcmag/features/utilities98/internetsecurity/cookie01.html

CHAPTER 16

Performance, Load, and Stress Tests

When a user clicks on the Buy button on your e-commerce site, you want to make sure that your customer will not have to wait long for service. Otherwise, the potential customer might leave and go do business somewhere else. To ensure that your system can endure the potential load due to business demands at the same time, and can serve your user in a reliable and timely manner, you need to conduct performance, load, and stress testing on your system. Although these tests are commonly done in a client-server environment, if you have not worked with a client-server sys-

Topics Covered in This Chapter

- Introduction
- Evaluating Performance Goals
- Performance Testing Concepts
- Web Transaction Scenario
- Understanding Workload
- Evaluating Workload
- Test Planning
- Testing Considerations
- Bibliography

tem before, or had an opportunity to do these tests before, it might take you some time to grasp the concept. This chapter is written to quickly introduce you to the issues involved with defining testing requirements; planning for the testing, identifying, and evaluating the needed tools; and knowing when to get help.

Introduction

One of the key benefits of Web applications is that they allow multiple users to access system resources simultaneously; multiple users may request differing services and gain access to varying features—all at the same time. Because multiuser support is central to the success of most every Web application, a system's ability to perform critical functions during periods of peak user activity must be evaluated carefully. In the effort of evaluating multiuser support capabilities, three types of tests are commonly conducted: (1) performance, (2) load, and (3) stress tests. Although these terms are often used interchangeably, each represents a test that is designed to address a different objective.

The primary goal of *performance testing* is to develop effective enhancement strategies for maintaining acceptable system performance. Performance testing is an information gathering and analyzing process in which measurement data are collected to predict when load levels will exhaust system resources.

Load testing evaluates system performance with predefined load level. Load testing measures how long it takes a system to perform various program tasks and functions under normal, or predefined, conditions. Bug reports are filed when tasks cannot be executed within the time limits (preferably defined by the product management or the marketing group). Because the objective of load testing is to determine if a system performance satisfies its load requirements, it is pertinent that minimum configuration and maximum activity levels be determined before testing begins.

Stress testing evaluates the behavior of systems that are pushed beyond their specified operational limits (this may be well above the requirements); it evaluates responses to bursts of peak activity that exceed system limitations. Determining whether a system crashes or recovers gracefully from such conditions is a primary goal of stress testing. Stress tests should be designed to push system resource limits to the point where their weak links are exposed.

The terms *performance* and *load* are often used interchangeably. A load test is done to determine if the system performance is acceptable at the predefined load level; a performance test is done to determine the system performance at various load levels. The similarities between performance and load tests lie in their execution strategies. Typically, these tests involve the simulation of hundreds, or even thousands, of users accessing a system simultaneously over a certain period. Due to the time and effort involved (i.e., money), it is often impractical to have human testers execute such testing without the aid of automated testing tools.

Unlike performance and load tests, stress tests push systems past their breaking points. System components that break are subsequently investigated and reinforced.

Performance and load tests simulate regular user activity. The results of these tests give developers insight into system performance and response time under real-world conditions. *Response time* is the amount of time a user must wait for a Web system to react to a request. For example, it might take 4 seconds to complete a purchase transaction on a particular e-commerce site after a user clicks a Submit button.

Performance, load, and stress tests use actual or simulated workload to exhaust system resources and other related problematic areas, including:

- Memory (physical, virtual, and storage, plus heap and stack space)
- Central processing unit (CPU) time
- Transmission Control Protocol/Internet Protocol TCP/IP addresses
- Network bandwidth
- File handles

These tests can also identify system errors, such as:

- Software failures caused by hardware interrupts
- Memory runtime errors (such as leakage, overwrite, and pointer errors)
- Database deadlocks
- Multithreading problems

Evaluating Performance Goals

Performance testing involves an extensive planning effort for the definition and simulation of workload. It also involves the analysis of collected data throughout the execution phase. Performance testing considers such key concerns as:

- Will the system be able to handle increases in Web traffic without compromising system response time, security, reliability, and accuracy?
- At what point will the performance degrade, and which components will be responsible for the degradation?
- What impact will performance degradation have on company sales and technical support costs?

Each of these preceding concerns requires that measurements be applied to a model of the system under test. System attributes, such as response time, can be evaluated as various workload scenarios are applied to the model. Conclusions can be drawn based on the collected data. (For example, when the number of concurrent users reaches X, response time equals Y. Therefore, the system cannot support more than X number of concurrent users.) The complication, however, is that even when the X number of concurrent users does not change, the Y value may vary due to differing user activities. For example, 1000 concurrent users requesting a 2K HTML page will result in a limited range of response times; whereas response times may vary dramatically if the same 1000 concurrent users simultaneously submit purchase transactions that require significant server-side processing. Designing a valid workload model that accurately reflects such real-world usage is no simple task.

Consider the following simplistic example to understand how increased traffic load—and, consequently, increased response time—can result in lost company revenue. (Refer to Figure 16.1 for detailed analysis of the traffic, percentage, and dollar amounts described in the following example.)

Suppose your e-commerce site currently handles 300,000 transactions per day. Three hundred thousand transactions divided by the amount of seconds in a day equates to about 3.47 transactions per second [300,000/(24 · 60 · 60) = ~3.47 transactions per second). Suppose a marketing survey is conducted, and the findings show that:

- The *transaction response time* is of an acceptable level as long as it does not exceed 4 seconds.

- If the transaction response time is greater than 4 but less than 9 seconds, 30 percent of users cancel their transactions.

- If the transaction response time is greater than 8 but less than 10 seconds, 60 percent of users cancel their transactions.

- If the transaction response time increases to over 10 seconds, over 90 percent of users cancel their transactions.

Suppose in the next 6 months, the number of transactions is expected to rise between 25 and 75 percent from the current level and the potential revenue for each transaction is $1. Management would like to learn how the performance would impact company revenue as the number of transactions per day increases.

A performance test is conducted and the findings show that the system cannot handle such increases in traffic without increasing response time; consequently, user transaction cancellations and/or failures result. If the number of transactions increases as expected, the company will face a potential revenue loss of between $112,500 and $472,500 per day.

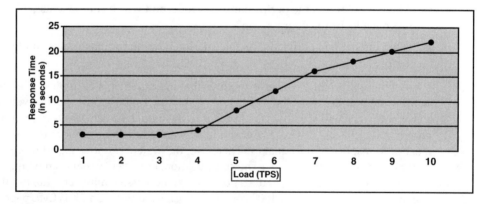

Figure 16.1   Response time to lost-revenue analysis.

It takes time, effort, and commitment to plan for and execute performance testing. Performance testing involves individuals from many different departments. A well-planned testing program requires the coordinated efforts of members of the product team, upper management, marketing, development, information technology (IT), and testing. Management's main objective in performance testing should be to avoid financial losses due to lost sales, technical support issues, and customer dissatisfaction.

Issues that management should consider before, during, and after performance testing include:

- Will the Web application be capable of supporting the projected number of users while preserving acceptable performance, and at what cost?
- At which point will the Web application load-handling capability begin to degrade?
- What will be the financial implications of the degradation?
- What can be done to increase the Web application load-handling capability, and at what cost?
- How can the system be monitored after deployment so that appropriate actions can be taken before system resources are saturated?

Performance Testing Concepts

Following are some key issues that should be understood and evaluated during performance testing planning.

Projected number of users.   It can be challenging to estimate the number of users that a system will likely support because user activities can vary, as can access time and activity frequency. Representing the projected number of users in a workload model requires careful thought, as does the simulation of real-world users.

Acceptable performance.   Determining the level of performance that is acceptable for a system requires input from marketing and product management. How performance will be measured, what it will cost, the tools that will be used, and the metrics that will be employed must be considered. Understanding which components affect system performance is also important.

Data analysis and corrective action planning.   Once performance testing results have been gathered, corrective measures for improving performance must be considered. For example, should additional system resources be added? Should network architecture be adjusted? Can programming improvements be made?

Performance testing involves the evaluation of three primary elements:

1. System environment and available resources.
2. Workload.
3. System response time.

One in Four Online Purchases Thwarted, Study Finds*

Palo Alto, California (Reuters)—The problem with the explosion of online stores is that more than a quarter of all the purchases attempted over the Internet never go through, according to a study. Andersen Consulting went shopping at 100 of the biggest and best-known online stores. Out of 480 gifts it tried to buy, it was able to complete only 350 purchases. The study found that more than one-quarter of the top Web sites either could not take orders, crashed in the process, were under construction, had entry blocked, or were otherwise inaccessible. "It was pretty eye-opening," said Robert Mann of Andersen's Supply Chain practice. He said he was stunned by the results of the survey, which had initially been designed to study only the time it took to complete and fulfill orders. Mann said he found instead that "speed is not really the issue. The issue is reliability." Although Andersen did not single out the best and the worst of these online stores, Mann said that none of them was problem-free. In general, though, the study found that the traditional retailers had a worse track record than the pure-play Internet stores, known as e-tailers. "The e-tailers who depend on this as their bread and butter have generally invested more on back-end systems. Many retailers have not invested as well," said Mann.

Another big problem was orders not arriving on time. The traditional retailers were once again the big offenders, according to the study, which found they delivered the order when promised only about 20 percent of the time. E-tailers, by comparison, were on time about 80 percent of the time. Curiously, some items took much longer to deliver. The average time for an electronics gift to arrive was 3.9 days, while music deliveries typically took 7.4 days.

Andersen plans to next study online merchants' ability to handle returns—which Mann said could be their next big challenge if consumers sent back all those gifts that did not arrive by Christmas Day.

*Reproduced with permission from Reuters Limited by Andrea Orr, December 20, 1999. Copyright 1999 Reuters Limited.

Figures 16.2 and 16.3 contrast how a naive view of expected workload and performance may differ from real-world results. Figure 16.2 illustrates a naive expectation of the relationship between traffic load and *aggregate response time* (i.e., the sum of server, network, and browser response time). Note that the server, network, and browser response times in Figure 16.2 increase in a predictable and regular manner as transactions per second increase. Figure 16.3, on the other hand, depicts a more likely system response scenario; note that system, network, and browser response times increase in a nonlinear manner. As the number of transactions rises, the transaction round-trip time increases. Ultimately, the number of transactions per second becomes saturated. The server response time eventually increases to such a point that the entire system stops responding to requests.

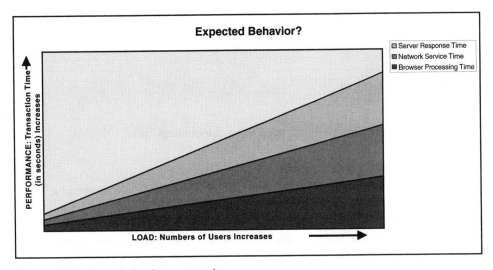

Figure 16.2 Naive behavior expectation.

Web Transaction Scenario

There are three primary components involved in any online transaction: (1) a browser on the client side, (2) a network, and (3) a server (Figure 16.4). A typical Web transaction proceeds as follows:

On the client side

- The user enters a URL or clicks a link within a browser to request a file from a server.

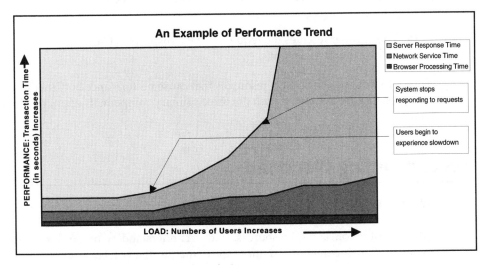

Figure 16.3 Actual workload and analysis.

Figure 16.4 Three primary transaction components.

- The Domain Name Server (DNS) converts the server's hostname into the appropriate Internet Protocol (IP) address.
- The client connects to Web server.
- Client sends a HyperText Transfer Protocol (HTTP) request (such as GET or POST) to the server.

On the Internet (network)

- The network delivers data from the client to the server.

On the server side

Once the request reaches the server, data are disassembled based on the appropriate communication protocol (such as HTTP).

- The server responds to the request.
- The server processes the request by retrieving data or writing to a database. Once the process is complete, the server returns the requested file or resultant information to the client.

Back on the Internet (network)

- The network delivers data from the server to the client.

Back on the client side

- The browser receives the requested data, displays HTML contents, and executes any active content.

Figure 16.5 defines the typical resources that cause performance bottlenecks and the activities that are associated with the three primary components of online transactions.

Understanding Workload

Workload is the amount of processing and traffic management that is demanded of a system. To evaluate system workload, three elements must be considered: (1) users, (2) the application, and (3) resources. With an understanding of the amount of users (along with their common activities), the demands that will be required of the application to process user activities (such as HTTP requests), and the system's resource requirements, one can calculate a system's workload.

Browser	Network	Server
Typical Resource Bottlenecks	**Typical Resource Bottlenecks**	**Typical Resource Bottlenecks**
CPU Time	Latency--Delays introduced by network devices & data queuing.	CPU time.
	Throughput or bandwidth.	I/O access time: I/O bus, disk controller and disk access.
Typical Activities	**Typical Activities**	**Typical Activities**
Receiving/Sending data	Packets routing from clients to servers.	Receives hits.
Formatting data	Packet routing from servers to servers.	Run scripts, library-functions, stored-procedures, executables, etc.
Displaying data	Packet routing from servers to clients.	
Executing scripts & active contents		

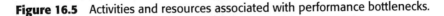

Transaction Time

Client Processing Time | Connect Time + Send Time + Receive Time | Response Time

Figure 16.5 Activities and resources associated with performance bottlenecks.

Consider the following when calculating workload:

Users.   The amount of users in each class.

- The maximum amount of concurrent users in each class
- The percentage of concurrent users in each class
- The length of user sessions in each class
- The amounts of each kind of unique activity

The application

- Activities can be expressed in terms of service rates, such as transactions per second (TPS), or throughput, such as kilobits per second (Kbps).

Resources

- System resources need to handle workload while preserving acceptable performance, which is normally expressed in *response time*.

Evaluating Workload

There are a few steps that one should take in determining workload.

- Before the system is deployed, consult any available performance requirement documents.
- Assemble a small group of users who can act as a cross-section of real-world users—simulating different personnel types and performing associated activities. Configure the server and use a log analysis tool to log user activity. Use the collected data to estimate workload.
- Estimate the number of concurrent users that the system will handle, classify the users into groups, estimate the percentage of each class of user, the length of their sessions, their activities, and activity frequency (as illustrated in the previous section).
- After system deployment, use log analysis tools or a proxy server to collect workload data.

Testing the Sample Application

The following tables offer a detailed example of how one might analyze the workload of the sample application (a Web-based bug tracking application) in a hypothetical scenario where 10,000 concurrent users are using the system to report news bugs, work with existing bug reports, and generate charts.

Requirement documents (if you are lucky enough to get them) should detail the workload that Web applications are designed to support. For systems that are already employed, the network administration group might be able to provide information regarding system traffic. This can normally be done by using log analysis tools such as Web Trends Log Analyzer (www.webtrends.com) or Analog (www.statslab.cam.ac.uk/~sret1/analog/). Be advised that whichever log analysis tool you choose to use, use it consistently because each tool will produce slightly different statistics for the same amount of network traffic.

The three types of users that are factored into the following calculations are (1) testing, (2) development, and (3) project management. Note that, normally, there would be more types of users. However, the sample application is a defect tracking system. Therefore, these are the primary users it details. The percentage of user type is also detailed (i.e., the testing group makes up 60 percent of the system's 10,000 users, equating to 6000 users), as is the average session length of each user type. From there, user activities and the frequency at which each activity is performed per session are detailed. Finally, the activities that are requested of the application and the TPS are covered.

Using the first row of the table as an example, TPS calculations are arrived at using the following formula:

$$\frac{\text{User type \% (0.60)} \times \text{Total users (10,000)} \times \text{Frequency per session (1)}}{\text{(60 minutes} \times \text{60 seconds)}}$$

User activity data such as that detailed in Table 16.1 should be analyzed to determine how often each transaction type is executed per second—regardless of which user type requests the transaction. Note that each activity type (reporting, obtaining

Table 16.1 Calculating Transactions per Second

USER TYPE	USER TYPE %	SESSION LENGTH	USER ACTIVITY	USER SUB-ACTIVITY	FREQUENCY PER SESSION	APPLICATION ACTIVITY	TRANSACTIONS PER SECOND
Testing	60%	60 minutes	Reporting	Reporting	1	Respond to a report submission by displaying the next blank report form	1.7

Table 16.1   *(Continued)*

USER TYPE	USER TYPE %	SESSION LENGTH	USER ACTIVITY	USER SUB-ACTIVITY	FREQUENCY PER SESSION	APPLICATION ACTIVITY	TRANSACTIONS PER SECOND
	60%		Working with existing reports	Simple query	2	Respond by displaying the result in a single-report view	3.3
	60%			Complex query	1	Respond by displaying the result in a single-report view	1.7
	60%			Navigate from one report to another	8	Respond by displaying the result in a single-report view	13.3
	60%			Submit an updated report	0.5	Respond by displaying the updated information in the current report	0.8
	60%		Obtaining metrics	The first time	0.5	Respond by displaying a chart in a Java applet	0.8
	60%			Subsequent times	0.5	Respond by displaying a chart in a Java applet	0.8
Development	30%	30 minutes	Working with existing reports	Simple query	2	Respond by displaying the result in a single-report view	3.3
	30%			Complex query	1	Respond by displaying the result in a single-report view	1.7
	30%			Navigate from one report to another	8	Respond by displaying the result in a single-report view	13.3

Continues

Testing the Sample Application *(Continued)*

Table 16.1 *(Continued)*

USER TYPE	USER TYPE %	SESSION LENGTH	USER ACTIVITY	USER SUB-ACTIVITY	FREQUENCY PER SESSION	APPLICATION ACTIVITY	TRANSACTIONS PER SECOND
	30%			Submit an updated report	0.5	Respond by displaying the updated information in the current report	0.8
Project management	10%	90 minutes	Working with existing reports	Simple query	2	Respond by displaying the result in a single-report view	0.4
	10%			Complex query	1	Respond by displaying the result in a single-report view	0.2
	10%			Navigate from one report to another	8	Respond by displaying the result in a single-report view	1.5
	10%			Submit an updated report	0.5	Respond by displaying the updated information in the current report	0.1
	10%		Obtaining metrics	The first time	0.5	Respond by displaying a chart in a Java applet	0.1
	10%			Subsequent times	0.5	Respond by displaying a chart in a Java applet	0.1

metrics, etc.) performed by all user types (testing, development, product management) is aggregated in Table 16.2—and an aggregate TPS rate is thereby calculated. The aggregate TPS rate is juxtaposed against the "acceptable" response time that has been established by management and the marketing group.

Table 16.2 Evaluating Transactions per Second

USER ACTIVITY	USER SUB-ACTIVITY	FREQUENCY PER SESSION	APPLICATION ACTIVITY	TRANSACTIONS PER SECOND (TPS)	AGGREGATE TPS	ACCEPTABLE RESPONSE TIME (SEC)
Reporting	Reporting	1	Respond to a report submission by displaying the next blank report form	1.7	1.7	2
Obtaining metrics	Subsequent times	0.5	Respond by displaying a chart in a Java applet	0.8		
	Subsequent times	0.5	Respond by displaying a chart in a Java applet	0.1	0.9	5
Obtaining metrics	The first time	0.5	Respond by displaying a chart in a Java applet	0.8		
	The first time	0.5	Respond by displaying a chart in a Java applet	0.1	0.9	30
Working with existing reports	Complex query	1	Respond by displaying the result in a single-report view	1.7		
	Complex query	1	Respond by displaying the result in a single-report view	1.7		
	Complex query	1	Respond by displaying the result in a single-report view	0.2	3.5	5
Working with existing reports	Navigate from one report to another	8	Respond by displaying the result in a single-report view	13.3		
	Navigate from one report to another	8	Respond by displaying the result in a single-report view	13.3		
	Navigate from one report to another	8	Respond by displaying the result in a single-report view	1.5	28.1	2

Continues

Testing the Sample Application *(Continued)*

Table 16.2 *(Continued)*

USER ACTIVITY	USER SUB-ACTIVITY	FREQUENCY PER SESSION	APPLICATION ACTIVITY	TRANSACTIONS PER SECOND (TPS)	AGGREGATE TPS	ACCEPTABLE RESPONSE TIME (SEC)
Working with existing reports	Simple query	2	Respond by displaying the result in a single-report view	3.3		
	Simple query	2	Respond by displaying the result in a single-report view	3.3		
	Simple query	2	Respond by displaying the result in a single-report view	0.4	7.0	2
Working with existing reports	Submit an updated report	0.5	Respond by displaying the updated information in the current report	0.8		
	Submit an updated report	0.5	Respond by displaying the updated information in the current report	0.8		
	Submit an updated report	0.5	Respond by displaying the updated information in the current report	0.1	1.8	2

DETERMINING HOW MANY VIRTUAL USERS TO SIMULATE

The two factors to keep in mind when determining the appropriate number of virtual users are *response time* and *throughput.* Five transactions happening simultaneously, for example, may have an effect on response time, but should have little effect on throughput. Five hundred transactions spaced evenly apart, on the other hand, may not have an effect on response time, but may present a throughput issue.

The appropriate number of virtual users that load and performance testing require depends on the focus of testing. Considering the sample application, there are a few different ways that an appropriate number of virtual users can be calculated.

> To test only the performance of the application and database servers in terms of response time and throughput, 40 (the aggregate number of transactions per second) is a good number of virtual users to consider.
>
> To test the performance handling of concurrent open sessions on each server, as well as response time and throughput, 10,000 (the actual number of concurrent users) is a good number of virtual users to consider.
>
> Perhaps an arbitrary number of users between 40 and 10,000 should be considered to test certain performance scaling models that must be validated.

Response and Performance Terms

Performance testing often requires the aid of automated testing tools to simulate workload, collect measurement data, and present data in a format that can be used for performance analysis. Each tool vendor uses slightly different terms to describe similar concepts. The following list includes many of the commonly used response and performance testing terms.

Throughput Calculation Example

The objective of throughput calculation is to determine what level of bandwidth is required to support system workload. For example, consider a Web server supporting 10,000 concurrent users who request documents from a pool of 10 different HTML documents (with an average size of 2K each) every 3.5 minutes. To calculate the bandwidth requirement for handling this throughput, use the following calculation:

$$\text{Throughput} = \frac{10,000 \cdot (2 \cdot 1024 \cdot 8)}{(3.5 \cdot 60)} = 780,190 \text{ bps}$$

Or

$$10,000 \text{ concurrent users} \cdot \frac{(2 \text{ Kbytes} \times 1024 \text{ bytes/Kbyte} \times 8 \text{ bits/byte})}{(3.5 \text{ min} \times \text{s/min})} = 780,190 \text{ bps}$$

To handle this throughput load, the network connection should be at least a T1 line (1,544,000 bps). Use the time, data size, and bandwidth conversion tables (Tables 16.4 through 16.6) to perform other workload assessments.

Test Planning

With the objectives of load and stress testing in mind, an effective test planning process can be developed. In addition to the software testing staff, the testing effort requires the involvement of the IT staff and the software engineering staff. Many of the following test planning activities are typical of all test planning projects.

Table 16.3 Response and Performance Testing Terms

ATTRIBUTE	TYPICAL DEFINITION	COMMENTS
Connect Time	The time (typically in seconds) required for the client and the server to establish a connection.	Time spent at network.
Send Time	The time (typically in seconds) required to send data from the client to the server.	Time spent at network
Receive Time	The time (typically in seconds) required to send the response data from the server to the client.	Time spent at network.
Process Time	The time (typically in seconds) required for the server to respond to a client request.	Time spent at client.
Response Time	The time (typically in seconds) required to complete a particular transaction.	Time spent at server.
Transaction Time	The time (typically in seconds) required for the client to process the data received.	The total amount of time spent at network, client, and server to complete a transaction. This is an interesting measurement because it represents the end-to-end performance of the system.
Transaction per Second	The total number of transactions such as Head, Get, or Post per second that the system received.	As the number of virtual users increases but the number of transactions per second decreases or is saturated, it will cause transactions to fail.
Failed Transactions per Second	The total number of transactions per second that the system failed to complete.	Failed transactions is one of the primary sources of technical support or sales loss problems.
Request per Second	The number of hits the Web servers received.	This details the interaction intensity between browsers and Web servers. When the number of requests per second is saturated, it will cause transactions with multiple requests to fail.
Failed Request per Second	The total number of failed requests.	The number of hits the Web server failed to serve.

Table 16.3 *(Continued)*

ATTRIBUTE	TYPICAL DEFINITION	COMMENTS
Concurrent Connections	The total number of concurrent connections over the elapsed time.	A Web server connection is opened when a request is generated from a browser. If the number of concurrent connections increases but the number of requests per second does not increase, it means that the request demands cause the connections to stay open longer to complete the service. This trend will eventually saturate the maximum number of open connections on a Web server, hence introducing a performance bottleneck.
Throughput-Kilobytes per Second	The amount of data transmitted during client-server interactions.	When the number of virtual users or transactions increases but the amount of data transmitted is saturated, data throughput has become a performance bottleneck.

Defining Baseline Configuration and Performance Requirements

In defining baseline configuration and performance requirements, identify system requirements for the client, server, and network. Consider hardware and software configurations, network bandwidth, memory requirements, disk space, connectivity technologies, and so on. To determine system workload, the system's users and their respective activities will also have to be evaluated.

Determining the Workload

Please see "Understanding Workload," earlier in this chapter.

Table 16.4 Time Conversion

WEEK	DAY	HOUR	MINUTE	SECOND	MILLISECOND
1	7	168	10,080	604,800	604,800,000
	1	24	1,440	86,400	86,400,000
		1	60	3,600	3,600,000
			1	60	60,000
				1	1,000
					1

Table 16.5 Data Size Conversion

GIGABYTE	MEGABYTE	KILOBYTE	BYTE	BIT
1	1,024	1,048,576	1,073,741,824	8,589,934,592
	1	1,024	1,048,576	8,388,608
		1	1,024	8,192
			1	8
				1

Determining When Testing Should Begin

Testing should be performed as early in the testing process as possible. It is far cheaper, easier, and more feasible to correct errors early in the development process than it is to fix them late in the development process. Additionally, the earlier that testing begins, the more that tests can be repeated; and the more often that tests are repeated, the more opportunity the development team will have to improve product performance.

Table 16.6 Bandwidth Conversion

LINE	MBPS	KBPS	BPS
28K dial-up	0.028	28	28,000
56K dial-up	0.056	56	56,000
ISDN single	0.064	64	64,000
ISDN double	0.128	128	128,000
T1	1.544	1,544	1,544,000
Token ring	4.000	4,000	4,000,000
10-baseT	10.000	10,000	10,000,000
Token ring	16.000	16,000	16,000,000
T3	45.000	45,000	45,000,000
100-baseT	100.000	100,000	100,000,000
FDDI (Fiber Distribution Data Interface)	100.000	100,000	100,000,000
Gigabit Ethernet	1.000	1,000	1,000,000
ATM	155.520	155,520	155,520,000
ATM	622.080	622,080	622,080,000

Performance, load, and stress tests can be a part of the regression testing suite that is performed with each build. Regression testing determines whether new errors have been introduced into previously bug-free code. Early detection of performance requirement failures can be critically important because it offers developers the maximum amount of time to address errors.

Determine if the Testing Process Will Be Hardware-Intensive or Software-Intensive

The *hardware-intensive approach* involves the use of multiple client workstations in the simulation of real-world activity. The advantage of this approach is that one can perform load and stress testing on a wide variety of machines simultaneously—closely simulating real-world use. The disadvantage is that one must acquire and dedicate a large number of workstations to perform such testing.

The *software-intensive approach* involves the virtual simulation of numerous workstations—over multiple connection types. The advantage of the software-intensive approach is that only a few physical systems are required to perform testing. The disadvantage is that some hardware-, software-, or network-specific errors may be missed.

Developing Test Cases

Generated loads may be designed to interact with servers via a Web browser user interface (UI), or via HTTP requests such as GET and POST (thereby bypassing the browser). Consideration must be given to the types of requests that are sent to the server under test by the load generator (and, hence, the amount of data per transaction that the server processes) and the resources available to the load generator.

Load and Stress Testing Tools

In deciding which testing tools would best assist the testing effort, determine the *operating environment* that the testing tool must support: operating system, hardware platform, network infrastructure (WAN or LAN), network protocols, and so on. Possibly, the tool has to work on multiple platforms. Also, consider the *number of users* that must be simulated; make sure that the tool can simulate enough users to produce an adequate test.

As far as test-script generation and execution is concerned, determine whether a tool that provides *script capturing* (as opposed to manual scripting) will be needed. Make sure that the tool can log all discrepancies. The tool should also be able to simulate multiple versions of browsers and network connections. Make sure that the tool also supports user *think time*. Finally, look for support of HTTPS, Java, ActiveX, scripts, and cookies.

Off-the-shelf tools, such as those listed in the chapter entitled "Web Testing Tools," can be expensive. Plus, it takes time to become proficient at them. Off-the-shelf tools may also not meet the needs of the project; one may end up paying for extra features that the test project does not require.

Homegrown tools can also be expensive due to the in-house costs related to their development. The significant maintenance and testing costs associated with the development of homegrown tools can be considerable. Internal engineering resources may be limited as well—making it challenging to develop tools in a reasonable time frame and maintain them over time.

The best solution may be a combination of off-the-shelf and homegrown tools. As with most decisions related to software testing, the earlier that one assesses testing needs, the better. Evaluate the tools that are available and assess the needs of the system under test as early in the testing effort as possible. For a list of available testing tools, see the chapter entitled "Web Testing Tools," or visit the Software QA/Test Resources Web site at www.softwareqatest.com/qatweb1.html#LOAD.

Analyzing and Reporting Collected Data

When considering tools for the gathering and analysis of data, consider whether a tool that provides result analysis and publishing features will be needed. Without such features, manual collection, analysis, and report tabulation of test results will be required. Also consider what type of data analysis the tool will need to perform: Will specific Structured Query Language (SQL) statements need to be captured? Should the tool monitor system resource usage and network communication activity?

Performance Testing Example

During beta testing phase, the testing objective of this performance test is to determine if the system can handle 100 concurrent users logging in within a reasonably acceptable response time without any transaction failure.

The process of setting up this test goes something like this:

1. Record a log-in script.

2. Modify the recorded script in such a way that it can rerun the same login procedure by just reading from an external text file a line at a time. Each line has two fields holding the user ID and password in each field. The modified script is shown next.

```
// This is an example of load testing on the sample
// application, TRACKGEAR

function InitAgenda() {
CopyFile("c:\\login.txt", "c:\\login.txt")

}
```

```
//Setup the array
login = GetLine("c:\\login.txt" ,",")

//Synchronize the Data points
SynchronizationPoint(3000)

//Go to the Web site
wlHttp.Get("http://engservices.logigear.com/trackgear/default.asp")

wlHttp.FormData["company"] = "trackgear"
wlHttp.Get("http://engservices.logigear.com/bts/bin/login.asp")

wlHttp.FormData["company"] = "trackgear"
wlHttp.Get("http://engservices.logigear.com/bts/bin/login.asp")

//Post Username & Password

Sleep(8840)

wlHttp.FormData["user_name"] = login[1]
wlHttp.FormData["password"] = login[2]
wlHttp.FormData["Login"] = "Login"
wlHttp.FormData["PageNumber"] = "2"
wlHttp.FormData["company"] = "y"
wlHttp.Post("http://engservices.logigear.com/bts/bin/login.asp")

if (login.LineNum = 100) InfoMessage("done with read")

//Time the Login Process, and return that value

SetTimer("LoginTime")

wlHttp.Get("http://engservices.logigear.com/bts/bin/usercont.asp")
wlHttp.Get("http://engservices.logigear.com/bts/bin/title.asp")

wlHttp.Get("http://engservices.logigear.com/bts/bin/mainuser.asp")
wlHttp.Get("http://engservices.logigear.com/bts/bin/refresh.asp")
SendTimer("loginTime")
```

3. Next is the content of the text file named user.txt (100 users' IDs and passwords) that the performance test script reads in when it begins to execute the test.

```
beno, beno
chrisv, chrisv
.., ..
ursulap, john
```

4. Prepare the controlling and the monitoring consoles as well as a computer to be used as a load generator spawning threads to simulate hundreds (if not thousands) of users.

5. Set up the test script to be run with the tool. In this example, the performance test tool used in this example is RadView's WebLoad.

In this particular test, we discover the response time is within expected limits, but transaction failures are occurring at the Web server. As shown in Figure 16.6, three of the 100 transactions failed to respond.

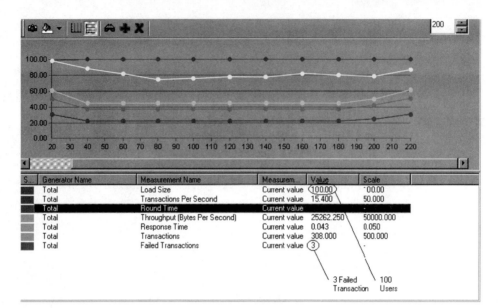

Figure 16.6 Three transactions failed to respond.

Testing Considerations

■ It takes time, effort, and commitment to plan and execute performance, load, and stress tests. Performance testing involves more people in an organization than just testers. A well-planned testing program requires a joint effort between all members of the product team, including upper management, marketing, development, IT, and testing.

■ Aggregate response time is a sum of browser processing time, network service time, and server response time. Performance analysis takes all of these factors into consideration.

■ Server-side analysis of *performance bottlenecks* often includes examination of the Web server, the application server, and the database server. Bottlenecks at any of these servers may result in server-side performance problems, which may ultimately affect overall response time.

■ Begin performance testing as early in the development process as possible to allow time for the analysis of data and the resolution of performance issues.

■ Repeat performance tests as many times as possible prior to deployment so that performance degradation issues can be identified early on. Allow plenty of time to isolate and troubleshoot performance issues.

■ Determining a *projected number of users* can be complex. Consider the following issues:

  ■ User activities vary.

- User-access behavior and activity frequencies vary from one time period to the next.

- Projected numbers of users must be considered within an appropriate *workload model.*

- Virtual users do not necessarily behave in the same ways that real users do.

- What happens if the product is wildly successful? That is to say, what happens if the number of users is grossly underestimated?

■ The number of users or the volume of transactions is predictable for the intranet (controlled environment) but is unpredictable for the Web site, such as an e-commerce site on the Internet (uncontrolled environment).

Determining *acceptable performance* can be challenging. Consider the following issues:

■ There are different means of measuring performance (metrics); each has different associated costs.

■ What factors affect performance in the system under test?

■ Many different tools are available on the market; each offers unique benefits and drawbacks.

Regarding *data analysis* and *corrective action planning,* consider how performance degradation can be resolved.

■ By adding system resources.

■ By adjusting network system architecture.

■ Through programming.

■ How can user workload be monitored so that appropriate actions can be taken to avoid saturation?

■ Continue monitoring system performance after deployment so that scalability issues can be addressed in a timely manner.

■ Performance testing is a capability planning process, not pass/fail testing.

■ Systems often have multiple performance bottlenecks.

■ Test script creation often requires programming skills. Prepare to train your testing staff.

There are several ways of improving server-side performance issues:

■ Upgrade hardware to improve service.

■ Reconfigure server parameters such as cache size and virtual-memory size.

■ Redesign network architecture to better distribute load and thereby improve service.

■ Redesign or optimize application code, stored-procedure code, or database tables.

■ Does the system's performance meet user expectations during standard operation (when the load is within specified limits)? If the answer is yes, then how is performance affected when the load exceeds specified limits?

- When the system is overloaded (i.e., when user demand exceeds system resource availability) and forced into an error condition, does the system accurately detect, handle, and recover gracefully from the condition? Does the system crash or begin to behave erratically?

- How scalable is the system? Can the system be upgraded easily and quickly (server memory, disk space, software, etc.) to accommodate increased load demand?

- Focusing testing on individual objects rather than entire systems yields more detailed and, consequently, more practical information regarding load limitations.

- In defining baseline configuration and performance requirements, you should identify system requirements for the client, server, and network. Consider hardware and software configurations, network bandwidth, memory requirements, disk space, and connectivity technologies.

- Consider whether your test execution will be hardware-intensive or software-intensive. Regardless of the method you choose, complete testing is not possible. One can only identify the best possible risk-based testing strategy available and then plan testing accordingly. Keep in mind that the risk of a failure in a Web site on the Internet is much more visible and costly compared with one in an intranet application (exposed internally only).

Determining workload involves the following issues:

- How many groups of users will be involved in a load test?

- How frequently will each user in each group access and interact with the application during a load test?

- What will be the typical activities performed by each group of users?

Performance testing is a server-capacity planning process that involves three fundamental steps:

1. Establishing a baseline.
2. Gathering and analyzing data.
3. Predicting future server capacity based on gathered data.

Common attributes that should be considered in Web application load testing include:

- Concurrent Operation Tests
- Web Server Load Tests
- Database Load Tests

In determining which tools are most appropriate for your test project, you should consider the following:

- What are the operating systems, hardware platforms, network infrastructure types (WANs and LANs), and network protocols that the tool must support? Must the tool work on multiple platforms?

- How many users must the tool simulate to produce an effective test?

- Must the tool provide script-capturing functionality in addition to manual scripting?

- Look for a tool that can run unattended and accurately log all discrepancies.

- Does the script support user think time, which more realistically simulates real-world conditions?

Bibliography

Anderson, M. D. "13 Mistakes in Load Testing Applications." *Software Testing and Quality Engineering* (September/October, 1999).

Menasce, D. A., and V. A. F. Almeida. *Capacity Planning for Web Performance.* Upper Saddle River, NJ: Prentice-Hall, 1998.

Menasce, D. A., and V. A. F. Almeida. *Scaling for E-Business.* Upper Saddle River, NJ: Prentice-Hall, 2000.

Nguyen, N. Q. "Testing Web Applications." *LogiGear Corporation Training Handbook* (2000).

Radview Software, Inc. "The Web Load User's Guide." Lexington, MA: 1998.

Savoia, A. "The Science and Art of Web Site Load Testing." *STQE STAREAST* (2000).

Schelstrate, M. "Stress Testing Data Access Components in Windows DNA Applications." *MSDN News* (March/April, 2000). http://msdn.microsoft.com/voices/news.

CHAPTER 17

Web Testing Tools

Why Read This Chapter?

Web applications operate in dynamic environments. Occasionally, testing tools are required to complement manual testing efforts. Some test types (e.g., load and performance testing) would be impractical without the help of tools that can simulate the actions of thousands of users. The value of various tools varies according to the specific testing needs, budget, and staffing constraints associated with the system under test.

Introduction

This chapter describes various types of Web testing tools, how the tools are used, and where the tools can be acquired. Many of the software vendors listed in this chapter offer evaluation copies of their products. Return-on-investment calculations (both short-term and long-term) can help you decide which tool makes the most sense for your particular project.

Topics Covered in This Chapter

- Introduction
- Types of Tools
- Additional Resources

Types of Tools

Following are lists of various Web testing tools and descriptions of each.

Rule-Based Analyzers

- Type: Static analyzer
- Note: The notion of *static analyzer* means that the code does not have to be compiled and executed.
- Input: Source (code)
- Output: Various analytical and error reports
- Primary user: Developer
- Secondary user: Tester

Technology principle. This type of tool reads the input source and compares the written code with the coding standards or language-specific rules in an effort to uncover inconsistencies and potential errors. They are, in some ways, comparable with grammar and spell checkers found in word processors.

In some cases, the tool also includes an agent or a *bot* (short for *robot*) that simulates human activities, accessing commands such as hyperlinks in HTML pages. On the content side of Web development, the two common rule-based analyzers are HTML validators and link checkers. Often, they are fully integrated into commercial-off-the-shelf products.

A Sample List of Link Checkers and HTML Validators

These tools check for bad links and HTML tags, browser compatibility (to a certain extent), dead links, popular links, load time, page design, spelling errors, and so on.

Watchfire Linkbot

Description: Link checker and HTML validator

Source: Watchfire

URL: www.watchfire.com

Platform: Windows

Evaluation copy: Yes

ParaSoft SiteRuler

Description: Link checker and HTML validator

Source: ParaSoft

URL: www.parasoft.com

Platform: Windows, Linux, and Sun Solaris

Evaluation copy: Yes

Matterform Media Theseus

Description: Link checker and HTML validator

Source: Matterform Media

URL: www.matterform.com

Platform: Macintosh

Evaluation copy: Yes

Allaire Homesite

Description: More than Link checker and HTML validator (HTML Editor)

Source: Matterform Media

URL: www.allaire.com/products/homesite/

Platform: Windows

Evaluation copy: Yes

Free Online HTML Validation and Link-Checking Services

W3C HTML Validation Service: http://validator.w3.org/

Bobby: www.cast.org/bobby/

NetMechanic: www.netmechanic.com/

Web Site Garage: http://websitegarage.netscape.com/

Dr. Watson: http://watson.addy.com/

A Sample List of Rule-Based Analyzers for C/C++, Java, Visual Basic, and Other Programming and Scripting Languages

These tools generally check for bad syntax, logic, and other language-specific programming errors at the source level. This level of testing is often referred to as *unit testing* and *server component testing*. The developer executes this testing.

Compuware Numega CodeReview

Description: Source code analysis

Language: Visual Basic

Source: Compuware

URL: www.compuware.com

Platform: Windows

Evaluation copy: Yes

ParaSoft Codewizard

Description: Source code analysis

Language: C/C++

Source: ParaSoft

URL: www.parasoft.com

Platform: Unix and Windows

Evaluation copy: Yes

ParaSoft Jtest

Description: Source code analyzer with automation features for test-case design and test execution

Language: Java

Source: ParaSoft

URL: www.parasoft.com

Platform: Windows

Evaluation copy: Yes

Reasoning InstantQA

Description: Code inspection services on the Web

Language: C, C++, Cobol, Java, and others

Source: Reasoning

URL: www.reasoning.com

Platform: N/A

Evaluation copy: Yes

Load/Performance Testing Tools

Type: Web-load simulator and performance analysis

Input: Simulated user requests

Output: Various performance and analytical reports

Primary user: Tester

Secondary user: Developer

Technology principle.   This type of tool enables you to simulate thousands of users accessing the Web site/application requesting data and submitting transactions, in addition to other e-commerce and e-business activities. Virtual load can also simulate various versions of Web browsers and network bandwidth. While the simulated load is applied to the server, performance data is collected and plotted in several useful report formats for further analysis. See Chapter 16, "Performance, Load, and Stress Tests," for more information on this type of test.

Web Load and Performance Testing Tools

These tools generate test scripts by recording user activities and combining them with scripting languages. They can spawn multiple threads, each thread running a specific test script or scenario to simulate real-world requests being sent to the servers. Performance metrics such as response time and data throughput can be tracked and reported in tabular as well as graphical formats for performance analysis.

Envive Prophecy

Description: Hosted services for load, performance, and scalability testing

Source: Envive

URL: www.envive.com

Platform: Web-based

Evaluation copy: Yes

Mercury Interactive LoadRunner

Description: Load, performance, and scalability testing

Source: Mercury Interactive

URL: www.mercuryinteractive.com

Platform: Windows

Evaluation copy: Yes

RadView WebLoad

Description: Load, performance, and scalability testing

Source: RadView

URL: www.radview.com

Platform: Windows

Evaluation copy: Yes

Rational Performance Studio

Description: Load, performance, and scalability testing

Source: Rational

URL: www.rational.com

Platform: Windows and Unix

Evaluation copy: Yes

RSW eLoad

Description: Load, performance, and scalability testing

Source: RSW Software

URL: www.rswsoftware.com

Platform: Windows

Evaluation copy: Yes

Segue SilkPerformer

Description: Load, performance, and scalability testing

Source: Segue

URL: www.segue.com

Platform: Windows

Evaluation copy: Yes

GUI Capture (Recording/Scripting) and Playback Tools

- Description: Captured user activities that are played back, enabling unattended functionality and regression testing
- Input: Recorded/scripted events or messages applied on GUI controls
- Output: Error logs indicating discrepancies discovered during playback
- Primary user: Tester
- Secondary user: Developer

Technology principle.   This type of tool enables you to consistently rerun repetitive test cases with little to no human interaction. These tools have the capability of recognizing GUI controls such as form buttons, tables, links, Java applets, and so on in Web browser pages. During the capturing phase, these tools track input events (generally from keyboard and mouse) as they are applied to specific GUI control objects. The events represent user activities and are converted into scripts that, at a later time, the playback engine will use as input to replay the prerecorded activities. The event-capturing process can also be done via scripting. During playback the program-state information, as well as output results (whether data or user interface settings), are compared with the original results. If there is any discrepancy, the tool makes the condition known. Keep in mind that to fully utilize the capability of this type of tool, a significant amount of training and planning is required. Otherwise, the return on investment (or lack thereof) may be disappointing.

A Sample List of Automated GUI Functional and Regression Testing Tools

These tools generate test scripts by recording user activities and combining them with scripting languages. The recorded or scripted events can then be played back repeatedly. This type of tool is also commonly used for acceptance tests and functionality-regression tests, because the test cases are so well defined.

Rational VisualTest

Description: Load, performance, and scalability testing

Source: Rational

URL: www.rational.com

Platform: Windows

Evaluation copy: Yes

RSW eTester

Description: Automated GUI functional and regression testing

Source: RSW Software

URL: www.rswsoftware.com

Platform: Windows

Evaluation copy: Yes

Segue SilkTest

Description: Automated GUI functional and regression testing tool

Source: Segue

URL: www.segue.com

Platform: Windows and Unix

Evaluation copy: Yes

Runtime Error Detectors

- Type: Dynamic analyzer
- Note: Code needs to be compiled and executed before dynamic analyzers can catch errors.
- Input: Execution of test cases
- Output: Trap and track runtime errors
- Primary user: Developer
- Secondary user: Tester

Technology principle.   This type of tool either inserts its code into the production code prior to compilation and execution, or it tracks memory read/write activities between the program (and its components) and the operating system. During the execution of the program, it looks for invalid and erroneous operations that are requested by the application so that the errors can be trapped and reported. This type of tool catches errors like memory overwrites, memory leaks, read errors, and memory double-freezes. Without a way of tracking such errors, memory-related bugs are difficult to reproduce.

Memory is a dynamic environment condition. When there is an error such as a memory overwrite problem, the symptoms from the black-box testing perspective may vary from nothing happening at all to a total system crash. This is due to the fact that the environment required for the symptom of the error to expose itself varies. This type of tool helps detect errors at the source level rather than at the symptomatic level.

A Sample List of Runtime Error Detection Tools

These tools check memory and operating system API-specific errors.

MicroQuill HeapAgent

Description: Detecting memory-related and other errors at runtime

Source: MicroQuill

URL: www.microquill.com

Platform: Windows

Evaluation copy: Yes

ParaSoft Insure++

Description: Detecting memory-related and other errors at runtime

Source: ParaSoft

URL: www.parasoft.com

Platform: Unix and Windows

Evaluation copy: Yes

Onyx QC

Description: Memory runtime error detection and stress testing

Source: Onyx Technology

URL: www.onyx-tech.com

Platform: Macintosh

Evaluation copy: Yes

Rational Purify

Description: Detecting memory-related and other errors at runtime

Source: Rational

URL: www.rational.com

Platform: Windows NT and Unix

Evaluation copy: Yes

Compuware BoundsChecker

Description: Detecting memory-related and other errors at runtime

Source: Compuware

URL: www.compuware.com

Platform: Windows

Evaluation copy: Yes

A Sample List of Web Security Testing Tools

These tools can be used to detect and analyze potential security issues in a network or Web application.

Network Toolbox

Description: Suite of tools for analyzing security weaknesses on Windows systems

Source: J.River

URL: www.jriver.com/products/network-toolbox.html

Platform: Windows

Evaluation copy: Yes

NetScan Tools

Description: Traditional Unix network tools ported for use on Windows systems

Source: Northwest Performance Software, Inc.

URL: www.nwpsw.com/

Platform: Windows

Evaluation copy: No

Surfincheck Firewall

Description: Personal firewall detects malicious VBScript, Java, and ActiveX applications

Source: Finjan Software

URL: www.finjan.com

Platform: Windows

Evaluation copy: Yes

PrivaSuite

Description: Easy-to-use encryption tools for use on Windows systems

Source: Aliroo

URL: www.aliroo.com/privsuit.html

Platform: Windows

Evaluation copy: No

Windows Task-Lock

Description: Controls access to applications

Source: Posum Software Security Technologies

URL: http://posum.com/

Platform: Windows

Evaluation copy: Yes

WebTrends Security Analyzer

Description: Analyzes Internet and intranet for security problems

Source: Webtrends

URL: www.webtrends.com/products/wsa/

Platform: Windows, Solaris, Linux

Evaluation copy: Yes

Java-Specific Testing Tools

Sun Micro Systems offers a suite of tools for testing Java applications including the following tools:

JavaSpec

Description: Tests Java applications and applets through their APIs

Source: Sun Micro Systems

URL: http://industry.java.sun.com/solutions/

Platform: Windows, Solaris, JavaOS

Evaluation copy: Yes

JavaStar

Description: Tests Java applications and applets through their GUIs

Source: Sun Micro Systems

URL: http://industry.java.sun.com/solutions/

Platform: Windows, Solaris, JavaOS

Evaluation copy: Yes

Several Other Types of Useful Tools

- Database testing tools
- Web-based defect tracking tools
- Development/test management tools
- Code-based performance and profiling tools
- Code-based coverage analyzers

Additional Resources

On the Internet

Rick Hower's Software QA/Test Resource Center

A software testing and QA related site that offers a collection of Quality Assurance FAQs and useful links to other QA/Testing organizations and tool vendors. It has a compilation of links to miscellaneous Web testing tools. www.softwareqatest.com.

Bret Pettichord's Software Testing Hotlist

A well-organized page offering links to several interesting papers on test automation, testing-related white papers, and other useful information. www.io.com/~wazmo/qa.html.

Marick's Testing Foundations

A thorough site with lists of test tools, contractors, training courses, papers, and essays. From Paul Marick, the author of The Craft of Software Testing. www.testing.com and www.rstcorp.com/marick/

DBMS Online Buyer's Guide Testing and Software Quality

A compilation of various software testing tools, including Web and load testing tools. www.dbmsmag.com/pctest.html.

LogiGear Corporation

The producer of TRACKGEAR™, the Web-based issue tracking and resolution management solution. Offering information on testing tools, software testing training, and outsourced testing services. www.loggear.com or www.qacity.com.

Development and Testing Tool Mail-Order Catalogs

These catalogs supply development and testing tools.

Programmer's Paradise, Internet Paradise, and Components Paradise

www.pparadise.com.

The Programmer's Supershop Buyer's Guide

www.supershops.com.

VBxtras

www.vbxtras.com.

CHAPTER 18

Finding Additional Information

Why Read This Chapter?

Web technologies (and the testing methods that are appropriate for them) are evolving at a rapid rate. Inevitably, new technologies have become available since this book went to print. This chapter will help you gain access to the most up-to-date information regarding Web-application testing.

Introduction

This chapter lists textbooks, Web sites, and professional societies that are great sources of information for test-case design and Web-application test planning.

Topics Covered in This Chapter

- ■ Introduction
- ■ Textbooks
- ■ Web Resources
- ■ Professional Societies

Textbooks

About Face: The Essentials of User Interface Design, by A. Cooper, IDG Books Worldwide, 1995, ISBN: 1568843224.

Administrating Web Servers, Security, and Maintenance, by E. Larson and B. Stephens, Prentice-Hall, 1999, ISBN: 0130225347.

Beginning Active Server Pages 3.0, by D. Buser et al., Wrox Press, 2000, ISBN: 1861003382.

The Craft of Software Testing: Subsystems Testing Including Object-Based and Object-Oriented Testing, by B. Marick, Prentice-Hall, 1997, ISBN: 0131774115.

Designing Web Usability, by J. Nielsen, New Riders, 1999, ISBN: 156205810X.

Dynamic HTML: The Definitive Reference, by D. Goodman, O'Reilly and Associates, Inc., 1998, ISBN: 1565924940.

Information Architecture for the World Wide Web: Designing Large-Scale Web Sites, by L. Rosenfeld and P. Morville, O'Reilly & Associates, 1998, ISBN: 1565922824.

Internetworking with TCP/IP: Client-Server Programming and Applications: Windows Sockets Version, Volume 3, by D. Comer and D. Stevens, 1997, ISBN: 0138487146.

Internetworking with TCP/IP: Design, Implementation, and Internals, Volume 2, 2nd edition, by D. Comer and D. Stevens, Douglas, Prentice-Hall, 1994, ISBN: 0131255274.

Internetworking with TCP/IP: Principles, Protocols, and Architecture, Volume 1, by D. Comer, Prentice Hall, 1991, ISBN: 0134685059.

JavaScript Bible, by D. Goodman and Eich, IDG Books Worldwide, 1998, ISBN: 0764531883.

Learning Perl on Win32 Systems, by R. Schwartz et al., O'Reilly & Associates, ISBN: 1-56592-324-3.

Scaling for E-Business: Technologies, Models, Performance, and Capacity Planning, by D. Menasce and V. Almeida, Prentice-Hall, 2000, ISBN: 0130863289.

Software Test Automation: Effective Use of Test Execution Tools, by M. Fewster and D. Graham, ACM Press, 1999, ISBN: 0201331403.

Sql Server 7 Beginner's Guide, by D. Petkovic, McGraw-Hill, 1999, ISBN: 0072118911.

Testing Computer Software, 2nd edition, by C. Kaner et al., VNR/ITP, 1993, ISBN: 1850328471.

Web Resources

Useful Links

www.QACITY.com

An online resource on Web testing and other testing-related subjects hosted by Hung Q. Nguyen and LogiGear Corporation. www.qacity.com.

Amjad Alhait's BetaSoft Inc.

Hosts QA discussion forums, many QA links, and download directories for automated testing. www.betasoft.com.

Bret Pettichord's Software Testing Hotlist

A well-organized page offering links to several interesting papers on test automation, testing-related white papers, and other useful information. www.io.com/~wazmo/qa.html.

Brian Marick's Testing Foundations

A thorough site with lists and descriptions of tools, contractors, training courses, papers, and essays from Brian Marick, the author of *The Craft of Software Testing.* www.testing.com.

Cem Kaner's Web Site

Kaner's site has information on software testing, software quality, and his own work. It includes several of Cem's papers on quality, software testing, outsourcing, technical support, and contracts. www.kaner.com/writing.htm.

Elisabeth Hendrickson's Quality Tree Web Site

Offers various papers on automated testing and useful QA-related links. www.qualitytree.com.

James Bach's Web Site

Offers various useful presentations and articles on software testing. www.satisfice.com.

Kerry Zallar's Software Testing Resources

Includes numerous links and information about test automation. www.crl.com/~zallar/testing.html.

Rick Hower's Software QA/Test Resource Center

A software-testing and QA-related site that offers a collection of QA FAQs, plus useful links to QA/Testing organizations and tool vendors. www.charm.net/~dmg/qatest/index.html.

Software-Engineer.org

A community of software engineers dedicated to free information sharing between software engineers (i.e., industrials, faculty members, and students). This is a very useful site. www.software-engineer.org.

STORM

Software Testing Online Resources is hosted by Middle Tennessee State University. A well-organized site with links to many software testing and QA sites, including directories of software testers, consultants, and software testing consulting companies. www.mtsu.edu/~storm/.

Center for Software Development

Established in 1993, the Center for Software Development provides the key resources software developers need to start and grow the next generation of successful technology companies. www.center.org/.

Software Productivity Center

Methodology, training, and research center that supports software development in the Vancouver, British Columbia, area. The SPC is a member-driven technical resource center that caters to day-to-day problems faced by software development companies. www.spc.ca/.

Centre for Software Engineering

The Centre for Software Engineering is committed to raising the standards of quality and productivity within the software development community, both in Ireland and internationally. www.cse.dcu.ie/.

European Software Institute

An industry organization founded by leading European companies to improve the competitiveness of the European software industry. Particularly interesting for information about the Euromethod contracted-software lifecycle and related documents. www.esi.es/.

Software Testing Institute

A membership-funded institute that promotes professionalism in the software test industry. Includes links to industry resources, including quality publications, industry research, and online services (Online STI Resource Guide). www.ondaweb.com/sti.

Anybrowser.org

Organization that advocates a nonbrowser-specific World Wide Web. www.anybrowser.org.

Building a Windows 2000 Test Lab

Includes general considerations for designing and running a test lab to meet the needs of organizations. www.microsoft.com/technet/win2000/dguide/chapt4.asp.

CSS2 Selector Support Chart

Lists features of the Cascading Style Sheets 2 standard. webreview.com/wr/pub/guides/style/css2select.html.

Carnegie Mellon SEI Software Technology Review

Contains papers on many Web-related software technologies. www.sei.cmu.edu/str/.

Counterpane Internet Security, Inc.

Information on Web security and other security-related issues. www.counterpane.com/about.html.

Cookie Central

A site dedicated to information about cookies. www.cookiecentral.com/.

CNET's "BROWSERS.COM"

Information, resources, and download page for browsers. www.browsers.com.

DevEdge Online Home Page

Netscape's Web site that's dedicated to developing Web applications. http://developer.netscape.com/index.htm.

Internet.com Browser Watch Home Page

Source for various versions of different browsers for several platforms. http://browserwatch.internet.com/.

MSDN

Microsoft's online resource for developers. http://msdn.microsoft.com.

PC Magazine's 1999 Utilities Guide

Comprehensive listing and analysis of system tools. www.zdnet.com/pcmag/features/utilities99/index.html.

Tech Encyclopedia

A database that offers definitions for various computer-related jargons. www.techweb.com/encyclopedia.

Whatis.com

A very cool search engine that serves definitions for and links to various technological terms. www.whatis.com.

ZD Net's Browser Help and How-To Page

Information regarding browser plug-ins, settings, and more. www.zdnet.com/zdhelp/filters/subfilter/0,7212,6002396,00.html.

webmonkey Home Page-Resource for Web Developers

Extensive how-to resource for Web technologies. http://hotwired.lycos.com/webmonkey/.

webmonkey Brower Reference Chart

Details on what features are supported by which versions of various browsers. http://hotwired.lycos.com/webmonkey/reference/browser_chart/index.html.

Useful Magazines and Newsletters

Software Testing and Quality Engineering

www.stqemagazine.com.

Software Development

www.sdmagazine.com.

Java Developer's Journal

www.javadevelopersjournal.com.

MSDN News

http://msdn.microsoft.com/voices/news

Miscellaneous Papers on the Web from Carnegie Mellon Software Engineering Institute

Client/Server Software Architecture—An Overview
www.sei.cmu.edu/str/descriptions/clientserver.html.

Common Object Request Broker Architecture (CORBA)
www.sei.cmu.edu/str/descriptions/corba.html.

Component Object Model (COM), DCOM, and Related Capabilities
www.sei.cmu.edu/str/descriptions/com.html.

Computer System Security—An Overview
www.sei.cmu.edu/str/descriptions/security.html.

Firewalls and Proxies
www.sei.cmu.edu/str/descriptions/firewalls.html.

Java
www.sei.cmu.edu/str/descriptions/java.html.

MiddleWare
www.sei.cmu.edu/str/descriptions/middleware.html.

Multi-Level Secure Database Management Schemes
www.sei.cmu.edu/str/descriptions/mlsdms.html.

Object-Request Broker
www.sei.cmu.edu/str/descriptions/orb.html.

Software Inspections
www.sei.cmu.edu/str/descriptions/inspections.html.

Three-Tier Software Architecture
www.sei.cmu.edu/str/descriptions/threetier.html.

Two-Tier Software Architecture
www.sei.cmu.edu/str/descriptions/twotier.html.

COTS and Open Systems—An Overview
Explains the decisions involved in choosing off-the-shelf software products.
www.sei.cmu.edu/str/descriptions/cots.html#110707.

Professional Societies

American Society for Quality (ASQ)

The ASQ is a society of both individual and organizational members that is dedicated to the ongoing development of quality concepts, principles, and techniques. The ASQ was founded in 1946 to enable local quality societies in the United States to share information about statistical quality control in an effort to improve the quality of defense materials. The ASQ has since grown to more than

130,000 individual and 1000 organizational members. Most of the quality methods now used throughout the world—including statistical process control, quality cost measurement, total quality management, and zero defects—were initiated by ASQ members.

This site describes the organization and its activities. It offers information on quality standards, certification programs (including Certified Software Quality Engineer and Certified Quality Engineers), and a useful ASQuality Glossary of Terms search engine. www.asq.org/.

Special Interest Group in Software Testing (SIGIST)

Testing branch of the British Computer Society (BCS). www.bcs.org.uk/sigist/index.html.

American National Standards Institute (ANSI)

American National Standards Institute. www.ansi.org/.

The Institute of Electrical and Electronics Engineers (IEEE)

The Institute of Electrical and Electronics Engineers (IEEE) is the world's largest technical professional society. Founded in 1884 by a handful of practitioners of the new electrical engineering discipline, today's Institute comprises more than 320,000 members who conduct and participate in activities around the world. www.ieee.org/.

International Organization for Standardization (ISO)

Describes International Organization for Standardization (ISO) with links to other standards organizations. www.iso.ch/.

National Standards Systems Network (NSSN)

National Standards Systems Network. Lots of links to standards providers, developers, and sellers. www.nssn.org/.

Society For Technical Communication (STC)

Society's diverse membership includes writers, editors, illustrators, printers, publishers, educators, students, engineers, and scientists who are employed in a variety of technological fields. STC is the largest professional organization serving the technical communication profession. This site (www.stc.org/) provides many links to research materials on documentation process and quality, including:

- Links to technical communication conferences
- Links to STC special-interest groups
- Links to technical communication seminars
- Links to educational technical communication–related resources, from indexing to online help, to usability

LogiGear Test Plan Template

Product Name
Test Plan

LG-WI-TPT-HQN-0-01-080500

Date

Copyright © 2000, LogiGear Corporation

All Rights Reserved

W.650.572.1400
F.650.572.2822

E-mail: info@logigear.com

www.logigear.com

Contents

Product Name

Test Plan

Author Name   Version 1.0

I. Overview

1. Test Plan Identifier

[LG]-[client's init]-[project's init]-[author's init]-[phase#][serial#]-[dist. date]
Example:
LG-WI-TPT-HQN-0-01-080500

LG	LogiGear Corporation
WI	Widget Inc.
TPT	Test Plan Template project
HQN	Hung Q. Nguyen
0	0 = Development Phase; 1 = Final Phase
01	The first distributed draft
080500	Distributed date: August 5, 2000

2. Introduction

An introduction of the overall project

3. Objective

What we strive to accomplish, taking the following factors into account: quality, schedule, and cost

4. Approach

The overall testing strategy to satisfy the testing objectives

II. Testing Synopsis

1. Test Items

Deliverable products or applications to be tested

1.1. Software Application Items

1.1.1. Main Application Executables

1.1.2. Installer/Uninstaller

1.1.3. Utilities/Tool Kits

1.1.4. Online Help

1.2. Software Collateral Items

1.2.1. Font

1.2.2. Clip Art

1.2.3. Related Multimedia Items

1.2.4. Sample/Tutorial

1.2.5. Readme

1.2.7. Others

1.3. Publishing Items

1.3.1. Reference/User Guide

1.3.2. CD/Disk Label

1.3.3. Packaging

1.3.4. Marketing/Product Fact Sheet/Advertising Blurb

2. Features to Be Tested

List of features to be tested. The list may include the environment to be tested under.

3. Features Not to Be Tested

List of features that will not be covered in this test plan

4. System Requirements

SERVER HARDWARE AND SOFTWARE CONFIGURATION REQUIREMENTS

- Pentium® PC (Pentium II or higher recommended)
- 128Mb RAM
- 100Mb of free disk space
- Microsoft® Windows NT Server 4.0 with Latest Service Pack or Windows 2000 Server
- Microsoft® Internet Information Server 4.0 or higher
- Microsoft® SQL Server 7.0 with Service Pack

CLIENT REQUIREMENTS

- An active LAN or Internet connection
- Microsoft® Internet Explorer 4.x or higher
- Netscape® Navigator 4.x

MICROSOFT® INTERNET INFORMATION SERVER

- Microsoft® IIS 5 is bundled as part of the Windows 2000 Server and Windows 2000 Advanced Server Operating Systems.
- Microsoft® IIS 4 is available, free of charge, as part of the Windows NT 4.0 Option Pack.

DATABASE SUPPORT

- Microsoft® SQL Server 7.0

SUPPORTED BROWSERS

- Supports clients using Microsoft® Internet Explorer 4.x or higher, or Netscape® Navigator 4.x on any hardware platform

[The software and hardware requirements to run the application. Normally, this information is found in the product specification or user manual. See the preceding example.]

5. Product Entrance/Exit

Describe the milestone/acceptance criteria.

6. Standard/Reference

- *IEEE Standard for Software Test Documentation* (ANSI/IEEE std 829-1983).
- Kaner et al. *Testing Computer Software,* 2nd edition. New York: Wiley, 1993.
- LogiGear Corporation *Test Plan Template.*
- XXXX 3.0 *Test Matrix.*

[List of any standards, references used in the creation of this test plan. See the preceding example.]

7. Test Deliverables

List of test materials developed by the test group during the test cycle to be delivered upon the completion of this project.

7.1. Test Plan

7.1.1. The Original Approved Development Test Plan

Essentially, this complete document with appropriate approvals

7.1.2. The Executed Development Test Plan

Test-case tables, matrices, and other test-related materials (as part of this test plan) with appropriate check marking as verification of test completion.

7.1.3. The Original Approved Final Test Plan

Usually, the final test plan is a scaled-down version of the development test plan. This plan is produced and used in the final testing cycle. Appropriate approvals should also be included.

7.1.4. The Executed Final Test Plan

Test-case tables, matrices, and other test-related materials (as part of the final test plan) with appropriate check marking as verification of test completion.

7.2. Bug Tracking System

7.2.1. Bug Reports

- Summary list of all bugs found
- Full description copies of all bugs found

7.2.2. Bug Database

A soft copy of the bugbase containing all bugs found during the testing cycles, including paper-form reports.

7.3. Final Release Report

The Final Release Report should be submitted prior to the release of this project. This report is a quality assessment document that describes the scope of the testing project, testing completeness, test results focused primarily on the areas of concern, and release recommendation (for or against).

III. Testing Project Management

1. The Product Team

List of product team members and their roles

2. Testing Responsibilities

Who will lead up the testing efforts? Other people resource and responsibilities.

3. Testing Tasks

- Develop test plans including test cases, matrices, schedule, etc.
- Conduct test-plan reviews and obtain appropriate approvals.
- Procure hardware/software/tools required.
- Create bug database.
- Perform tests.
- Report bugs.
- Conduct bug deferral meeting.
- Produce weekly status report.
- Produce final release report.

4. Development Plan and Schedule

What is to be delivered for testing. Schedule—When the preceding items will be delivered.

5. Milestone Entrance/Exit Criteria

Milestone definitions, descriptions, and measurable criteria

6. Test Schedule and Resource

6.1. Schedule

Testing task grouping—List of task groups and their descriptions. Preliminary schedule matched with resource needs and test tasks.

6.2. Resource Estimate

Estimates of people resource required for completing the project.

7. Training Needs

Identify training needs.

8. Environmental Needs

8.1. Test Components

List of all software and hardware resources needed to complete the project. Resources availability and strategies to acquire them.

- Hardware
- Software
- Online account

8.2. Test Tools

- Off-the-shelf tools
- In-house tools
- Tools to be developed

8.3. Facilities

All testing will be done at [Company Name's] lab. If there are needs to outsource some of the testing tasks, we'll update this plan accordingly.

9. Integration Plan

Is there an integration plan? If yes, how it would fit in the testing strategy?

10. Test Suspension & Resumption

When should testing be suspended? When should a suspended testing process be resumed?

11. Test Completion Criteria

When should testing stop?

12. The Problem Tracking Process

12.1. The Process

Describe the bug tracking process.

12.2. The Bug Tracking Tool (database)

Describe the bug tracking tool.

12.3. Definition of Bug Severity

Bug severity is a subjective method used by reporters to grade the severity level of each report. Following are guidelines for grading bug severity.

12.3.1. 1–Critical

Severity 1—*Critical* (show-stopper) *bugs* are those that result in loss of key functionality, usability, and performance of a product in normal operation; there is no workaround solution available. These also include nonprogrammatic bugs such as an obviously embarrassing misspell of a product or company name in the splash screen, wrong video clip in the intro screen, erroneous instructions for a frequently used feature, and so on. Following are a few sample categories:

- Crash or core dump
- Data loss or corruption
- Failure of key feature

12.3.2. 2–Serious

Severity 2—*Serious bugs* include key features that don't function under certain conditions or nonkey features that don't function at all, degradation of functionality or performance in normal operation, difficult-to-use key features, and so on. Usually, these bugs should be fixed during the normal development cycles. Only during the final testing phase, these bugs might be carefully assessed and perhaps considered defer as appropriate.

12.3.3. 3—Noncritical

Severity 3—*Noncritical bugs* are those that represent some inconvenience to the user but perhaps don't happen frequently. These include minor display/redraw problems, poorly worded error messages, minor design issues, and the like. Usually, these bugs should be fixed provided time permitting or minimum efforts required by the programming team. Keep in mind that if many Severity 3 Noncritical bugs get deferred, there will be a definite quality-degradation effect to the product.

13. Status Tracking & Reporting

In what form will the status be reported?
What is the reporting frequency?
What types of information will be reported?

14. Risks & Contingencies

Risks and possible adjustments to the plan

15. The Approval Process

15.1. Test Plan Approval

How is the test plan approved?

15.2. Final Release Approval

What is the approval process for releasing the tested product?

Appendix I
Setup/Installation Test Case

Table A1.1   Functional Test: The Installer Executable

ID	CAT.	TEST PROCEDURE	EXPECTED RESULT	P/F	COMMENTS
	N				
	P				
	N				
	P				
	P				
	P				
	S				
	N				
	P				
	N				

Table A1.2   Functional Test: XXX

ID	CAT.	TEST PROCEDURE	EXPECTED RESULT	P/F	COMMENTS
	P				
	P				
	P				
	P				
	P				
	N				
	P				
	P				
	P				

Appendix II
Test Case for Application Shell

Table A2.1 Fast: XXX

ID	CAT.	TEST PROCEDURE	EXPECTED RESULT	P/F	COMMENTS
	P				
	N				
	P				
	N				
	P				
	P				
	P				
	P				
	P				

Table A2.2 Fast:

ID	CAT.	TEST PROCEDURE	EXPECTED RESULT	P/F	COMMENTS
	P				
	P				
	P				
	P				
	P				
	P				
	P				
	P				
	P				
	P				
	P				
	P				
	P				
	P				
	P				
	P				
	P				
	P				

Appendix III
Test Matrix for XXXXX

Table A3.1   Task-Oriented Functional Test

ID	CAT.	TEST PROCEDURE	EXPECTED RESULT	P/F	COMMENTS
	P				
	P				
	P				
	P				
	P				
	P				
	P				
	P				
	P				
	P				
	P				
	P				
	P				
	P				
	P				
	P				
	P				
	P				

Appendix IV
Compatibility Test Systems

- Acer Altos 330 Intel® Pentium® II Processor, 300MHz, 512KB 4.3GB Ultrawide 64MB ECC SDRAM 32X
- Compaq Proliant 1600R Intel® Pentium® III Processor, 550MHz, 128MB RAM
- Hewlett-Packard 9780C Minitower, AMD Athlon Processor 900MHz, 128MB RAM, 60 GIG Hard Drive, DVD, CD-ROM
- Hewlett-Packard Netserver LH4 Intel® Pentium® III Processor, 550MHz, 512K
- IBM 300GL P3 733 128MB 20.4GB 48X SDRAM 32MB AGP4 256KB NT
- IBM 300PL P3 733 20.4GB 128MB 48X 16MB ENET SND 98 256KB

Weekly Status Report Template

Product Name Status Report

Report No. 23

Week Ending *Month XX, 200X*

Author
Month XX, 200X

I. Testing Project Management

1. Project schedule.

DEVELOPMENT MILESTONE	DATE	TESTING* MILESTONE	DATE
Pre-alpha	*xx/xx/xx*	*Test plan 1st draft delivered*	*xx/xx/xx*
		Test plan 2nd draft delivered	*xx/xx/xx*
		Test plan completed/approved	*xx/xx/xx*
Alpha	*xx/xx/xx*	*Begin alpha test phase*	*xx/xx/xx*
Beta	*xx/xx/xx*	*Begin beta test phase*	*xx/xx/xx*
Release candidate	*xx/xx/xx*	Begin final test phase[†]	*xx/xx/xx*
Golden master	*xx/xx/xx*	Testing completed	*xx/xx/xx*

Italicized milestones are completed milestones.

* Also see the detail test schedule in the test plan.

† Assuming the release candidate is accepted.

2. Progress and changes since last week

- Completed Install/Uninstall tests.
- Completed configuration/compatibility tests.
- Regressed all outstanding fixed bugs.
- Completed testing the online help system.
- Reported 16 new bugs.

3. Urgent items

- LogiGear Testing group still has not received the xxxxx and xxxxx to be included with the product. The missing items might cause a schedule delay of the release candidate.
- It has been 3 weeks, the majority of memory bugs are still unfixed. This is a very high risk issue. This might cause a delay in the shipping schedule.

4. Issue bin

Nonurgent issues to be addressed in the next week or so park here.

5. To-do Tasks by Next Report

- Complete regressing all fixed bugs.
- Deliver final test plan for review and approval.
- Review executed test plans to verify testing completeness.
- Complete all procedures in preparation of final testing phase.
- Perform acceptance test for the release candidate.

II. Problem Report Status

1. Bug report tabulation

	LAST WEEK	THIS WEEK
Bugs Found & Reported	15	9

Bugs found this week = Total bugs this week – Total bugs last week

STATUS	LAST WEEK	THIS WEEK
New	15	9
Open	183	149
Total new and open	198	158
Resolved	65	98
Closed	252	275
Total resolved and closed	317	373
Grand Total	515	531

2. Summary List of Open Bugs

Summary lines of open bug reports.

III. Trend Analysis Report

Stability Trend Chart

This line chart Figure B.1 shows the curves of the total number of bug reports and its breakdowns in term of [open + new] and [closed + resolved] status. As the [closed + resolved] curve rises and the [open + new] curve drops, they will eventually intersect. This intersection indicates the beginning of the *maturity phase*. Ultimately, at the time the product is ready for release, the [closed + resolved] curve will meet the Total Bug Reports curve and the [open + new] curve will drop to zero. Observing the progressing trend from the beginning of the *maturity point* onward will give you reasonable predictability of the schedule.

For definitions of *open, new, closed,* and *resolved,* see the section entitled "Problem Report Status."

Quality Trend Chart

Valid bugs may be resolved by either fixing or deferring them. A high number of closed (fixed) bugs and a low number of deferred bugs indicate that the quality level

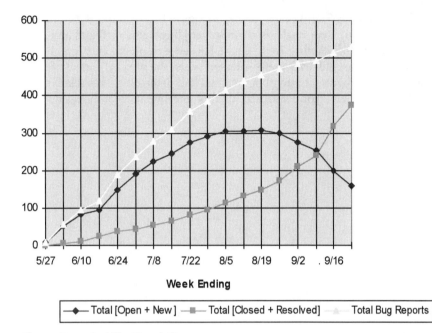

Figure B.1 Stability Trend Chart.

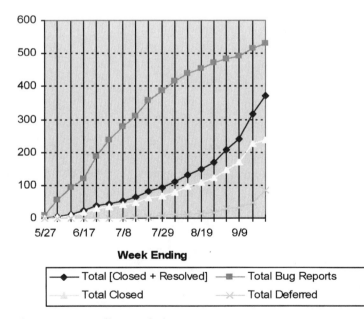

Figure B.2 Quality Trend Chart.

is high. The Quality Trend Chart (shown in Figure B.2) includes the cumulative curves of Total Bug Reports, [closed + resolved] bugs, closed (fixed) and deferred bugs. Similar to the Stability Trend Chart, [closed + resolved] and Total Bug Reports curves in this chart will eventually intersect when the product is ready for release. Observing the progressing trend of the fixed and deferred curves relative to the closed curve will give you reasonable quality interpretation of the tested product.

Error Analysis Checklist—
Web Error Examples

Check for the Existence of DNS Entry

Symptoms

No response when clicking on certain links. This only happens when you are outside of the intranet.

Possible Problems

This symptom may be caused by a number of problems. The most common is that the server cannot be found due to a missing DNS entry rather than coding error.

Examples

When you are outside of the intranet and click on the QA Training or TRACKGEAR button in the page illustrated in Figure C.1, the browser appears to hang or you don't get any response from the server. However, when you report the problem, your developer who accesses the same links could not reproduce it.

One of the possible problems is the DNS entry for the server in the links is only available in the DNS server on the intranet and is not known to the outside world.

Figure C.1

Tips

1. Use the View Source menu command to inspect the HTML source.

2. Look for the information that's relevant to the links.

   In this example, you will find that clicking on the QA Training and the TRACKGEAR button will result in requests to the server authorize in the qacity.com domain.

   ```
   ...
   <td>
   <map name=01b238de91a99ed9>
   <area shape=rect coords="0,0,88,20"
   href=https://authorize.qacity.com/training-login.asp?>
   <area shape=rect coords="0,20,88,40"
   href=https://authorize.qacity.com/trackgear-login.asp?>
   ...
   ...
   </td>
   ...
   ```

3. Try to ping authorize.qacity.com to see if it can be pinged.

4. If the server cannot be pinged, tell your developer or IS staff so the problem can be resolved.

Check for Proper Configuration of the Client Machine and Browser Settings

Symptoms

Cannot get response from a server after entering a URL.

Possible Problems

This symptom may be caused by a number of problems. The two most common problems are:

1. The client machine is not properly configured to connect to the network.

2. One or more browser settings are not properly configured.

Examples

- Your machine is not connected to the network. Therefore, there is no TCP/IP connection for your browser to be served.

- Your browser is configured to use proxy server. However, the address of the proxy server in your browser settings is invalid (see Figure C.2) or the proxy server is not accessible. Therefore, the browser can't be served.

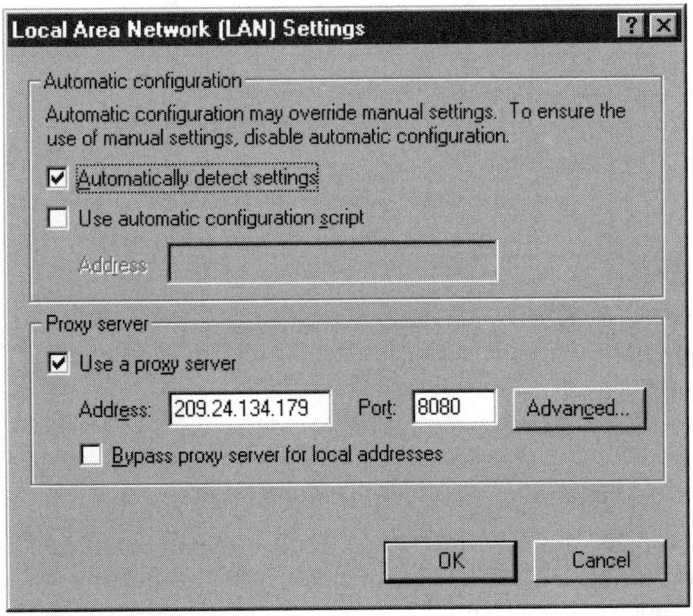

Figure C.2

Tips

To check your network connection on a Windows machine:

1. Run IPCONFIG or WINIPCFG to obtain the default gateway IP and the default DNS IP address.

2. Ping the default gateway machine to ensure that your machine is properly connected with it.

3. Ping the DNS server to see if it can be found from your machine.

4. Ping one of the known servers on the Internet to ensure that your machine can access a server outside of your LAN.

To check your browser settings to ensure accessibility:

- Pick a couple of intranet pages on a remote server and try to access those pages to test your browser accessibility within the LAN.

- Pick a couple of popular nonrestricted Web sites and go there when you need to test your browser accessibility. I normally use www.cnn.com and www.cnet.com.

- Identify if the proxy server is used. If yes, try to ping the proxy server to ensure it can be found.

- Check the security settings to ensure that the site you are trying to get to is not part of the restricted sites.

Check the HTTP Settings on the Browser

Symptoms

Cannot connect to certain Web servers.

Possible Problems

This symptom may be caused by a number of problems. One possible issue is the browser is having difficulties connecting to server that can only support HTTP 1.0 through proxy server.

Examples

If your Web server only supports HTTP 1.0 by using proxy server and your browser is configured to only use HTTP 1.1, the communication between the browser and the Web server will not work. See Figure C.3.

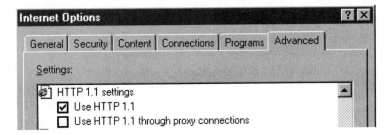

Figure C.3

Tips

- Try to connect to the server with the HTTP 1.1 boxes cleared to see if the problem reoccurs.
- Verify that server can support HTTP 1.1.

Check the JIT Compiler–Enabled Setting on the Browser

Symptoms

Java applet works properly on one browser but not on another, although both browsers are on the same platform, produced by the same vendor, and their release versions are identical.

Possible Problems

This symptom may be caused by a number of problems. One possible issue is that the Java JIT (Just-In-Time) compiler enable option is checked. See Figure C.4.

Figure C.4

Examples

If a Java JIT compiler is incompatible with a Java applet, having the compiler setting turned on may prevent the Java applet from operating successfully. On the browser that has this option cleared, the Java applet works correctly.

Tips

Before reporting an error, check the Java JIT compiler setting on both browsers to see if they are different.

Check the Multimedia Settings on the Browser

Symptoms

Unable to play animations, sounds, and videos, or display pictures properly on one browser, but able to do so on another, although both browsers are on the same platform, produced by the same vendor, and their release versions are identical.

Possible Problems

This symptom may be caused by a number of problems. The most common problem is that the multimedia options are not checked to enable multimedia contents to be played in the browser.

Examples

If the "Show pictures" check box is cleared as illustrated in Figure C.5, the graphics will not display in the browser as shown in the next screen shot.

Tips

Before filing a bug report related to the execution or display of multimedia contents, check the multimedia settings to see if they are properly enabled.

Check the Security Settings on the Browser

Symptoms

Unable to process purchase transactions or connect in secured mode (HTTPS).

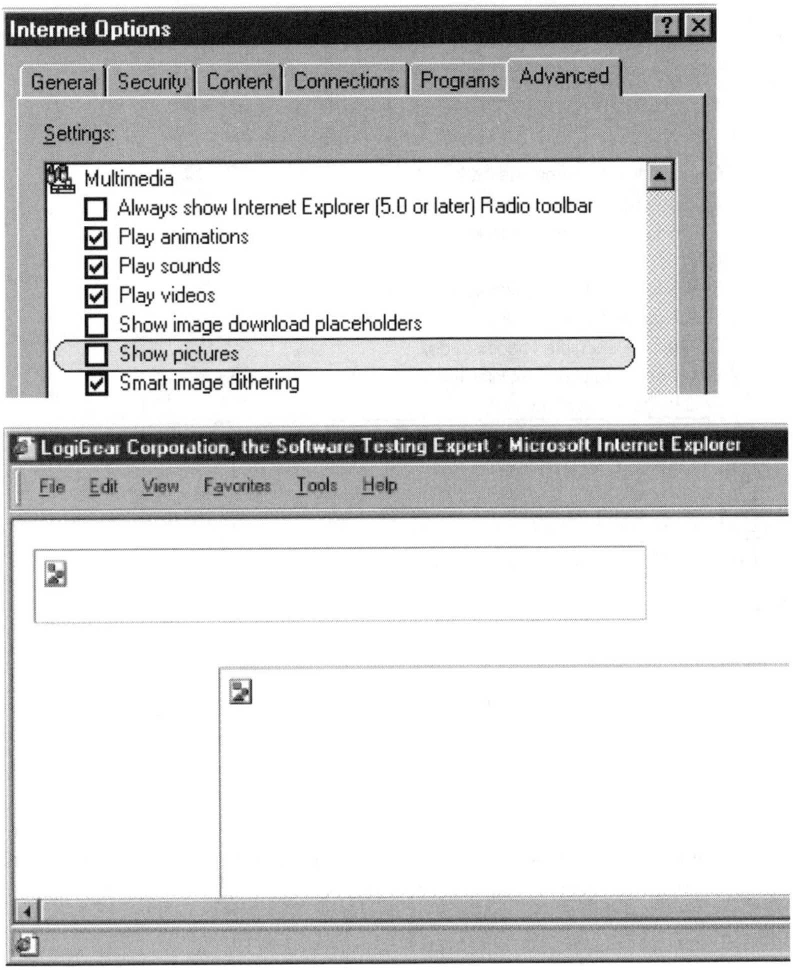

Figure C.5

Possible Problems

This symptom may be caused by a number of problems. One common issue is that the supported version of the security protocol by the server is not enabled on the server side.

Examples

If your server only supports encryption through SSL 2.0 protocol, but the SSL 2.0 security on the browser side is cleared, the browser will not be able to connect to the Web server through HTTPS. See Figure C.6.

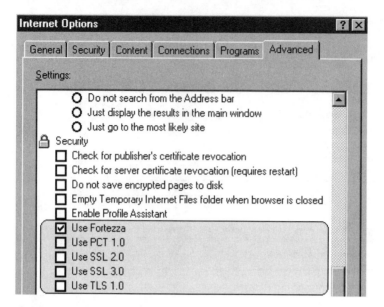

Figure C.6

Tips

Before filing a bug report related to public/private encryption, check the security options to ensure that they are configured properly.

Check for a Slow Connection

Symptoms

Login fails to authenticate with certain types of connection.

Possible Problems

This symptom may be caused by a number of problems. One common issue is that you might have a slow connection that causes a time-out in the login or authentication process.

Examples

With certain types of connections, such as dial-up, it may take too long (longer than the script time-out value) for the client-server to send/receive packets of data, the script will eventually time-out, causing the login or authentication process to fail. The problem could not be reproduced when your developer tries to do so on an intranet or a LAN connection.

Tips

- Use an alternate dial-up configuration (RAS, a different ISP, or a different modem) with the same bandwidth to see if the problem is reproducible. This process helps you eliminate the configuration dependency (other than a slow connection) theories.

- Connect with a slower connection to see if the problem reproduces. If yes, than the slow connection theory can be further validated.

- Connect with a faster connection to see if the problem reproduces. If no, then the slow connection theory can be further validated.

Check for Proper Configuration on the Web Server

Symptoms

Unable to access certain pages (on certain servers).

Possible Problems

This symptom may be caused by a number of reasons. One of the possible issues is the application server has not been configured to allow running scripts or executables.

Examples

When you click on certain links or buttons on a Web page from your "TEST" server, you get the error message shown in Figure C.7. When your developer tries the same links or buttons on another serve such as "DEVELOPMENT" server, the problem does not reproduce. On an IIS server, this may mean that the "TEST" server is not configured to allow running scripts or executables. For example, the screen-shot in Figure C.8a shows the Execute Permissions setting on the "TEST" server for myApp configured to None, and the next screen shot (Figure C.8b) shows the Execute Permissions setting on the "DEVELOPMENT" server configured to Scripts and Executables.

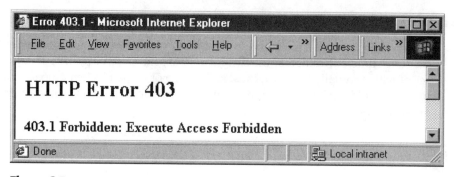

Figure C.7

Tips

1. Identify the server names by examining the URL or the HTML source.

2. Once the servers are identified, examine the settings on both servers to identify any discrepancies.

Note: Is this a software error? It depends. If the documentation instructs the system administrator to configure the Web server properly but it was not done, then it's a user error, not a software error. On the other hand, if the installer is supposed to configure the Web server programmatically but failed to do so, then it's a software error.

Check for the Deletion of Your Browser Cache (Temporary Internet Files)

Symptoms

The recent fixed bug appears to be fixed on your developer's browser but not on yours, although both browsers are from the same publisher with identical release version.

Possible Problems

This symptom may be caused by a number of problems. The possible reason is that the data is still cached memory on the browser side.

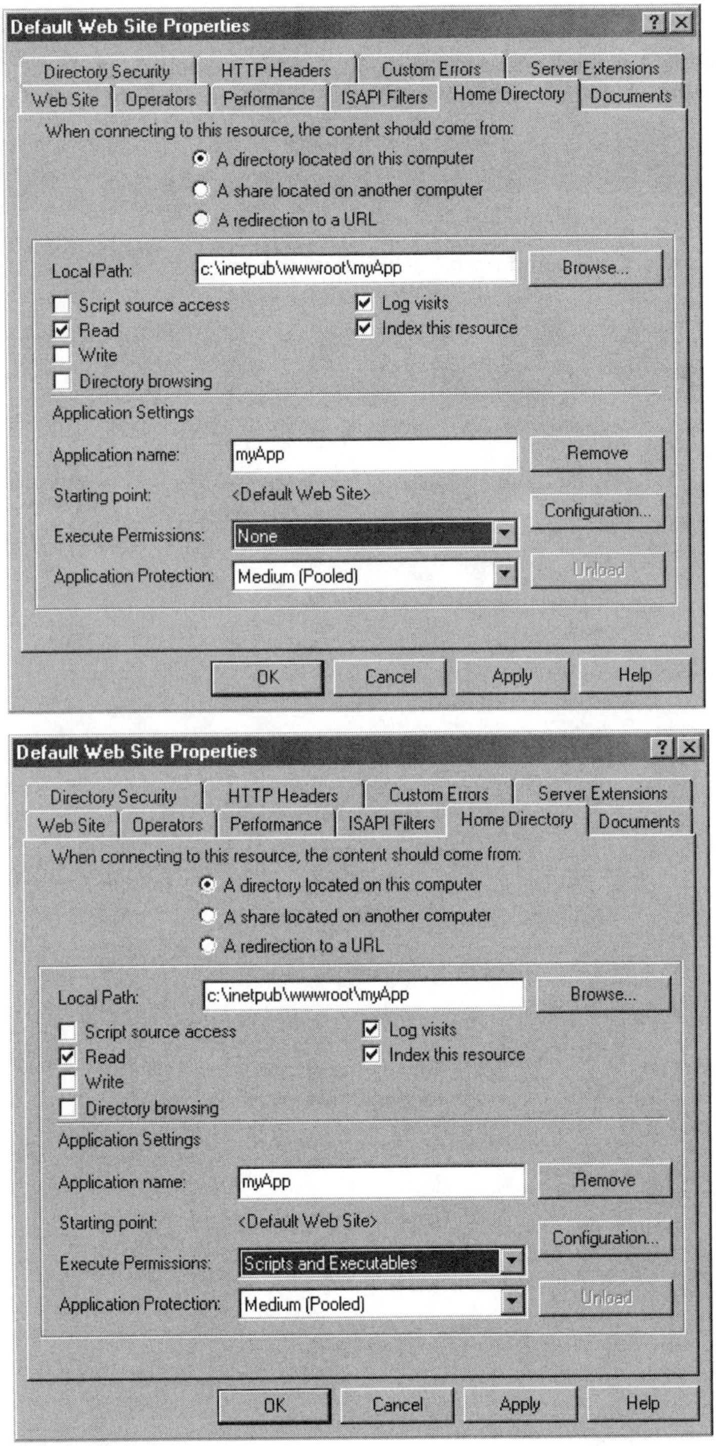
Default Web Site Properties
Directory Security
HTTP Headers
Custom Errors
Server Extensions
Web Site
Operators
Performance
ISAPI Filters
Home Directory
Documents
When connecting to this resource, the content should come from:
A directory located on this computer
A share located on another computer
A redirection to a URL
Local Path:
c:\inetpub\wwwroot\myApp
Browse...
Script source access
Read
Write
Directory browsing
Log visits
Index this resource
Application Settings
Application name:
myApp
Remove
Starting point:
<Default Web Site>
Configuration...
Execute Permissions:
None
Application Protection:
Medium (Pooled)
Unload
OK
Cancel
Apply
Help
Default Web Site Properties
Directory Security
HTTP Headers
Custom Errors
Server Extensions
Web Site
Operators
Performance
ISAPI Filters
Home Directory
Documents
When connecting to this resource, the content should come from:
A directory located on this computer
A share located on another computer
A redirection to a URL
Local Path:
c:\inetpub\wwwroot\myApp
Browse...
Script source access
Read
Write
Directory browsing
Log visits
Index this resource
Application Settings
Application name:
myApp
Remove
Starting point:
<Default Web Site>
Configuration...
Execute Permissions:
Scripts and Executables
Application Protection:
Medium (Pooled)
Unload
OK
Cancel
Apply
Help

Figure C.8 *(a)*. *(b)*.

Examples

You report a bug. Your developer immediately fixed it and asked you to regression-test the fix. You execute the test script and discover the problem is still not fixed, although the fix has been validated on your developer's browser.

Tips

Delete your browser cache and try reexecuting your regression test.

UI Test-Case Design Guideline: Common Keyboard Navigation and Shortcut Matrix

Key	Left Arrow	Right Arrow	Up Arrow	Down Arrow	Home	End	Page Up	Page Down	Tab	Tab	Tab	Tab	Left Arrow	Right Arrow	Up Arrow	Down Arrow	Home	End	Page Up	Page Down	C	O	P	S	V	X	Z	Esc	Esc	Esc
Modifier Key																														
None	♦	♦	♦	♦	♦	♦	♦	♦	♦																			♦		
SHIFT											♦		♦	♦	♦	♦	♦	♦	♦	♦										
CTRL										♦											♦	♦	♦	♦	♦	♦	♦		♦	
ALT												♦																		♦
Page/Dialog/Java applet/ActiveX/ UI elements																														

UI Test-Case Design Guideline: Mouse Action Matrix

Mouse Actions	Pointing (mouse-over)	Pressing	Dragging	Clicking	Double-clicking	Pressing	Dragging	Clicking	Double-clicking	Pointing	Pressing	Dragging	Clicking	Double-clicking	Pressing	Dragging	Clicking	Double-clicking	Pointing	Pressing	Dragging	Clicking	Double-clicking	Pressing	Dragging	Clicking	Double-clicking	Mouse Action Invalid Cases	Mouse Action Invalid Cases	Mouse Action Invalid Cases
Mouse Button 1	♦	♦	♦	♦	♦					♦	♦	♦	♦						♦	♦	♦	♦								
Mouse Button 2						♦	♦	♦	♦						♦	♦	♦	♦						♦	♦	♦	♦			
SHIFT						♦	♦	♦	♦	♦	♦	♦	♦	♦	♦	♦	♦	♦												
CTRL																			♦	♦	♦	♦	♦	♦	♦	♦	♦			

Page/Dialog/Java Applet/ActiveX/ UI elements

Web Test-Case Design Guideline:
Input Boundary and Validation Matrix I

Additional Instructions:

	Type in each of the entry field, one at the time	Problematic characters for SQL	\ Back slash	/ Slash	: Colon	* Asterisk	' Single quotation mark	< Greater than	> Less than	| Pipe	Other interesting characters	! ~ " # $ % & . ' ( ) + - = ` @ [ ] ^	Additional Invalid cases						
Web Page Text Fields																			
Text boxes																			
Examples																			
Save As dialog																			
File name																			
Schedule an activity dialog																			
Date																			
Time																			
Enter "My Record" Information																			
Company																			
Name																			
Address 1																			
Address 2																			
Address 3																			
City																			
State																			
Zip																			
Phone																			
Extension																			

Web Test-Case Design Guideline:
Input Boundary and Validation Matrix II

Additional Instructions:

	Type in each of the entry field, one at the time	NULL	Valid value	At Lower Boundary of value	At Upper Boundary of value	At Lower Boundary of value -1	At Lower Boundary of value +1	At Upper Boundary of value -1	At Upper Boundary of value +1	Outside of Lower Boundary of value	Outside of Upper Boundary of value	0	Negative value	Valid number of digits or characters	At Lower Boundary of number of digits or characters	At Upper Boundary of number of digits or characters	At Lower Boundary of number of digits or characters +1	At Upper Boundary of number of digits or characters -1	At Upper Boundary of number of digits or characters +1
Web Page Text Fields																			
Text boxes																			
Examples																			
Save As dialog																			
File name																			
Schedule an activity dialog																			
Date																			
Time																			
Enter "My Record" Information																			
Company																			
Name																			
Address 1																			
Address 2																			
Address 3																			
City																			
State																			
Zip																			
Phone																			
Extension																			

Display Compatibility Test Matrix

DISPLAY COMPATIBILITY TEST MATRIX
Logigear Premium Compatibility Test Lab

Client: _____

Project: _____

Version: _____

Tester: _____

Date: _____

Config ID: _____

Resolution	Font Size	Color Depth				
		4-bit	8-bit	16-bit	24-bit	32-bit
640x480	Small					
	Large					
	Custom					
800x600	Small					
	Large					
	Custom					
1024x768	Small					
	Large					
	Custom					
1280x1024	Small					
	Large					
	Custom					

Release	OS			
	95	98	NT 4.0	2000
Original				
Upgrade A				
OSR2 B				
SE				
SP3				
SP4				
SP5				
SP6				

Browsers	
Navigator 3.02	IE 3.0
Navigator 3.04	IE 3.02
Communicator 4.01	IE 3.04
Communicator 4.02	IE 4.0 *
Communicator 4.04	IE 4.01 *
Communicator 4.06	IE 4.01 SP1 *
Communicator 4.07	IE 5.0 *
Communicator 4.08	IE 5.0a
Communicator 4.5	IE 5.01
Communicator 4.51	IE 5.5 Beta
Communicator 4.6	
Communicator 4.61	
Communicator 4.72	
Communicator 6.0	

* Active Desktop   yes   no

Browser OS Configuration Matrix

BROWSER/OS CONFIGURATION MATRIX

BROWSERS			
Internet Explorer		Netscape Communicator	America Online
IE 3.02		NS 3.01	AOL 3.0
IE 4.0	ver. 4.71.1712.6	NS 3.02	AOL 4.0
IE 4.01	ver. 4.72.2106.8	NS 3.03	AOL 5.0
IE 4.01 SP1	ver. 4.72.3110	NS 3.04	
IE 4.01 SP1a	ver. 4.72.3110.8	NS 4.04	
IE 4.01 SP2	ver. 4.72.3612.1713	NS 4.05	
IE 5.0	ver. 5.00.0910.1309	NS 4.06	
IE 5.0	ver. 5.00.2014.0216	NS 4.07	
IE 5.0	ver. 5.00.2014.0216IC	NS 4.08	
IE 5.0a	ver 5.00.2314.1003	NS 4.5	
IE 5.01	ver 5.00.2516.1900 (W98 SE)	NS 4.51	
		NS 4.6	
		NS 4.61	
		NS 4.72	
		NS 6.0	

OS	day1	day2	day3	day4	day5
W95					
W95a					
W95b					
W98					
W98 SE					
W2000					
W NT					
W NT SP 3					
W NT SP 4					
MAC OS 7.6.1					
MAC OS 8.1					
MAC OS 8.5.1					
MAC OS 8.6					